Arthur Charles Champneys

History of English

A sketch of the origin and development of the English language. With examples,

down to the present day

Arthur Charles Champneys

History of English
A sketch of the origin and development of the English language. With examples, down to the present day

ISBN/EAN: 9783337096984

Printed in Europe, USA, Canada, Australia, Japan

Cover: Foto ©ninafisch / pixelio.de

More available books at **www.hansebooks.com**

HISTORY OF ENGLISH

A SKETCH OF THE ORIGIN
AND DEVELOPMENT OF THE ENGLISH LANGUAGE
WITH EXAMPLES, DOWN TO THE
PRESENT DAY

BY

A. C. CHAMPNEYS, M.A.
ASSISTANT MASTER AT MARLBOROUGH COLLEGE

RIVINGTON, PERCIVAL & CO.
KING STREET, COVENT GARDEN
LONDON
1893

PREFACE

THIS book does not profess to be more than an introduction to a large subject. Still, I am quite aware that it is somewhat daring for an amateur like myself to write a book of any kind on the History of the English Language. My excuse must be that, having tried at various times to teach different parts of the subject, I thought that the experience so gained might perhaps enable me to present it in such a way as should be more or less intelligible and interesting.

With this object in view I have as much as possible kept clear of technical terms (except such as are used in every grammar), explaining those which I did not see my way to avoid. I have also kept out abbreviations from the text. Though these are in some cases necessary, they must plainly tend to increase the labour of reading. And I have tried in most cases to give some at least of the grounds on which conclusions have been arrived at, believing from my own early experience that philology, put as a mass of unsupported statements, is neither easy to understand nor readily credible. It appeared to me also that a certain limited amount of repetition would make the thread of the subject easier to follow.

As to the arrangement of the chapters, a more strictly logical plan would, no doubt, have been to follow exclusively either order of time or order of subject—that is to say, either to discuss at one time the progress of the English language as a whole during a certain period, or to take one subject (as *e.g.* the verb) throughout the history of the language. But it appeared to me that the former plan would necessarily lead either to much repetition or to obscurity, while the latter would not give any general idea of the progress of English towards its present state. I have therefore preferred a compromise between the two methods.

In order to make the book complete there should, no doubt, have been an introductory chapter on 'Sounds, and how they are made.' This is omitted, partly in order to limit the book to some moderate length; partly because of the extreme difficulty of making such a chapter at once scientifically adequate and interesting to the ordinary reader. I have done my best to make what is stated in the course of the book intelligible without such an introduction.

The book may perhaps seem in some places rather encumbered with notes. My principle has been to keep the text as short as possible, adding at the foot of the page such further explanations, illustrations, and cautions against mistake as some readers might be likely to wish for or require. Where any of these necessarily exceeded the limits of a footnote I have put it as an appendix.

Next as to the maps. The one which is intended to illustrate European languages at the present day, being founded on others of good authority previously made,[1] ought to give the main facts as correctly as can be expected from a small map of the kind. As regards the one which is meant

---

[1] Debes, Kirchhoff, and Kropatscheck, *Schul-Atlas*, Leipzig, 1888; and Spruner and Menke, *Hand-Atlas für die Geschichte des Mittelalters und der neueren Zeit*, Gotha, 1880.

to illustrate the distribution of English dialects in the fourteenth century (on p. 256), it is, I hope, approximately correct. It is founded on the statements contained in Professor Skeat's *Principles of English Etymology*, First Series, and in Dr. Morris's and Professor Skeat's *Specimens of Early English*. I have also been helped by Mr. Kington Oliphant's *Old and Middle English*, and I have taken into consideration such other evidence as I could find, including the present distribution of dialects as marked on Prince Louis Lucien Bonaparte's map (to be found in the *Transactions of the Philological Society* for 1875-76), and the general probabilities of the case. It is very possible that the boundaries are capable of being more accurately defined by others, but in general the evidence is defective, and in some points uncertain. On account of the mixture of dialects for some distance from their edges such a map can at best be only approximate. Under these circumstances it might appear the safer course not to attempt its construction at all. But there is no doubt that one of the first things which an intelligent reader would do is to apply the statements in the text to a map of England, and I thought it my duty to help him to the best of my ability.

My obligations to the work of others have of course been great, and I wish to do my best to acknowledge them fully. I have tried to give the reference wherever I have actually quoted or paraphrased from a particular book. I have also noted, especially at the beginning of each chapter, the works to which I am chiefly indebted in the different parts of the subject. But there are some books to which my debt is certainly larger than has been expressed in this way. These are dictionaries and grammars, Bosworth's *Anglo-Saxon Dictionary*, both the earlier edition, and also such parts of the greatly improved edition by Professor Toller as were published in time for me to use, Professor Skeat's *Etymological Dictionary*, both in its full and in its abridged form, Stratmann's *Dictionary of the Old English Language*, Koch's *Historische Grammatik der Englischen Sprache*, the grammar at the beginning of Mr. Sweet's *Anglo-Saxon Reader*, Professor Earle's *Anglo-Saxon Primer*, and Dr. Morris's *Historical Outlines of English Accidence*; Mr. Sweet's *New English Grammar* appeared too late for me to be able to make more than a very limited use of it. If my debt in any particular is still unacknowledged, I can only apologise beforehand for the omission.

My personal thanks are also due to Professor Earle, Dr. Morris, Professor Skeat, and Mr. Sweet, for kindly allowing me to use several extracts from texts published by them in illustration of the English of different periods. I must also especially thank the two Professors of Anglo-Saxon for their kindness in explaining a passage (on p. 155), where a mistake in the manuscript had quite puzzled me. To Professor Earle I am also permanently indebted for my first training in Old English, which, if it is not likely to be of material benefit to others, has at least been a source of much interest to me. I must also thank Mr. H. F. Stewart and Mr. F. V. E. Brughera, of Marlborough College, for help with the specimens of Norman or Anglo-French; my brother, Mr. Basil Champneys, for many valuable criticisms and suggestions, especially on the style of Modern English Prose and Poetry, as well as for help in revising the proofs; and my sister, Miss Mary Champneys, for much help clerical and otherwise.

A. C. CHAMPNEYS.

MARLBOROUGH, 1892.

CONTENTS

CHAPTER I
THE 'LIFE' OF A LANGUAGE

What the 'life' of a language really means—How children learn words and grammar—'Analogy'—Changes in grammar by 'false analogy'—Changes in vocabulary, in form and meaning—How these begin—How they are checked—And how fresh words are supplied.

Pages 1-13

CHAPTER II
DIALECTS AND LANGUAGES

The difference between a dialect and a language—How one grows out of the other—English as an example of this—How the relationship of two languages can be proved 14-21

CHAPTER III
ENGLISH RELATED TO OTHER LANGUAGES

Proof of the relationship of English to the other Indo-European languages —'Shifting of consonant sounds' in different languages of the family, or Grimm's Law—What it proves, and its use in deriving words.

22-31

CHAPTER IV
THE INDO-EUROPEAN FAMILY OF LANGUAGES

Divisions of the Indo-European family of languages—Position of Sanskrit —The other branches—Impossibility of grouping these . . 32-40

CHAPTER V

THE INDO-EUROPEAN PEOPLE

Condition, life, and manners of the Indo-European people—The evidence The conclusions—Uncertainty about their original home.

Pages 41-51

CHAPTER VI

THE PRIMITIVE INDO-EUROPEAN LANGUAGE

Character of the Indo-European language—Can we trace it back to roots, and can we explain the origin of these ? 52-64

CHAPTER VII

THE NEAR RELATIONS OF ENGLISH

Speech of the Teutonic branch, and the position in it of English—Its history—Position of Gothic among Teutonic languages . . 65-75

CHAPTER VIII

THE ENGLISH LANGUAGE PLANTED IN BRITAIN

How the English language came to Britain and was established there

76-80

CHAPTER IX

ENGLISH IN ITS EARLY FORM

Old English or Anglo-Saxon—The Verb—'Strong' Perfects (1), (2)—'Weak' Perfects — Subjunctive — Declensions of Substantives — Genders—Plurals formed by change of vowel—'Strong' and 'weak' declension of Adjectives—The definite Article: its origin—Pronouns—Use of the cases—Anglo-Saxon an inflexional language, and the parent of Modern English 81-117

CHAPTER X

HISTORY OF ENGLISH BEFORE THE NORMAN CONQUEST

Dialects of Old English and their history—Beginnings of English literature—Early predominance of Northumbrian—Settlement of the Danes in England—Their influence on the speech of those districts where they settled—Alfred the Great's influence on English. Pages 118-130

CHAPTER XI

ENGLISH DIALECTS BEFORE THE NORMAN CONQUEST

General sketch of the dialects of English before the Conquest—Their peculiarities, and descendants at the present time . . 131-135

CHAPTER XII

THE VOCABULARY, OR STOCK OF WORDS IN ENGLISH BEFORE THE CONQUEST

Native words—Latin words, brought in at different periods—Celtic words—Danish (or Norwegian) words—The mass of the vocabulary pure English 136-155

CHAPTER XIII

FOREIGN ASCENDENCY

English dialects and English literature at the time of the Norman Conquest—How Norman French gained its ascendency—Character of Norman French—Its history in England, and how it went out of use—Position of Latin in England—Latin, French, and English literature after the Conquest 156-173

CHAPTER XIV

EFFECTS OF THE NORMAN CONQUEST UPON ENGLISH

Loss of Old English poetical style—Dialects put on an equality—Simplification and shortening of inflexions—English spelt as French—

French idioms—French words in English—Their first appearance—How they were introduced—Duplicate words—French words with English terminations—'Hybrid' words—Influx of French words about 1280 — French words of Government, War, Architecture, Medicine, Sport, Religion—Words related in French and English—Pronunciation—French and English accent . . Pages 174-208

CHAPTER XV

CHANGES IN THE SOUNDS OF ENGLISH

Changes in English sounds—Not directly traceable to French influence—Changes of long A—of C—of SC—of G—ȝ and þ lost . 209-222

CHAPTER XVI

DIALECTS OF ENGLISH AFTER THE CONQUEST, ESPECIALLY THE EAST MIDLAND

The four main dialects of English—Where spoken—All have contributed to Modern English—But especially East Midland—First appearance of that dialect—The *Peterborough Chronicle*—Inflexions dying out—Orm—His grammar—Danish influence on English—Contrast of the Southern dialect—Northumbrian the parent of Lowland Scotch
223-254

CHAPTER XVII

ENGLISH DIALECTS IN THE FOURTEENTH CENTURY

East Midland English in the first half of the fourteenth century—The ancestor of 'standard' English—Robert of Brunne—The Southern dialect of Gloucestershire, and of Kent—The West Midland dialect
255-266

CHAPTER XVIII

THE BEGINNINGS OF 'STANDARD' ENGLISH

No fixed 'standard' English in Chaucer's time—Chaucer's dialect—His grammar — Wycliffe and Purvey — Contemporary letter-writing — Southern English still written 267-282

CHAPTER XIX

EARLY 'STANDARD' ENGLISH

The changes of the fifteenth century—East Midland becomes 'standard' English—Causes of this—Changes in the language itself—Confusion and loss of final -*e*'s—Other terminations dropped or compressed—*their, them,* displace *her, hem—give* or *yeve—that—those—y-(clept)*—Caxton's English . . . . Pages 283-301

CHAPTER XX

ADDITIONS TO THE ENGLISH VOCABULARY DOWN TO 1625

French words—French words Latinised—New Latin words—'Doublets' — Latin words in Shakespeare — Dutch words, how they were borrowed, and how they are to be recognised—Spanish and Portuguese words—Italian words—Celtic words—Hebrew and Aramaic words—Words from Arabic—American and Indian words—How words pass from one language to another—Why English is not swamped with foreign words 302-313

CHAPTER XXI

SIXTEENTH-CENTURY ENGLISH

Character of sixteenth-century English—Some of its literature—Translations of the Bible in the sixteenth century—Our present Bible a revision of these, hence its language was old-fashioned in 1611—Prayer-Book of 1549—Latimer—Spenser—Shakespeare—Specimens of sixteenth-century English—Differences of sixteenth-century English from our own: the Verb, Substantives, Adjectives, Pronouns; Soft G or Y; 'ax'—Idioms—Freedom of sixteenth-century English—Dialects which have contributed to form 'standard' English . . 314-348

CHAPTER XXII

CHANGES IN 'STANDARD' ENGLISH SINCE 1625

Changes in English mostly small since 1625—Changes in pronunciation since Chaucer—Not marked by spelling—How the former pronunciation is ascertained—Traces of it in English dialects—Changes of English vowel-sounds—Changes of EA, OI proved—Dropping and changes of consonants—Changes in grammar—Additions to vocabulary—Latin and Greek words—French words—Words from European languages other than French—Words from distant countries—Changes in style—What style is—Latin influence on English prose—The choice of words—The Johnsonian style—French words and idioms dragged into English—German intruders—English poetical style—Specimens of English prose—Hooker, Bacon, Milton, Addison, Johnson, Scott, Thackeray, the Modern Johnsonian style, Macaulay

Pages 349-384

CHAPTER XXIII

ENGLISH DIALECTS AT THE PRESENT DAY

The Southern (or South-Western) dialect—The West Midland dialect—The Northern dialect—East Midland, or 'standard' English

385-392

APPENDICES

A. RACE AND LANGUAGE 393
B. THE ENGLISH OF THE CONTINENT 394
C. THE KENTISH DIALECT 395
D. NOTE TO P. 167 396
E. VERBAL SUBSTANTIVES AND PRESENT PARTICIPLES IN '-ING' . 398

INDEX 401

MAP OF INDO-EUROPEAN LANGUAGES AT THE PRESENT DAY . xvi

PLAN OF INDO-EUROPEAN LANGUAGES 33

APPROXIMATE MAP OF ENGLISH DIALECTS IN THE FOURTEENTH CENTURY 256

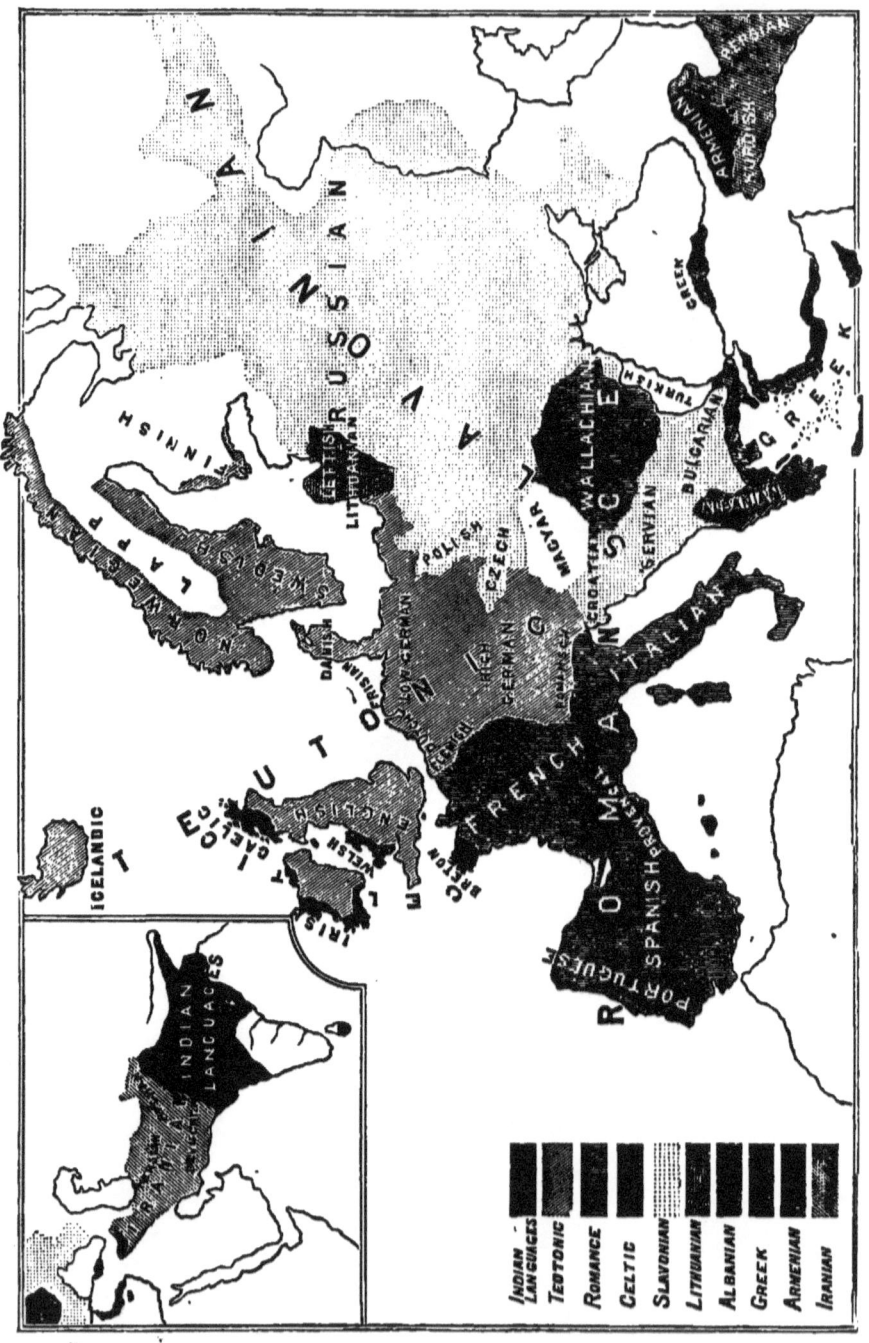

HISTORY OF ENGLISH

CHAPTER I

THE 'LIFE' OF A LANGUAGE

What the 'life' of a language really means—How children learn words and grammar—'Analogy'—Changes in grammar by 'false analogy'—Changes in vocabulary, in form and meaning—How these begin—How they are checked—And how fresh words are supplied.[1]

IT will probably be best, first of all, to get some idea of what is meant by the 'life' of a language, how it is handed on from one generation to another, how it gets altered in the process, and in what way it is in the main kept the same from one generation to the next. A 'living' language, such as English, is constantly changing more or less, like a living man or animal; but just as 'the child is father to the man,' so a language at a later stage is not totally distinct from what it was even centuries before, and certainly, as we know, does not undergo any very startling alterations in fifty or a hundred years, any more than the human being does in two or four years. For the 'life' of a language is far longer than the life of a man. If we take English at the present time and see how it is and has been altering, and how gradual this alteration is, we shall understand better the way in which a language is

[1] See Whitney, *Language and its Study*, edited by Morris.

preserved, and to what extent it changes. But we must always remember that in speaking of the 'life' of a language we are really using a metaphor, a sort of parable condensed. No language has really an existence of its own apart from those who speak it. So far as those who speak it continue to speak in the same way, the language remains unaltered; so far as they change their mode of speaking, the language is changed. Writing is of course nothing but a set of signs for the spoken words. And the language of books follows the language as spoken, though slowly. Changes are almost always made first in the *spoken* language.

It is quite true that people in talking do not, as a rule, think of altering their way of speaking from the speech which they are used to; they do not even think of keeping it the same. In speaking our own language we usually think merely of the ideas which we wish to convey to others, and not of the words which we shall use for the purpose. Thus the preservation of words and phrases and pronunciation in a language is unconscious, just as the gradual alteration in them is. But for all that, whether we think of what we are saying or not, language has plainly no existence apart from people speaking it, or representing the words which they would use by written signs.

Now, if we look at the way in which a child learns to speak, we shall not only see how language is handed on from one to another, but we shall also get some hints as to the way in which it changes. For the child is a human being after all, and the same tendencies will be found in it after it has grown up. Let us see, then, how children learn to speak.

First of all they learn single words[1] by imitation. They learn them imperfectly at first, disliking or being unable to pronounce the more difficult sounds, or combinations of sounds. Thus some children say *de* for *the*, *free* for *three*. The sound

---

[1] Or very short sentences, such as 'How d'you do?'

TH is as difficult to them as it is to most European nations. So, too, S is often dropped, as in, *'ing* for *sing*, or turned into an H, as when a child says *horry* for *sorry*. In this it shows a fellow-feeling with the Greeks, who dropped an S between two vowels, and also changed σί-στημι into ἵ-στημι. Again, hardly any young children can pronounce an R, just as educated Englishmen in general now pronounce no R's except those immediately before a vowel. Some persons throughout their life never learn to pronounce one or other of these sounds. We must remember that different people are differently constituted, both in the formation of their mouths and in their power of accurate imitation ; and that what is hard to one is not always hard to another, though all prefer a short word to a long one, a single to a double consonant. Thus children almost always clip their longer or harder words, as *pocket-handkerchief* is degraded into *pocky-nantcher*, or something of the kind, and *star* into *'tar*.

So far we have spoken of the way in which single words are picked up; we next come to the way in which these are combined in sentences ; and now grammar makes its appearance. How then do children learn English grammar? Plainly, in the same way as they learn the words, by imitation, and for the most part unconsciously. They do not learn the cases or other inflexions of each word separately, but as they hear *papa's* used in a way implying possession on the part of papa, so *Frank's* is used where possession by Frank is implied, and this process is extended to all words by 'analogy'—that is, words which resemble other words (for instance as being nouns, or verbs) are treated in the same way.

This principle of 'analogy' is extended by children further than the practice of the English language at present allows. So we get *us's, we's, foots, oxes, lended, hurted*. This use of new forms is checked by 'chaff' on the part of their brothers and sisters, by admonition from parents, and by noticing the correct inflexions of these 'irregular' words when they hear them said, or see them written, so that each fresh generation is not allowed to change and simplify the language at its pleasure. We have already had some hints that these tendencies to change the language are not confined to children. And we may now look more in detail into the ways in which a language changes. In doing this we shall confine ourselves as much as possible to recent times. But as all languages change gradually, and as English at the present day is changing at a remarkably slow rate, it will be necessary sometimes to go back two or three centuries or more in order to observe the changes which are and have been taking place.

(1) The desire for ease of pronunciation, the preference for an easy sound, or a short word, is the cause of many changes, as we saw in the case of children. Thus many names of places or surnames have been shortened while their old and longer form is retained in the spelling. Thus *Cirencester* is pronounced *Cicester*; *Leominster, Lemster*; *Marjoribanks, March-banks*. In the same way we write *boatswain*, but say *bo'sun*, and most of its members call the University the *'Varsity*. *'Bus* for *omnibus* is a very recent instance of this shortening of a word, since the thing itself has only been introduced within the last sixty years. So too our many silent letters, which we write but do not pronounce, the K in *knave* and *knight*, the W in *write*, represent sounds which have been dropped since 1500, and some of them in much more recent times. Again, two hard (or 'breathed'[1]) sounds, two soft (or 'voiced'[1]) letters are easier to pronounce together. Thus we say, 'he *rubbed*,' but 'he *crept*,' though the termination is evidently, to begin with, the same in both words.

---

[1] The difference between 'breath' and 'voice' is made by the vocal chords. In a 'voiced' letter (such as B) the breath is modified by the vocal chords, in a 'breathed' letter (such as P) it is not. A vowel is, of course, made with 'voice,' but this is modified by the shape of the mouth and position of the tongue, which form a 'resonance-chamber,' somewhat like the mouth of a trumpet.

(2) We saw in the case of children that they imitate the usual inflexions beyond what the practice of the language allows. This is called 'false analogy.' Thus the commonest form of the past tense of verbs, in *-ed*, has been gaining ground in English. We now say 'he *helped*,' and not 'he *holp*,' *seethed*, and not *sod*.[1] *Beseeched* is now trying to gain its position in the language as the past tense of *beseech*, instead of *besought*, and may be found in the newspapers at all events. So Bunyan uses *catcht* for *caught*, and this form, sometimes in the shape *ketch'd* or *cotch'd*, is commonly heard, though it is still branded as 'vulgar,' as was no doubt the case with *helped* and many other 'regular' past tenses when they were first used.

There has been a similar levelling in the declension of substantives. The old plural of *cow* was *ky*, as it still is in 'Lowland Scotch,' the descendant of one of the Old English dialects. 'Analogy' has made this into *cows*. So too the plural *horses* has become established in English since 1500,[2] the old plural being *horse*, the same as the singular. It seems to be a mere accident that the child's plurals, *foots* and *oxes*, are not now the correct English forms.

If we pass from changes in pronunciation and grammar to changes in the stock of words or 'vocabulary' of the language, we shall see further alterations.

(3) New words come in to express new ideas or things newly discovered. These are sometimes made up from two or more words or parts of words already in the language, as *steamboat, type-writer*; often by making a Latin or Greek compound and cutting off its termination to make it like the numerous words of this kind already in the language. In this way we have got *telegraph, telephone, phonograph*, and many others. Sometimes we join a Greek or Latin tail to an English head, and produce a monstrous word like

---

[1] Gen. xxv. 29, 'And Jacob sod pottage.' *Seethe* is now only used intransitively.
[2] But *horses* is to be found much earlier.

cablegram, though this is not really more extraordinary than our attaching an ending or 'suffix' like *-able*, which comes to us from Latin through French, to a purely English word like *love*, as in *lovable*. But *cablegram*, being a new word, strikes us as unusual, while *lovable* does not.

One of the most recent additions to the language is the verb to *boycott*, not, as we know, a compound word of any kind, but merely a proper name applied in a new sense, being the name of the gentleman, Captain Boycott, who first suffered from the process now marked out by the term. We cannot exactly give its birthday, but the word was born in the end of the year 1880.[1] At first applied only to persons, it is now used of things as well. We not only say 'he was *boycotted*,' but a member of Parliament lately spoke of the Government '*boycotting* the Paris Exhibition.' Like other new words received into the language, it is inflected like any other English word, and we can speak of 'boycott*ing*,' 'boycott*ers*,' just as we say 'he telegraph*ed*,' 'telegraph*ing*,' 'telephone*s*,' applying the ordinary English inflexions by imitating other words, unconsciously, just as a child does.[2]

Sometimes too new words are introduced which are formed from the stock of the language itself (such as *knowingness*, *unknowable*), not to mark out any new thing, but either because they are found useful from their shortness, or to express some shade of meaning which has no word attached to it, or perhaps for no reason that we can see. These sometimes gain admission into the language through being used by some author. Thus Sir Walter Scott introduced (or reintroduced) the substantive *following*, meaning 'body of retainers.' Coleridge established *reliable* and *reliability*.

(4) Then too sometimes one word crowds another out of the language and takes its place, just as the brown or 'Hanover' rat has driven the native black rat out of England. The

---

[1] See Skeat, *Principles of English Etymology*, First Series, p. 6.

[2] The word has also been naturalised in German, appearing in the form *Boycottierung*.

victorious word may be wholly new, or the two words may have existed side by side for generations, as is still the case with

begin	*commence*
belief	*creed*
herb	*plant*
like	*similar*

and a host of other pairs. But if we compare English of the present day with the English of the Authorised Version of the Bible, or with Shakespeare, we shall see that many words have been superseded by others. Thus—

wont	by	*accustomed*
come to pass	by	*happen*
draught	by	*haul*
sundry	by	*various*
anon	by	*directly*

just as *wire* may very possibly turn *telegraph* out of the English language.

(5) But words not only change their form, are born and die, but also shift their meaning more or less completely. Thus, as we know, *prevent*[1] meant merely 'anticipate' when the Bible and Prayer-book were written, it now means 'stop,' and cannot be used in its older sense. *Artillery*[2] originally meant warlike machines, and is used of Jonathan's bow and arrows in the Bible. It can now mean nothing but cannon. *Fowl*[3] in the Bible meant any bird, as in the phrase 'the *fowls* of the air,' and retains this meaning in the words derived from it, *fowler, wild-fowl*; it now means one kind of bird only, a chicken. So *meat* meant any food, as when Elijah 'went in the strength of that *meat*,' which was 'cakes' or loaves.[4]

These are merely some specimens of the ways in which the language has been altering in recent times. We can see from many of these examples that the change has not stopped

---

[1] Matt. xvii. 25.   Collect for the Seventeenth Sunday after Trinity.
[2] 1 Sam. xx. 40.   [3] Gen. i. 20.   [4] 1 Kings xix. 8.

yet. There are some people still alive who say, *'erb*, and *'umble*. Both these, *laylock* for *lilac*, *pardner* for *partner*, and perhaps *Prooshia* for *Prussia*, were the 'correct' or received pronunciation at the beginning of the century. Many persons now think it correct to pronounce the H in *where*, *when*, which a generation ago was never heard except from Scotchmen or Irishmen who had never dropped the sound. Perhaps in a generation or two it will be once more universally pronounced.

Now all changes in language must begin from some individual person, though we can hardly hope to trace the process throughout. From one man they spread to a family, a school, or college. If they do not gain ground outside these, they remain as family, school, or college slang. If they spread to a district, they become part of a local dialect. If they are imitated by the whole nation, they of course become part of its language. Now no two persons are alike in their pronunciation, or in the words which they use by preference. There are few persons who do not at some time or other invent words, mostly for a joke, or use an old word in a new sense. Thus the conditions necessary for starting some change in the language are constantly present, and people are inclined to imitate what they hear, whether it is new or old. And, as a fact, we have seen that English is constantly changing. And yet we know that the Bible, translated in 1611,[1] and Shakespeare's plays, written a few years earlier, are in the main readily intelligible so far as the language is concerned, to the silent reader at least, though, if we heard them read as they were pronounced by the translators and author, they would certainly sound very strange. How is it then that a language does not change more rapidly? what are the causes which preserve it?

(1) The use of language is to express our thoughts to

---

[1] The language of the Bible is really older than the date of our translation, as will be seen later on.

others, and plainly in order to do so we must use language which they understand. This is one of the chief causes which hinders the spread of slang, since it is not readily understood outside the circle in which it grew up, and is consequently soon dropped.

(2) Imitation, if it is the means by which changes in language spread, also tends much oftener to keep it the same. By imitating other people, our talk (or what we write) tends on the whole to a sort of average, steering midway between extremes of pronunciation and style. Thus, though one form of imitation, the copying of the commoner forms of grammar by 'analogy,' has a tendency to level 'irregularities' of grammar (such as *holp*), yet the imitation of the ordinary speech tends to keep the forms the same as before.

(3) We always prefer what we are used to. New words or grammatical forms strike people who hear them as unusual, and therefore as 'incorrect.' This is especially the case in a country where many people are educated, since the most highly educated class sets the standard of language, and these persons are particularly hostile to change. And, besides this, books, if they are really first-rate, are read for generations, as has been the case with the Authorised Version of the Bible, the Pilgrim's Progress, and Shakespeare. These do not alter. Other writers model their style on them. And people in their talk naturally imitate to some extent, for the most part unconsciously, the books which they read, though we never speak quite 'like a book,' so that thus we come round again to the second head. There are many persons to be found in the country districts whose talk is obviously modelled on the English Bible. This literary influence and influence of the educated class is unusually strong at the present day, and consequently it is far harder for the language to change to any great and obvious extent. But at any time the conservative forces in language will fall under one of these three heads: (1) The necessity of being understood; (2) Imitation of the

average speech of those with whom we come in contact; (3) Preference for what we are used to, or for what the educated classes are used to, and which they tell us is 'correct.' Of these conservative influences the first is by far the strongest.

Besides the processes of change in a living language, and the forces which prevent this change from being rapid, we must also say something of the way in which it repairs its waste like a living body. As this is a part of the change which takes place in language, something has been said of it already.

We have seen that words have a constant tendency to wear down. This loss usually stops before the word becomes unintelligible or ambiguous, but not always. Thus *right* in 'I have done it *right*,' *fair* in

'So, *fair* and softly, John he cried,'

stand for *rightë* and *fairë*, where the final E once marked them as adverbs. There is now no distinction between the adjective and the adverb apart from the context. Again, as we have seen, words become obsolete altogether. Now in English this waste is and has long been repaired and the fresh words needed have been supplied chiefly by borrowing from other languages. But this is exceptional among languages in general, and even in English borrowing is rare till a considerable time after the Norman Conquest. The usual way in which fresh words are made is by forming compound words, as in German at the present day. And we can trace the stages of their formation.

First,[1] we have a loose compound, two words put together but hardly joined into one word. As examples of this class we may take two or three of the compound words which Shakespeare uses, *sky-aspiring*, *senseless-obstinate*, *eagle-winged*. Now the sense of these words is the same whether we write each of them as one word or two; they have not acquired

[1] Whitney, *Language and its Study*, p. 71, etc.

any sense different from the sum of the parts composing them.[1] Besides this, we more naturally pronounce them with an accent on each part, and, if we think for a moment, we shall see that every English word has one main accent and no more. These combinations of words then are merely two words put close to one another and have not become joined into a single word. They are compounds of the loosest kind.

Secondly, we have an example of a closer compound in the name *Newfoundland*. We can still see its derivation clearly; no part of it has begun to wear down. But, in the first place, it has only one main accent, and is thus one word; and secondly, it has a special meaning of its own different from the joint meaning of the words composing it. Originally given to an island off the mouth of the St. Lawrence, because it was the land then most recently discovered (in much the same way as a certain college at Oxford is called New College), it is no longer applied to *any* newly-discovered country, as according to its derivation it might be, but is crystallised or hardened into a name for one particular country. Thus the combination of the three words *new found land* has become a new word with a new meaning. An excellent example of the difference made by uniting two words into a compound with one accent is *blackbird*. We can say 'the crow is a *black bird*,' but certainly not, 'the crow is a *blackbird*.'

Thirdly, we have the combination drawn still tighter in *needful*. This word, like *Newfoundland*, is shown by its single accent to be really one word, and its meaning is not the same as that of the sum of the parts that make it up. It does not mean 'full of need,' but 'needed' or necessary. Thus the second part *full*, though we can easily see from what separate word it is derived, does not retain its meaning, it has become little more than a suffix, such as the *-ed* in need*ed*. But besides

[1] Earle, *English Prose*, p. 50.

this, as the accent falls upon the earlier syllable,[1] the *ful* has begun to wear down, being pronounced less distinctly than its free brother *full*, and having this fact marked by the omission of the second L.

Fourthly, we have compounds which have been so much worn down that they no longer show clearly from what they are derived. No one would suppose that the *-ly* in *truly* was originally a distinct word like *-ful* in *needful*. And yet, if we look at the older form of English, we shall see that such is the case; *-ly* is the worn-down form of *-líce*,[2] the dative case of *líc*, 'a body' (as in *lych*-gate, the gate at the entrance of a churchyard), and so *truly* originally means 'with a true body or shape.' So too *-ship* in *friendship, lordship*, is originally a distinct word meaning 'shape,' and so state or condition. Again, *-hood* in *manhood*, *-head* in *Godhead*, is a distinct word, *hád*, in Old English, meaning 'position in society,' 'state,' or 'quality,' so that *manhood* meant and means still the qualities of a man. And *-less* in *needless* is the same word as *loose* (*léas* is the old form); thus *needless* means 'loose, or free from need.' In some of these compounds the latter part of the word has become disguised either in consonant or vowel. The reason is that, as the accent falls further back on the main part of the word, the latter part was not so fully pronounced, and consequently was often shortened in some way for ease of pronunciation. And its different pronunciation from the free word with which it was identical would not strike any one as strange. As soon as a compound word is definitely formed, those who use it seldom think of its derivation, even when it is still so obvious as in *needful* and *Newfoundland*, or in *selfish*.

It is well to bear in mind these facts about the formation of compound words, since they are most important in the

---

[1] Also, no doubt, because in saying it we do not think of *-ful* as identical with *full*, and so do not feel bound to pronounce it the same.

[2] So in Somersetshire they still say ''ard-like,' 'quiet-like.'—*Transactions of the Philological Society*, 1875-76, p. 197.

history of language. Think how many different ideas may be expressed, for instance, by compounding the one verb *bear* with various prepositions and suffixes. There are *forbear, bearing, overbearing, underbearing* (in Shakespeare), *bearable, unbearable.* And later on we shall see more clearly what an important part this formation of compound words has probably played in making our language.

CHAPTER II

DIALECTS AND LANGUAGES

The difference between a dialect and a language—How one grows out of the other—English as an example of this—How the relationship of two languages can be proved.

BEFORE speaking of the relation to each other of dialects and languages it will be well to understand what these two words mean.

To begin with, in speaking of the English language as opposed to dialects, we often mean that form of the language which is used in books and by the educated classes, as opposed to the local speech of different parts of the country, which is seldom written. But in fact, as we shall see more clearly further on, this literary language is merely one dialect out of many, which, with some admixture of other dialects, has by force of circumstances gained a predominant position. But it is only one dialect after all. The same is the case with the French and German which we read in books, and which educated Frenchmen and Germans imitate in their talk. It will be well then to call this 'standard' English the literary dialect, for the English language includes all dialects of English. What then is a language as opposed to a dialect? We speak of the German language and of the English language, while we call the varieties of speech in Devonshire, Lancashire, Northumberland, and the Scotch Lowlands dialects of English. The principle on which we distinguish languages from dialects

Dialects and Languages

must be this, that those who speak one dialect of a language can be more or less well understood by those who speak another, whereas those who speak English and German are not mutually intelligible. It is a question of degree, for as a matter of fact dialects may and do develop into languages.

We shall see their relation better if we take the steps by which language diverges.

We have seen already, and it is easy for each of us to notice, that no two persons speak quite alike. Further, each family, from one member of it copying another, has common peculiarities of speech. Some of these spread to a district, and so we have the beginnings of a local dialect. We saw in the last chapter that there are certain conservative forces which tend to keep language as it was before. If these are removed or weakened the language will go on diverging, so that

(1) Personal or family peculiarities of speech will develop into
(2) Local dialects, which again may in time become
(3) Distinct languages, such as English and German.

This will be clearer if we take an imaginary instance of the process.

Suppose two English Families Robinson to be cast upon a desert island without books. Each family will have some peculiarities in pronunciation and in the stock of words which it uses. If it should happen that both families have a difficulty in pronouncing some sound, R, or TH, or S, it is plain that this sound will die out among the community, for the children will never hear it and so cannot imitate it. As for those peculiarities which extend to one family only, as well as those which are certain to crop up afterwards (since no two people speak quite alike), some of these will be generally adopted, and some will not, according as the rest choose (unconsciously) to imitate them. In any case words will get clipped so as to be easier to pronounce (as has happened with *bo'sun* and *'bus*), grammar will be simplified by analogy (as *catch'd*, and 'I *see'd* it'). And these changes will not all be the same as those which establish themselves in England at the same time, though some, no doubt, will be.

Further, as to their stock of words. Those words which neither family happens to be fond of will die out of the language; their children cannot imitate what they never hear. In this way too the names of all animals will be lost except of such as exist on the island, or which may be preserved in stories handed down. And if the families come from a town they will not know the ordinary names for many agricultural implements, and if they invent these, they will give them different names from those which are in use in England. They will also invent words, and give old words new meanings. Thus their speech will diverge from ordinary English. For they have no need to be intelligible except to each other. They have only each other's speech to imitate. And we have said that they are to have no books. Therefore their speech will soon become a distinct dialect of English. And if they are left undisturbed long enough (perhaps four or five centuries would be required), they will be unintelligible to Englishmen who may rediscover them,—that is, they will have developed a distinct language.

Now, in order that their speech may vary, a family, village, or tribe need not necessarily be separated from the rest of their nation by the sea. A forest, a river, mere distance were until recent times quite enough to separate one village or tribe from another so that strong local peculiarities could grow up. As long as they act together even occasionally, as by forming alliances for war, there will be strong influences at work to prevent them from becoming quite unintelligible to each other. As soon as intercourse between them ceases altogether, the divergence goes on unchecked. And literature in very early times had very little influence in keeping the dialects together. For it was not made permanent by being written down; and if a fable, or legend, or poem spread from one tribe to another, the person who repeated it naturally adapted it to his own dialect.

At the present time everything tends to level dialects; to make the speech of the whole country similar. For the forests have been cleared, or at least have good roads through them, rivers have been bridged, railways have brought the different districts close to one another, children are taught 'standard' English in schools; there is a common literature in this one dialect, and most people can read it; every one tries to copy the speech or dialect of the educated classes; the whole country is one State. In former times none of these influences were present.

And yet there are still plenty of traces left of the older condition of things. Lancashire people, talking to each other, are, both from their pronunciation and from the local words which they use, hard enough for the 'Southerner' to understand. There are plays, or dialogues, and poems in this dialect, and the poems of William Barnes in the dialect of Dorsetshire. A Scotchman or Irishman can generally be detected by his use of *will* for *shall*, as when he says 'I *will* be fourteen next May.' Then there is the peculiar way of pronouncing R found in Northumberland, the Northumberland 'burr' as it is called, and the Devonshire U, like a French U, or ü in German. There are plenty of local words or local uses of words in most districts, as in the Midlands they say 'to be *starved* with cold and *clemmed* with hunger.' And many of these local forms of speech are of great antiquity. The Midland *nobbut* (= only) is found in Wycliffe (1388), who wrote Midland English. And the Lowland Scotch (or modern Northumbrian) use of *till* for *to*, as in ' *till* hame,' *intill*, is found in some of the earliest English which we possess, which is in the Northumbrian dialect (see p. 146).

As we have seen then, before the world was civilised the conditions necessary for producing dialects were present everywhere And a migration of a tribe or tribes even to a small distance, as, for instance, to the other side of a community of different race and language, or, as in the case of the English, across a sea, was sufficient to stop intercourse almost or altogether, and consequently remove all necessity for the emigrants to make their stay-at-home relations understand them, as well as all possibility of one part imitating the other. And there was no fixed or standard literary dialect in which poems were composed, though there may have been a poetical style. Hence two parts of the same tribe, two families of the same village, would, when separated, develop different languages, since the peculiarities which each had would become fixed, and fresh differences would crop up,[1] till in course of time two distinct languages were formed, as in the case of the language of Schleswig-Holstein and English.

We know from history that the Angles came from Schleswig-Holstein, and the Saxons and Frisians, who also settled in 'Britain' (as it was then), came from the part immediately to the south and west of this. Their speech was thus, to begin with, the same as Low German or Platt-Deutsch and Frisian or 'Friese.' Now an Englishman cannot understand those languages unless he learns them almost as he might learn French or Latin, since each dialect or language has diverged from its older form.[2] And yet there are a great many resemblances both in the grammar and in the stock of words, which mark the common origin of the languages. As the rhyme says—

'Bread, butter, and cheese,
Is good English, and good Friese.'

We know, then, in this case[3] from History that the resemblances between English on the one hand, and Frisian

---

[1] We shall see later on that it requires several centuries for two dialects to diverge so much that the one is quite unintelligible to those who speak the other.   [2] See Appendix B.

[3] The derivation of French, Spanish, Portuguese, Italian, Romansch, and Wallachian as distinct languages from the Low or popular Latin is also known from history.

and Low German on the other, are due to the fact that these languages were once one and the same language. Can we conclude, wherever we find similar resemblances between two or more languages, that these also are due to the same cause, to their having been originally one language?

Let us see what are the other possible causes of a general resemblance between two languages. These are—

(1) Chance.
(2) One language borrowing from another.
(3) It may be said, 'There is a natural way of expressing ideas in language.'

(1) Words do occasionally resemble each other by accident. *Cura* is very much like *care* both in form and meaning, but the two words have nothing to do with each other. The same is true of *whole* and ὅλος.

But if we find large numbers of words alike in two or more languages, we plainly cannot attribute this to chance or coincidence.

(2) English is full of words borrowed from Latin, either directly or through French. Can there then be such a general borrowing by one language from another as to make it appear that the two languages are originally connected?

There are certain essential words in a language, for instance, the pronouns, and names for near relations, and (almost always) the simple numerals,[1] which, first, a language cannot have done without until they were supplied from a foreign speech, and which, in the second place, are much too commonly used, too familiar, too firmly rooted in the language to be changed for foreign words. Occasionally, it is true, such a word is changed. In English, for instance, we have adopted *uncle* from French *oncle*, which comes from Latin *avunculus*, and dropped our

[1] In many parts of Wales the English numerals are commonly used by the Welsh-speaking inhabitants.

native word *éam*. So too *second* (French, from Latin *secundus*) has taken the place of *other* as a numeral, except in the phrase 'every *other* day' (= 'every second day ').[1] But English has borrowed more words than any European language. And if we find many words of the sort mentioned above corresponding in two languages, this cannot be due to borrowing even in English.

And then no language ever borrows its grammar, the inflexions of its verbs and substantives. An Englishman might know Latin or German ever so well, and yet he would not feel the least inclination to make the genitive of *jackass*, *jackatis*, or the plural of *hare*, *haren*. Rather we transfer our own grammar to foreign words which we adopt, and say 'he telegraph*ed*,' 'omnibus*es*, and 'octopus*es*.'

(3) A good instance of the idea that notions are 'naturally' expressed by some particular combination of sounds is given in the answer of the man who, on being asked why a particular kind of ball was called a 'yorker,' said, 'Why, I don't see what else you could call it!' As a matter of fact, the same ball is or was called a 'lob' at Winchester College. And if we compare English or Latin with Hungarian, for instance, we shall see that, whether or not all languages may originally have had some very simple elements in common (which has not been proved), at all events these are now hardly possible to recognise, and certainly have not produced the very numerous and distinct resemblances which we find between English and most of the languages of Europe, living and dead, along with many Asiatic languages. That certain definite languages are allied, while others, so far as we can see at present, have no connection with them, is a result to which we are led, whether we compare their stock of words or their grammar.

[1] The White Queen, in *Through the Looking-Glass*, draws absurd conclusions by using 'other' in this expression according to the ordinary meaning of the word in Modern English.

We may say, then, that if two languages closely resemble each other in many of their pronouns, names of near relations, and numerals, this can be due only to the fact that they were formerly mere dialects of one language.

CHAPTER III

ENGLISH RELATED TO OTHER LANGUAGES

Proof of the relationship of English to the other Indo-European languages—'Shifting of consonant sounds' in different languages of the family, or Grimm's Law—What it proves, and its use in deriving words.[1]

It will be well to have some facts to go upon, and consequently there are here inserted, to begin with, some examples of the resemblance of certain languages to English and to each other.[2] Celtic and Slavonic are not single languages, but branches of language (see plan, p. 33), each containing several more or less distinct languages from some one of which these words are taken. The first list is of similar words from nearly all the branches of the Indo-European family of languages. In the second and third table four languages are selected as specimens of the whole family, not as having any specially close relationship to each other, which is not the case.

I

Sanskrit.	Greek.	Latin.	Celtic.	Slavonic.	Lithuanian.	English.	Arabic.	Hungarian.
dwa	δύο	duo	dau	dwa	du	two	ithn	ket
tri	τρεῖς	tres	tri	tri	tri	three	thalath	harom
tritija	τρίτος	tertius	tryde	tretii	trĕczias	third	anta	te
twam	σύ, τύ	tu	tu	tii	tu	thou	ana	engem
mâ	μὲ	me	me	man	manen	me	umm	anya
mátár	μήτηρ	mater	mathir	mati	moté	mother	akh	fiver
bhrâtar	φράτηρ	frater	brathir	bratru	broterélis	brother		
yuga	ζύγον	jugum	iau	igo	jungas	yoke		
rudhira	ἐρυθρός	ruber[3]	rhudd	rudru		red		

[1] Skeat, *Principles of English Etymology*, First Series. Whitney, *Language and its Study*. Schrader, *Sprachvergleichung und Urgeschichte*. Kington Oliphant, *Old and Middle English*.

[2] Chiefly from Whitney, *Language and its Study*; and Kington Oliphant, *Old and Middle English*.

[3] Supposed to be a corruption of 'rudher.'

II

Sanskrit.	Greek.	Latin.	English.
nâ-man	ő-νο-μα	no-men	na-me
râj-an	...	reg-em	(bishop)ric [1]
yuk-ta	ζευκ-τός	junc-tus	yok-ed
as-mi	εἰ-μί (ἐσμί)	s-um	a-m
an-	ἀν-, ἀ-	in-(sons)	un(seen)
antar	...	inter	under
...	ἀεί	aevum	ever

III

1st sing.	vêd-a	(F)οἶδ-α	vidi	wât (Old Eng.)
2nd ,,	vêt-tha	(F)οἶσ-θα	vidisti	wâst
3rd ,,	vêda	(F)οἶδ-ε	vidit	wât
1st plur.	vid-ma	{ (F)ἴδ-μεν / (F)ἴσ-μεν }	vidimus	witon
2nd ,,	vid-a	(F)ἴσ-τε	vidistis	witon
3rd ,,	vid-us	(F)ἴσ-ασι	viderunt -re	witon

I. Now, if we look at the first list of words, we shall see

(1) That most of them belong to the class of words which can scarcely be borrowed. We can hardly imagine a language without words for *me* or *mother*, or its changing the native words for foreign ones. And at all events, with so many words of this kind, borrowing is impossible.

(2) That such numerous coincidences cannot be due to chance.

(3) That there is no 'natural' way of expressing our thoughts in language. If we look at the corresponding words in Arabic and Hungarian, languages belonging to two other families, we see how entirely different these are.

II. In the words *name, yoked, am*, we see that (1) the root, or main part of the word, and (2) the suffix, which fixes it as a part of speech, or the termination, are similar in the four languages selected, widely separated as these are in space (see Map). In *un-* we find a syllable with a distinct meaning, but not capable of standing by itself, similar in these four languages and still ready to be used in English at the present

---

[1] Also *rix* in Gaulish (Celtic) proper names, such as Dumnorix, Vercingetorix; *rex* is of course for *reg-s*, as is seen in the accusative *reg-em*.

day for forming new words, such as *unknowable* or *unreliable* which are certainly of recent formation.

III. Here we have further evidence that the terminations in the different languages were originally the same; we must remember that no language borrows its grammar from another. But besides this we find another most striking resemblance. It is believed that in the earliest periods, when the languages were still one, the accent fell on the 'stem' in the singular, on the termination in the plural.[1] Thus the stem was more strongly pronounced in the singular, the termination in the plural. The marks of this primitive accent have lasted in three of the four languages, Latin being the exception. The English form given is that which was used before the Norman Conquest, and even so late as Wycliffe's Translation of the Bible (1388), this distinction between singular and plural is preserved (He *woot*, they *witen*).

Now all the correspondences between the languages of the Indo-European family are not so easy to detect as those given above. We have seen that a dialect develops peculiarities of its own, like the Devonshire Ü, and the peculiar Northumbrian R, and we know that over a large part of England an H is never heard except among educated people, who acquire or keep the habit of pronouncing the letter because it is 'vulgar' to do otherwise. On the other hand, it is plain that the H must once have been commonly pronounced or it would not have been written, and the English in America do not drop their H's. In the same way, when the dialects of the Indo-European speech were becoming separated into different languages, certain 'shiftings of sound' took place; one branch, for instance, saying T where another said D, as in *two, duo*. Whether we can find out which was the original sound is a different question. We saw above

---

[1] Stress or accent belongs either to a word or a sentence. As an example of the former we may compare the subst. *ob*ject with the verb to *object*; as an example of the latter, '*He* won't do it,' with 'He *won't* do it,' which have a somewhat different meaning.

that the tendency is to change the more difficult sound into one easier to pronounce. But it is not always clear which of two sounds is the easier, though, for various reasons, the D is in all probability the more original sound. The sound is, as we should expect, seldom altered into a totally different one, though, through various stages, this does sometimes happen. Thus τέσσαρες, πίσυρες (Æolic Greek), *quattuor*, *four*, are originally the same word. But as a rule the sound continues to be made in the same sort of way, and the changes run between hard, soft, and aspirated 'gutturals,' or labials, or 'dentals' as the case may be, and not from 'gutturals' to 'dentals,' or 'dentals' to labials.

We are supposing then that the ancestors of the English, Romans, and Greeks, of the Indians who spoke Sanskrit, and of the other nations related to these in language, originally all pronounced the sounds D, or T, or G, in the same way, and that afterwards, when the speech of each of these had developed into a dialect of Indo-European, or when it had split off into a separate language, a 'shifting of sounds' took place, beginning, no doubt, like other changes, with some one family or tribe, but spreading to all the members of the branch, who must have still been in tolerably close contact with each other, until, in the speech of that branch, all D's of the original language had been changed into T's, all T's into TH's.

This theory will become much more probable if we can give some instance where such a shifting of sounds has certainly taken place. And as a matter of fact this has happened in comparatively recent times within the Teutonic branch of the Indo-European family to which English and German belong. It has taken place so recently (600-900 A.D.) that its progress can be traced from writings, from evidence, and not by conjecture. These changes of sound, such as—

    T   to   Z
    TH to   D,

took place in 'High'[1] or inland German, and spread, some farther, some less far, northwards towards the coast. The English had left Germany before these shiftings began, and thus many of the differences between the English and German forms of the same word are accounted for; for instance

two and *zwei*
thief and *dieb*.

As to the causes of it we know nothing, any more than we can assign a cause why the Northumbrian 'burr' differs from the ordinary English R.

To return to the earlier 'shifting of sounds' which has now been supported and illustrated by an undoubted example of a similar change, the regular correspondence between these different sounds, the 'law' by which a T in one language is represented by a D in another, was discovered (not invented, or passed in the German Parliament) by a German named Grimm, and is consequently known as 'Grimm's Law.' The simplest way to state it is as follows. Let Latin, Greek, and Sanskrit[2] (which in the main go together as far as these consonants are concerned), be considered as one group, and Teutonic, represented by English,[3] as the other. Let us suppose (as is probable) that the first group keeps the older sound, the sound which was used in these words in the Indo-European language. Then in each of the following series it will be found that this Indo-European sound is 'shifted' in the Teutonic language to the sound next following it. Thus—

In the 'Dental' series DH becomes D, D becomes T, T becomes TH
,, Labial ,, BH ,, B, B ,, P, P ,, PH
,, 'Guttural' ,, GH ,, G, G ,, K, K ,, KH

---

[1] Literary German, which we read in books, is a High German dialect, with some modifications. Only a few of these shiftings are found in the Low German of the Continent; *e.g.* in Low German or Platt-Deutsch *that* is *dat*. Here the TH at the beginning is changed, but not the T, as in High Germ. *das*.

[2] Skeat, *Principles of English Etymology*, First Series, chap. viii., from which work a very large part of this chapter is derived.

[3] High German, as we have seen, has undergone a 'shifting' peculiar to itself.

English related to other Languages

Or we may put it thus: If we take a Latin or Greek word and wish to find the corresponding English one, we must take each 'dental,' labial, and 'guttural,' and move one place on in the series, as in the 'Mad Tea-party.'

'Dental' Series

DH (*Greek* θ).	D.	T.	TH.
θαρσεῖν	dare		
θυγάτηρ	daughter		
θρῆνος	drone		
	δαμᾶν / domare	tame	
	dwa¹ (*Skr.*) / δύο / duo	two	
	δρῦs	tree	
	ad (*Skr.*) / ἔδομαι / edere	eat	
	ad	at	
		tad ² (*Skr.*) / τό / (is-)tud	that
		tenuis	thin
		pat-ra (*Skr.*) / πέτ-ομαι	feather
		bhara-ti (*Skr.*) / fer-t	beareth

Labial Series

BH (*Greek* φ, *Latin* f).	B.	P.	PH (*English* f).
bhrátar (*Skr.*) / φράτηρ / frater	brother		

---

¹ *Skr.* = Sanskrit.
² It will be noticed that this and many other words illustrate two changes at once.

BH (*Greek* φ, *Latin* f).	B.	P.	PH (*English* f).
bhu (*Skr.* = be) φύω fui	be		
φηγός fagus	beech		
bhid (*Skr.*) fīdi (*Perf. of* findo)	bite		
		pitár (*Skr.*) πατήρ pater	father
		pad (*Skr.*) πόδ-α ped-em	foot
		πῶλος pullus	foal
		ἀπό	of, off
		σκάπτειν	shave (*Old English* scafan)

It appears that an example of the shifting of B to P cannot be found in the languages which we have selected. An original P has sometimes remained unchanged.[1]

'GUTTURAL' (OR PALATAL) SERIES

GH (*Skr.* h, *Gr.* χ, *Lat.* h, f, g).	G (*Skr.* j).	K (*or hard* c, *Skr.* ç).	KH (*Eng.* h).[2]
hams-a (= swan, *Skr.*) χήν (h)anser	goose (gans, *Gothic and German*)		
vehere	wain (*Old Eng.* wægn)		

---

[1] See Skeat, *Principles of English Etymology*, First Series, pp. 137, 138.

[2] Originally often or always *guttural*, as in German *ch*; *e.g.* in *night* pronounced *nicht*.

English related to other Languages

GH (Skr. h, Gr. χ, Lat. h, f, g).	G (Skr. j).	K (or hard c, Skr. ç).	KH (Eng. h).
	jánu (Skr.) γόνυ genu	} knee[1]	
	jná (Skr.) γνῶ-ναι gno-sco	} know[1]	
	gelu gelidus (F)έργον	cool cold work	
		νύκ-τα noct-em }	night
		καρδία cord-is }	heart
		cornu	horn
		çata (Skr.) ἑ-κατόν centum }	hund(-red)

There is another series about which a word or two must be said, though the subject is far too complicated to be followed out at all thoroughly here. It appears that in the original language there were certain sounds resembling 'gutturals,' but differing from them in that they had a tendency to join a W to the GH, G, or K, just like a Q in English. Now W is of course a labial, a sound formed by the lips, and sometimes this W has got the better of the G or K, and converted the sound altogether into a labial, or even into a dental, where the vowel following it made this easier to say,[2] though sometimes, on the other hand, all trace of the W disappears. Thus we get *quatuor* in Latin, πίσυρες and τέσσαρες in Greek, *pedwar* in

---

[1] The K was of course still pronounced at the time when English spelling became fixed.

[2] In forming E and I the tongue is very nearly in the right position for pronouncing a dental letter, D or T.

Welsh, *féower* in Old, and *four* in Modern English. The original form is supposed to have been *qetwar*.

And for other reasons as well the examples do not always work out so clearly as those given above. We have seen that even in these the aspirates of the original language (DH, BH, GH) especially assume various forms in the languages which we have grouped together—Greek, Latin, and Sanskrit, since each of these had its own tendency to shift particular sounds. And we saw that a still more extensive shifting has taken place in High German. So too the Law has been made difficult to follow by further changes in English, or some one or more of the other languages.[1] Old English *þæc*[2] is connected with Latin *tego*, but the C has since been softened, and the word has become *thatch*. And in other cases one consonant has preserved another close to it (just as two sticks tied together are harder to break or bend than each is separately), as, for instance, the Latin *stella* (for *ster-ula*) is the same word as English *star*. But even from the examples given above the connection of the languages comes out clearly, and the result is the same if we compare examples from the remaining languages of the Indo-European family. The argument is this: If we assume the rule, the connection of the languages is clear, and on no other ground but their connection with each other can the regular correspondence of the consonants be explained.

This rule is also most necessary to bear in mind in order to derive words correctly, for derivation or etymology is not a matter of guess-work, but requires a knowledge of the laws of sound of the language or languages through which a word has passed, and of the shape which the word would thus assume in it or them. For instance, *castle* and *castellum* are evidently the same word. But if *castle* were one of the words which both English and Latin inherited

---

[1] Some of these have been formulated in what are known as Verner's and Grassmann's Laws. [2] þ=th.

from the original Indo-European language, the C would appear in English as H, since it would have been a part of the Teutonic language before English and German and the other Teutonic dialects separated from each other—that is, at the time when the sound of C or K was in all words altered to KH or H by our Teutonic ancestors. Just as if we were to find a coat hung up in a room where pastilles or sulphur had recently been burnt, and it had no special smell, we should conclude that it had been brought into the room after the fumigation took place. Now, as a matter of fact, we happen to know that the word *castle* was brought into English from Latin at or after our conversion to Christianity, and became more widely spread[1] from its use by Edward the Confessor's Norman friends, and from the castles built by William the Conqueror and others, the French word which they used being almost exactly similar to the Latin one from which both it and the English word were derived. But we could have known that English borrowed the word directly or indirectly from Latin simply by means of Grimm's 'Law,' the 'Law' or rule of the regular correspondence of consonant sounds in certain languages, which Grimm did not make or pass but discovered. In the same way we cannot connect *call* with καλεῖν.

[1] With a change of meaning. In English it originally meant 'village.'

CHAPTER IV

THE INDO-EUROPEAN FAMILY OF LANGUAGES

Divisions of the Indo-European family of languages—Position of Sanskrit —The other branches—Impossibility of grouping these.[1]

WE may then conclude that English, Greek, Latin, Sanskrit, and the other languages of the Indo-European family are all related to each other, that they were in fact once mere dialects of one Indo-European speech, and that they developed into separate languages when the tribes or nations which spoke these dialects parted off from each other, and there was thus no longer any intercourse between them to keep those who spoke one dialect intelligible to those who spoke another. On the opposite page will be found a plan of the branches or divisions into which the Indo-European family of languages has parted.

A question which has often been asked is, 'Which of these languages is the oldest?' by which must be meant 'Which of them is most like the primitive language?' In order to answer this question it is plainly necessary to find out what the original language was like, and how can this be done when no fragment of it has survived? Of course it is impossible to reconstruct it completely, but it is possible to find out with some approach to accuracy what the primitive form

[1] See Whitney, *Language and its Study*; and Schrader, *Sprachvergleichung und Urgeschichte.*

The Indo-European Family of Languages

was by comparing the varieties of a particular word in the different kindred languages, and judging what form could, according to the laws of language which we know, lie at the root of them all. Among these laws of language are the

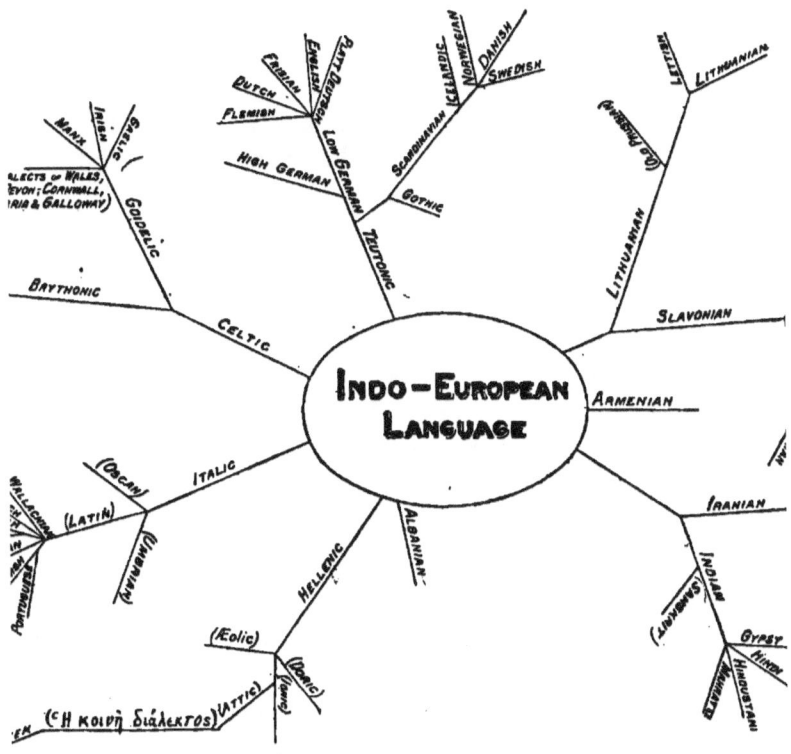

A plan of this kind is perhaps somewhat misleading, see below, p. 38, etc.

Dead languages are enclosed in brackets. Of course too the earlier single form of language in each branch is dead, and no specimen of these has been preserved.

There were doubtless many other languages, and even branches of language, which have perished, leaving no trace in writing behind them. Probably these, if we had them, would serve to bridge over with intermediate forms many of the wide gaps between the branches. Some of the less important known dialects are omitted in the plan.

following : (1) An easier sound is not changed to a harder one. (2) Languages do not increase the length of a word, except occasionally to make it easier to pronounce,[1] or in order to modify its meaning by adding what are called suffixes, and case or personal endings. But the conclusions as to the primitive form of words are plainly liable to mistake, and are altered as fresh laws or uniformities are discovered according to which language changes.

It was formerly thought that in Sanskrit we should almost always find a very close copy of the primitive Indo-European language. But Sanskrit often has A in words where the European languages have E or O, and yet there is the strongest reason for supposing that both E and O belong to the original form in the Indo-European language. In fact, it now appears that Sanskrit is close to the primitive language rather in its consonants than in its vowels, Greek being a more faithful copy of the original vowels, which are a no less important part of a language. And even as regards the consonants Sanskrit has not got a monopoly of old forms. We said, for instance, that it modifies or softens K into Ç (= S).[2] The original sound must have been some sort of K, for K is found in other languages, such as Greek (Skr. *çata*, Gr. ἑκάτον, Lat. *centum*), and Ç could never have changed to this sound, which is harder to pronounce. In the same way Sanskrit softens G to J, and γένος is less altered from the primitive word than Sanskrit *jan*; even the English form *kin* is here nearer to the primitive language than Sanskrit. On the whole, however, we may say that Sanskrit gives us forms more nearly resembling those in the primitive language than any other language does, though Greek is not far behind. This is not unnatural, as the oldest works in Sanskrit date from before 1000 B.C., and it has been a dead language (such

---

[1] *e.g.* e-scuyer (esquire, now *écuyer*) from *scutarius*.
[2] So Latin C (= K) has been softened in French into Ç or Ch : *recipere—recevoir, cantare—chanter*.

The Indo-European Family of Languages 35

as Latin is now), and therefore unchangeable, since about 500 B.C. If we had such early specimens of Latin or of a Teutonic language, they might have been as little altered from the primitive speech. We must, therefore, remember that Sanskrit is not the original Indo-European language, but merely one of its descendants, like Latin and English, only, on the whole, less altered than the rest. Accordingly English is not derived from Sanskrit.

Thus we get our first knowledge of the different languages at all kinds of periods. Sanskrit, as we have seen, supplies the earliest documents. The Homeric poems in Greek are of some date between 1000 and 700 B.C. On the other hand, the earliest writing in Lithuanian which we possess dates only from the sixteenth century A.D. Of course this makes a great difference to the 'antiquity' of any language, since languages are always changing, always becoming less like their primitive form. On the other hand, this change goes on at very different rates in different languages. English in the last 900 years has altered to an extraordinary extent, and Modern Persian is like it in this respect. On the other hand, Lithuanian, which comes almost latest within the field of our knowledge, has some wonderfully old-fashioned forms, retaining, for instance, 'verbs in $\mu\iota$,'—that is, it has as person-endings -*mi*, -*si*, -*ti*, like Greek or Sanskrit. We have a relic of these in English in 'I a-*m*.'

We may now say a word or two about some of these related languages, though the map and plan for the most part explain themselves.

Sanskrit is the language of the Indo-European invaders of India, who entered it from the North, probably not very long before the earliest works which we possess in the language were composed. Sanskrit or something like it was at first, of course, the ordinary spoken language of the people; but about 500 B.C. it ceased to be spoken, though it was still used as a sacred and literary language, just as Latin was commonly used for learned works down to quite recent times,[1] and is still in use in the services of the Roman Catholic Church. Closely allied to Sanskrit are the spoken languages of the northern half of India, such as Hindustani, Hindi, and Mahratti, as well as the language of the Gypsies. The Cuneiform Inscriptions (*cuneus* = wedge) are the Old Persian writings in wedge-shaped or arrow-headed letters found on the walls of Persepolis and elsewhere, containing records of the reigns of Darius, Xerxes, and other kings of Persia from about 500 B.C. The inscriptions at Nineveh and Babylon, though written with similar letters, are in an entirely different language. By Zend is meant the language in which the Zend-Avesta, the sacred book of the Old Persians, was written, which was brought to India by the Parsees, who migrated there to preserve their religion when Persia was conquered by the Mahometans. Parsi is the language spoken and written by the Parsees shortly before their migration.

The Old Slavonic, or Church Slavonic, is the language into which the Bible was translated for the ancestors of the Bulgarians late in the ninth century A.D. It is still used in the services of the Russian Church, like Latin further west.

The Old Prussian was the language of North-East Prussia, now displaced by Platt-Deutsch and literary High German. Of Lithuanian enough has been said already, and the relations of the Teutonic languages to each other will be discussed later on.

The earliest writings in any Celtic language (except some inscriptions) are Irish, late in the eighth century A.D. The Celtic languages, at the time when our first adequate knowledge of them begins, have already been greatly altered from what is known to have been their primitive form. The Goidels must have settled in Britain before the Brythonic branch of the Celts. They were driven west by the Brythons,

---

[1] *e.g.* many of Lord Bacon's works were in Latin.

The Indo-European Family of Languages   37

and afterwards, when the English came over, many of the Brythons were driven to seek refuge among the Goidels. Except in the Scotch Highlands, Galloway, the Isle of Man, and Ireland, the Goidels finally adopted the Brythonic language or dialect.[1]

Latin was not the only language of the Indo-European family spoken in the Italian peninsula. There are considerable remains both of Umbrian and Oscan (the language of the Samnites), showing both that these were related to Latin and yet that the three languages had diverged very widely from each other. The oldest Latin inscription which affords clear information about the language is still to be read on one of the tombs of the Scipios (about 250 B.C.) The other languages of Italy are dead, and have left no descendants, but Latin has numerous children still alive which are often called the Romance languages. These are not descended directly from the literary Latin which we read, the language written and spoken by educated men at Rome, but from the 'vulgar' dialect of the soldiers, colonists, and traders, by whom the knowledge of Latin was brought into the provinces. And there are still remaining enough documents of different periods to show the steps by which French and the other Romance languages were formed from Latin. These languages are especially interesting to us, since one of them, namely French, has contributed a very large number of words to Modern English, as we shall see presently.

The Greek language was split up into numerous dialects. The Doric forms in the Choruses of Greek Tragedies (the rest of which are in Attic Greek), the dialect of Herodotus and of Homer, will remind us of this. But Attic became the prevailing form of speech, and spread more or less over the whole extent of Alexander's conquests. It was in this popular Attic ('the common dialect,' ἡ κοινὴ διαλεκτός) that the New Testament was written, and upon it that modern literary

[1] Rhys, *Celtic Britain*.

Greek is founded, and from constant imitation has become once more a very close copy of its original.

We have now glanced at the various branches into which the original Indo-European language has become divided. Can these be further classified so that, for instance, the North European languages shall form one group, the South European another, and so on? The attempt has often been made, but on the whole it is impossible to carry this grouping very far. Sanskrit and the Old Persian languages undoubtedly have so many characteristics common to both, and besides, have so many words in common which are not shared by the other Indo-European languages, that we may believe that there was a time, *after* the tribes speaking the other dialects became separated from them, when the ancestors of the Hindoos and Persians still lived close to one another, the dialect of the one tribe being still intelligible to the men of the other, so that, for instance, improvements in their weapons made by the one tribe became known to the other and carried their name with them. The same seems to have been the case with the ancestors of the Lithuanians and the Slavs. But when we try to carry this grouping further we are met by great difficulties. We might, for instance, be inclined to say that the formation of the dative[1] plural in *-bhi, -bhis, -bhyas* (*-bhyams*), Latin *hosti-bus*, Greek εὐνῆφι, Irish *doir-ibh*, Sanskrit *daru-bhyas* (= δόρυ = wood) on the one hand, and in *-m*, as in the Teutonic and Slavonic and Lithuanian branches, on the other (Old English *wulfum*, Gothic *wulfam*, Old High German *wulfum*, Old Norse *ulfum*, Old Slavonic *vluko-mu*, Lithuanian *wilka-mus*), is so marked a characteristic of their grammar that we are justified in throwing Sanskrit, Greek, Latin, and Celtic into one group, and the Teutonic, Slavonic, and Lithuanian languages into another. But surely the fondness for softening a K into Ç or S or Z is an equally distinct characteristic; and if we attend to this, we shall throw Sanskrit, Iranian, Slavonic,

[1] Or instrumental.

The Indo-European Family of Languages 39

and Lithuanian into one group, while Greek, Latin, Celtic, and Teutonic will form another (Sanskrit *çata*, Iranian *satu*, Old Slavonian *suto*, Lithuanian *szimtas*; Greek ἑκατόν, Latin *centum*, Irish *cét*, English *hund-red*). And if we take other points as our principle of division, we shall be led again to different groupings, and be landed in inextricable confusion. Now we must remember that this grouping of the languages is not to be merely an artificial classification, made by ourselves for the sake of aiding our memories, but that we wish to discover what parts of the original Indo-European nation, after their wanderings had begun, still remained close enough to each other for the dialects of that part to develop common characteristics, or, perhaps, which divisions were nearest to each other in the original home. The more probable account seems to be this. While the Indo-European nation still lived together, the tribes composing it undoubtedly spoke or got to speak different dialects. Each of these dialects was the parent of one of the 'branches' of the language. There was a Celtic dialect, a Lithuanian and Slavonic dialect or dialects, and so on. As language is constantly shifting, new characteristics developed themselves. Thus a tendency to soften the K,[1] beginning, for example, with the Sanskrit and Iranian dialect, spread to those who spoke the early form of Lithuanian and Slavonic. On the other hand, the new form of the dative plural in -*m*, beginning perhaps with the Teutons, spread to the Lithuanians and Slavs. And this is made more probable by the fact that each of these characteristics is shared by a group of nations which still remain near to each other (as, in the two cases mentioned, a glance at the map will show), and which, therefore, were probably next to each other in the original home.[2] It is like the wave when a stone is thrown

---

[1] As has happened in French in much later times; *e.g.* Latin *centum*, French *cent*, pronounced *sent*.

[2] That is, we can draw a boundary line on the map, cutting off those nations which, for instance, had softened K to Ç or S, without including other Indo-European nations.

into the water, which spreads a certain distance and then dies away. So too in England the dialects of Somerset and Dorset both soften an S to Z, and are alike in many other respects; but each has its peculiar characteristics besides, which are confined to itself. And finally, the processes or 'waves' of sound-shifting in Germany, which have separated the Low German dialects, more especially English, so far from High German (as in *that—das*, by which one word two of these processes are illustrated), though they all apparently [1] started from Southern Germany, have some of them influenced even Modern Dutch, and Platt-Deutsch,[2] while others have spread over a much smaller extent of country.

[1] In the change of TH—D the progress of the 'wave' can be distinctly traced. [2] See Appendix B.

CHAPTER V

THE INDO-EUROPEAN PEOPLE

Condition, life, and manners of the Indo-European people—The evidence—The conclusions—Uncertainty about their original home.[1]

AND now is it possible to discover anything about the early condition of this Indo-European people whose thought and speech made our language in its earliest form? Well, it is plain that if a word appears in the same form and with the same sense in all or many of the languages, and has not been borrowed by one language from another, then those who spoke the original language must have possessed the word, and consequently the thing named. For instance, the correspondence of *jugum*, ζύγον, *yoke* (p. 22), and the similar words in the other languages, show that the Indo-Europeans, while they still lived together, knew how to harness animals to a cart or plough. *Ruber*, ἐρυθρός, *red*, show that they could discriminate red from other colours. *Centum*, ἑκατόν, *hund-red*, prove that they could reckon up to 100, which all uncivilised peoples cannot easily do. But, as we go further, we are met by difficulties, and have to be cautious as to our conclusions. The same word for copper, for instance, is shared by Latin (*cuprum, aes cyprium*) with the Teutonic and Celtic languages; but there can be no doubt that these have borrowed it from the Romans. So too the same word for tin appears in Greek

[1] See Schrader, *Sprachvergleichung und Urgeschichte.*

(κασσίτερος), and also in the Slavonic languages, Wallachian, and Sanskrit. But the word was first brought to Greece by the Phœnicians; from the Greeks the name spread, along with the knowledge of the metal, to the Slavonians (from whom it was, at a much later date, borrowed by the Wallachians), and by Alexander's conquests it was introduced into India. We must not therefore conclude that tin and forged or smelted copper were known to our original ancestors.

Again, we must not attribute to this primitive and half-savage people notions and thoughts which are due to ages of civilisation and Christianity. Their life, manners, and thought, must have been rough and coarse to a degree which we find it hard to realise, though these contained, no doubt, the germs or seeds of future progress. Still, by careful study of the words which can be proved to be parts of the original language, and not borrowed or developed later on, checking the conclusions by what we learn of the Indo-European peoples from the earliest records of each of the divisions—that is, from the earliest Sanskrit writings, from Homer, Herodotus, Strabo, Caesar, Tacitus, the last three of whom tell us a good deal about those branches of the family which had a later development, as, for example, the Germans—as well as from mythology, and from relics of early civilisation or the want of it (as in the lake-dwellings of Switzerland and the Valley of the Po), a good deal can be found out about what the condition of our ancestors must have been just before they began to part on their wanderings. It would be too long to give the proofs for the correctness of our picture; but a list of words will be found at the end of the chapter which illustrate the different portions of it, in the same order as the subjects have been taken.

First of all then, they knew nothing of any metals except copper. But even as regards this, since there are no words common to the different families which imply any knowledge of forging or smelting metals, we must conclude that even copper was only known as a striking natural substance, which it is, on account of its red or green colour, and its frequent occurrence. They may perhaps with stones have hammered bits of it, cold, into axe-heads or other implements; but even then copper is not a very valuable substance unless hardened into bronze by a mixture of tin, a metal which they were unacquainted with. So their implements and weapons must have been almost entirely of stone, horn, bone, and wood, and this alone shows that they had not reached a high stage of development.

They were mainly a pastoral people, having already tamed cattle, sheep, goats, and the dog to take care of them,—perhaps pigs as well. They had also a name for the horse, but it is not certain that they knew it otherwise than as a wild animal, since the languages have no word in common meaning 'to ride.' They lived in huts with doors, doubtless of no very solid construction, since they were quite ready to change their place of abode on small provocation. But though their chief wealth (like that of the Patriarchs) was in flocks and herds, yet they were certainly not entirely ignorant of agriculture, being in this respect in the position of Isaac and Jacob.[1] They grew barley, spelt, millet, and almost certainly wheat, besides peas, beans, and onions, and also flax. Out of the flax they would not only twist or spin threads, but seem to have known also the rudiments of weaving, since they had names for the warp (the threads arranged upwards, side by side, Latin *stamen*, 'standing'), between which the horizontal threads, called the woof, were run in and out, as in basket-weaving. They may have woven wool as well; they certainly made it into a kind of felt. They could make rough pottery. They had waggons on wheels to convey their families and belongings from place to place, when, for the sake of fresh pasture, from the pressure of their enemies, or for other causes, they changed their home. Finally, they had boats moved

[1] Genesis xxvi. 12; xxxvii. 7.

with oars, and not with sails; but they do not seem to have lived near the sea.

As to their food, besides the flesh of their flocks and herds, they made milk into curds and whey, and into butter, which last was also used for anointing themselves. Their corn they probably ate, for the most part, simply roasted in the ear, or ground and made into a kind of porridge, though they seem also to have baked bread in some primitive fashion. Besides water and milk they drank mead, an intoxicating drink made with honey.

Like all savage peoples they lived in constant fear of their enemies, not only those nations which were of a totally different stock; for the separate tribes would frequently be at war with each other, from chance quarrels or for spoil, just like civilised nations. And a murder or manslaughter might convert two families of the same tribe, that of the slayer and the slain, into deadly enemies, unless those who were trying to revenge their relation could be bought off by a payment of money. Therefore arms, made of stone and wood, were a very important part of the property of each family. These were the bow, javelin, spear, club,[1] a short stone knife or dagger, and probably the shield.

As to their government, it can hardly be proved that there was any, except that each family was ruled by the father, or on his death by the eldest brother, who governed his mother and sisters at least, perhaps too his younger brothers and their children. But we cannot tell whether all the brothers, with their children, remained under the government of the eldest member of the family; if they did, they would of course soon become a tribe like those of the Israelites, but no doubt the practice varied. At any rate they seem to have had words meaning 'tribe.' Beyond this, there cannot have been a very close connection, except when two or more settlements or tribes may have united to fortify a hill or some other

---

[1] Some stone-clubs or axes were used even at the Battle of Hastings.

place easy to defend (the germ of the 'city'), with ditch, mound, and palisade, somewhat like the British camps still existing in England, and described by Caesar,[1] as a refuge for themselves and their cattle in time of danger. And, when the danger came, this loose alliance would be drawn closer by choosing for the time a war-chief or 'king.'

Their religion was a worship of the powers of nature themselves, not, it must be borne in mind, of a being or beings who controlled them. Father Zeus was at first the sky which embraces the world and gives rain, which makes the grass and crops grow (Ζεὺς ὕει, Zeus rains). Hermes was the storm, the swift messenger of the gods. The Sun and Moon were two gods, husband and wife, though the Teutons differed from the Greeks and Latins as to which was the god and which the goddess. And so the other great natural objects were regarded as persons and worshipped; motion especially being thought to imply life, as it did in their own bodies.

No doubt they had also a mass of minor superstitions, though it is impossible to say with certainty what superstitions are primitive. But there is an old German charm for healing a lame horse which bears a very striking resemblance to one in Sanskrit. No doubt charms were a most important part of medicine in those days, and the belief in them is not quite extinct even yet.

As to the manners and customs of our ancestors, there can be no doubt that, occasionally at least, especially in times of scarcity, aged people had their lives shortened for the common benefit, and, probably, not contrary to their own desire; that they stole or bought their wives; that the husband had the power of life and death over his wife, and exercised it if he

---

[1] Caesar, *Gallic War*, v. xxi. § 3. 'Oppidum autem Britanni vocant, cum silvas impeditas vallo atque fossa munierunt, quo incursionis hostium vitandae causa convenire consuerunt.' This is in a forest-country; but the camps on the Downs were no doubt analogous.

thought fit; that children were exposed and left to perish if the father did not choose to have them reared; and that wives were commonly burnt with their husbands, which last 'pious custom' has been put down in quite recent times among one branch of the Indo-Europeans by another family of the same stock. The dream of a 'golden age' long ago is a very pleasing one, but it is a dream all the same.

And now, if we know so much about the Indo-European race while they still lived in their old home, we ought surely to be able to find out where the home was. Such guidance as is given by a comparison of the names of trees and animals known to them all, which must therefore have existed in their original home, and an inquiry into the regions in which a mass of tribes living chiefly on their flocks and herds could maintain themselves, ought, one would think, to guide us to some certainty on the point. Some have thought that the fact of Sanskrit being the oldest language (that is, having more forms closely resembling the primitive language than any other) shows that those who spoke it cannot have moved far from their primitive home, and that, if we can find a region in Central Asia where they and the Iranians can have lived together, we shall have the original home of the Indo-European people. But we must not forget that we have Sanskrit of an earlier date than any relics of the other languages; it therefore naturally supplies us with older forms. On the other hand, those who think that the original home was in Europe urge that all the earliest migrations of Indo-European peoples of which we can learn anything for certain, such as the invasions of Italy[1] and Greece[2] by the Gauls, were in a southerly or easterly direction. But this too does not absolutely prove the point; these smaller migrations may have been a back eddy, after the main

---

[1] Rome was captured by the Gauls about 390 B.C.
[2] About 280 B.C. This led to their establishment in Galatia.

stream of migration had exhausted its force, and due to different causes. On the whole the question where the original home of the Indo-European race was is one which cannot be answered with certainty from the facts which we know at present.[1]

[1] See Appendix A, 'Race and Language.'

Sanskrit.	Iranian.	Greek.	Latin.	Celtic.	Slavonic.
áyas	ayanh	...	aes	...	...
paçú	pasu	...	pecus	...	...
sthûrá	staora	ταῦρος	taurus	tarb	turu
vaçâ	...	...	vacca	...	...
ávi	...	ὄϊς	ovis	ói	ovica
ajá	iza (?)	αἴξ	...	...	...
çván, çun	spâ	κύων	canis	cú	...
sû-kará (?)	hû	ὗς, σῦς	sus	...	svinija
áçva	aspa	ἵππος	equos	ech	...
damá	...	δόμος	domus	dam	domu
dvâra (*for* dhvâra)	...	θύρα	fores	dorus	...
...	...	...	granum	grán	zruno
urvárâ	urvara	ἄρουρα	arvum	...	...
...	...	ἄγρος	ager	...	...
...	...	ἀρόω	aro	airim	orati
...	...	ὀξίνη	occa	...	...
...	...	ἅρπη	sarpere (verb)	...	srupu
laví, lavaka	...	λαῖον	...	...	...
...	...	κριθή	hordeum	...	...
...	...	...	far	...	buru
...	...	μελίνη	milium	...	...
...	...	...	faba	...	bobu
...	...	ἐρέβινθος	ervum	...	...
... —	...	κρόμυον	...	crem	...
...	...	λίνον	linum	lín, léine	linu
...	...	χόρτος	hortus	gort (=*seed*)	gradu (=*wall*)
...	...	μύλη	mola	melim	melja
...	..	πόλτος	puls	...	...
dhânâs	dâna	...	...	...	...
..	...	κλίβανος (=*oven*)	libum (=*cake*)	...	...
anjana	...	...	unguentum (=*oil for anointing*)	imb (*for* ing)	...
mádhu	madhu	μέθυ (=*strong*)	...	mid	medu (=*honey*

nan.[1]	Old English.	Mod. English.	Original Meaning.
iz	ár	ore	copper
hu	feoh	fee	herd of cattle
iur	stéor	steer	bull, or draught-ox
..	...	...	cow
..	...	...	sheep
..	...	...	goat
nds	hund	hound	dog
ú	sú, sugu	sow	sow
hu	...	...	horse
..	...	...	house
úr	dór	door	door
orn	corn	corn	corn
..	...	...	corn-field
krs	æcer	acre	field
..	erian (*inf.*)	ear	to plough
ida	...	...	harrow
..	...	...	sickle
(orse)	...	...	sickle
rsta	...	...	barley
ıris	bere	bar-ley	barley(?) spelt(?)
..	...	...	millet (*borrowed*)
...	...	...	bean
awîz	...	...	pea
ıms	...	...	onion
ein	lín	lin-en	flax
ırds	geard	yard	courtyard, or garden (*borrowed* from French)
iouse)			
alan	...	...	to grind, mill (*borrowed* from Latin)
...	...	...	pulse (*borrowed*), porridge
...	...	...	bread
aifs	hláf	loaf	loaf, baking

Sanskrit.	Iranian.	Greek.	Latin.	Celtic.
sthávi (=*weaver*)	...	(ἰστός), στήμων	stamen	...
...	...	πῆνος	pannus (=*piece of cloth*)	...
...	...	πῖλος	pileus (=*felt hat*)	...
...	tashta	...	testa	...
rátha	ratha (=*waggon*)	...	rota	roth
áksha	...	ἄξων	axis	echel
nau	nâvi	ναῦς	navis	nau
arítra	...	ἐρετμός	remus	rám
ci	ci	τί-νο-μαι	...	...
jyâ	jya	βιός (=*bow*)	...	...
íshu	ishu	ἰός	...	...
açan	asan	ἄκων	...	...
ásí	ahi	ἄ-ορ[2]	ensis	...
...	...	...	saxum (=*stone*)	...
...	...	σκῦτος (=*leather*)	scutum	sciath[2]
...	...	...	touta (*Umbrian and Oscan*)	tuath
pur	...	πόλις	...	...
râj-an	...	...	rex	rí, -rix
dyâús pitâ	...	Ζεὺς πατήρ (Δί-α)	Ju-piter	...
dévá	...	...	deus	...
sarámâ	...	Ἑρμῆς	...	...

German.[1]	Old English.	Mod. English.	Original Meaning.
...	...	...	warp (=the *upright* threads)
fana	...	...	woof (*cross*-threads)
filz	felt	felt	felt
...	...	...	jar
rad	...	...	wheel
ahsa	eaxl (=*shoulder-joint, shoulder*)	axle	axle
naue (*Bavarian*)	...	...	boat
rieme	...	...	oar
...	...	...	compensation for injury
...	...	...	bowstring
...	...	...	arrow
...	...	...	a weapon for throwing—stone or javelin
...	...	...	dagger
sahs	seax	Sax(-on)	stone-knife
skildus[2]	scild	shield	shield
þiuda	þéod	...	tribe
...	...	...	camp of refuge
reiks	ríce (=*kingdom*)	(bishop)-ric	war-chief
Tiu, Zio	Tiw	Tues(-day)	the sky
tívar (*Norse*)	...	...	a god
sturm[2] (*for* srum?)	storm	storm	wind, as the messenger of the gods

CHAPTER VI

THE PRIMITIVE INDO-EUROPEAN LANGUAGE

Character of the Indo-European language—Can we trace it back to roots, and can we explain the origin of these?[1]

WE have now seen that the ancestors of the nations of Europe (with a few exceptions, such as the Hungarians and the Turks) and of those of South-West Asia once spoke one language, though no doubt with some smaller distinctions such as those of the English dialects at present, yet so that each individual could make himself understood by any other in the whole nation, or set of kindred tribes. As to the general characteristics of this language there can be no doubt. It was 'inflexional,' —that is, it marked the relation of words to each other, and so expressed its meaning clearly, by their terminations, as in Greek or Latin, not by their order and stress[2] or accent, as is mainly the case in Modern English. Its substantives had seven cases at least—Nominative, Accusative, Genitive, Dative, Ablative, Locative (Greek, οἴκοι = at home; Latin, *Carthagini* = at Carthage), and Instrumental (Greek, ἅμα, εὐνῆφι). The Vocative is, of course, not properly a case. It has no termination or case-ending, but is the stem of the word used as an interjection. The verb must have been very much like a Greek verb in its tenses and moods, except that it did not

---

[1] Schrader, *Sprachvergleichung und Urgeschichte*. Sweet, *History of English Sounds*. Brachet, *Historical French Grammar*, translated by Kitchin.

[2] Stress may have played a more prominent part at a still earlier period.

possess any exclusively Passive tenses,[1] but a Middle-and-Passive, or Reflexive voice only.

And now, can we trace back this language to a still earlier stage?

We have seen (p. 10, etc.) how new words are and have been formed in English, by putting together two separate words, which are then accented as a single word. The next step is for one or both of these formerly distinct parts, usually the less important one which loses its accent, to become more or less disguised. Examples of words thus formed have been given before, *truth-ful, need-less, lord-ship*; and we saw that the latter part of each had a distinct existence (which we still find in *full, loose,* and *shape*) before the compound was made.

Now, in every word that is declined or conjugated, by comparing its different forms we can distinguish between the root or stem, the central part of the word which gives the main part of its meaning, and the suffix or inflexion which modifies this. So in *yok-ed, junc-tus, ζευκ-τός, yuk-ta,* the first part of the word *yoke-, junc-* (for *jung-*), *ζευκ-* (for *ζευγ-*), *yuk-* gives the general notion of 'yoking' or 'joining,' while *-ed, -tus, -τος, -ta* show that a person, animal, or thing spoken of undergoes the operation described. Besides this, in *junctus* and *ζευκτός* there are two further notions implied: (1) That the word refers to the 'subject' or chief thing spoken of in the sentence, which does the action described by the verb (or suffers it, if the verb is in the Passive voice); (2) That the person or thing spoken of is of the masculine gender, as in the sentences—

ζευκτὸς	ἵππος	ἕλκει	τὴν	ἅμαξαν
junctus	equos	trahit		carrum
ζευκτὸς		ἵππος		ἐλαύνεται
junctus		equos		agitur

[1] It is quite possible to express ideas with sufficient accuracy without a Passive Voice. The French, *e.g.*, usually manage to use *on* or a reflexive instead—'on les tue' = they are killed; 'tout ce qui se mange' = everything that is eaten. The same is the case to a less degree in German.

And by comparing the different cases and genders of ζευκτός and *junctos* (the older form of *junctus*) we can see that -το, -*to* is the masculine form of a suffix implying that a thing is acted on, and -ς, -*s* the sign of the nominative case with the meaning given above. In a similar way we might dissect some part of a substantive or verb.

Now what is the value of this breaking up of a word? Is it merely useful for teaching grammar, just as the word 'maritime,' for instance, might be broken up into three parts to teach the spelling (ma-ri-time), or were the parts ζευκ, *jung*, on the one hand, το, *to*, on the other, as well as the *s* at the end, originally distinct words like *truth-ful* and *need-less*? That is to say—Are we cutting up an apple which was originally one, or taking to pieces a puzzle, the parts of which were originally distinct? There is no direct evidence on the subject. We have no remains of the Indo-European language, even at the stage when it had a complete system of inflexions attached to its stems, as in Greek and Latin and, to a less extent, German. We can only find out what this language was like by a comparison of its descendants (see p. 32, etc.), and there is plainly a considerable chance of making mistakes in the process. And, of course, if we try to go back further still the subject becomes still more obscure. The further we go from the light the darker the room gets.

Is there, then, any guide to be found in some other language, where we can, so to speak, see its formation still going on; a language of later date, that is, still forming at a time when writing was more or less common, to prove to us that inflexions are sometimes actually made from distinct words? We have already seen (p. 12) that -*ly*, the termination of most English adverbs, in *rarely*, for instance, is originally the dative case of the substantive *lîc* = a body. And the languages of modern Europe which have developed out of Latin supply further instances.[1]

---

[1] Brachet, *Historical French Grammar*, translated by Kitchin.

(1) Where does the termination of French adverbs, *-ment*, come from, since there is nothing like it used in Latin to form an adverb, and why is it attached to the feminine form of the adjective? Why do we write *nulle-ment, bonne-ment*?

In classical Latin expressions are found like '*bona mente faciam*,' '*devota mente tuentur*.' Both of these, the latter especially, are very like an adverb; 'they observe with a devout mind' hardly differs in meaning from 'they observe devoutly.' Now the provincial Latin, which was to become French, was in want of a fresh termination for its adverbs, to mark them off from other words and make speech intelligible; for the proper Latin terminations *-e, -ter* (as in *rit-e, felici-ter*), being of little weight and unaccented, were hardly pronounced by the provincials, just as we in English have lost the *-e* of adverbs like *right, fast* (see p. 10), ('he did it *right*,' 'we drive *fast*'), which marked them off from the adjectives. Expressions, then, like *devota mente, bona mente* being constantly heard and used, the two words got to be regarded as one word, and, the original meaning of the *mente* being little thought of, it seemed to be merely an inflexion or termination characteristic of adverbs, and thus, in imitation of these compounds, other words were formed in which the sense of *mente* was not appropriate. Thus in French, or corrupt popular Latin as spoken in France, of the eighth century A.D., *solamente* is found meaning 'only.' Accordingly in French we have not merely *bonne-ment, dévote-ment*, but *seule-ment*, and a host of other adverbs where the *-ment* is really quite inappropriate if we consider its original sense.[1] However, as *mens* is feminine in Latin, it is the feminine form of the adjective to which *-ment* is attached. Perhaps this *-ment* is not an inflexion in the strict sense of the word, though it is hard to make a reasonable distinction between the two. The next example will be one of the formation of an inflexion in the strictest sense.

[1] So in the English word *scientifically* 'with a scientific body' gives no sense.

(2) Any one who is at all acquainted with Latin, and realises that French is a modern form of it, will probably notice in reading French that the future, *aimerai*, for instance, cannot possibly be derived from the Latin future *amabo*, or *finirai* from *finiam*.

Now even in classical Latin we sometimes find a way of expressing the future different from the form found in grammars—that is to say, instead of a tense formed by inflexion, a phrase made up of the infinitive and *habeo*. *Ire habeo, venire habeo*, 'I have to go,' 'I have to come,' give the same general sense as 'I shall go,' and 'I shall come.'

In the popular Latin, from which French is derived—the Latin which the Gauls picked up from Roman soldiers, colonists, and shopkeepers—this roundabout way of expressing the future was more common than the other. So the Gauls learnt to say *amare habeo, ire habeo*, and, as the words were worn down, *aimer-ai, ir-ai*.[1] In the dialect of Southern France, or Provençal, the two parts of the word are still distinct, so that one can say '*dir vos ai*,' just as well as '*vos dir-ai*.' And yet no one who speaks French, unless he happens to have learnt the derivation of this form, thinks of *-ai* as being a part of *avoir*. *Aimer-ai*, to the ordinary Frenchman, shows that the verb is in future time and nothing else. So in this case we can trace the formation throughout its history, and prove that the termination *-ai*, from being originally a distinct word, has, by being constantly attached to an infinitive, come to be regarded as a mere part of the verb, modifying its meaning so as to give the notion of future time—that is, it has become an inflexion. Now, are there reasonable grounds for believing that the inflexions of the Indo-European language were formed in the same way?

Take the termination, *-mi*, or *-m*, of the first person

---

[1] The derivation is confirmed by the forms in the other Romance languages.

singular of certain verbs called 'verbs in μι,' such as εἰ-μί in Greek, *su-m* in Latin, *es-mi* in Lithuanian, *a-m* in English. This is almost certainly the same as με, *me*, the stem (or root) of all cases of the pronoun of the first person except the nominative. Thus ἵστη-μι is precisely the same as *I stand*, only in the Greek word the pronoun comes last. So the -τι in ἐσ-τί, *es-t*, German *is-t*, is most probably originally identical with το, '(is-)*te*,' *that*.[1] Then ἐσ-τί is precisely equivalent to *it is*, or rather *it be*,[2] as they say in the country, but with the pronoun last, the two words having become one word, just like *tru-ly*, *seule-ment*, and *aimer-ai*.

These are the clearest instances that we have. But if these terminations were formed in this way it is certainly probable that the rest were made on the same principle, even though we may not now have the facts which would enable us to derive them. At any rate we know of no other way in which they can be really explained. And, if this is the true account, we may be quite sure that, when our remote ancestors had once got into the habit of attaching these pronouns or other words to the end of a stem meaning 'be,' 'stand,' 'bear,' or whatever it was, they soon forgot that the last part was a separate word, and joined it on (by 'analogy,' or imitation) to other verbs as a mere termination, not thinking of its meaning, just as we attach -*ly* to an adjective to form an adverb, if we want one (as in *rowdily*), without any thought of its original sense. And the pronoun, treated as a mere inflexion, and having as a rule parted with its accent, would soon begin to wear down.

According to this theory, which is at least the most probable one, the Indo-European language had at one time no inflexions, but expressed the meaning of the speaker by

---

[1] See Delbrück, *Introduction to the Study of Language*, p. 71, etc., and p. 97, etc.

[2] But this *be* is more probably from *bið*, which in Old English is an alternative form for *is*. At all events *I'll* for 'I will,' *he'd* for 'he would' are similar instances, only that we remind ourselves that they are abbreviations by writing them with an apostrophe.

putting together separate words in a particular order, and with a particular accent. So English has but few inflexions [1] left, and yet we can express our meaning in that language with sufficient clearness. And there are languages existing which are entirely destitute of inflexions.

'Languages such as Chinese and Japanese have no inflexions. Tenses are expressed by adverbs, the Present by a word like our "now"; the Past by a word meaning "past," "spent," "enough"; the Future by "will," "desire," "intend,"[2] (the last as in English). In the same way it is only natural that they should have no real compound words, for inflexion, on our theory, is merely one kind of compound.

A curious specimen of this kind of language is supplied by what is called 'Pidgin'[3] (that is, 'Business') English. This medium of communication between Chinamen and Englishmen consists of words mainly English in origin, though adapted to Chinese powers of pronunciation, but these are strung together according to the rules of Chinese grammar— that is, there is in it, strictly speaking, nothing which can be called grammar at all. It has no inflexion to express tense or person in the verb, or cases in the noun. 'My look-see' may be 'I see,' 'I saw,' 'I will see,' or 'See!' Here is a longer specimen. A Chinaman is wishing to see the Chinese Ambassador, and is vainly trying, in Pidgin-English, to explain his wants to the porters at the Langham Hotel. An Englishman acquainted with this language fortunately appears, and this conversation follows.

Englishman. Wat ting you wantchee? (What do you want?)

Chinaman. Hab look-see Chinaman? (Have you seen a Chinaman here?)

---

[1] We mostly use phrases for inflexions, *e.g.* 'conscious *of innocence,*' though we still have the genitive to mark possession, as 'my brother's dog.'

[2] Morris, Introduction to Whitney's *Language and its Study.*

[3] Chinese Pidgin-English, C. G. Leland, *St. James's Gazette,* 11th July 1888.

The Primitive Indo-European Language   59

Englishman. My look-see two piecee numpa-one Chinaman wailo top-side house-o galow. (I saw two Chinese gentlemen go upstairs, aye.)

Chinaman. Maskee—chin-chin. (All right, respects.)

In this language then (as in Chinese, which supplies its syntax) there is no inflexion, and yet the meaning can be clearly expressed. As has been said, it has no real compound words, such as *nameless, childhood* (p. 10, etc.), though a number of words can be put side by side to express a complex idea, as when a three-masted paddle-steamer is described as 'three-piecee-bamboo-makee-outside-walkee.'

Thus a language without any inflexions is by no means impossible after all.

We have now shown

(1) That, in some languages, what were once separate words have become mere inflexions.

(2) That we can trace this in some parts of the verb in Indo-European languages with something like certainty, and that it is a reasonable explanation of the other inflexions.

(3) That languages do actually exist in the state which we are supposing for an earlier stage of the Indo-European language.

These arguments combined give a strong probability to the theory that the Indo-European language, before it assumed the inflexional form which the languages descended from it still more or less possess, was once nothing but 'roots.' Thus STA gave the notion of 'standing,' AS or ES of 'breathing' or 'living,' and each of these roots might be either verb, or substantive, or adjective, according to the context, since the endings which fixed the parts of speech (*e.g. men* in *stamen, t* in *sta-t*) were still at large as independent words.[1] So too there were no cases, or persons,

---

[1] So in English, as we have worn off most of the 'suffixes' which distinguish the parts of speech, we have almost gone back to this primitive state of things. *State* is a substantive in the last sentence, a verb in 'I *state* it as a fact,' an adjective in '*State* trials.'

or tenses, or moods, for the words destined to become terminations were still free and had not sunk into the position of dependents.

Now, since the Indo-European Language had not only acquired a complete set of inflexions, but had also broken up into distinct languages before we get our earliest glimpse of it through its descendant Sanskrit (see p. 34, etc.), its uninflected stage (if it is a fact, which it probably is) must be a very long way off from us. However, not content with following it thus far, many people have attempted to trace our speech back to its very origin and to show how language itself came into being. But since we can only get general outlines of the one Indo-European language itself, and since its existence as a number of uninflected roots, though most probable, cannot be absolutely proved, there can plainly be no certainty if we try to go further back still. And yet something must be said on this question which is often asked, How did language originate?

There have been two theories of the origin of language, irreverently called the 'Pooh-pooh' and the 'Bow-wow' theory. The first derives roots from interjections, the second from imitations of natural sounds. But the two run into each other, and must be combined to give anything like a probable account of the beginnings of human speech. To the 'Bow-wow' or 'onomatopœic' theory the language of children certainly gives strong support. By them imitations of natural sounds are not merely added to the ordinary names for things in order to give point to them (as in *moo-cow, baa-lamb*), but are also used by themselves to form new words, such as *puff-puff* (= engine) and *bow-wow* (= dog). Besides, words like *cuckoo, peewit* are undoubtedly formed in this way. The 'Pooh-pooh theory' has less obvious facts on its side, but in some cases it seems most probable that words have been thus formed. The root AGH,[1] ANG, for instance, seems

[1] As in German, *Ach!*

The Primitive Indo-European Language 61

very much like the exclamation of a person choking. If this was used, as it very well might be, to express pain or distress, we may easily derive from it ἄχος, pain; *angor*, distress of body, and then distress of mind; *anxius*, distressed, anxious; and, through Norse *agi* (= fear), the English word *awe*. So AS or ES seems to be an imitation of a long-drawn breath; the notions of breathing and living are very closely connected; and Sanskrit *asmi*, Greek εἰμί (for ἐσ-μι), English *a-m* are certainly derived from this root.

But when we try to explain all words by means of these two theories, we are met by great difficulties. For instance, what natural sound, or what interjection, can be expressive of 'standing,' and account for the root STA? On the other hand, we should remember that in its origin language must have consisted largely of acting or gestures, with appropriate cries to draw attention and to point the meaning. There are still traces of this state of things in the gestures which foreigners use to explain and point their remarks. And if a sound came to be associated with a particular gesture, as a cry expressive of hunger, with pointing to the mouth,[1] this cry by itself would, by association, come to have a definite meaning alone, just as a tune may remind us of a particular house, or place, or occasion on which we have heard it. And besides this, before we say that it is impossible to account for all words on this theory, we must remind ourselves of one great characteristic of language. We have seen that it is always changing, not only in form, but in meaning (p. 7). *Meat*, for instance, 300 years ago, and after English had for the most part settled into its present form, meant something different from what it does now. In the Bible it means 'food' in general,[2] now it means only 'flesh used as food.' By a custom, the cause of which we cannot trace, those who spoke or wrote the word gradually got to use it only in the latter sense.

---

[1] Sweet, *History of English Sounds*, p. 51.
[2] Gen. i. 30.

Thus the meaning of the word was 'specialised,' or narrowed. On the other hand, we may extend the meaning of a word, and use it of all things which bear some resemblance to its first meaning. Thus there is, to begin with, only one sun. But, as the fixed stars are believed to stand to planets of their own in the same position as our sun does to us, we speak of them as 'so many *suns*,' thus 'generalising' the word.[1] Further, we often think of only one of the qualities possessed by the thing to which the name originally belonged, and so transfer the word to something very different, which happens to share this quality. Take the word *horn*, for instance, in English, and *cornu* (the same word) in Latin. This meant originally, or at an early stage, only the projections or weapons on the head of an animal. These are hard, pointed, and so on. But some one's mind catches hold of the idea of 'projection,' putting out of sight the other qualities of horns,—the points of the crescent moon project like horns, therefore both in English and Latin we speak of 'the *horns* of the moon.' So too the extremities of an army in line project at each end, and are therefore in Latin called *cornua*, 'horns,' though we (and the Romans too for that matter) by a similar process of thought call them 'wings.' Thus also in Latin the projections or ends of sail-yards are called *cornua*. Again, horn is hard. We forget its other qualities for the moment and speak of 'a *horny*-handed son of toil.' Once more, a cow's or ram's horn may be made into a musical instrument. So we come to speak of a 'French *horn*,' though this instrument is made of metal. In fact, there is hardly any end to the changes of meaning which a word can undergo through one or other of these two processes: (1) 'specialising,' or limiting it to one part of its meaning; (2) generalising it, by attending to some one or more of its qualities only, and so extending its meaning, and often transferring it to something quite different from the thing originally meant by the word. Poets are freer

[1] Whitney, *Language and its Study*, edited by Morris, pp. 103, 104.

The Primitive Indo-European Language 63

and more daring in these matters, but all language is full of these two processes, and by means of them the meaning of words is varied to an extraordinary extent. *Organ*, for instance, originally meant an instrument or tool, being borrowed from Greek ὄργανον.[1] But, when we speak of an organ, we generally mean an instrument for the production of music, and, further, one particular kind of musical instrument. We have already seen (pp. 48, 49) that *fee* originally meant cattle, as the same word *vieh* still does in German. As payments were in early times made in cattle, it was used to mean specially 'cattle as payment,' and so 'payment in cattle,' then 'payment,' the word shifting its meaning by short stages, for all changes in language are gradual. And yet there is a wide enough interval between a herd of cattle and a doctor's fee. There is a similar process of comparison when poets speak of ripples as 'the many-twinkling smile of Ocean,' or of midnight as 'the very noon of night,' only these expressions are unusual and therefore striking. Our examples have been of changes of meaning in substantives, but the sense of verbs is transferred in the same way. It is a 'metaphor,' a comparison and a change of meaning, every time we speak of 'bearing' misfortune. We are thinking of it (or rather some one long ago thought of it for us) as a load to be endured, just as a man toils along with a heavy weight on his back, like Christian in the Pilgrim's Progress.

So then if we think of the marvellous extent to which our imagination can, by gradual changes, alter the meanings of words, we ought not to be too hasty in saying that language *may* not originally have sprung from a limited number of very simple words. On the other hand, we can have no proof that all language actually did arise from exclamations and imitations of natural sounds, assisted and explained by gestures. We have no record of a race, speechless before, acquiring speech. We cannot watch the process, as we saw inflexions

[1] Through Latin and French.

growing. And consequently, though we may think this theory possibly or even probably true, it is safer to say about the whole question of the first beginnings of language that 'we do not know.'[1]

[1] As Professor Earle remarks (*English Prose*, pp. 306, 307), quoting from the New English Dictionary, there is every reason to suppose that words are even now created, and not merely formed by compounding or otherwise from pre-existing roots. This is certainly the case with some words which children invent, and also with some slang terms, which seem to have no derivation. It is exceedingly dangerous to quote instances of such newly-created words, since their derivation may be discovered at any moment. But there seems to be no doubt that some words are being so made, and there is no reason whatever why primeval times should have had a monopoly in manufacturing the raw material of language, though no doubt the number of fresh root-words, which really become recognised in the language, is and has long been extremely small.

CHAPTER VII

THE NEAR RELATIONS OF ENGLISH

Speech of the Teutonic branch, and the position in it of English—Its history—Position of Gothic among Teutonic languages.

WE have lately been working, or trying to work, backwards into times far removed from all written records. We will now turn our heads the other way, and, taking up the Teutonic branch of the Indo-European family of languages, make our way down to English.

In dealing with a Teutonic language, we are plainly nearer to our own tongue. Take, for example, any ordinary sentence in English, German, and Latin, such as—

> My father is gone out
> Mein Vater ist ausgegangen
> Meus pater exivit

or,

> The man is at home (Devonshire and American,
>   '*to* home,' or 'hum')
> Der Mann ist zu Hause
> Homo est domi

and we shall find that, while many of the Latin words have a common origin with those in German and English, in the two latter languages it is the exception (among the simpler words) not to find this correspondence, and also that it is much closer and more obvious. And besides, as we shall see, they agree (or did agree) very closely in grammar, and English and German have a large number of idioms and proverbs in common. The fact is that English, German, and Latin all belong to the same great family of languages, but that English and German are members of the same branch of it. Or we might say that English and Latin are cousins (as being children respectively of the brothers Teutonic and Italic [1]), but that English and German, being children of the Teutonic language, are own-brothers. Now we are sometimes told that 'English is derived from German.' If by 'German' were meant the original Germanic or Teutonic speech of which Low German (including English) and High German, and Norse, and Gothic were once mere dialects, this would be quite true. If it means (as it does) Modern High German, the language of Luther's Bible and of German books,[2] it is quite false. In fact, English is in many respects more 'ancient,'—that is, nearer to the earlier Germanic or Teutonic language than High German is. We saw (pp. 25, 40) that High German has had a 'shifting of sounds' peculiar to itself, which has disarranged many of its consonants. So, although English vowels have altered to a surprising extent from their original pronunciation, yet, so far as its consonants are concerned, *three* is more primitive than *drei, that* than *das*. The connection between the two languages is that they are both of them originally dialects of the Teutonic language. Even so far as borrowing goes, English owes far fewer words to German than to any other of the more important European languages.

And now we must bring in the other members of the family, and show that Old English (with the other Low German dialects), High German, Gothic, and Norse, are all closely related to each other. Look at the declension of the substantive *fish*, and of the pronoun *thou*, and the present indicative of the verb *find*. All three words, substantive, pronoun, verb, show the connection of these languages with Latin, but much more clearly their close relationship with each other.

---

[1] Which languages developed out of dialects of the Indo-European language.

[2] The literary dialect of Germany is mainly High German, though not exclusively so.

And their nearness in grammar is much more important evidence of their connection than even the fact that they have so many words in common (see p. 20).

FISH

	Old English.	Low German.		Gothic.	Old High German.	Old Norse.
		Old Saxon.				
		SINGULAR				
Nom.	fisc	fisc		fisks	visk	fiskr
Gen.	fisces	fiscas, fisces		fiskis	viskes	fisks
Dat.	fisce	fisca, fisce		fiska	viska	fiski
Acc.	fisc	fisc		fisk	visk	fisk
Instr.		fiscu			visku	
		PLURAL				
Nom.	fiscas	fiscos, fiscas		fiskos	viska	fiskar
Gen.	fisca	fisco, fisca		fiske	visko	fiska
Dat.	fiscum	fiscun, fiscon		fiskam	viskum	fiskum, fiskom
Acc.	fiscas	fiscos, fiscas		fiskans	viska	fiska

THOU

	Old English.	Low German.		Gothic.	Modern High German.	Old Norse.
		Old Saxon. Old Frisian.				
Nom.	þú [1]	þu	þu	þu	du	þû
Gen.	þín	þîn		þeina	dein	þîn
Dat.	þé	þi		þus	dir	þer
Acc.	þec, þé	þi		þuk	dich	þik

I FIND [2]

PRESENT INDICATIVE

	Old English.	Low German.		Gothic.	Old High German.	Old Norse.
		Old Frisian.				
		SINGULAR				
1st.	ic finde	finde		finþa	findu	finn
2nd.	þú findest	findest		finþis	findis	finnr
3rd.	hé findeþ	findeþ		finþiþ	findit	finnr

[1] þ, þ=th. An accent (e.g. þú) in Old English marks a long vowel.
[2] Helfenstein, *Comparative Grammar of the Teutonic Languages*, 1870. Helfenstein gives an instrumental case to Old English, *fiscé*. The form seems to be doubtful, and at all events only differs from the dative in the length of the vowel.

	Low German.				
	Old English.	Old Frisian.	Gothic.	Old High German.	Old Norse.

DUAL

1st.			finþôs		
2nd.			finþats		

PLURAL

1st.	wé findaþ	findaþ	finþam	findames	finnum
2nd.	gé findaþ	findaþ	finþiþ	findat	finniþ
3rd.	hí findaþ	findaþ	finþand	findant	finna

Now, as to the condition of the Teutonic branch, while its members were still in contact with each other,[1] we can learn something by noticing what words are common to the different languages of the branch, just as we found out something about the condition of the undivided Indo-European race by the same method. What the language teaches us agrees in the main with what we learn about our ancestors from Caesar and Tacitus, at the time when the Romans first came in contact with them. But, though in some cases inventions and the names for them were no doubt learnt by one tribe from another, carried across the sea to or from Scandinavia, or derived from other Indo-European peoples, such as the Lithuanians and Slavs, on the whole the picture of their civilisation or of the want of it, given us by their language, will apply to a much earlier period than that of these authors—to a time when the divisions of the branch, Low Germans, and High Germans, and Scandinavians, and Goths still had practically the same language.

Our ancestors had then made considerable progress since they parted from the other members of the Indo-European family. They had become acquainted with a variety of metals, and had learnt to work them, which meant, of course,

---

[1] We cannot say, 'while they were intelligible to each other.' It appears that down to a period long after the Christian era, a member of any Teutonic race could have made himself at least partially understood by a member of any other.

a vast improvement in their weapons and implements. They were now in contact with the sea, and had words not only for sea-animals and sea-birds, but for sails and masts. We can see in some cases how they (probably) formed names for these new discoveries. A sail (Old English *segel*) is 'that which bears or endures the wind,' from a root SEGH, Greek ἔχω, meaning 'to endure.' So too *mast* originally means 'a branch of a tree,' 'specialised' (like *meat*, see p. 61, etc.) to mean the branch cut and shaped to support the sail.[1] They also made or borrowed names for the new land-animals that they came across—fox, deer, and reindeer. They had a word in common for 'to ride,' as well as two new names for the horse, a word for letters, and a verb for 'to write.' Here again we can trace the way in which they got a name for the new art. *Write* is 'specialised' from the meaning 'scratch' (German *reissen* = tear), since the first Teutonic writing was carved on tablets of beech (*book*, Old English *bóc*, means originally 'beech'). Their letters, the Runes, were derived from the Latin, or more probably from the Greek alphabet, modified so as to be more easily carved on wood, though it is doubtful through what means the knowledge of the letters came to them. They had learnt to grow oats and rye, as well as the crops with which the whole Indo-European family were acquainted, to make beer, and to wear breeches. They had also advanced in government. There are at least two new words meaning 'people' or 'tribe,' a fresh word for 'king,' and again a separate name for the 'duke,' or elective general for those tribes which were not governed by kings. These points are illustrated by the list of words to be found at the end of the chapter.

Of their condition about the beginning of the Christian era, Caesar gives us some account, and more detailed information is to be found in Tacitus's *Germany*.

---

[1] Neither of the above derivations is quite certain. See Skeat, *Etymological Dictionary*.

We will now give a slight sketch of the first appearance of the Teutonic tribes in history, and see what territory they occupied before our forefathers crossed the sea, and (nearly at the same time) other Teutonic peoples swarmed over other parts of the Roman Empire and conquered them.

The earliest information [1] which we get from history about the mass of Teutonic tribes is from Pytheas, of the Greek colony of Marseilles, who, about 325 B.C., made a voyage of discovery along the northern coast of Europe. As he passed the mouth of the Rhine, he found that the nationality of the tribes changed. He had passed from Celts to Germans. Early in the second century B.C. the Bastarnae, a German tribe who had migrated into Dacia (now Roumania), helped Perseus, King of Macedon, in his war with the Romans, and shortly before 100 B.C. the Cimbri and Teutones, of whom the latter at all events were Germans, brought the Romans into a state of extreme alarm by their attempted migration into Italy, which ended in their own destruction. But it is only in Caesar's time, about 50 B.C., that we get a connected view of the Germans. Their boundaries were, roughly, the Rhine on the west, the Vistula on the east, the Baltic on the north, and on the south the Hercynian Forest, stretching from where the Main joins the Rhine to the Carpathians. That is to say, except on the south, where the great forest and Celtic tribes held territories now filled by Germans, they occupied much the same extent of country as modern Germany. And this territory they continued to occupy, until, breaking through the frontiers of the Roman Empire, where they had been kept at bay for more than four centuries, they swarmed over France, and Spain, and Italy, and northern Africa, while another part of them, our ancestors on the shores of the North Sea and the Baltic, began the conquest of Britain.

And now, what sort of speech was the yet undivided language of the whole Teutonic race? Of course we have no

---

[1] See Schrader, *Sprachvergleichung und Urgeschichte*, p. 445, etc.

specimen of it left. We may get some vague notion of it by comparing the words in the various Teutonic languages which are to be found at the end of the chapter. It must have been something, roughly speaking, midway between the undivided Indo-European language and Old English, commonly called Anglo-Saxon. And so we shall probably get an idea of it when we come to speak of the oldest form of English which we have, noticing those points in it which are relics of an earlier stage of the language. But there is one language which is nearer to Teutonic than Old English is, namely Gothic. The Goths who spoke it were once a great and widely-extended people, who at various times conquered Dacia (Roumania), and Moesia (Bulgaria), and southern Russia, and Italy, and southern Gaul, and Spain; yet there is very little of their language now remaining, except part of a translation of the Bible, made for the Goths of Moesia by Wulfila (the 'little wolf') or Ulphilas, according to the Greek form of the name, in the fourth century A.D.[1] This, except some few fragments, is the oldest specimen of any Teutonic language extant. And besides, Gothic seems to have been a conservative language (p. 35), so that for both reasons it gives us much information about what the undivided Teutonic language was like. For instance, Gothic keeps the stems and the suffixes and inflexions of words in a far more distinct shape than Old English does, so that they can be easily marked off from each other. It shows some of its cases almost in what must have been their original form in the Indo-European language; for instance, the accusative plural *wulfans*,[2] that is, the accusative singular with -*s* added to it, which is much less worn down than the Latin *lupos* (= *lupon-s*) or Greek λύκους (= λυκον-s). It retains

---

[1] Gothic was spoken in the Crimea down to the sixteenth century A.D.

[2] In Gothic substantives the accusative singular is often the same as the nominative, and it does not end in -*an*. But the original termination appears in the accusative singular of the adjective ('strong' form), *blindana*, e.g., and in Old High German the accusative of the substantive *got* (god) is *gotan*.

the *s* of the nominative singular, which is so common in Greek and Latin. It has a form for the passive voice, not a phrase, as in the other Teutonic languages (Old English *Ic eom*, or *weorþe gelufod* = I am loved; German *Ich bin* or *werde geliebt*)—

ik	hait-ada
þu	hait-aza
is	hait-ada
weis ⎫	
jus ⎬	hait-anda
eis ⎭	

= 'I, thou, he, we, you, they are called.'

It has just a trace of these forms used in a middle sense (which must have been their original use, see p. 52), and finally it keeps a dual, not only in the personal pronouns (as Old English does), but also in the terminations of the verb.[1]

Gothic, then, is the oldest form of a Teutonic language with which we are acquainted. But Old English has some forms older than the corresponding forms in Gothic. Thus Gothic has only one 'verb in μι,'—that is, a verb in which the first person singular keeps the old personal ending in *mi* or *m*—*ik im* (Old English *ic eom*). But in Old English we find besides this *ic beom*, 'I be,' as some people say in the country, *ic geséom*, 'I see,' *ic gedóm*, 'I do.' Plainly, therefore, English cannot be derived from Gothic. We cannot derive earlier forms from later ones. And if it is said, 'Oh, but English is derived from an earlier stage of Gothic in which these forms were still found!' this is the same as saying that English is derived from the original Teutonic language, just as Gothic is. And this happens to be the fact. Old English and Gothic are brothers, but Gothic is the elder brother.

---

[1] But not in the passive.

The near Relations of English

Gothic	Norse	Old High German	German	Old English	English
smiþa	smiðr	smid	schmied	smiþ	smith
eisarn	isarn	îsarn	eisen	îsen, iren	iron
...	stâl	stahal	stahl	style	steel
gulþ	guld	gold	gold	gold	gold
silubr	silfr	silabar, silber	silber	silfor	silver
...	tin	zin	zinn	tin	tin
...	lod	lôt	loth	léad	lead
...	hvalr	wal	wall(-fisch)	hwæl	whale
...	selr	selah	...	seolh	seal
...	segl	segal, segel	segel	segel	sail
...	mast	mast	mast	mæst	mast
...	hreinn	...	renn-thier (from *Norse*)	hrán	reindeer (from *Norse*)
fauho	fox	fuhs	fuchs	fox	fox
...	rá	rêho	reh	ráh	roe
...	rípa	rîdan	reiten	rídan	ride
...	hros	hros	ross	hors	horse
...	vigg	wigg	...	wicg	(=*horse*)
boka (=*letter*)	bókstafr	buohstap	buchstabe	bócstæf	(=*letter of the alphabet*)
writs (=*stroke with a pen*)	ríta	rîzan	reissen (=*tear*)	writan	write
hwaiteis	hveiti	hwaizi	weizen	hwǽte	wheat
...	rûgr	rocco, roggo	roggen	ryge	rye (=*oats*)
...	hafr	habaro	hafer	...	(=*oats*)
...	bjórr	bior	bier	béor	beer
...	hosa	hosa	hose	hosa	hose (*meant* trousers)
...	fölk	folc	volk	folc	folk
...	konungr	chuning	könig	cyning	king
...	hertogi	herizoho	herzog	heretoga	(=*duke*)

Several of these words are shared by the Lithuanians or Slavs, or by both.

ST. MARK III. 9-12 IN GOTHIC (BEFORE 381 A.D.)[1]

9 Jah kwath thaim siponjam seinaim ei skip habaith wesi
   And he-spake to-the dis-ciples his that a-ship had be
at imma in thizos manageins, ei ni thraih-eina
near him on-account of-the multitude, that not they-might-throng
  (dat.)

10 ina. Managans auk ga-hailida, swa-swe drusun ana
   him (acc.) *Many also he-healed so that they-pressed on*
ina ei imma at-tai-tok-eina, jah swa managai swe
him (acc.) *that him* (dat.) *they-might-touch, and so many as*

11 habai-dedun wundufnjos jah ahmans unhrainjans, thaih than
   had plagues and spirits unclean, they when
ina ga-sehwun, drusun du imma jah hropi-dedun
him saw, pressed to him and cried

12 kwithandans, thatei thu is sunus guths. Jah filu
   saying that thou art Son of-God. And much
and-bait ins ei ina ni ga-swi-kunthi-ded-eina.
he-rebuked them that him not they-should-make-known.

(It will be useful to look back at this example of Gothic after reading the sketch of Old English.)

[1] Skeat, *Gospel of St. Mark in Gothic.*

THE SAME IN ANGLO-SAXON (WEST SAXON DIALECT,
ABOUT 1000 A.D.[1])

9. And he cwæð to his cnihtum þæt hi him   on scipe
    And he spake to his dis-ciples that they on-him, (dat.) *in a-ship*
þenodon. for þære menigu þæt hi hine ne of-þrungon;
should wait, on-account-of the multitude that they him (acc.) *not might-throng;*

10. Soþlice manega he ge-hælde; Swa þæt hi æt-hrinon
    Indeed many he healed, so that they touched
his. and swa fela swa untrumnessa
him (gen.)*, and so many as infirmities*

11. And unclæne gastas hæfdon; Þa hi hine gesawon.
    And unclean spirits had, when they him saw,
hi to-foran him a-strehton. and þus cweðende clypedon.
they before him bowed-down, and thus saying cried,
þu eart godes sunu.
thou art God's Son.

12. And he him swyðe forbead þæt hi hine ne
    And he them strongly forbade that they him not
ge-swutelodon.
should-make-known.

[1] Skeat, *The Gospels in Anglo-Saxon, Northumbrian, and Old Mercian Versions.*

CHAPTER VIII

THE ENGLISH LANGUAGE PLANTED IN BRITAIN

How the English language came to Britain and was established there.[1]

IT is clear from what has been said above that the place where English was first spoken was not what we now call England. Our forefathers, when they came over with Hengest and Horsa and their other leaders in 449 A.D. and later years, brought their language with them. And if we see from what part of Germany they came, we shall at the same time find the place where the English language was first developed.

Now, if we look at a map of Germany as it was in the later times of the Roman Empire, we shall find a tribe called 'Angli.'[2] They are placed on the neck of the Danish peninsula, in the part now called Schleswig. And north of them are the 'Juti,' on the part of Denmark still called Jutland.[3] South and south-west of the Angles, near the mouth of the Elbe, we find the 'Saxones' or Saxons, and, mostly west of these, the Frisians. All these were kindred tribes, speaking Low German dialects, and no doubt an Angle would understand a Saxon, Jute,[4] or Frisian, about as easily

---

[1] See especially Freeman's *Norman Conquest*, vol. i.

[2] There is a district on the east coast of Schleswig, then called Angel, now Angeln, which marks their original home. Of course our ancestors did not use Latin terminations, but called themselves Angle, Iotas, Seaxe, and Frysan.

[3] The Danes may have occupied Denmark from the North after our ancestors left it, or there may have been some there before side by side with the Jutes.   [4] See Appendix C, the Kentish Dialect.

as we understand a Somersetshire peasant, or a man from the wilder parts of Lancashire. Their descendants, who have remained on the Continent and in the islands off the west coast of Schleswig, still speak a language nearly allied to English.

These Angles, Saxons, Jutes, and Frisians had long known the coasts of Britain well. Bodies of Saxons, and no doubt also of the other tribes, had been in the habit of making plundering expeditions to Britain as early as the third century after Christ, and under the Romans there had been a 'Count[1] of the Saxon Shore,' that is, an officer whose duty it was to protect the east and south-east coasts of Britain from the pirates—our ancestors. And when the Roman garrison was withdrawn, about 410 A.D., these plundering expeditions would become safer, and therefore more frequent. But it was just like the Danish invasion in later times. Some of the pirates very soon made up their minds to settle. Such land as could be cultivated without much trouble was perhaps overcrowded in Schleswig-Holstein and along the coast of North Germany, and by merely driving back the Britons they would find fields ready for cultivation in this island. First the Jutes settled in Kent, and later on in the Isle of Wight and on the shores of Southampton Water. The Saxons gradually conquered those parts of England which still bear their name— Sussex (the South Saxons), Essex (the East Saxons), Middlesex (the Middle Saxons), as well as all the country bounded on the east by Kent (or more probably by Surrey), and on the west by 'West Wales' or Cornwall, on the north by the Thames, and on the south by the sea, which was called Wessex (West Saxons) down to the Norman Conquest.[2] The rest of Britain

---

[1] 'Comes,' or 'count,' was under the later Roman Empire a title given to officers of high rank. It means, of course, honorary 'companion, or comrade, of the Emperor.'

[2] They conquered also Gloucestershire, Worcestershire, and Herefordshire, and some of the country east of these towards Middlesex and Hertfordshire. Though these districts were afterwards lost to Mercia, they retained their Saxon dialect.

as far north as the Forth, and as far west as the frontiers of Strathclyde and Wales, was conquered and occupied by the Angles. It is quite uncertain in which part of the country we are to place the Frisian settlements, and consequently we must now and henceforward leave them out of our calculations. All these tribes, as we have seen, spoke one language, though in different dialects. And since the Angles occupied the greater part of the country, and also perhaps because it was the Anglian dialect, in its Northumbrian form, which first became a cultivated and literary language on our conversion to Christianity, the speech of all was called by one name, 'English.'

The way in which the conquest of Britain was carried out influenced our language in one point especially. The Britons, from whom the Welsh are descended, made a very stubborn resistance. The conquest of the bulk of the country took 150 years, roughly speaking. The Britons did not attempt to make terms with the invaders, who most probably would not have made or kept terms with them. They did not, for instance, give up a part of their lands to save the rest, or let the English have the ownership of the land, while they tilled it and paid rent in labour or with a share of the crop, but when they could not hold a part of the country—the coast, for instance—they withdrew farther to the west or north, and were ready to make just as stubborn a fight behind their next line of defence—a river, or forest, or marsh. Now, if they had remained among the conquerors, English would probably have included many more Celtic and Latin words in its early stage. We might even have lost our own language altogether, as did our relations the Franks, the German invaders of Gaul. There the inhabitants, who were Celts like the Britons, but who had dropped their own language, except a very few words, and adopted Latin, submitted readily to the Franks. And as the invaders were in the minority, they gradually adopted the debased Latin which they heard spoken everywhere around them; and so, though French contains a large number of German words, such as *guerre* (Old High German *werra*), *garder* (Old High German *warten*), *danser* (Old High German *dansón*), and many others, yet the majority of the words in it and all its grammar are from Latin. Just in the same way the descendants of the Normans in England at last completely adopted English, as we shall see, though they brought a great many French words into the language. But as for the English who invaded Britain, at least before they became Christians, they and the Britons were like oil and vinegar, they did not easily mix. And so our ancestors did not adopt Welsh or Latin as their language, but went on speaking English as they or their fathers had done in Schleswig-Holstein and North Germany. Before the conquest of Britain by the English, it appears that Welsh was spoken in the country by the large majority of the Britons, Latin by the educated classes in the towns. But our forefathers borrowed very few words from either of these languages at this time. Still, they took some of the Britons as slaves, and from these they learnt the names of the rivers in Britain, for it is natural when you see a river to ask its name, expecting it to have one already. And so nearly all the rivers of England have Celtic names. The name *Ouse*, applied to several rivers in England, the same word as *Usk* in Wales, *Esk* in Scotland, and *Exe* in Devonshire, is derived from a Celtic word meaning 'water,'[1] and *Avon* is also a Celtic word of the same meaning. There was a *Tamesis* when the Romans conquered Britain, and there is a *Thames* now.

As regards the towns, the smaller places mostly lost their name together with their existence. But the invaders kept something like the Celtic names for the Roman garrison-towns, usually with the addition of *ceaster* (*castrum*) to describe them. So *Venta* (Icenorum) became *Wintanceaster* (*Winchester*),

---

[1] *Usque-baugh* (Irish) means 'water of life,' like 'eau-de-vie,' and *whiskey* is a shorter form of the word.

Glevum, Gléawceaster (*Gloucester*), and *Lindum colonia, Lindcylene* (*Lincoln*). *Ceaster* was one of the few Latin words which came into our language at this time. A Roman town with stone walls was like a great natural object, and could hardly change its proper name any more than a river. And the whole class of such towns required a special name, since the invaders had never seen anything like them before. Some few Latin words (such as *mile* and *pound*) had already made their way into the German languages through Roman traders, or German soldiers who had served in the Roman legions. These our ancestors of course brought with them, and they added a few others, such as *ceaster* or *caster*, already mentioned, and *wīc* (*vicus*), as in 'North*wīc*,' 'Nor*wich*.' They also borrowed a very few Celtic words, such as *cart, down,* and *slough*. There will be more to say on this part of the subject later on.[1]

---

[1] The small amount of Celtic in the earliest English supports the account given above of the slight intermixture of Celtic blood in the Anglo-Saxons (which is probable on other grounds), but by itself it does not absolutely prove it (see Appendix A, Race and Language).

The number of Latin words borrowed from such of the Britons as were sufficiently Romanised to speak Latin may have been somewhat greater than is suggested above. But it cannot have been very large. We had certainly adopted some few Latin words on the Continent, and many must have been borrowed at and after our conversion. If we subtract these from the Latin words in Anglo-Saxon it will not leave a large number which can have been borrowed from the Britons (see chap. xii.).

CHAPTER IX

ENGLISH IN ITS EARLY FORM

Old English or Anglo-Saxon—The Verb—'Strong' Perfects (1),(2)—'Weak' Perfects — Subjunctive — Declensions of Substantives — Genders — Plurals formed by change of vowel—'Strong' and 'weak' declension of Adjectives—The definite Article: its origin—Pronouns—Use of the cases—Anglo-Saxon an inflexional language, and the parent of Modern English.[1]

WE must next see what the language which our ancestors brought with them was like, and at the same time try to get some idea of the changes which had taken place while one variety of the Indo-European tongue developed into Teutonic, and Teutonic into the various dialects of which English was one.

It has been already said that the Greek verb gives us a very fair general notion of what a verb was like in the Indo-European language. In a Greek verb we see that almost all the modifications of the meaning of the stem, those of person, tense, mood, and voice, are expressed by inflexions, which have become so closely joined to the stem as to form one word with it, though originally, as we saw reason to believe, these were separate words. That is to say, the perfected Indo-European language was purely inflexional. But when we get our first view of the Teutonic languages, we see that a change has set in. The tide has begun to ebb. Instead of retaining the old inflexions for the pluperfect, the future, and

---

[1] Skeat, *Principles of English Etymology*, First Series. Sweet, *Anglo-Saxon Reader*. Koch, *Historische Grammatik der Englischen Sprache*. Kington Oliphant, *Old and Middle English*. Thompson's *Greek Syntax*. King and Cookson, *Sounds and Inflexions in Greek and Latin*.

so on, modifying the stem or root so that the whole idea is expressed in one word, as in ἐ-δέ-δε-το (he had been bound), we find it expressed by two or more separate words, as in English at the present day,—the notion is conveyed by a phrase and not by a single word. This is called the 'analytic' tendency in a language (from ἀναλύω, 'to break up into parts'). We have met with it before when we saw that the Latin provincials preferred to say $\begin{Bmatrix} amare\ habeo,^1 \\ aimer\text{-}ai \end{Bmatrix}$ rather than some simplified form of *amabo*. It is the same tendency which makes the Modern German say in ordinary conversation, 'Ich *habe* ihn gestern *gesehen*,' and the Frenchman, 'Je l'*ai vu* hier,' instead of using 'Ich *sah*,' and 'Je *vis*,' past tenses formed by inflexion. This change from inflexions to phrases is due partly to inaccurate use of the terminations, making one inflexion, for instance, do duty for all persons of the plural, as in the Old English verb. This often makes it needful to use a pronoun with it, for the sake of clearness, and then again the termination becomes unnecessary. It is also partly due to what we may call the natural decay of the old inflexions, which, as we saw (pp. 12, 56, 57), begin to wear down as soon as they have become one word with the stem, as in English *án-líce, anlíȝe*,[2] *only*. Thus in time they often become too indistinct to be at once intelligible, and as the object of language is to convey our thoughts to others, some other means of doing this had to be discovered.[3] Now, our meaning can be equally well expressed by joining together two or more words to express the idea, and by putting words in a particular order according to what they have to do in the sentence.

[1] It is curious that what seems the opposite tendency, namely, to form new terminations out of separate words, was still more or less active. It is only necessary to refer to the later history of *amare habeo*, to *seule-ment*, and *rare-ly*, all formed in times when the general tendency both of French and English was to use groups of words or 'phrases,' rather than inflexions. We shall see another instance in the English verb presently (p. 92).

[2] ȝ, ʒ in the middle of a word usually = a soft GH, like German CH, as in *ich*.

[3] The 'analytic tendency' may also be due partly to a habit of mind. In this case we know nothing of the causes which produced it.

A comparison of Latin with Modern English will at once show the difference between an 'inflexional' and an 'analytic' language. Thus, in Latin we put 'oblitus *tui*.' In English we break up the *tui* into two words, and say 'forgetful *of you*.' Again, in Latin, we can say either 'Homo occidit lupum' or 'Lupum occidit homo.' The terminations distinguish the nominative from the accusative, and both sentences mean the same. In English there is a very serious difference between 'The man killed the wolf,' and 'The wolf killed the man.' The inflexions of the cases having been lost, we must take care to put the subject or nominative first (as is customary in the language) if we wish to be understood. Modern English is a language in which the tendency to substitute groups of words for inflexions has been almost completely carried out. But we must not expect to find that Old English (or Anglo-Saxon) has carried out this tendency with any approach to completeness. A sister-language, namely German, has even been surprised, so to speak, in the midst of the change, by an age of education, and above all by printing; and so its forms, at least those which appear in books and in polite conversation, have been for the most part fixed at a particular stage in this process of change from inflexion to phrases. This was not the case with English until it had parted with the vast majority of its inflexions, as will be seen hereafter. But, when the earliest works in our language were composed, it was still to a large extent an inflexional language. Though it had parted with many of its inflexions, English, or rather the Teutonic language from which it sprang, had made some new ones peculiar to itself, and had also seized upon certain variations in words, which did not originally serve this purpose, as means of expressing differences of tense and number.

We will now look at the oldest form of English which we have, and see how it bears out these statements. In order that the writing may give a correct idea of the language, we must bear in mind

(1) That the vowels sounded as they do in the 'new' or correct pronunciation of Latin, or nearly as in Modern German.[1]

(2) That the sound of diphthongs can be recovered most nearly by pronouncing the two vowels rapidly one after the other.

(3) That no letters are silent (like K in *knight*).

(4) That a variety of spelling nearly always points to a variety in pronunciation.

We shall say something more on some of these points later on; at present they must be taken for granted.

If we look at the present tense of any verb in Old English (West Saxon dialect), we shall find the personal endings of the singular in a tolerably complete form—

Present Indicative ic binde
Singular þú[2] bindest
(*West Saxon*) hé bindeþ[3] (*or by contraction*, bint)

While in the plural there is only one ending for all the persons—

Present Indicative Plural wé ⎫
(*West Saxon*) gé ⎬ bindaþ
  hí ⎭

The subjunctive is still constantly used, but its personal endings are much weakened—

Present Subjunctive ic ⎫
(*West Saxon*) þú ⎬ binde
  hé ⎭

  wé ⎫
  gé ⎬ binden, *or* bindon
  hí ⎭

---

[1] An accent, thus á, ǽ, denotes a long letter, á = ā. (A as in *father*.)
[2] Þ, þ, and Ð, ð = th.
[3] *Originally* -bindis -bindiþ.

The Imperative is—

Imperative	2nd Pers. Sing. bind
(*West Saxon*)	2nd Pers. Plur. bindaþ

But the personal endings can be discarded as unnecessary, where the pronoun immediately follows. So we find *wite gé*, 'you know' (present indicative), *ne sléa gé*, 'do not kill' (imperative plural).

We must not leave out the forms in the other dialects, for a part of our modern verb ('he speaks') cannot be accounted for from the West Saxon forms.

In the Northumbrian[1] verb we find a variety of forms—

Present Indicative	ic spreco, *or* sprecu
(*Northumbrian*)	þú spreces, *or* sprecis
	hé spreces, sprecas, spreceþ, sprecaþ
wé	
gé	sprecas, spreces, sprecaþ, spreceþ
hí	

In the 3rd person singular we sometimes find two forms combined in the same sentence—

hé ettes and drincaþ
he eats and drinketh (St. Mark ii. 16).

And the Northern plural will also account for some constructions in Shakespeare, which cannot be otherwise explained, as in *Macbeth*—

Whiles I threat, he lives;
Words to the heat of deeds too cold breath *gives*.[2]

On the other hand, Northumbrian retains some very ancient forms not found in West Saxon. Thus it has some 'verbs in

---

[1] Durham Gospels. Skeat, *The Gospels in Anglo-Saxon, Northumbrian, Old and Mercian Versions*.   [2] II. i. 60, 61.

μι᾽ besides West Saxon *ic eom* (Northumbrian *ic am*, Modern English *I am*), such as *ic geséom*, 'I see,' *ic gedóm* or *doam*, 'I do.'

Mercian or Midland too had the 2nd person singular ending in -*s*, as þú *sis*, 'thou seest.' So in Lancashire they still say, 'thou *names*,' 'thou *thinks*.' And we find one example in this dialect of the plural in the present indicative ending in -*n* —*doan*,[1] 'they do,' a form which we shall be meeting with constantly in Midland English after the Norman Conquest. The Southern or West Saxon plural, -*a*þ, is still preserved in the proverb (made at Winchester), 'Manners mak*yth* man.'

We must now say something about the past tense, which Teutonic languages show in forms which are in great measure peculiar to them.

In the primitive Indo-European language a very large number of perfects, if not all of them, must have been formed by 'Reduplication,'—that is, by saying the root or base of the word twice over. This repetition is often met with in language. It is familiar to our earliest years in the form *puff-puff*. But many other words have been made in English in the same way, such as *chit-chat* and *riff-raff*. Now this repetition of a root (which in some languages is used to form a plural) was in the undivided Indo-European language employed to form a perfect tense. But, as in the case of other compound words, as soon as the two parts were inseparably joined together, one of them began to wear down. So in Greek, while the perfects of all verbs that begin with a single consonant are formed by reduplication, we do not find the root (or base of the word) repeated in full, but usually only a part of it, while the vowel is altered, as in τέ-τυπ-α, λέ-λυ-κα. The same is the case with the reduplicated perfects in Latin, such

[1] Swa hǽðene doan, St. Matthew vi. 7. Rushworth Gospels, quoted by Kington Oliphant, *Old and Middle English*, p. 121. The plural in the past tense, and in the subjunctive, both present and past, ends in -*n* in all three dialects.

as *ce-cĭd-i* and *ce-cīd-i*, and the old form *te-tul-i*. Now, in Gothic many verbs have their perfects formed by reduplication—*hai-hait* (I called), from *haitan*; *sai-slep* (I slept), from *slepan*; and, with a change of vowel (very much like λείπω, λέλοιπα; ῥήγνυμι, ἔρρωγα), *tai-tok* (I touched), from *tekan* [see specimen of Gothic, p. 74, (*at-*) *tai-tok* (*-eina*)]. In English one obviously reduplicated perfect has lived down to our own day, which, as we shall presently see, has more work to do than any other perfect tense in the language—*ic dy-de* (from present *ic dó*), 'I did.' But in the oldest form of English which has come down to us there are other verbs which still bear the marks of the reduplication. As in Gothic the diphthong peculiar to the reduplication is AI (*sai-slep*), and, as in Greek, its vowel is E (τέ-τυφα), so in the very oldest English, older than any specimens of it which have survived, the reduplication seems to have been regularly formed with the diphthong EO.[1] Thus we actually find *lácan* (to spring) making its perfect *léo-lc*, *rǽdan* (to advise) with a perfect *réo-rd*, and *on-drǽdan* (to fear) perfect *on-dréo-rd*. If we suppose that in English of an earlier date these tenses were respectively *leo-lac, reo-rǽd, on-dreo-drǽd*, their form is at once explained, and the similar forms in Gothic make this explanation tolerably certain. A like formation in Greek (if such existed) would be λε-λπα for λέ-λοιπα. *Ste-ti*, the reduplicated perfect of *sto*, shows the same preservation of the reduplication at the expense of the central part of the word. But these forms *léo-lc, réo-rd, on-dréo-rd* are only 'survivals,' and soon all distinct traces of the reduplication are lost in the forms *léc, réd, on-dréd*. Still, as we have seen that the diphthong of the reduplication was EO, we may conclude that nearly all the verbs which in Old English (or Anglo-Saxon) make their perfects in EO were originally formed by reduplication. Among these verbs are—

[1] Perhaps developed from I, as in $\begin{Bmatrix} \text{di-de} \\ \text{dy-de} \end{Bmatrix}$ did.

Present.		Past, or Perfect.[1]	
Old English (West Saxon).	Modern English.	Old English (West Saxon).	Modern English.
cráwan	crow	créow	crew
feallan	fall	féoll	fell
grówan	grow	gréow	grew
healdan	hold	héold	held.[2]

The second class of perfects, of which we may take *sing—sang, bind—bound* as examples, consists of those which are formed by a change ('gradation') of the vowel of the stem, but which show no trace of reduplication.

Of this 'vowel-gradation' we find distinct traces in other languages. Thus the verb *teg-o* in Latin has E, but the substantive *tog-a* ('a garment for covering') has O. *Prec-or* is 'I pray,' but 'the person who prays' or 'suitor' is *proc-us*. In Greek—besides such examples as γέν-ος, γόν-ος; ἔ-τεκ-ον, τόκ-ος; πλέκ-ω, πλόκ-η,—we find this change in the formation of the perfect, as λείπω, λέλοιπα; ῥήγνυμι, ἔρρωγα. It is supposed that this change of the vowel was accidental, that it arose from the difference of accent or tone with which the word was originally pronounced. Now, if these verbs once had the reduplication to mark the perfect (as is probable), it has simply fallen off, leaving merely the change of vowel to show the difference of tense, and this is quite sufficient for the purpose. It is like the use of *tuli* for the older *te-tuli*, or as if in Greek the perfect of λείπω were λοιπα.

This then is the probable explanation of these verbs, and it is all that appears necessary to explain them in Modern English. But in the old form of the language this alteration ('gradation') of the vowel went further in many of these verbs, as we may see in our former example, the verb *bind*. Its perfect ran thus in the form of the language used before the Norman Conquest—

[1] These perfects have and had in English the *meaning* of a simple past tense, like the Greek Aorist, with whose *form* they have nothing in common.

[2] Several of this class have now 'weak' perfects, such as rówan, réow, now rowed; flówan, fléow, now flowed.

ic band
þú bunde
hé band
wé ⎫
gé ⎬ bundon.
hí ⎭

Whereas in Modern English the tense has the same vowel throughout—

I bound
thou boundest
he bound
we bound
you bound
they bound.

This looks very much as if we had got to using the vowel of the plural throughout, just as we use the vowel of the singular for the whole tense, 'I began,' etc. But from the history of these verbs it appears that, while a few past tenses come from the A being turned into O (as in *rád, rode*, see p. 210, etc.), *spun, swung, burst*, and *bound, found*,[1] etc., as well as the 'incorrect' forms, 'I *swum*,' 'I *sung*,' and so on, come from the past participle, as if one change of vowel were enough in the verb. This is also the best explanation of 'I broke' (Old English *ic bræc, wé brǽcon*).[2] We shall have to say something more about this very confusing part of English grammar.

To return to our English 'strong' verb as it stood before the Conquest, we see that in *ic band* the vowel is varied in the 2nd person singular and in the plural. Now, if we look back to pp. 23, 24, we shall see that in *ic wát* (which is also originally a perfect tense like its brother οἶδα) there is a similar difference of vowel between the singular *ic wát* and

---

[1] If not, *bound, found*, etc., come from the A being first turned to O.— Morris, *Historical Outlines of English Accidence*, p. 161.
[2] See Morris, *Historical Outlines of English Accidence*, p. 160, etc. Skeat, *Principles of English Etymology*, Second Series, pp. 459, 460. Koch, *Historische Grammatik der Englischen Sprache*.

the plural *wé witon*, a variation which also appears in Greek and Sanskrit. And as that was attributed to a difference of accent in the original language, since in the singular the stem and not the short termination took the accent, while in the plural it fell on the longer termination and not on the stem, so the difference between *ic band* and *wé bundon* is probably to be accounted for in the same way. Only under 'difference of accent' must be included not merely the greater or less force with which a syllable is pronounced (as in 'they *say*,' as opposed to '*they* say,' '*manly*,' as opposed to '*gentleman*'), but also any such difference of tone as when we raise our voice in asking a question, or drop it at the end of the sentence when we make a statement. Both 'accent' and 'tone' have apparently a tendency to alter a vowel. But the whole subject is rather obscure.

These two classes of verbs—those which form their perfect originally by reduplication, and those which appear to form it merely by change of vowel—are usually called the 'strong' verbs. In their past participles the vowel is sometimes the same as in the present, sometimes as in the plural of the preterite, sometimes a different vowel from either of these, as—

		Present Infinitive.	*Perfect Singular.*	*Perfect Plural.*	*Past Participle.*
Reduplicated	{	feallan (*fall*)	féoll	féollon	feallen
		bláwan (*blow*)	bléow	bléowon	bláwen
(1)	{	bindan (*bind*)	band	bundon	bunden
		swimman (*swim*)	swamm	swummon	swummen
(2)	{	brecan (*break*)	bræc	brǽcon	brocen
		teran (*tear*)	tær	tǽron	toren
		sprecan (*speak*)	spræc	sprǽcon	sprecen
(3)	{	gifan (*give*)	geaf	géafon	gifen
		etan (*eat*)	æt	ǽton	eten
(4)	{	scacan (*shake*)	scóc	scócon	scacen
		wacan (*wake*)	wóc	wócon	wacen

	Present Infinitive.	Perfect Singular.	Perfect Plural.	Past Participle.
(5)	rídan (*ride*)	rád	ridon	riden
	scínan (*shine*)	scán	scinon	scinen
	wrítan (*write*)	wrát	writon	writen
(6)	cléofan (*cleave*)	cléaf	clufon	clofen
	céosan (*choose*)	céas	curon	coren.[1]

Whatever the vowel may be, the past participle of a 'strong' verb always ended in -*en*, though the termination has often dropped in Modern English. We say *fallen, given, grown*, but 'he was *bound* to do it,' though by an 'archaism,' an old-fashioned form of speaking, we can speak of 'his *bounden* duty.' Sometimes too we now use the perfect for the past participle, as when we say, 'I have *stood* there,' whereas the old past participle was *standen*. This -*en* was used to form adjectives as well, such as *open, heathen* (originally 'a dweller on the *heath*,' or in the wilds).

So much, then, for the 'strong' verbs, those, that is, which form the perfect with a change of vowel, in whatever way the change arose. But we all know that such verbs are the exception. They were certainly more numerous in the older English, or Anglo-Saxon,[2] for we have made many of them 'regular,' such as *weep*, perfect *wept* (Anglo-Saxon *wéop*, a reduplicated verb), *bake*, perfect *baked* (Anglo-Saxon *bóc*, by 'gradation' of the vowel), just as children say 'he *falled*,' or '*fallded*,' 'he *growed*,' for 'he *fell*,' 'he *grew*,' imitating the common or 'regular' formation of the perfect. Now this -*ed* or -*t* (in Old English -*ode*, -*ede*, -*de*, -*te*) has nothing to do with the -*ed* or -*t* of the past participle (Old English -*od*, -*ed*, -*t*), as in 'he has *baked*,' or '*a lost* cause.' It is a mere coincidence, such as often occurs in language, that their form

---

[1] For an explanation of the changes of the vowels see Skeat, *Principles of English Etymology*, Second Series, p. 463, etc.

[2] Rarely the resemblance or attraction of a 'strong' verb has made a 'weak' perfect 'strong.' So even Chaucer (died 1400) says—

'Of fustian he *wered* a gipoun' (or short coat).

We now say 'he *wore*,' on the analogy of *bear, tear*. So we sometimes hear I *arrove*, on the analogy of *strive, strove*.

should have become the same. *Show-ed,* in 'I have *showed,*' *yok-ed,* in 'an ox *yoked* to the plough,' is the same formation as in the Greek verbal adjective (λύ-τος, ζευκ-τός), in the Latin past participle (*scrip-tus, junc-tus*), as the *-ta* in Sanskrit *yuk-ta* (see pp. 53, 54). But the *-ed* in 'I *showed*' has a totally different history, and is a means of expressing past time which the ancestors of the Goths, Norsemen, English, and Germans developed for themselves later on, but while the Teutonic people still spoke one language, just as the provincials of the Roman Empire, the ancestors of the French, made their new future *aimer-ai* out of 'amare habeo.'

We might have guessed at the origin of this *-ed* or *-t* from English or German,[1] but a comparison of Gothic converts this guess into a certainty. Look at the plural of the past tense of *wiljan* (to will) in Gothic; this is *wil-dedun.* So *habaidedun* from *haban* (to have), *hropi-dedun,* from *hropjan* (to cry out) appear in the sample of Gothic on p. 74. Now, there is no separate form answering to the verb 'to *do*' in Gothic, but since it appears in English and other Low German dialects, and in literary High German[2] (the German of books), it is not difficult to believe that Gothic once possessed it. The Old English reduplicated perfect of this verb makes in the plural *dy-don.* We can see then that 'weis *wil-dedun*' (Old English 'wé *wol-don*') is 'we did will,' only the 'did' is put at the end instead of the beginning. And this *dyde, dydon,* having been frequently attached to verbs, its origin was forgotten, and it underwent the common fate of terminations in being worn down and altered (as *lîce* got changed to *-ly*), just as a coin wears down with use. In English one of the commonest changes of this *-ode, -ede, -de* (Modern English *-ed,* or *-d,* as it is pronounced) is for the D to be altered to T by the influence of the preceding consonant. So the 'hard' or 'breathed' letter P has made it into a T in the past tenses,

[1] As in *ich weinte, ich liebte, ich hatte.*   [2] *Thun,* past tense *that.*

'he *crept*,' 'he *wept*'; and in *whipped, dropped, blessed*, and other perfects it is pronounced as T, though not usually so written.¹ In *led, fed*, the double D has made the preceding vowel short (Old English *ic lǽd-de, ic féd-de*) and the *-de* has then dropped off; for the final E was lost, like other E's at the end of words which were the relics of terminations, and there is no difference of pronunciation between 'fed' and 'fedd,' to preserve the second D. The shortness of the vowel was quite sufficient to mark the past tense in speaking. This shortening of the vowel is like the footprint of an extinct animal of which no other trace is left. Sometimes, however, as in *hit, sit*, where the present tense already had a short vowel, there was no mark of distinction left at all, and the present must be distinguished from the past by the rest of the sentence. *Sought, thought, wrought*,² are also 'weak' perfects. 'I *made*' is an abbreviation of *maked*, which, of course, is for *make-did*.

A 'weak' perfect indicative was thus conjugated—

Weak Perfect Indicative	ic	sóhte ('I sought')
(West Saxon)	þú	sóhtest
	hé	sóhte
	wé	
	gé	} sóhton.
	hí	

And both 'strong' and 'weak' perfects are alike in the subjunctive mood—

Perfect Subjunctive	ic		ic	
(West Saxon)	þú } bunde		þú } sóhte	
	hé		hé	
	wé		wé	
	gé } bunden, *or*		gé } sóhten, *or*
	hí } bundon		hí } sóhton.

---

¹ It is well to make these changes a matter of experiment with our own mouths. It is very difficult to pronounce *creepd*, or *crepd*, just as it is to pronounce *whipped* as it is written, unless we make it two syllables. Even then a T comes easier.

² We also have the 'regular' form *worked*.

In speaking of 'strong' and 'weak' past tenses we have also spoken of the past participles corresponding to them. It is only necessary to add that both kinds of past participle can alike be declined as adjectives, and that both usually take *ge-* before them, unless they already have some other prefix (much as in German of the present day), such as *be-* in *beréafian* ('bereave'), *to-* in *to-brecan* (*to-break* or 'break to pieces,' as in 'and all *to brake* his scull,' Judges ix. 53). This *ge-* appears in the form of *y-* not unfrequently in Spenser, as *yfed, yborn*,[1] rarely in Shakespeare, as *yclad* (*Second Part of Henry VI.*, I. i. 33), and in Milton's line—

In heaven *y-clept*[2] Euphrosyne.

And having been retained longest in the dialect of the South and West (West Saxon), it still remains in the speech of Dorsetshire, which is a modern representative of the West Saxon dialect, as in the lines of William Barnes—

Vorgi'e me, Jenny, do! an rise
Thy hangèn head an' teary eyes
An' speak, vor I've *a-took* in lies
An' I've *a-done* thee wrong.

But this prefix was also used with other parts of verbs, and with nouns, adjectives, and adverbs, sometimes merely to strengthen their meaning, and so we have further traces of it in *handiwork* (*hand-ge-weorc*), *aware* (*ge-wær*), *everywhere* (*ǽfre-ge-hwǽr*), *enough* (*genóg, genóh*, German *genug*), and in Macaulay's lines—

I wis, in all the Senate
There was no heart so bold,

where *I wis* is written and treated as a verb. But it is really nothing but *gewis*, 'certain,' worn down to *ywis, iwis*, like Milton's *yclept* above.

Besides these forms, Old English had a present participle in

---

[1] But Spenser wrote in an 'archaic' or old-fashioned style, and we must not suppose that his language is the ordinary English of his day.

[2] In West Saxon *ge-cleopod* = called.

-ende, berende (bearing) for instance. This still survives in the substantives *friend* and *fiend* (which used to mean merely 'enemy,' like German *feind*); for these were, to begin with, participles, from *fréon*, 'to free, honour, love,' and *féon*, 'to hate' (see p. 148). The Old English verb also has a present infinitive in -*an*,[1] which it declines in the dative to form a kind of gerund. Thus, nominative *cweþan*, 'to say,' dative *cweþanne* or *cweþenne*. For instance, 'Úre drihten is to *cweþenne*' = 'Our Lord is to say' (or, 'will say'), 'Ic dó éow to *witanne*' = 'I do you to wit,' that is, 'I make you to know.'

We have now gone through the different inflexions of the verb. We may notice that Old English had no future tense; none, that is, formed by inflexion, as in Latin and Greek; and as the other Teutonic languages, including Gothic, do not possess one either, it seems probable that it had perished before the dialects of Teutonic separated into languages. Its place is supplied in three ways. First, by using the present, a somewhat clumsy device, though we still say, 'I *am going* away to-morrow,' or 'I *am sending* the carriage on Thursday.' This is a very common plan, but one example will be sufficient—

Gé sittaðˇ ofer twelf setl. démende twelf mægðˇa israhel.[2]
Ye shall-sit on twelve thrones, judging (the) twelve tribes of Israel.

The second and third ways are by using 'will' and 'shall' with the infinitive. This is of course the plan which we now employ. But in English before the Conquest *willan* and *sculan* (present *ic sceal*) have hardly become mere auxiliaries attached to a verb. There is often a notion of 'must' or 'ought' connected with *shall*, of wishing or resolve attached to *will*. This is of course sometimes the case in our own talk, only we now have to make the *will* and *shall* very emphatic

---

[1] Which has survived in the verb *chast-en*, where -*en* is merely the infinitive termination, which it is not in "embold*en*,' for instance. See Skeat, *Etymological Dictionary*.

[2] St. Matthew xix. 28. Skeat, *West Saxon Gospels*.

to show that they are anything but the mark of future time, as in 'he *will* go out,' 'you *shall* do it.'

The other tenses of the verb, pluperfect, 'perfect with have,' imperfect, as well as the tenses of the passive voice, are formed much as in Modern English, with the auxiliaries 'to have' and 'to be,' and also with a third verb *weorþan*, 'to become' (German *werden*) which only survives in Modern English in the poetical expression 'woe *worth* the day,'[1]—that is, 'evil be, or happen, to the unlucky day.' This verb, like its German brother, generally implies that an action is going on, as 'ic *wearþ* gebunden,' 'I $\left\{\begin{array}{l}\text{was}\\\text{became}\end{array}\right\}$ tied, 'ic *wæs* gebunden,' 'I had fetters on.' But this distinction is not very scrupulously observed, nor is that of the past tenses from each other so exactly kept as in Modern English. There was just a trace of a passive voice, formed by inflexion, in one verb, *ic hátte*, 'I am called,' or 'I was called' (later *hight*);[2] its plural was *hátton*. In Gothic this appears in a fuller form as—

ik haitada
þu haitaza
is haitada
weis ⎫
jus ⎬ haitanda.
eis ⎭

And a similar form is found in many verbs in that language. The still undivided Teutonic language must have had a passive voice in all verbs. Now, some of these compound forms explain themselves, such as 'I *was* bound,' 'I *became* bound.' But why should 'I *have*,' which originally means merely 'I possess,' give the notion of past time? We are so accustomed

---

[1] Scott, *Lady of the Lake*, I. ix. Ezekiel xxx. 2.
[2] As in Shakespeare—
   This grisly beast, which Lion *hight* by name.
Midsummer-Night's Dream, V. i. 140, quoted by Skeat. Or in Spenser, *Faery Queene*, I. ix. 14—
   And at her parting said, She Queene of Faeries *hight*.

to using 'I *have* seen it,' in much the same sense as 'I saw it,' that we do not think of the exact or original meaning of the words so long as we find other people understand them. And yet 'I possess it seen,' which should mean the same thing, does not do so at all. The account of the phrase or expression seems to be somewhat as follows. With many verbs, such as 'receive,' 'buy,' 'take,' the verb 'to have' plainly gives the meaning of a past tense. 'I *have* it bought' (or, 'I possess it bought') is much the same as the conventional past tense, 'I *have* bought it.' And from such expressions as this the use of 'have' must have been extended to others where it was really inappropriate (like the *mente* in *seulement*, see p. 55), to such expressions as 'I *have* given it,' where 'I possess it given' would have a very different sense. But, as has been said above, when a phrase has once become fixed with a particular sense, we do not think of the meaning of its separate parts. 'I *have* it taken' is used as a past tense, and therefore 'I *have* it given' is formed in imitation of it to express past time as well. In the older Anglo-Saxon there is this trace of the origin of the phrase, that the past participle is in the accusative case agreeing with the accusative governed by *have*, as—

<blockquote>
Hé hæfð mon geworht-ne.[1]
He hath man wrought (acc.)
</blockquote>

What shows that this is a tolerably natural line of thought is that we also find the beginnings of it in Latin, carried to completion in French. Thus

<blockquote>
'Dumnorigem . . . omnia Haeduorum vectigalia . . . redempta habere'
</blockquote>

may be translated either 'that Dumnorix *owned* all the taxes of the Ædui bought up,' or 'that Dumnorix *had* bought up all the taxes of the Ædui.'[2] And there are other examples

---

[1] Cædmon, quoted by Koch.
[2] Caesar, *Gallic War*, i. xviii. § 2; quoted by Brachet, *Historical French Grammar*, translated by Kitchin.

in Latin where 'habeo' is evidently tending to become an auxiliary.[1] In French, in such a sentence as 'J'ai vu les hommes,' ai (habeo) is nothing more than a sign of past time.

Before parting with the verb we ought to say a few words about the use of the subjunctive in Anglo-Saxon. In form it is greatly worn down and obscured, if we compare it with the Gothic verb (thraih-*eina*, ga-swi-kunthi-ded-*eina* on p. 74), but in nearly all persons of the present, and in some of the past tense of the subjunctive, it is still distinct from the indicative, which is all that is required for practical purposes. Accordingly we find it used to a very considerable extent, in ways that remind us of the uses of the subjunctive in Latin, and of the subjunctive and optative in Greek. Thus it is not only used—

(1) As a substitute for the imperative mood, as in

Sí[2] þín nama gehalgod,

in the Lord's Prayer, like 'Sanctificetur nomen tuum,' but also,

(2) In reporting what somebody else said (like the optative in Greek, especially in Xenophon)—

ǽgþer sý[2] sixtig elna lang.
each is (he said) sixty ells long.

---

[1] *e.g.* milites, quos in classem scriptos habebat.—Livy, xxii. 57, § 5.
[2] Present subjunctive of *béon*, 'to be,' 3rd sing. It will be best to give the commonest forms of the verb 'to be' for reference—

	Special Northern Forms.	West Saxon.
Present Indicative	ic am	ic eom, béom, béo
		þú eart, bist
		hé is, biþ
	wé, gé, hí } aron, earon (also Mercian)	wé, gé, hí } béoþ, sind, sindon
	(vér erum is the Norse form).	
Present Subjunctive		ic, þú, hé } béo, sí (or sý)
		wé, gé, hí } béon, sín (or sýn)

(3) In asking a question indirectly—

    Saga me, hwæt fisccynna   *sý*   on   wætere.
    Tell me, what of-fish-kinds (there) is in (the) water.

(4) To express a wish or purpose—

    (Hí) woldon þæt hér þý mára wísdóm on londe
    They would that here the more wisdom in (the) land

    wǽre,   þý wé má geþéoda cúþon.
    { *were / should be* } { *the / as* } *we more languages knew.*

(5) With an indefinite relative, or relative expressing a class—

    Syle þám þe þé *bidde.*
    Give to-the-one who thee asks.

(6) In conditional and concessive clauses [1]—

    Gyf hwá *slá* þé.
    If any strike thee.

These are merely samples of the uses of the subjunctive in Anglo-Saxon. In Modern English they are greatly contracted; we have lost the habit of using the subjunctive chiefly because the distinction in form between the two

		West Saxon.	
Perfect Indicative		ic	wæs
		þú	wǽre
		hé	wæs
		wé, gé, hí	wǽron
Perfect Subjunctive		ic	wǽre
		þú	wǽre
		hé	wǽre
		wé, gé, hí	wǽren, wǽron
Imperative	sing.	wes,	béo
	plur.	wesaþ,	béoþ

Infinitive, wesan, béon.
Present Participle, wesende.

[1] Such clauses also have the indicative, as in Latin and Greek.

moods has been for the most part lost. Therefore, in such sentences, we mostly use the indicative, or else insert an auxiliary verb, such as 'may,' 'should' (see (4) above). But our version of the Bible keeps it in tolerably frequent use, as in, '*Be* it known unto you all'[1] (1); 'Whether he *be* a sinner or no, I know not'[2] (3); 'See thou *tell* no man'[3] (4), not indicative *tellest*; 'If it *be*, give me thy hand'[4] (6).

This last is the only use of the subjunctive which is still alive in ordinary speech, as when we say, 'If I *were* to do so.' It is true that even here people often put the indicative, 'If I *was* to go,' but this is hardly correct English at the present time. German of course still makes a considerable use of the subjunctive, as, for instance—

Er sagte mir, es *sei* nicht nöthig (2).
He said to-me, it is not necessary.

Next, we pass to the substantives. If we take any substantive in Modern English, there is not much difficulty in declining it. The declension of the word *day*, for instance, would be as follows —

Singular.		*Plural.*	
Nom. Acc.	day	Nom. Acc.	days
Gen.	day's	Gen.	days'

So we should decline *soul, eye,* and, in fact, all nouns with but few exceptions. The apostrophe (') in the genitive plural suggests that if that case did not end in -*s* already, the plural, like the singular, would take an -*s* for the genitive, as it does in 'men's labour.' The other cases, which in the older form of the language were formed as in Greek or Latin, or in German, by means of inflexions, the dative, for instance, are made up by phrases, by using *to, from,* and such words with the nominative or accusative of the noun, or are implied by

---

[1] *Be* representing the subjunctive form, *ic béo*, etc., Acts iv. 10.
[2] St. John ix. 25.   [3] St. Matt. viii. 4.   [4] 2 Kings x. 15.

position in the sentence, as in 'Tell *the man* I said so'; where *the man* is in the dative case. And even the genitive is limited in its use. It is hardly used except as the possessive case. We could not now say, 'my brother*'s* love,' meaning 'love for my brother,'[1] except in poetry, which is always fond of imitating old forms and uses of language. But in English, before the Conquest, the analytical process, by which we put little words in the place of inflexions, had not gone nearly so far as this. Let us see what the declension of these same words is like in Old English.

DÆG (day, *Masculine*)

	Singular.		Plural.
Nom. Acc.	dæg	Nom. Acc.	dag-as
Gen.	dæg-es	Gen.	dag-a
Dat.	dæg-e	Dat.	dag-um

SÁWOL (soul, *Feminine*)

	Singular.		Plural.
Nom.	sáwol	Nom. Acc.	sáwl-a
Acc.	sáwl-e	Gen.	sáwl-a
Gen.	sáwl-e	Dat.	sáwl-um
Dat.	sáwl-e		

In the declension of *sáwol* a number of different endings have been worn down to a similar form, just as *a-* at the beginning of different words in English—*aboard, aware, ago, ado*—represents both *on* and *ge-*, and the prefix *á-*, and *at*.

ÉAGE[2] (eye, *Neuter*)

	Singular.		Plural.
Nom. Acc.	éag-e	Nom. Acc.	éag-an
Gen.	éag-an	Gen.	éag-ena
Dat.	éag-an	Dat.	éag-um

Of the nominative plural of such words as *éage*, we have some surviving relics in Modern English, *oxen (ox-an)*; *hosen*

[1] Shakespeare, *Richard III.*, I. iv. 229, 230.
[2] A masculine or feminine word would have an accusative in *-an*. The declension is not specially of neuter words. From a comparison with Gothic, more of the word should be included in the stem, less in the case-ending. But the arrangement in the text gives practically a better notion of the declension of such words.

(*hos-an*) in the Bible,[1] and *eyne* in Shakespeare and Milton,[2] *een* in Lowland Scotch or Modern Northumbrian.

Of the dative plural we have traces in *whilom*, Old English *hwīl-um*, 'at whiles' or 'at times,' so 'in certain times' (past). *Seldom* is a dative case of an old adjective *seld*, which also appears in German *selt-en, selt-sam*.

From the examples given above we see that almost all English words now follow *dæg* in the declension of such cases as they have preserved. But even in Anglo-Saxon there had been a great loss of cases out of the seven which existed in the Indo-European language. The ablative and locative are gone; the instrumental is lost in the nouns,[3] though we shall find it still kept in the adjectives and the definite article; and the functions of these three cases are discharged by the dative. Besides this, the accusative is often the same as the nominative. The nominative singular has lost its termination -*s*, which is mostly retained in Gothic (for instance, *hunds*, Anglo-Saxon *hund*, Modern English *hound*), and which forms such an obvious link between Gothic, Greek, and Latin. The nominative has in Old English become the mere stem, or less, like the vocative in Greek or Latin, and so again the distinction between nominative and vocative has been obliterated.

It must not be supposed that we have exhausted the declensions in Anglo-Saxon with our three examples. The substantives of any language may be classed in a varying number of declensions, just as in Greek, while the older grammars (such as Wordsworth's)[4] gave five declensions, the recent ones give only three. But for practical purposes Anglo-Saxon nouns cannot be divided among less than nine or ten declensions, and even these numbers leave plenty of room for irregularities.[5]

---

[1] Daniel iii. 21.
[2] *Midsummer-Night's Dream*, V. i. 178. Milton, *Ode on the Nativity*, line 203.   [3] See p. 67.   [4] In the earlier editions.
[5] There are fifteen examples of the declension of nouns given in full in Sweet's *Anglo-Saxon Reader*.

The declensions follow the gender of the noun to a considerable extent. And this brings us to another characteristic of Old English, which we have lost. In the older form of the language we cannot by any means conclude that males will be masculine, females feminine, and things without life neuter. There an ox was masculine, but a sheep neuter; one word for a woman, *wif*, was neuter;[1] while others, *ides*, as well as *fǽmne* (borrowed from Latin *femina*), are feminine. *Child*[1] (*cild*), *maiden*[1] (*mǽden*), are neuter. Old age (*ildu* or *eldu*, Modern English *eld*) and a street are feminine, a brook masculine, though a burn is feminine. The genders seem as unreasonable as those in Latin, Greek, French, and German.

One other mode of forming the plural of some English substantives is worth a few words of explanation. We know that the plural of *man* is *men*, of *goose*, *geese*, of *foot*, *feet*, and that *mouse* makes *mice* in the plural, although we do not say *hice* for *houses*; and in Old English there were other words forming their plural in a similar way, which have since been made 'regular,' such as *bóc*, plural *béc*, now *books*. But this seems to be contrary to all laws of the Indo-European languages. For it has been said before that the root (or the stem) gives the main notion or meaning of the word, while the terminations express modifications of this, such as, that there are more things than one (the plural), or that the thing, whatever it may be, is the possessor of something else (the genitive), as in 'houses,' 'man's life.' And we saw that there is good reason to suppose that these terminations were originally separate words. But here the same modification of meaning seems to be expressed by a change in the vowel of the stem itself.[2] The way in which it is to be accounted for

---

[1] So in German, *Weib*, *Kind*, *Mädchen*.

[2] In Hebrew and the languages related to it (the Semitic languages), a change of vowel is a common way of modifying the meaning of the root. Thus, in Arabic, *malikun* is *a king*, *mulûkun*, *kings*. But this has nothing to do with the present question, for the only possible connection of English with this family of languages (except for a few words borrowed) would be through the primitive Indo-European language. And no such connection has as yet

is as follows. A sound which is just coming may affect a sound before it, since we have the whole word or sentence in our minds. A boy, for instance, in saying the line of Ovid—

Haec implet lento calathos e vimine textos,

is inclined to say 'implent' from the attraction of the 'lento' just coming. Thus, too, in carelessly saying, '*Though* I allow it,' one is inclined to say, '*Thou* I allow it.' It seems still more natural that a vowel just coming in the same word should affect the vowel before it by a sort of anticipation, through our getting our mouths into position for the second vowel before we have finished the first. Yet it is difficult to find instances of this in Modern English; our vowels are most of them too indistinct to influence each other much, and our unalterable spelling is there to hinder the word from changing permanently at all events.[1] But the pronunciation 'parsiminy' for *parsimony*, and 'chiffinch' for *chaffinch*, is probably due to this looking forward to the next vowel.

Having now shown that it is possible for a sound just coming to affect a sound before it, we may state the principle on which these plurals can be explained. We must bear in mind how English vowels were pronounced, namely, like 'new pronunciation' Latin.

The changes[2] of the vowels then, which are shown in *men, feet, geese, teeth*, and *mice*, as the plurals of *man, foot, goose, tooth*, and *mouse*, are accounted for by the presence of an I in the termination, which has since dropped off, partly, no doubt, because, after the change of vowel took place, this was quite enough by itself to distinguish the plural from the singular.[3]

been shown to be probable. Besides, this method of forming the plural cannot even have been part of the one Teutonic language, since Gothic does not show it.

[1] Except in the direction of the indistinct vowel, as in 'gard*en*,' as the last syllable is pronounced in conversation.

[2] See Skeat, *Principles of English Etymology*, First Series, chap. xi. Helfenstein, *Comparative Grammar of the Teutonic Languages*.

[3] As the reduplication was (probably) dropped in the strong verbs (see p. 88).

English in its Early Form

(1) First, then *mann* became *menn* in the plural through the influence of an I following in the termination. In order to make things clear, let us first take two other instances of an I producing the same result on a preceding A. Now these changes did not take place before the Teutonic dialects separated into languages, and Gothic does not show them. Thus, we can compare Gothic *fani* (mud) with Old English *fenn*, and Gothic *marei* (sea) with Old English *mere* (lake). It seems clear that the change of vowel is due to the attraction of the I which was once at the end of the words. It is true that we can find no form *mannis* or *manni* for the plural of *mann*. But, as it happens, the dative singular of *mann* in Old English is *menn* as well. And the dative of *mann* in Old Norse, a language closely related to English, is *manni*. If this was at one time the case in our own language, the dative *menn* is accounted for, and we can hardly doubt that the plural *menn* is to be explained by there having once been a form *manni*. It is not very difficult to understand the change. E is certainly half-way between A and I, according to the former pronunciation of the vowels, as any one can tell by trying the experiment with his own mouth.

This plural *men* is by no means the only example of this change in English. The word *English* itself is another instance. The tribe which settled in Britain were called *Angli* by the Romans, just as the country in Schleswig from which they came is still called *Angeln*, and they called themselves *Angle*[1] and *Angelcyn*. The change of vowel from *Angle* to the adjective *Englisc, English*, is explained by the I in the suffix (*-isc, -ish*) which marks the word as an adjective. In the same way *Francisc* (p. 78) has become *Frencisc*,[2] and this has been 'crushed' into *French*.

[1] Also *Engle, Engla-land*, which must be due either to the attraction of *English*, or to a plural ending with an I in it.
[2] This change is exactly the same as that of *Mann* to *männ-isch* (pronounced *menn-isch*) in German. We have more recently formed an adjective *Frankish* again, and it has remained unaltered, since the principle of 'mutation' has long been dead for all practical purposes.

(2) Next let us take the forms *feet, geese, teeth*, with the plural of *book* in Old English, namely *béc*, though this has long ago been made into the 'regular' form *books*. Here long O passes into long E through the attraction of an I following.

In this case the evidence is still more distinct. Old Saxon, a language of course very near akin to English as being the form of Saxon or Southern English which was developed at home on the Continent, actually has *fóti* as the nominative plural of *fót*, and its form of the word *book* is declined in the same way. But it is not quite so easy to say for certain the precise way in which I changed long O into long E. Ē is in a way intermediate between Ō and I. So too is German O modified (ö), which again has passed into Ē in some German dialects, and the two are near enough together to be allowed as a rhyme in that language:[1] In one or other of these ways, either directly or through an intermediate step, Ō must have passed into Ē, *fóti* into *fét*. And in the same way are explained *gós, gés; tóð, téð*. There are plenty more examples of this change in English. For instance, a large class of verbs are formed from substantives or adjectives by adding *-jan* in Gothic, *-ian* in Old English. Then through the influence of the I the vowel is often modified, after which the I has dropped or been absorbed. Thus we can explain *feed* (*fédan*) from *food* (*fóda*), and *deem* (*déman*) from *doom* (*dóm*).[2]

(3) Lastly, as to the plural of *mouse* (*mús*), namely *mice* (*mýs*). We have one word in Old English which has kept the termination with I—*burh*, nominative plural (and dative singular) *byrig*—so that here there is no mistake about the cause of

[1] *e.g.* Und wüssten sie mein *Wehe*,
Die goldenen Sternelein,
Sie kämen aus ihrer *Höhe*,
Und sprächen Trost mir ein.—*Heine*.

[2] Short O on the other hand becomes Y. Thus *vixen* is for *foxin*, with the F pronounced soft in the manner of Southern English, and *gold-ian* has become *gyldan*, and *gild* (see next page). This tendency to change the vowel was certainly still alive while we were adopting Latin words into Anglo-Saxon. Thus *coquina* became *cocin*, *cycene*, afterwards *kitchen*; and *molina, molin, mylen, myln*, and *mill*.

the U being changed. And U closely followed by I gives exactly the sound of a German ü (French, or Devonshire U), and this was the sound of an Old English Y. This Y again became confused with I towards the time of the Norman Conquest. In the same way ü in popular German is constantly sounded as I, and is allowed to rhyme with it.[1]

This 'mutation' or modification of the U is also found in the class of verbs above mentioned, with an original suffix *-jan* or *-ian*. *Full* and *fill* are obviously connected. *To fill* is in Gothic *full-jan*. In English the I has modified the vowel before it and then has dropped or been absorbed, so that the verb is *fyllan* (for *full-ian*).

But if *mice* is the plural of *mouse*, why do we not talk of 'town and country-*hice*'? The reason is that *house* (*hús*) was in Old English a substantive which, like many other neuters, had no inflexion for the nominative and accusative plural. So we now say 'three *sheep*,' or '*deer*,' and in the Poacher's song he says—

'I served my master truly for more than seven *year*.'

Horse too was used as a plural so late as 1512.[2] *Houses*, like *horses*, was a plural formed at a tolerably recent date by 'analogy,' in imitation of the 'regular' plural.[3]

[1] *e.g.* Das ist's ja was den Menschen *zieret*
Und dazu ward ihm der Verstand
Dass er im innern Herzen *spüret*
Was er vollbracht mit seiner Hand.—*Schiller*.

and

Dann reitet mein Kaiser wohl über mein Grab,
Viel Schwerter klirren und *blitzen*,
Dann steig' ich gewaffnet hervor aus dem Grab'
Den Kaiser, den Kaiser zu *schützen* !'—*Heine*.

[2] See Badminton Library, *Hunting*, p. 160. But *horses* is to be found much earlier, about 1200 A.D.

[3] In German we find this mutation of the vowel in *Mann, männisch*, already mentioned, *gut, gütig*, and many other words, some of which do not show its origin clearly. But we are not now concerned with the laws of the German language.

We now come to the adjective. It will be best to give an example both of the 'strong' and 'weak' declension of adjectives. The 'weak' form was used with the article and demonstrative and possessive pronouns much as in German.

Strong Declension

BLIND (= blind)

	Masculine.	Feminine.	Neuter.
Singular			
Nom.	blind	blind-u, blind	blind
Acc.	blind-ne	blind-e	blind
Gen.	blind-es	blind-re	blind-es
Dat.	blind-um	blind-re	blind-um
Instrumental	blind-e	(as Dative)	blind-e
Plural			
Nom. Acc.	blind-e	blind-e, blind-a	blindu, blind-e
Gen.		blind-ra	
Dat.		blind-um	

Weak Declension (with the Definite Article) [1]

Singular

	Masculine	Feminine	Neuter
Nom.	se blind-a	séo blind-e	þæt blind-e
Acc.	þone blind-an	þá blind-an	þæt blind-e
Gen.	þæs blind-an	þǽre blind-an	þæs blind-an
Dat.	þám, þǽm blind-an	þǽre blind-an	þám, þǽm blind-an
Instrumental	þý blind-an	(as Dative)	þý blind-an

Plural

Nom. Acc.	þá blind-an
Gen.	þára, þǽra blind-ena
Dat.	þám, þǽm blind-um

It is hardly necessary to call attention to the resemblance of the cases to those of the German article, and of the German

---

[1] From a comparison with Gothic it appears that the end of the stem should come later. See note on substantives above, p. 101.

adjective, especially in its 'weak' form. But as the Old English vowels are less corrupted, German, for instance, having a colourless E throughout the adjective, the Old English declension is plainly not 'derived from German.' If we were to look at the Gothic Grammar, we should see that there the terminations are preserved in a much fuller form. Anglo-Saxon is on the whole further removed from the original Teutonic language than Gothic is. However, Old English still keeps an instrumental case in the 'strong' form of the adjective where Gothic has lost it. Therefore, again, we see that English is not 'derived from Gothic,' but both from a common parent—the Teutonic language.

Of the 'weak' declension of the adjective we have just a trace left in the expression 'in *the olden* time.'[1] There is, of course, no verb 'to old' of which it could be a participle,[2] nor is there any trace of *olden* as an adjective distinct from *old*. *Olden* must therefore be for *ealdan* or *aldan*, the dative of the 'weak' form of the adjective *eald* or *ald* with the article, with which, in fact, it is nearly always connected in the Modern English phrase. This is one of the very few traces of the declension of adjectives to be found in Modern English. *Once (ánes), unawares,* and other words like them, are adverbs formed from the genitive singular of the 'strong' form, mostly after the Norman Conquest. One word containing the genitive plural survives in Shakespeare,[3] *alder-liefest*, that is $\begin{Bmatrix} ealra\ léofesta \\ of\text{-}all\ dearest \end{Bmatrix}$, where the D is inserted for ease of pronunciation, as in *thunder* from *þunor*.

The declension of the article has left more considerable traces. In our table of the article the instrumental case is *þý*. This is kept in such sentences as, '*the* more you ask me *the* more I won't come,' where *the* is plainly not the nominative of the definite article, but is equivalent to '*quo* magis,

---

[1] Morris, *Specimens of Early English*, Part I. p. 306.
[2] *Eald-ian* (to grow old) makes *eald-od* in the past participle.
[3] *Second Part of Henry VI.*, I. i. 28.

eo minus' in Latin, the ablative of 'the measure of difference,' a sort of instrumental case.[1] *Hwá?* (*who?* masculine and feminine), *hwæt?* (neuter), is declined much like the article, and *hwý?* is its instrumental case, meaning 'through, or on account of what?' This appears both in the ordinary interrogative *why?* and in the line—

For *why* the Lord our God is good.

Here *why* is the instrumental case of the relative, governed by the preposition *for*. And this *for why*, meaning 'because,' may still be heard in country districts.[2]

The dative feminine singular of the article *þǽre* appears in *there-fore, there-with*, and so on, where it is governed by the prepositions, such as *for, with*, which follow it. It is also found in the surname *Atterbury*, 'at ter bury'; in Anglo-Saxon *æt þǽre byrig*. *Byrig* is the dative singular of *burh* (*borough*),[3] and the phrase must originally have been a description of some Edward, or John, or Richard, who lived by a town or *borough*, to distinguish him from others of the same name, like 'Jack o' lane-tops' in Lancashire, though it afterwards hardened into a surname for his descendants, and so was retained when they no longer lived near the town. So too the name *Attenborough* is from *at ten borough*, and represents *æt þám burh*, or *buruh*, though this shows a confusion of grammar and genders.[4] Again, in the curious expression, *for the nonce*, we find the dative of the article. It is really, *for þám ánes* (for the once), *for then ones*; *ánes, ones, once* being treated as a substantive. But the N has become attached to the wrong word, as when we say *a newt* for *an*

---

[1] Hí woldon ðæt hér ðý mára wísdóm on londe wǽre ðý wé má
    They would that here the more wisdom in (the) land were the we more
geðéoda cúðon. (King Alfred, in Sweet's *Anglo-Saxon Reader*.)
languages knew.

[2] But *hwá* (*who*) is only interrogative, not a relative in the oldest English.

[3] See p. 106.

[4] Skeat, *Principles of English Etymology*, First Series, pp. 193, 194.

eft (Old English *efeta*).¹ Just in the same way *the tother*, or *tother day*, comes from þæt óþer, þæt being the neuter of the definite article.²

Now, we must bear in mind that there is no very distinct line to be drawn as to their meaning, and none as to their origin, between a definite article and a demonstrative pronoun, which is often also a personal pronoun of the third person. The history of the definite article, in Greek, in the languages derived from Latin, and in the Teutonic languages, is that some demonstrative pronoun became specially used to mean simply 'the.' So in Homer, ὁ, ἡ, τό, is much oftener a personal or demonstrative pronoun than the article. In later Greek, too, in such a sentence as—

Ἰνάρως . . . Ἀθηναίους ἐπηγάγετο · οἱ δὲ . . . ἦλθον,³
Inarus invited the Athenians; and they *came.*

οἱ is certainly not the article. This use of οἱ δὲ is particularly common in Xenophon. So too in the modern form of Latin called French, both *il* (personal pronoun) and *le* (definite article) are derived from *ille*. And in German, *der, die, das* are constantly used as demonstrative pronouns, as in—

Das ist mein Buch.
That *is my book.*

So too even in Modern English, we can give the article almost the force of a demonstrative pronoun by putting stress on it, as if we say—

Those are not *the* books.

But this is not the end of the confusion. For the relative pronoun, too, is not a very early creation, but originally a demonstrative (or sometimes an interrogative ⁴) pronoun. In Homer, ὅ, ἥ, τό, is frequently a relative. Later Greek poetry

---

¹ On the other hand, *an adder* for *a nadder* (Old English *næddre*) shows the reverse process. ² Wycliffe also has *the toon* = *that* (the) *one.*
³ Thuc. i. 104, quoted in Thompson's *Greek Syntax.*
⁴ As, for instance, our relative *who, what.*

as well, with the fondness of all poetry for what is antique or old-fashioned, has such lines as—

$$\delta\iota\pi\lambda\hat{\eta}\ \mu\acute{a}\sigma\tau\iota\gamma\iota\ \tau\grave{\eta}\nu\ \text{Ἄρης}\ \phi\iota\lambda\epsilon\hat{\iota}.^{1}$$
With the double scourge which *Ares loves.*

So too the regular Greek relative ὅς is still a demonstrative pronoun (or pronoun of the third person) in the phrase ἦ δ' ὅς, 'said *he*.' Again, in German, the article is commonly used for the relative, as in—

Der Mann *den* ich gesehen habe.
The man whom *I seen have.*

And finally, in English at the present time, we can and do constantly say, 'I have told you all *that* I know.' So too in the lines—

That I had, that I gave,
That I gave, that I have ;

the first *that* in each pair is equivalent to the relative *what*. The fact is, that 'pointing out' ('demonstrating') the same thing twice gives the same sense as 'referring back' to it with a relative.

To sum up, then, there is no original distinction between a demonstrative pronoun, a relative, and the definite article.

Now, in Old English (West Saxon dialect) the article is—

se   séo   þæt

declined as above. But this was originally a demonstrative pronoun, or (which is much the same thing) a personal pronoun of the third person, just as *that man* is equivalent to *he*. And, according to this old use, we sometimes find in Anglo-Saxon *se*[2] used for *hé* (he). So too *séo, scœ, she*[3] has superseded the feminine of *hé*, which is *héo* (*hoo* = she in the Lancashire dialect). *That* (þæt), properly the neuter of the definite article,[4] is now, as we all know, a demonstrative pronoun for all genders. Again, while the nominative of the

---

[1] Æschylus, *Agamemnon*, 642, quoted in Thompson's *Greek Syntax*.
[2] *Sin* (his, her, its), the possessive of this, is used in Old English poetry. It is obsolete in the prose.   [3] Like *sie* (she) in German.
[4] See above, p. 111, as in *the tother*.

definite article was *se* in the South (West Saxon), in Northumbria it was *þe*, which is the definite article in Modern English. But this *þe* had in the South come to be employed only for the relative, in which use it is undeclined. If cases were wanted, *se* was put before it in the proper case, and here again *se* is a demonstrative (or personal) pronoun. Thus *þone þe* means *whom*. We have seen that both relative and definite article are originally demonstrative pronouns.[1] In these examples they are 'harking back' to their original use.

We must now say something about the personal pronouns proper, which are declined as follows—

	I	*Singular*	*Thou*
Nom.	ic		þú
Acc.	mec, meh, *later* mé		þec, þeh, *later* þé
Gen.	mín		þín
Dat.	mé		þé
		Dual	
Nom.	wit		git
Acc.	uncit, *later* unc		incit, *later* inc
Gen.	uncer		incer
Dat.	unc		inc
		Plural	
Nom.	wé		gé
Acc.	úsic, *later* ús		éowic, *later* éow
Gen.	úser, *later* úre		éower
Dat.	ús		éow

		Singular	
	He	*She*	*It*
Nom.	hé	héo	hit
Acc.	hine	hí	hit
Gen.	his	hire	his
Dat.	him	hire	him

Plural (They)

| *Nom. Acc.* hí, hig | *Gen.* hira | *Dat.* him |

'(In the declension of *hé* there are some other duplicate forms.)

---

[1] *Se* is also sometimes used by itself as a relative.
As has been said above, some relatives are originally interrogatives. But the use of *who* as a relative in English is later than the Norman Conquest.

I

In each of the pronouns, *I, thou, he,* we have in the singular retained as many as three cases in our Modern English. But it is curious that in each of them the dative has 'crowded out' the accusative, and discharges its functions with its own. *Me, thee, him,* were originally datives, as they still are in such sentences as 'Tell *him*,' 'Knock *me* on this door' (Shakespeare), '*Methinks*' (that is, 'It seems to me'). The genitive and dative cases of *héo* are the same, and this form is now the accusative as well. $\left\{ {Éow \atop You} \right\}$, like a young cuckoo, has crowded out not only the accusative *éowic*, but also, in more recent times, the nominative, as when we say, '*You* see,' where the Bible has the proper nominative, '*Ye* see.' The nominative and the accusative (originally dative) were first confused and used for each other, as in 'I grant *ye*' (Shakespeare), 'thankee' ('thank-*ye*'). It is also to be noticed that the 1st personal pronoun requires two stems to form it in English (and the other Teutonic languages) as well as in Sanskrit, Greek, and Latin. *Ic* of course corresponds to ἐγώ, *ego*, according to Grimm's Law (p. 29), G. changing to K or hard C. *My, thy, our, your,* are in Modern English only the possessive case. In Old English they discharged other functions of the genitive as well, as in $\left\{ {\textit{Úre déghwilc} \atop \textit{of-us each}} \right\}$.[1] The dual lasted on more or less till about 1280.[2]

There is a curious survival of the accusative of *he* (*hine*) in Southern Provincial English, for instance, 'Let '*un* bide.' In *it* for *hit* we see an early instance of the dropping of H's. *Its* for *his* is a far later formation.[3]

Án (one) and *sum* (some, also used in the singular) occasionally stand for the indefinite article, *an, a* (the same word as *one*). But it is usually left out altogether.

---

[1] Forms like the genitives are also declined and used as possessive adjectives.
[2] Kington Oliphant, *Old and Middle English,* p. 355.
[3] *Its* was just coming into use about 1600.

So ends our sketch of Old English Grammar, and we may now shortly state the view which it gives us of the language. Though it had lost a good many inflexions it was still distinctly an inflexional language. And these inflexions were not mere ornamental endings, attached to words for the sake of 'euphony,' or from some other mysterious cause. The differences of gender, indeed, with the variety of terminations involved in them, are to us at present very unintelligible. However they originated, they must be preserved 'by ear'— that is, without them the word or sentence does not sound right; they are only in a secondary degree of importance as giving the key to the meaning of the sentence.[1] But, in the main, the inflexions were a most essential part of the language, just as they were in Greek or Latin, a fact which will be clearly seen from a few examples.

Óhtere sǽde his hláforde (1), Ælfréde cyninge (2), þæt hé
Ohtere said to his lord, Alfred (the) king, that he
ealra (3) Norþmonna norþmest búde.
of-all Northmen northmost lived.

Ac him (1) wæs ealne weg (4) wéste land on þæt
But to-him was all (the) way waste land on the
stéorbord.
starboard.

Ne mæg nán man twám hláfordum (1) þéowian.
Not may no man two lords serve.

Þéah þe hǽðstapa hundum (5) ge swenced,
Although (a) { heath-stepper / stag } by-hounds pressed,

Heorot hornum (6) trum, holt-wudu séce.
(A) hart { of- / in- } horns strong, (the) wood seek.

---

[1] Yet, as many words are very much alike, and as we seldom hear every word in a sentence distinctly, even for understanding what is said, the variation of termination according to the gender may be of some use.
The genders of Old English have perished with the loss of the terminations which marked them.

Synnum (5) fág.
With-sins   stained.

Þý sumere (7) fór Ælfréd cyning út.
In-the summer   went Alfred (the) king out.

Þám bróþrum restendum (7).
The brothers   resting, or, while the brothers rested.

Swylcra (8) ys heofena   ríce.
Of-such   is of-heavens (the) kingdom.

Ic hæbbe   his (3).
I have (some) of it.

Here we have instances of our old friends in Greek and Latin, the Dative of the Recipient, of Advantage or Disadvantage (1), the Dative of Manner (6), the Dative of the Instrument or Cause (5), the 'Dative of time when,' used sometimes like the ablative absolute (7), of the Partitive Genitive (3), of the 'Genitive of appropriateness' (8), as in 'cujusvis hominis est errare,' of the Accusative of Measure of Space (4), and of 'a Substantive agreeing in case with another Substantive to which it is in apposition' (2). For some of these a phrase with a preposition may also be used,[1] as in—

on þissum géare.
in   this   year.
hé erede mid horsan.
he ploughed with horses.

This is a foretaste of the way in which, in Modern English, we supply the place of the lost cases. But, on the whole, Anglo-Saxon is still plainly an inflexional language. It ought also to be clear by this time that Anglo-Saxon is not one of several elements, all more or less on the same level, of which English is made up, but that English is nothing but a

---

[1] The meaning of the case is made clearer by a preposition (which is said to 'govern' it) being added.

corrupt form of Anglo-Saxon (just as French is a corrupt form of Latin), although our language (chiefly in later times) has borrowed an enormous number of words from other languages, the greater part of them, directly or indirectly, from Latin.[1]

[1] Examples of many of the grammatical forms and idioms mentioned above will be found in the extracts at the end of chapter xii.

CHAPTER X

HISTORY OF ENGLISH BEFORE THE NORMAN CONQUEST

Dialects of Old English and their history—Beginnings of English literature—Early predominance of Northumbrian—Settlement of the Danes in England—Their influence on the speech of those districts where they settled—Alfred the Great's influence on English.[1]

WE have seen already that the English began to settle in Britain about 449 A.D. We have seen that there were three main divisions of them which correspond more or less to the different English dialects. (1) There were, then, the Jutes, who conquered Kent and Surrey and the Isle of Wight with the part of Hampshire adjoining it;[2] (2) the Saxons, who (except those who came to Essex and Middlesex) landed in the South, and bit by bit got possession of nearly all Britain south of the Thames, and some land to the north of it, and spread up the valley of the Severn;[3] and (3) the Angles, who gradually conquered the rest of the country as far north as the Firth of Forth, and whose dialect branched off into Northumbrian and Mercian.[4] There is also no doubt that many Frisians came and settled in Britain, though we cannot

---

[1] Skeat, *Principles of English Etymology*, First Series. Earle, *Anglo-Saxon Literature*. Sweet, *History of English Sounds*. Kington Oliphant, *Old and Middle English*, etc.

[2] See Appendix C, the Kentish Dialect.

[3] Districts which they afterwards lost to Mercia, though they retained their Saxon dialect.

[4] It is not surprising that the same dialect should part into two well-marked varieties in two separate kingdoms (see p. 16). But there *may* have been some difference of race between Mercians and Northumbrians.

tell for certain in what part of it they made their home, or how their dialect affected the language. But no doubt any one of the dialects spoken in England could be understood with tolerable ease by those who spoke another.

As to the changes or progress in the language of these settlers, we know nothing till after their conversion to Christianity, a work which was commenced in 597 A.D. In fact, our first real acquaintance with our own language begins considerably later than this. Guesses may, no doubt, be made as to what it was like in the fifth and sixth centuries, from old forms, like the reduplication (p. 87), which survive, for instance, in the poetry of the later language. But without written documents we cannot say when such and such changes took place, though we may know that they did occur, either before or after the coming of the English to Britain. A few inscriptions in Runic letters upon rings and so on, such as the names *Beognoþ, Rœhœbul*,[1] will not enable us to reconstruct the grammar of the language in the fifth or sixth centuries, or whatever their date may be.[2] It is with the commencement of literature which followed our conversion that our first real knowledge of the language begins.

The first English writings appear to have been made in Kent. Perhaps, from its near neighbourhood to the Continent and other causes, Roman culture had not been so utterly extinguished there as in other parts of the country. But the real start in education and literature was in Northumbria.

Now, while the southern part of England was converted by missionaries from Rome, the North was converted by Irish missionaries from Iona. These discarded the Runic letters, and, like so many missionaries in modern times, used their

---

[1] Sweet, *Oldest English Texts*, p. 129.
[2] Two poems, 'The Traveller's Tale,' and 'Deor's Lament,' seem to have been composed (not *written*) before our ancestors crossed the sea. But those who wrote down these poems naturally modernised the dialect, and these works show no more distinct traces than other Old English poetry of an earlier form of the grammar.

own form of the Latin Alphabet for the language of the people whom they came to convert, writing down the English, just as it was pronounced, in the Latin letters which corresponded to the sounds, that is, in 'phonetic' spelling;[1]— no one until about the last 400 years was anxious to use letters which should *not* represent the sound of the word as far as possible. So that the 'new' or correct pronunciation of Latin will give us the true pronunciation of English before the Norman Conquest.[2] Even C still had its hard sound, though it had been softened down in the popular dialects of Latin on the Continent, as it is in Modern French and Italian which sprang from these; but Iona was far enough removed from such influences. *Cent*, the name of the county, is enough by itself to show this. We cannot suppose that it was ever pronounced as in 'five per *cent*,' or that the C was pronounced one way in *Cent*, and another in *Canterbury* (*Cantwara-burh*—that is, 'town of the Kent-men ').[3] That the way in which Old English was written is due to the missionaries from Iona, and not to those from Rome, is shown by the form of the letters, which are practically identical with those in the Old Irish Alphabet. But the Runic letters continued for some time to be used for inscriptions (not for books), and gradually two of these came into use in the ordinary English Alphabet, Þ, þ for W, for which the Irish Alphabet has no

---

[1] In other words, they wrote English as if it were Latin, that being the great literary language, and one with which they were well acquainted. It was just as if a German, who knew no English, were to write down in German letters the sounds of English words, for instance 'faunds,' 'inglifch.'

[2] The vowels are nearly the same as in German.

[3] But hard C (or K) can be pronounced either in the front or in the back of the mouth, as in *king, cart*, with a slight difference of sound, as any one can tell by noticing his own mouth in pronouncing them. Pronounced in the front of the mouth it naturally goes with the vowels E, I. This 'front' C is the progenitor of CH in *chin* (Old English *cin*), *churl* (Old English *ceorl*). But it had not gone so far as this before the Norman Conquest.

The case is much the same with G. And in some words G seems even in Old English to have been pronounced so far forward in the mouth as to have had almost or quite the sound of Y in *year*, or German J, as in *geoc*, also *ioc* (yoke); *geong*, also *iung* (young).

symbol, and Ƿ, þ for TH, which were at first written respectively U or UU and TH. For this latter sound our ancestors also used a modified D—Ð, ð. There is no difference in the pronunciation of these two letters þ and ð. Both stand indifferently for the hard sound of TH in *think*, and for its soft sound in *thine*. Æ, ǽ (long) was pronounced like the second A in *aware*; Æ, æ (short), as A in *cat*, *apple*; so that þǽr, *there*;[1] æt, *at*, are words which have not changed their sound but only their spelling. F stood both for F and V, as in *off*, *of* (pronounced *ov*), which are two forms of the same word. The diphthongs EA, EO, were formed by pronouncing the two vowels, with their Latin (or Italian, or German) sound, rapidly one after the other. Y, as has been said already, was pronounced like UE, ü in German, or French U, or U in the Devonshire dialect. Z hardly ever occurs except in foreign names.

And now, what use did they make of this Alphabet in Northumbria? It was chiefly used for copying Latin works, and composing books in Latin, such as the numerous writings of the Venerable Bede (died 735). But there was a good deal of Northumbrian English written as well, mostly verse. Bede himself wrote some poems in English (one of which is preserved), and, as is well known, he was turning the Gospel of St. John into English on his deathbed. This translation has, most unfortunately, been lost. Some parts of the poems of Cædmon, on the Fall of the Angels, the Creation, and the Fall of Man, have come down to us; only we have these in the West Saxon dialect for reasons which will be stated later on.[2] But the first lines of the earliest poem which he wrote, by which, according to the story, Hild, Abbess of Whitby (called Streoneshalh before the Danes settled there), was convinced

---

[1] *There-* in *thereon* corresponds more exactly, since of course the R was pronounced.
[2] But perhaps the poems of Cædmon, as we now have them in West Saxon English, are a later version of the poem actually written by him.

that he had been inspired to write sacred poetry, will be found in the original Northumbrian on p. 146.[1]

The period between the middle of the seventh and the middle of the eighth centuries A.D. was a glorious time for Northumbria. Literature and education, started by the Irish missionaries from Iona, flourished under the protection of the kings of Northumbria. As King Alfred says,[2] 'The kings who had the government of the people in those days honoured God and His messengers. . . . They prospered both in war and in wisdom, and also the clergy were in earnest both about teaching and learning . . . and from foreign lands men sought wisdom and teaching here in the land;' as Alcuin, for instance, was sent for by Charlemagne to be his chaplain, and to encourage learning among the Germans.[3] But even before the Danes came the literary glory of the kingdom had died away, partly owing to the incessant civil confusion. Though the Latin books were still in the monasteries, they had become useless, since the monks no longer understood Latin, and they had not been translated into English. Then came the Danish, or rather Norwegian invasion, which, as we shall see, has done more to form our present language than any event in English History (except perhaps the Norman Conquest) 'since first Angles and Saxons came up over the broad seas and sought Britain.'

But for the time it seemed mere destruction. 'All was harried and burned.' The libraries perished with the monasteries, especially those in Northumbria, where most of them were, and in Mercia. In 787 the first Danish, or rather Norwegian ships came to England. In 833 and the following years they troubled the end of Egbert's reign, the first king

---

[1] It was perhaps partly because nearly all the early literature was in this Anglian dialect that the language of the whole country was called English.
[2] Preface to the *Pastoral Care*. Sweet's *Anglo-Saxon Reader*.
[3] Alcuin went from York after the golden age of Northumbrian literature was past. But the Abbey of York had preserved the tradition of learning longer than the rest. Charlemagne was crowned Emperor 800 A.D.

to whom all the English kingdoms were really subject. In 855 they first stayed over the winter. In 866 and the following years they turned their chief attention to the more northerly parts of England—to Northumbria, Mercia, and, above all, East Anglia. But in 871 they invaded Wessex, evidently with a view to conquering it, and Æthelred and Alfred had to fight hard to keep them out of Wessex proper, the country west of Reading. It was hopeless to think of saving the rest of England, their vassal-kingdoms or provinces. In 876 the Danes divided Northumbria among themselves, and began to cultivate it, and next year they treated Mercia in the same way. In 877 and 878 they again made a serious attempt to conquer Wessex, and it seemed as if the English power was to be finally extinguished. How Alfred beat them, and obliged Guthrum to become a Christian, is to be found in any English History. But the rule of the English was sadly reduced. By the treaty between Alfred and Guthrum (which is still extant) [1] Alfred's boundaries ran as follows:—Along the Lea to its source, then to Bedford, then along the Ouse to Watling Street, and along Watling Street to Chester. All England north and east of this was left to the Norsemen, and it is from the language of this latter part that the English which we now speak and write is mainly derived. The parts in which the Norsemen settled are marked out by the ending -*by* [2] in names of places, which is commonest in Lincolnshire, but also occurs more or less frequently in Leicestershire, Northamptonshire, Nottinghamshire, Norfolk, and Yorkshire. Der*by* is one of the most westerly examples. We see then which is the part of England where the Danes settled permanently, with many of the former inhabitants among them,

---

[1] See Earle, *Anglo-Saxon Literature*, p. 157.
[2] It means a dwelling, or settlement, just as -*ham* (home) did in English. For instance, *Whitby* (from its white cliffs), *Derby, Naseby*; and, on the other hand, *West Ham, Ham, Cater-ham, Birming-ham* ('the home of the sons of Birm'). Norse settlements are also marked by the endings -*thwaite, -ness, -drop, -haugh, -garth* (English *geard, yard*).—Kington Oliphant, *Old and Middle English*, p. 98.

and it is necessary to bear its boundaries carefully in mind.¹ The centre of it, and perhaps its most Danish part, was the 'Five Boroughs,' which formed a League, something like the five cities of the Philistines.

But the English line of kings, the kings of Wessex, did not tamely submit to have the rest of England, which had been under their dominion, finally torn from them. Alfred, indeed, was fully occupied during his lifetime in building a navy and defending Wessex in other ways, in settling its laws, and providing for the education of its inhabitants, about which we shall have something to say presently. But his daughter Æthelflæd, the 'Lady of the Mercians' who till her death governed English Mercia (west of Watling Street), enlarged its borders eastwards at the expense of the Norsemen; and Edward, Alfred's son, who succeeded him, took up the same work, securing the land as he won it by building fortresses, until, in 924, not only Northumbria, the only part of England which was still independent of him, but also the people of Strath-Clyde and the Scotch chose him 'as their father and lord.' Still the Norsemen preferred their independence, and rebelled again and again under his successors, only to be subdued afresh. The 'Five Boroughs' were often the centre of resistance—

burga fife ·
Ligoraceaster · and Lindcylene ·
Leicester, *Lincoln,*
and Snotingaham · swylce Stanford éac ·
Nottingham, *so* *Stamford* *also,*
Deoraby · Dæne wæran ær ·
Derby; *Danish* *were-they* *before,*
under Norðmannum · nyde gebegde ·
Northmen *by need* *bowed.*²

At last, under Edgar and his great minister Dunstan (959), they settled down in peace as a part of England, retaining

¹ They do not seem to have penetrated into Southern Lancashire to any extent, though they settled on the coast of Northern Lancashire and Cumberland. ² Song in the *Anglo-Saxon Chronicle,* 942 A.D.

some rights of self-government, and their own laws. The Danish part of the country was called '*Denalagu*, or *Dane-law*.' But these earlier settlers, though the English called them Danes, were really Norwegians. The later Danish invasions, this time from Denmark itself, which began only five years after Edgar's death, and ended in establishing Cnut's Danish dynasty for a time on the English throne, must have strengthened the Scandinavian element in the population of the North and East, since the Danes who came over would naturally settle down mostly among people who were nearly of their own race and language. The difference between the Norwegians and the Danes in dialect must have been as slight in those times as it is at present, and so from the point of view of language we may call them collectively '.Danes' as our forefathers did.[1]

And now let us try to imagine the condition of this half-Danish part of the country from the reign of Alfred till after the Norman Conquest.

We have plenty of examples in the world of two nations intermingled on the same ground, living on friendly terms with each other, yet each keeping its own language. The Franks, for instance, who settled in Gaul, kept their own German language for centuries, while the provincials whom they had conquered spoke corrupt Latin. As a rule, where two nations thus live together, each learns at any rate something of the language of the other. So to this day most of the people in the greater part of Wales will speak English to an Englishman, though to their own countrymen they naturally talk Welsh, facts which may be observed in any third-class railway carriage in those districts. But, when the English and the Danes were thrown together in East Mercia and Northumbria, they were not like two nations speaking entirely different tongues. As the languages were then, an Englishman,

[1] The nearest representative which we have of the 'Danish' or Scandinavian brought into England is the Icelandic literature of the twelfth—fourteenth centuries.

and especially an Angle, must have been more or less intelligible to a Dane, and a Dane to an Englishman. The languages were, as we have seen, originally identical, and Anglian and Dane had not been far separated in their earlier home, even if some of the Danes did not already live on the Danish peninsula itself at the time when the mass of the Angles left it. Of course the two languages had been each going its own way since the Angles sailed to England, and so were now farther separated. But the difference which there already was between them in 500 A.D., added to the further varieties which developed in the three or four centuries which passed before the Danes settled in England, must have left each of the two languages more or less intelligible to those who spoke the other.[1] Let us now see what would be the result of this, when Angles and Danes were brought together, first on the inflexions, and secondly on the vocabulary, or stock of words, of the English language.

First of all, there is no doubt that the Danes would not pick up English inflexions correctly, except the commonest ones, and such as were the same in their own language. For they were not used from childhood to them and them alone; other Danes, whom they were accustomed to hear speak, would not use them, and they certainly did not study an English Grammar. All that they would aim at would be to make themselves understood, which is, after all, the chief object of language. Thus only some few of the commonest English inflexions would be used by the Danes in speaking English.[2] But we must also remember that by far the larger

[1] 'Englishmen write English with Latin letters such as represent the sound correctly. . . . Following their example, *since we are of one language, although the one may have changed greatly, or each of them to some extent* . . . I have framed an alphabet for us Icelanders.' Grammatical treatise prefixed to the Snorra Edda, about 1150, quoted in Skeat, *Principles of English Etymology*, First Series, p. 455.

[2] So an uneducated Englishman who had migrated to Germany would at first get hold of some common German plural termination, in -*en*, for instance, and decline all plurals in this way. Of course their Danish was also influenced by contact with English, but this side of the question does not concern us.

number of the words which the Danes themselves used had sister-words in our language. They would thus readily learn to speak a kind of English, omitting or altering many inflexions and introducing specially Danish words unconsciously.[1] And their example would easily infect the uneducated English who lived among them. For inflexions have, in all recent ages, led a somewhat precarious existence, as we have seen from the way in which the Roman provincials put phrases in their place, such as *aimer-ai* for *amare habeo*, and as we may see from their being constantly dropped in ' vulgar ' German of the present day, as is evident from the comic newspapers in that language. Those who clip *eine Pfeife* into *a' Pfeif'*, and who say, ' *Nix 'komme ?* ' for (*Haben Sie*) *nichts bekommen ?* are certainly in danger of losing the bulk of their inflexions, which are only saved by the example of 'educated people.' But these, though common enough in Germany now, were very rare among Englishmen of the ninth—twelfth centuries. So that the infection, the ' bad example ' of Danes speaking English with fewer and more 'regular' inflexions, must have spread rapidly to the Englishmen of those parts, at least to that far greater number of them who could not read the books which preserved the old inflexions, and who never came in contact with the court of Wessex, where the old inflected English was still spoken. It is not known when the Danish language became extinct in England. But at any rate before it died out it had produced a form of English with many of its inflexions rubbed off, and more ' regular' in its use of those which remained; altogether, more like the English which we speak at present.

As was only natural, many specially Danish words were introduced into this East Mercian and Northumbrian peasants' English. Among these were *Thurs-day* ('Thor's day'), *law,*

[1] As the German waiter says in *The Newcomes*, ' Her Excellency the Frau Gräfinn von Kew is even now *absteig*ing,' as if ' to *absteig* ' were an English verb. Or as an English lady, who had long lived in Switzerland, said of the stitches in a piece of work, ' And then you *diminue* ' (*diminuer*).

plough,[1] *booth, sky, wail,* and a mass of others. Many of these have words in Anglo-Saxon more or less resembling them, for instance Þ*unresdæg*, though the shape in which we have them in Modern English is certainly due to the Danes. Few Danish words found their way into English literature before the Norman Conquest, and the loss of inflexions in the popular speech had probably little effect even on those books which were written in Northumbria and Mercia before 1066, and certainly none whatever on West Saxon literature. And yet, as we shall see, it is to the East Midland popular or 'vulgar' English, as altered by contact with the Danes, that our Modern English is mainly due.[2]

We must now say a few words about Alfred the Great's influence on English. We have seen that before his time Northumbria had been the great centre of literature in England, and that the language in which this was written was either Latin or the Anglian dialect of English spoken in Northumbria. The result of the Danish invasions had been, by ruining the monasteries, to destroy most of the learning which still remained in England. This, as Alfred saw, could not be brought back, at once at all events; though he did his best to raise the intellectual standard of the clergy, by encouragement, and by bringing learned men from Wales and other foreign countries to be bishops. But, he thought, if his subjects could not learn Latin, they might at least read English. There were, however, few books in English for them to read. There were the works of Cædmon and other poets, but there seems to have been little English prose, except laws, charters, and deeds. And so, as he says, with the help of learned men, 'Plegmund,[3] my Archbishop, and Asser, my bishop (a Welshman), and Grimbald (from

---

[1] Perhaps a Slavonic word originally, borrowed by the Norsemen and some other Teutonic tribes. See Skeat, *Principles of English Etymology*, Second Series, pp. 399, 401.

[2] See Kington Oliphant, *Old and Middle English.*

[3] Preface to the *Pastoral Care.* Sweet's *Anglo-Saxon Reader*, pp. 6, 7.

Before the Norman Conquest

Flanders), my mass-priest, and John (from Saxony), my mass-priest,' he turned into English those books which he considered most necessary for all men to know. These were Gregory the Great's *Pastoral Care*, the *Comfort of Philosophy* by Boethius, Bede's *Church History of England*, and Orosius's History, which contains also a geographical sketch of the world as known in the time of its author, about 420 A.D. This last work Alfred 'brought up to date' by adding some discoveries in geography made in his own time, as related to him by Ohtere and Wulfstan, of whom the first had rounded the North Cape and sailed as far as Archangel, while the second had explored the Baltic (see p. 151). Thus there was some Theology, some Philosophy, English History, General History, and Geography, for those who could read their own language. The Bishop of Worcester also translated for Alfred another book by Pope Gregory, the king writing a preface to it. The record of his reign too in the Anglo-Saxon Chronicle is remarkably full; real history, not short jottings on the chief events of each year, or 'annals,' like the greater part of these Chronicles. What with poetry and prose, the literature in English at Alfred's death was far superior to that existing in any spoken or 'modern' language of Europe.

Now, in consequence of this impulse which Alfred gave to literature, Wessex became the literary centre of England. It was also England's political centre. For the line of English kings who subdued the Danes and made England more or less one kingdom were Wessex men, and their capital was Winchester; therefore West Saxon was the language spoken at Court. It is not surprising, then, that the Wessex dialect was 'standard English' from the latter part of Alfred's reign (about 890) to the Norman Conquest. Nearly all new books were written in it, and those which, like the poems of Cædmon, already existed in another dialect, were rewritten (one cannot talk of 'translation') in the speech of Wessex. And this is the dialect which is usually meant when we speak of 'Anglo-Saxon.' Thus the speech of which the Somersetshire, Wiltshire, Hampshire, and Dorset dialects (as in the poems of William Barnes) are the living representatives, was once the leading dialect of English, and, but for the Norman Conquest, would probably have remained so. But for that event we should now be speaking a language with the sounds of the Dorsetshire dialect, and probably with a more varied and inflexional grammar than at present, while the speech of Danish Mercia, from which our Modern English mostly springs, would still be an obscure local dialect, repulsive to educated ears, like peasants' German at the present day.

CHAPTER XI

ENGLISH DIALECTS BEFORE THE NORMAN CONQUEST

General sketch of the dialects of English before the Conquest—
Their peculiarities, and descendants at the present time.

WE may now take a general view of the dialects of English and their characteristics down to the Norman Conquest. We must bear in mind that, as the writing was intended to represent the sounds of the spoken language as nearly as possible, and was not fixed by custom, differences of spelling nearly always imply differences of pronunciation.

These dialects were—

(1) West Saxon, spoken south of the Thames, except in Kent and Surrey, in some districts to the north of that river, and in the counties of Gloucester, Worcester, and Hereford. A sketch of the characteristics of this dialect has been given above in chapter ix., and it is the only dialect of Old English of which there are enough specimens extant to give us a complete knowledge of it. It was the Court language, Winchester being the capital of England, and, ever since Alfred's time, the language of literature, colouring even those books which were written or copied by Mercians. It changed, of course, to some extent between Alfred's reign and the Norman Conquest, as all living languages must. The changes which are to be seen in its

spelling correspond to changes in pronunciation. But, on the whole, the alterations in Anglo-Saxon as written and as spoken by educated people were slight. The language was kept from changing much—(1) by the influence of the literature, which affected indirectly even those who could not read; (2) by the conservative habits of polite society in its speech (p. 9), as at the present day. The literature in this dialect, including the poems originally written in Northumbrian, was certainly superior, both in quantity, style, and general excellence, to that existing in any one living language at the time. Cultivated prose especially was hardly to be found in any other language spoken in Europe. It is this dialect which is usually meant when 'Anglo-Saxon' is spoken of. Its modern representatives are the dialects of the south-western counties.

(2) Kentish, spoken in Kent and Surrey. Whatever was the original language of those who settled in Kent,[1] the dialect became more and more like West Saxon.

(3) Mercian, reaching from the Humber southwards to a line drawn some distance north of the Thames. It was the dialect of South Lancashire, but not of Gloucestershire, Worcestershire, and Herefordshire (see p. 77). Mercia had no great literary period like Northumbria and Wessex, and its dialect was from Alfred's time so much overshadowed by that of Wessex that probably few books were written in it. In any case, very few have survived. But we have a Psalter to which 'glosses' (or equivalents written over the Latin words[2]) were added in Mercian English about 800-850 A.D.,[3] and also a Latin copy of the Gospels,[4] in which St. Matthew's Gospel has Mercian 'glosses' belonging to the latter part of the tenth century. From these English words we can see that Modern English is nearer to this dialect than to West Saxon, as a few specimens will show—

[1] See Appendix C, the Kentish Dialect.
[2] Just as on p. 148. [3] Sweet, *Oldest English Texts*.
[4] The Rushworth Manuscript.

Wessex.	Mercian.	Modern English.
eald	áld	old
eall	all	all
syndon	arun	are
falleþ	falleþ	falleth
féoh	feh	fee
geoc	ioc	yoke
léoht	líht	light
seolfor	sylfur	silver
slépon	sleptun	slept [1]

There are signs of the grammar becoming simpler, but, on the whole, this specimen of the dialect is probably little affected by Danish influence.[2]

(4) Northumbrian, spoken north of the Humber as far as the Firth of Forth. This was, as we have seen, the language of the earlier English literature; but in this character it was afterwards superseded by the West Saxon dialect. Consequently, there are but few specimens of it left. The most complete is in a manuscript of the Four Gospels in Latin,[3] where the equivalents in Northumbrian English are written over the Latin words. Now there is a certain difficulty in judging of this specimen of Northumbrian. The date of the 'glosses' is about 950, when the Danes had been settled in the country for seventy years. There are a considerable number of coincidences between this Northumbrian, and Norse, or Danish, which we do not find in West Saxon, besides that mentioned in the note to p. 98, *wé aron*, Northumbrian (and Mercian), Norse *vér erum* (we are). Now, are these due to the influence of the Danes settled in England, or to the original resemblance between Danish and Anglian, which, as we saw, were very closely related? The question can hardly

---

[1] Skeat, *Principles of English Etymology*, First Series, p. 44.
[2] Perhaps the frequent dropping of *ge-* in the past participle (as in Danish), e.g. *cweden* for *ge-cweden*, may be due to this; but its omission is not unknown elsewhere.
[3] The Lindisfarne Manuscript, or 'Durham Book.'

be answered with certainty, since we have not enough specimens of the earlier Northumbrian, before Danish influence was possible, to compare with the Northumbrian of the tenth century, so as to see whether the latter does or does not bear a closer resemblance to Danish. But it is probable that most of the points of agreement are not due to any recent influence of the Danes in England. Thus in Danish the infinitive ends in -a, and *til* is used for *to*. But *til* is used for *to* (as it still is in the Lowland Scotch, '*till* hame') in the verses of Cædmon, written down about 737; and in the lines on the Ruthwell Cross, which are probably not later than 750,[1] the infinitive ends in -a, not in -an, as it does in West Saxon. Thus both these peculiarities correspond to Danish (or Norse), but appear before the Danes came to England. On the other hand, the simplification of the grammar is probably largely due to contact with the Danes.

Let us now look at a few of the points where the Anglian of Northumbria is nearer to Modern English.

The definite article is þe, and not se, as in West Saxon.

Many words end in -es in the genitive singular and nominative plural which have other forms, especially -an, in West Saxon. Thus Northumbrian, nominative plural, *tunges* (*tongues*), West Saxon, *tungan*; Northumbrian, genitive singular, *fadores* (*father's*), West Saxon, *fæder*, undeclined.

The infinitive usually ends in -a, or sometimes in -e, instead of in -an, as in West Saxon. The Northumbrian form is weaker and more ready to drop off altogether. Thus we have Northumbrian *geflea* (to *flee*), West Saxon *fléon*.

The 3rd person singular of the verbs in Northumbrian often ends in -s, as in our ordinary speech; *hé spreces* (he speaks). And, in general, the grammar is simpler and more 'regular,' as in Modern English.

Further, Northumbrian was more like our present English in pronunciation, if we remember that the vowels had their

---

[1] Sweet, *Oldest English Texts*.

Latin (or Italian, or German) values. Thus, we find *hir* for *hér* (*here*), *scip* for *scéap* (*sheep*), *tahte* for *tǽhte* (*taught*), the first of each pair being more like our present pronunciation of these words.[1]

Though our Modern English comes chiefly from the East Mercian dialect, this dialect must itself have been greatly affected by its neighbour Northumbrian. Or it is quite possible that the ordinary speech of some parts of Mercia at least agreed with Northumbrian in these points before the Norman Conquest, as it certainly did later on. We might add, as varieties of Northumbrian and Mercian—

(5) The popular speech of Northumbria as affected by contact with the Danes, with many of its inflexions worn away, and the rest reduced to greater regularity. We have just seen that literary Northumbrian was more 'regular' than West Saxon, and, no doubt, popular Northumbrian was still poorer in inflexions. There are no specimens of it remaining; in fact, there was probably little or nothing written in the dialect. We can only guess what it must have been like, from the writings in its later form some time after the Norman Conquest. Its present representatives are Lowland Scotch (since Northumbria originally reached to the Firth of Forth), and the dialects of Northumberland, Durham, Westmoreland, and of Yorkshire, except the south of that county.

(6) Popular or 'vulgar' Mercian, altered by contact with the Danes, as in (5), but the core of the language was, of course, Mercian, and not Northumbrian. This dialect was the parent of East Midland, as we find it after the Conquest, and so, in the main, of Modern English. Both these last dialects must have admitted numbers of Danish words into their vocabulary.

---

[1] Kington Oliphant, *Old and Middle English*, p. 107.

CHAPTER XII

THE VOCABULARY, OR STOCK OF WORDS IN ENGLISH BEFORE
THE CONQUEST

Native words—Latin words, brought in at different periods—Celtic words—
Danish (or Norwegian) words—The mass of the vocabulary pure
English.[1]

So far we have spoken mainly of the grammar of the language in general and of its separate dialects. We must now say a little of its stock of words, or vocabulary. For this purpose we need not keep the different dialects separate. So far as their educated or literary forms were concerned, the same words were for the most part common to them all, with slight differences of pronunciation and grammar.[2] Of the words then which made up Old English by far the most important part was—

(1) The native words.

An enormous proportion of the words in Old English were Teutonic, brought over from the Continent by the English settlers, or formed by compounding these together. English was at this early time able to form new words, with prepositions and otherwise, as easily as German does now; that is, new compounds did not seem strange or uncouth

---

[1] See especially Skeat, *Principles of English Etymology*, First Series.
[2] All that we know of the other dialects points to this, as well as other considerations, but we have no complete acquaintance with any dialect except West Saxon.

when they were first heard. At the present day we usually borrow or make words from Latin or Greek to express new ideas for which new words are required (e.g. *telegraph, omnibus*). We have even dropped many of our old compound words, as, for instance, *for-scruncon* ('for-shrunk,' or shrank away), *forþrysmudon* (choked), *big-spell* (parable, see p. 154).

(2) The Latin words.

At the present time words borrowed directly or indirectly from Latin form a very considerable part of the whole stock of words in the language, and so it is necessary from the outset to be quite clear about this part of the subject in order to avoid confusion later on.

First of all, we must carefully distinguish the *borrowed* words from those which we have possessed from the first in common with Latin.[1] These last can of course only date from the infancy of the language, when Teutonic and Italic were mere dialects of the Indo-European language. One way then in which many of these can be identified is by their having shifted their sounds in Teutonic in accordance with 'Grimm's Law' (see pp. 24-31). For we have seen that this shifting of sounds took place at some early period, and no longer worked at the time when our first English writings were made, or even when the Teutonic nations on the Continent first came in contact with the Latin language (a developed dialect of Italic). So that it could not affect words *borrowed* from Latin. If the coat smells of pastilles or sulphur it was in the room when they were burnt. So *ic* (I) or *ego*, *two* or *duo*, *three* or *tres*, *father* or *pater*, were words already in the language when Teutonic and Italic were dialects of one speech, but *turtle* (-dove) and *candle* must have been borrowed later from Latin,—that is, they must have come into English *after* the tendency in Teutonic to shift T and C had passed away.

---

[1] A German is said to have proposed, in order to purify the language of all foreign words, to begin by turning out *Vater* and *Mutter* as being derived from *Pater* and *Mater*!

So too *cornu* and *horn* are originally the same word, but *ceaster*[1] or *caster* (Northern form, as in *Tad-caster*) must have been borrowed from Latin, or it would appear as *haster* or something of the kind. But, secondly, the words which have been borrowed from Latin have come into our language at several different periods, and have not even yet ceased to do so. In order, then, to see what words were borrowed from Latin before the Norman Conquest, we must exclude from these—

(A) Those words which came through French, when, after the Conquest, it was commonly spoken in England, and also in later times—such words as *voice* and *honour*, many of which, in their spelling at least, still show plainly that they have not come to us straight from Latin, the Norman-French forms of the two mentioned being *voice* and *honour*, as at present.

(B) Those words which, whether they came through French or not, were at a later period derived from the written Latin; 'learned' words, so to speak, which have hardly changed their form at all in passing from Latin into English, such as *episcopal* (*episcopal*-em), *resurrection* (*resurrection*-em), *salvation* (*salvation*-em). One of these has also a corresponding verb borrowed from the spoken French, a natural, and not a 'learned' form—*save*, from *saver* (or *sauver*), also derived from *salvare*. But in some cases words derived through French have had their spelling altered later to bring them nearer to their Latin original.

We see then (A) that words borrowed from Latin were *certainly* not in our language before the Conquest, if they show by their form that they have been a part of spoken French; and (B) that they were *probably* brought in after that date if they are exactly like Latin in spelling. For words adopted from Latin into Anglo-Saxon usually look just as if they were derived by ear from one spoken language by another.[2]

---

[1] The change of the word to *chester* took place after the Norman Conquest. Winchester is in Anglo-Saxon *Wintan-ceaster*.

[2] Some of them have had a vowel changed by the influence of a following vowel (like the *native* words *English*, *feet*), which shows that they were introduced while this early tendency was still in force; for instance, *coquina*, *cycene*, *kitchen*; *culina*, *cylin*, *kiln*, see p. 106.

Or, treating the matter historically, we may say that the enormous majority of the Latin words now in our language which do not appear in Anglo-Saxon writings were not a part of our language before the Norman Conquest,[1] and of course all those which are found in Old English books were already in the language. But the words which our forefathers borrowed from Latin before the Conquest were borrowed at three separate periods:—

(*a*) While they still lived on the Continent some words were borrowed from Latin through intercourse with the Roman frontier territory, from merchants, from Germans who had served in the Roman army, and so on.

(*b*) Some Latin words were borrowed from the Britons, either from those of them who spoke Latin, as was common in the towns, or through Welsh, into which the Latin words had made their way.

(*c*) A large number were introduced by the missionaries, both Roman and Irish, who both knew Latin almost equally well and used it as the Church language.[2] And others came in later on.

Now, though it is certain that words came into English from Latin at all three periods, it is usually difficult or impossible to say with certainty at which of the periods any one of those Latin words was introduced which were certainly in the language before the Norman Conquest. For there are no English writings until after the conversion of England. So that it is of no use to take books of different dates, and see when the word first appears. A Latin word found in the earliest Anglo-Saxon writing may have been introduced at

---

[1] We have not nearly all Anglo-Saxon literature remaining, so some other Latin words may have been used in those books which have been lost. But the amount of West Saxon writings preserved is quite enough to make the statement in the text correct.

[2] For instance, St. Chad's Gospels, in Lichfield Cathedral Library, probably brought to Lichfield (then the capital of Mercia) by St. Chad, or some other of the missionaries from Northumbria, are in Latin.

any one of the three periods. Still, there are some considerations to guide us.

(a) There is a certain probability that a Latin word was borrowed by our ancestors while they still lived on the Continent, if it appears in the other Teutonic dialects (and, as is sometimes the case, also in the languages spoken on their borders), unless, that is, it is the name for something connected with the Church, in which case the same word would be introduced by the missionaries into the different languages. Of course some words have been borrowed from Latin by the English in England, and by their relations who spoke High German, for instance, independently.[1] But the following are probably among the words borrowed before our ancestors came to Britain:—

Latin.	West Saxon.	Modern English.	German.
caseus	cése, cýse	cheese	käse
cuper, cuprum (æs cyprium)	copor	copper	kupfer
milia (passuum)	míl	mile	meile
pœna	pín	pine (verb)	pein
pondo	pund	pound	pfund
strata	strǽt (*Mercian* strét)	street	strasse
vallum	weall [2] (*Mercian* wall)	wall	wall
vinum	wín [2]	wine	wein

(b) *Ceaster*,[3] Northumbrian *caster* (Tad*caster*), Modern English *Chester*, *-chester* (as in *Rochester*), is a tolerably certain example of a word derived from Latin (*castrum*) through the Britons.

[1] Thus a word may have been adopted into High German from the Romans on the frontier, and may not have spread farther among the German dialects. And again, we must remember that a large part of Germany was converted by English missionaries. This would account for some coincidences in the words (besides ecclesiastical terms) borrowed from Latin by English and German.

[2] These words, as well as *wic*, show the old Latin pronunciation of V as W.

[3] In Old English not confined to names of places. *Chester*, for instance, appears in the Chronicle as 'a waste *chester*' (or Roman fortress) 'called Legaceaster.' So too *wic* is used not merely in compounds but like any native word.

Vocabulary before the Conquest

For it cannot have been learnt on the Continent, or it would appear in other Teutonic languages, and we cannot suppose that the names *Chester, Leicester, Tadcaster,* and so on, were first given to those places after the English were converted to Christianity. For similar reasons *wīc* (*vicus*), meaning a dwelling or settlement, as in *Norwich* (*North-wīc*), probably came into the language at the same time.

(c) The Latin words introduced at and after our conversion are much more numerous, though few compared with the total number of words derived from Latin which we now use in English. Like the other Latin words introduced before the Conquest, these too, curiously enough, mostly bear the appearance of having been derived by ear from a spoken language imperfectly reproduced. They are mainly substantives. Many of them are names for things connected with the Church, and of these a large number have been first borrowed by Latin from Greek, as, for instance—

Greek.	*Latin.*	*West Saxon.*	*Modern English.*[1]
	—abbat(-em)[2]	abbod	abbot
ἐλεημοσύνη	eleemosyna	ælmesse	alms
ἐπίσκοπος	episcopus	biscop	bishop
	candela	candel	candle
	credo	créda	creed
	missa	mæsse	mass
μοναστήριον	monasterium	mynster	minster

and many others.

There were also introduced into the language, partly at this time, many words connected with improvements in tools, and with civilised life in general, such as—

Greek.	*Latin.*	*West Saxon.*	*Modern English.*
ἄγκυρα	ancora	ancor, ancer	anchor
	cupa	cuppe	cup
δισκος	discus	disc	dish

[1] Skeat, *Principles of English Etymology,* First Series, p. 432, etc.
[2] Borrowed from Syriac *abba* (=father).

Greek.	Latin.	West Saxon.	Modern English.
	—molina	myln (mylen)	mill
	—moneta	mynet	mint
	—postis	post	post
	—coquus	cóc	cook [1]

and many others.

We also borrowed a good many names for birds, fishes, trees, and plants, such as—

Greek.	Latin.	West Saxon.	Modern English.
τα(F)ῶs [2]	pavo	páwe	pea(-cock), po(-cock) (*as a proper name and in Chaucer*)
	turtur	turtle	turtle(-dove)
	musculus	muscle, muxle	mussel
	pina (= *mussel*)	pine(-wincla)	'pennywinkle' periwinkle (*the shell-fish*)
τρώκτης (*gnawer, sharp-toothed creature*)	tructa	truht	trout
	buxus (*box-tree*) buxum (*a box, made of box-wood*) } box	box	box
	fœniculum	finugle, fenol	fennel
λείριον	lilium	lilie	lily
μίνθα	menta	minte	mint (*the plant*)
	pervinca	pervince	periwinkle (*the flower*)
	pinus	pín(-tréow)	pine(-tree)
	planta	plante	plant
ῥόδον	rosa	róse	rose

Also a number of miscellaneous nouns, a few verbs, and one adjective, as, for instance—

[1] Almost all of these *may* have been brought in at the first period (*a*) before the English came to Britain.

[2] Borrowed by Greek from Persian, and by Persian from Tamil.—Skeat, *Etymological Dictionary*.

Greek.	Latin.	West Saxon.	English.
	femina	fǽmne	(= woman)
	lacus	lacu	lake
	mont(-em)	munt	mount
	puteus	pyt	pit
σχολή	schola	scólu	{ school { shoal (*of fish*)
	offero	offrian	offer
	dispendo	spendan	spend
	stuppo (*cram up with tow*, stuppa)	stoppian	stop
	crispus (*curled*)	crisp	crisp

These are only specimens of the words which we had borrowed from Latin before the Norman Conquest. And besides, some Latin words which we then used have been lost, and others have either been superseded by the form of the Latin word which came through French, or have been brought into agreement with it. Thus, from *calic-em* the Anglo-Saxon word *calic* was derived. It is now *chalice*, the French form of the same Latin word.[1] So *lion* in Anglo-Saxon was *leo*, *saint* was *sanct*; we have now adopted the form which came through French. Thus our language had borrowed a good number of words from Latin before the Norman Conquest.

It must be repeated that in the case of most of them we cannot be certain at which of the three periods they were introduced. And it is curious to find some of them appearing at all, as we must have had native terms for many of the things described by them. But even now many people are fond of using a French word, for instance, where an English one would do just as well. The 'personnel' of a ship[2] is not different from its officers and crew. The 'locale' of a

---

[1] A much more complete list of words adopted from Latin into Anglo-Saxon is to be found in Skeat's *Principles of English Etymology*, First Series, p. 432, etc., from which the above examples are mostly taken.

[2] Kington Oliphant, *Old and Middle English*, p. 535.

murder is nothing but the place where it occurred. A 'dot' is precisely the same thing as a dowry. And among the extraordinary words formed recently on a basis of Latin, 'altruism' can scarcely be distinguished from 'unselfishness,' though it sounds grander.

(3) Celtic words.

We have a good number of words derived from Celtic languages in the English of the present day, but very few of these date from the time before the Conquest. This shows how very slight was the intercourse of the English with the Britons whom they conquered. Besides the words borrowed much later from Gaelic and Irish, a large number of the Celtic words now existing in English no doubt first made their way into the speech of the country bordering on Wales and Cornwall. And this would, of course, begin before the Conquest. Words may live for centuries without finding their way into books, as is the case with many provincial terms at the present day. (But at any rate the Celtic words which had become part of the ordinary speech of educated Englishmen before 1066, and which are therefore to be found in Anglo-Saxon books, are very few. The list given by Professor Skeat[1] is *bannock*, *brock* (badger), *cart*, *clout*, *combe*, *cradle*, *crock*, *down* (hill), *dun*, and *slough*.

(4) Danish or Norwegian words.

We have already seen that in the *spoken* language of Eastern Mercia and Northumbria these must have been numerous before the Conquest.[2] But they only appear later in literature. Very few Danish words are to be found in Anglo-Saxon writings. Among these are *lagu*, law, which superseded an English word *ǽ* ; *plóh*,[3] plough, just beginning to appear by the side of *sulh*, which (like its fellow-countryman,

---

[1] *Principles of English Etymology*, First Series, p. 452.

[2] As has been said above, a very large proportion of words were common to the two languages, see pp. 127, 128.

[3] Apparently used before the Conquest only in the sense of 'ploughland,' see also p. 128, note.

the brown rat of Norway) it has now turned out of the language; *wícing*, viking,[1] and *ceallian*, call.

From what has been said above, it is plain that the foreign elements in the stock of words or vocabulary then formed together a very small proportion of the words in our language as compared with the native element. Our religious terms especially were, before the Conquest, mainly English,[2] though with some exceptions, such as *mass*, *bishop*. Christ was almost always *se hǽlend* (the *healer*, or Saviour); our ancestors did not use the word *Resurrection* but *ǽryst* (rising). *Unity* was *ánnes* (*one - ness*), *Trinity*, *þrýnnes* (*three - ness*). Thus our Anglo-Saxon forefathers had only to think of what the words obviously meant in order to understand what their religion was, and had not to learn the meaning of words derived from a foreign tongue. Again, what we now call the *Cross* (probably a Provençal form of Latin *cruc-em*) was *ród* (*literally*, a gallows),[3] as in *rood-screen*, or *rood-loft*, so called from the great Crucifix that stood on it. So too our ancestors did not speak of *Communion* but of *húsel*, which is an old heathen word meaning 'sacrifice,' altered or specialised to this meaning (see pp. 61-63). From this was formed *húslian* (to give the Communion to), as Hamlet's father says that he was

> 'Cut off even in the blossoms of my sin,
> Unhousel'd,'[4]

and also *húsel-disc* (a paten), *húsel-gang* (going to, or attendance at the Communion), *húsel-genga*, *húsel-wer*, and *húsel-bearn* (all meaning 'a Communicant'), which also show the way in which compound words were formed in the language.

---

[1] 'Son of the Creek,' from Danish *wíc* (a creek), as in *Lerwick, Wick*; not from *wíc*, a dwelling, as in *Norwich* (see p. 141).

[2] That it is still possible to express the greatest and most abstruse facts of Christianity in pure English words, may be seen from the beginning of St. John's Gospel. Here, in the first ten verses, *comprehended* is the only word borrowed from any foreign language, unless we count the proper name *John*.

[3] A *rood* of land and a *rod* are the same word, from the original sense of 'pole,' for measuring or otherwise.

[4] *Hamlet*, I. v. 76, 77.

BEGINNING OF CÆDMON'S POEM

(From a Manuscript of Bede's History of about 737 A.D.)

NORTHUMBRIAN

Nu scylun hergan hefaenricaes uard,[1]
metudæs maecti end his modgidanc,
uerc[2] uuldurfadur;[1] sue he uundra gihuaes,
eci Dryctin, or astelidæ.
He aerist scop aelda[2] barnum
heben til[3] hrofe, haleg scepen.
Tha[1] middungeard, moncynnæs uard,
eci Dryctin, æfter tiadæ
firum fold[u], frea allmectig.

Primo cantavit Caedmon *istud carmen.*

From Sweet's *Oldest English Texts.*

---

[1] u, for the special Rune=w (ƿ), th for þ, as in the oldest English manuscripts (see pp. 120, 121).

[2] The words correspond to those in the West Saxon version, except *uerc*= work (*uerc uuldurfadur*=the work of the glorious father), *aelda*=of men.

[3] See p. 134.

BEGINNING OF CÆDMON'S POEM

(From Alfred's Translation of Bede's History, Manuscript of about 1000 A.D.)

WEST SAXON

Nú[1] wé sceolon herian heofonríces Weard,
Now we must praise heaven's-kingdom's Guardian,
Metodes mihte ond his módgeðonc,
(the) Lord's might and his mind-thoughts,
wera Wuldorfæder; swá hé wundra gehwǽs,
of-men (the) glorious Father; as he of-wonders of-each
éce Dryhten, ord onstealde.
everlasting Lord, (the) beginning established.
Hé ǽrest gescéop eorðan bearnum
He first created for earth's children
heofon tó hrófe, hálig Scippend;
heaven for (a) roof, holy Creator;
ðá middangeard, moncynnes Weard,
then earth, mankind's Guardian,
éce Dryhten, æfter téode
the everlasting Lord, after adorned
firum foldan, Fréa Ælmihtig.
for-men (the) ground, (the) King 'Almighty.

From Sweet's *Anglo-Saxon Reader.*

[1] The accents, except in this extract, are left as in the manuscript. They did not usually put accents to those vowels which any one who could read the language would know at the first glance to be long, without thinking. Some manuscripts have no accents at all, or hardly any. Sometimes, too, they are put in incorrectly.

CANTICUM ZACHARIAE SACERDOTIS

MERCIAN, 800-850

Gebledsad dryhten god Israel forðon neasede ⟋
Benedictus Dominus Deus Israhel quia visitavit et

dyde alesnisse folces his ⟋ arehte horn hælu
fecit redemptionem plebis suae Et erexit cornu salutis

us in huse Dauiðes cnehtes his swe spreocende
nobis in domo David pueri sui Sicut locutus

wes ðorh muð haligra his witgena ða from
est per os sanctorum suorum prophetarum qui a

weorulde sind ⟋ gefreade usic from fiondum[1] urum
saeculo sunt Et liberavit nos ab inimicis nostris

⟋ of honda alra da[2] usic fiodun[1] to donne
et de manu omnium qui nos oderunt Ad faciendam

mildheortnisse mid fedrum urum ⟋ gemunan cyðnisse
misericordiam cum patribus nostris et memorare testamenti

his haligre ðone swergendan að ðone he swor to
sui sancti Jusjurandum quod juravit ad

Abrahame feder urum sellende hine[3] us ðet butan
Abraham patrem nostrum daturum se nobis Ut sine

ege of hondum fionda[1] ura gefreade we ðiwgen
timore de manibus inimicorum nostrorum liberati serviamus

him in halignisse and rehtwisnisse biforan him allum
illi In sanctitate et justitia coram ipso omnibus

dægum urum.
diebus nostris.

From Sweet's *Oldest English Texts.*

---

[1] *Fiond*, or *fiond* ('fiend' = enemy) is evidently the participle of *féon*, or *fion* (see above, p. 95). [2] For ða.

[3] The gloss translates as much as possible word for word, and the result is not always ordinary Old English; see also next page.

SONG OF ZACHARIAS
WEST SAXON, about 1000 A.D.
(Luke i. 68-75)

68. Gebletsud sí drihten israhela god . forþam þe he
     Blessed   be the Lord   Israel's God,   for that he
geneosode . ꝛ his folces alysednesse dyde;
visited   and his people's deliverance made;

69. ꝛ he ús hǽle horn arǽrde . on dauides huse
    And he to-us of-salvation a horn reared-up, in David's house
hys cnihtes;
his servant's;

70. Swa he spræc þurh hys halegra witegena muð. þa he[1]
    As he spake through his holy prophets' mouth, who
of worldes frymðe sprǽcon .
from world's beginning spake,

71. ꝛ he alysde us of urum feondum . ꝛ of ealra[2] þara
    And he delivered us from our enemies and from of-all[2] those
handa þe ús hatedon.
(the) hands that us hated.

72. Mildheortnesse to wyrcænne mid úrum fæderum . ꝛ
    Mercy to perform with our fathers, and
gemunan his halegan cyþnesse;
to-remember his holy testament;

73. Hyne[3] us to syllenne þone að . þe he úrum
    to-us to give the oath which he to-our
fæder abrahame swór .
father Abraham swore,

74. Þæt we butan ege of ure feonda handa alýsede him
    That we without fear of our enemies' hands delivered him
þeowian.
should-serve,

75. On halignesse beforan him . eallum urum dagum.
    In holiness before him, in-all our days.

From Skeat's *Gospels in Anglo-Saxon, Northumbrian, and Old Mercian Versions.*

---

[1] Probably wrongly written for þe; þe, Hatton MS. (a later version) and Northumbrian.   [2] See p. 109.

[3] The *se* (*daturum*) in the Latin seems to have confused the translator.

BÉOWULF
WEST SAXON, 800–900 A.D. (?)
(The home of the monster Grendel and his mother)

. . . Hie dygel lond
They (an) unknown land
warigeað, wulf-hleoðu, windige næssas,
hold, wolf-hills, windy nesses,
frecne fen-gelad, þær fyrgen-stream
(the) dangerous fen-tract, where (the) mountain-stream
under næssa genipu niðer gewiteð,
under nesses' mists down cometh,
flod under foldan ; nis þæt feor heonon
the flood under (the) ground; not-is that far hence
mil-gemearces, þæt se mere standeð
of-mile-distance, that the mere standeth
ofer þæm hongiað hrinde bearwas,
over which hang rustling trees,
wudu wyrtum fæst, wæter oferhelmað.
(a) wood with-roots fast, (the) water overhangeth.
Þær mæg [man] nihta gehwæm nið-wundor séon,
There may one of-nights on-any (a) horrid-wonder see,
fyr on flode ; no þæs frod leofað
fire on (the) flood; not so wise liveth
gumena bearna, þæt þone grund wite ;
(any) of-men's children, that the bottom he-should-know ;
þeah þe hæð-stapa hundum geswenced,
though (the) heath-stepper by-hounds pressed,
heorot hornum trum, holt-wudu sece
(the) hart in-horns strong (the) holt-wood seek
feorran geflymed, ær he feorh seleð,
from-far driven, first he (his) soul gives-up,
aldor on ofre, ær he in wille,
(his) life on (the) bank, ere he in will,
hafelan [hydan]. Nis þæt heoru stow :
(his) head to hide. Not-is that (a) pleasant place :
þonon yð-geblond up astigeð
whence (the) wave-surge up riseth
won to wolcnum, þonne wind styreð
wan to (the) clouds, when wind stirreth
lað gewidru, oð þæt lyft drysmað,
hateful tempests, till that (the) air darkens,
roderas reotað. . . .
(the) heavens weep.[1]

---

[1] *Béowulf*, Moritz Heyne. Paderborn, 1879 ; and Grein, *Bibliothek der Angelsächsischen Poesie*, edited by Wülcker. Cassel, 1883.

ALFRED'S ADDITIONS TO OROSIUS

(Composed end of Ninth Century, Manuscript of the Eleventh Century)

WEST SAXON

(Ohtere's account of his position and life in Norway)

He wæs swyþe spedig man on þæm æhtum þe heora
(a) very wealthy   in the possessions which their
speda on beoþ, þæt is, on wildrum.   He hæfde þagyt,
wealth (pl.) in consists,   in deer.   had   still,
þa he þone cyninge sohte, tamra deora unbebohtra syx
when the king sought, of-tame deer unbought
hund. Þa deor hi hataþ 'hranas'; þara wæron syx
hundred. The they call 'reindeer'; of-those
stælhranas; þa beoþ swyþe dyre mid Finnum, for þæm
decoy-reindeer; those are   dear with (the) Fins   that
hy foþ þa wildan hranas mid.   He wæs mid þæm
they catch   with (them).   among
fyrstum mannum on þæm lande: næfde he þeah ma
men   had-not he though more
þonne twentig hryþera, and twentig sceapa, and twentig
than   of-cattle   of-sheep
swyna; and þæt lytle þæt he erede[1] he erede mid horsan.
the little ploughed with horses.
Ac hyra ár is mæst on þæm gafole þe þa Finnas him
But their property most tribute which the to-them
gyldaþ. Þæt gafol biþ on deora fellum, and on fugela
pay.   is   deers' skins,   fowls'

---

[1] *Eared*, as in the Bible, Isaiah xxx. 24, for instance.

feþerum, and hwales bane, and on þæm sciprapum, þe
              bone   *ship-ropes, which*

beoþ of hwæles hyde geworht, and of seoles. Æghwilc
are   *wrought*   *seal's.*   *Each*

gylt be hys gebyrdum. Se byrdesta sceall gyldan
pays according-to   *rank.*   *The most-noble must*

fiftyne mearþes fell, and fif hranes, and an beran fell, and
      marten's skins   *reindeer's*   *one bear's*

tyn ambra[1] feþra, and berenne kyrtel[2] oþþe yterenne, and
ten ambers of-feathers   *of-bear (a) kirtle*   *or*   *of-otter*

twegen scíprapas; ægþer sy syxtig elna[3] lang, oþer[4] sy
two   *each is (he said)*   *ells*   *the-one*

of hwæles hyde geworht, oþer[4] of sioles.

From Sweet, *Extracts from Alfred's Orosius.*

---

[1] An amber equalled 4 bushels.

[2] K is an uncommon letter in Anglo-Saxon manuscripts, and is only used as an alternative to C.

[3] A Scandinavian ell equalled 2 feet.

[4] As in Latin *alter . . . alter* = the one . . . the other.

ANGLO-SAXON CHRONICLE

This particular chronicle (Ā) was probably compiled at Winchester, and the entries of this period were written down not very long after the events, therefore the date is about 945-975 A.D.

WEST SAXON

944. Her   Eadmund   cyning   ge eode   eal
    Here   *king*   *conquered*   *all*
Norþ hymbra land him   to ge wealdan . and aflymde ut
                      for-him to   *rule*   *drove*   *out*
twegen cyningas . Anlaf Syhtrices sunu . and Rægenald
two   *son*
Guð ferþes sunu.

945. Her Eadmund cyning ofer hergode eal Cumbra ·
                             over-harried
land . and   hit   let   to   eal Malculme Scotta cyninge .
          it *let* *to* *all* *to-Malcolm*
ón   þæt   gerad   þæt   he   wære   his   mid wyrhta
        condition   *should-be*   *fellow-worker*
ægþer ge ón sǽ ge ón lande.
both   *and*

From Earle, *Two of the Saxon Chronicles Parallel.*

GOSPEL OF ST. MATTHEW
(Chap. xiii. Verses 3-9)
WEST SAXON, about 1000 A.D.

3. And he spræc to hym fela on big-spellum cweþende;
     spake them many (things) in parables saying
Soþlice ut-eode se sǽdere hys sǽd to sawenne [1]
Truly out went the sower his seed sow

4. And þa þa he seow. sume hig feollon wiþ weg. and
     as sowed, some they fell by (the) way, and
fuglas comun and ǽton þá;
fowls came ate them;

5. Soþlice sume feollon on stænihte þær hyt næfde mycle
     some fell on (a) stony (place) where it not-had much
eorþan. and hrædlice upsprungon for-þam þe hig næfdon
earth. quickly up-sprang because that they not-had
þære eorþan dypan;
of-the earth depth;

6. Soþlice upsprungenre sunnan [2] hig adruwudon and
     up-having-sprung sun they dried-up
forscruncon. for þam þe hig næfdon wyrtrum; [3]
shrank-away they not-had root;

7. Soþlice sume feollon on þornas. and þa þornas weoxon
     some fell thorns the thorns waxed
and for-þrysmudon þa.
choked them.

8. sume soþlice feollon on gode eorþan and sealdon [4] weastm.
   some fell good gave fruit,
sum hund-fealdne. sum sixtig-fealdne. sum þrittig-fealdne;
some hundred-fold sixty thirty

9. Se þe hæbbe [5] earan to gehyrenne [1] gehyre. [6]
   He who has ears hear let-him-hear.

From Skeat's *Gospels in Anglo-Saxon, Northumbrian, and Old Mercian Versions.*

---

[1] Gerund = *ad serendum*, etc., p. 95.   [2] Dative 'absolute' or 'of time when.'
[3] Like 'St. John's *wort.*'
[4] The same word as *sold*, now specialised in meaning, see pp. 61-63.
[5] Subjunctive, see p. 99, (5).   [6] Subjunctive, see p. 98, (1).

GOSPEL OF ST. MATTHEW
(Chap. xiii. Verses 3-9)
MERCIAN, about 970 A.D.
(Gloss to the Latin Version)

3. And he sprec to heom feola in gelicnissum cweþende
   parables
henu ut eode se sawend to sawenne
behold!   *sower*

4. and þa he seow sume gefeollun bi wæge and cuomun
fuglas heofun and frætun   *came*
of-heaven   *ate*

5. þæt[1] oþere þonne gefeollun on stanig lond þær ne
   that *others* *then*   *stony*
hefde eorðe miccle and hræþe[2] cuomun upp forþon þe hie
had   *much*   *quickly*   *because that*
næfdon heanisse[3] eorðe
       highness of-earth

6. sunne þa upp cuom hatedun and forðon þe hie nefdun·
         then   *they-heated*
wy[r]tryme for-wisnadun
           they-withered away

7. sume þonne gefetun[4] in þornas and wexon þa þornas
                  fell   *waxed*
and smoradun hiæ
smothered   *them*

8. Sume þonne gefetun[4] on eorðe gode and saldun[5]
wæstem sume hund-teontig sume sextig sume þritig
              hundred

9. seþe hæbbe eara gehernesse gehere.
             ears *of-hearing.*

From Skeat's *Gospels in Anglo-Saxon, Northumbrian, and Old Mercian Versions.*

---

[1] *þæt* should be in the former verse.
[2] Positive of *rather* (=more quickly, sooner). The adjective occurs in Milton, *Lycidas*, l. 142—'Bring the *rathe* (=early) primrose.'
[3] Latin *altitudinem.*
[4] Should be *gefellun*; it is a slip on the part of the scribe, the man who wrote it.
[5] Nearer to Modern English than *sealdon*, the West Saxon form. A often turned into O, as we shall see.

For notes (1) and (4) I am indebted to the kindness of Professor Earle and also of Professor Skeat.

CHAPTER XIII

FOREIGN ASCENDENCY

English dialects and English literature at the time of the Norman Conquest—How Norman French gained its ascendency—Character of Norman French—Its history in England, and how it went out of use—Position of Latin in England—Latin, French, and English literature after the Conquest.[1]

IT is very important to have an accurate notion of the character and position of English, in its various dialects, at the time of the Norman Conquest, so as to understand the changes which took place after, or in consequence of that event. Of these changes some were directly due to the coming of the Normans, and the rest were, as we shall see, for the most part indirectly affected by it.

English, then, as written at the time of the Norman Conquest, was an 'inflexional' language, as may be seen from the specimens of it already given. The language was divided into five main dialects (see chap. xi.), excluding Kentish, which, for practical purposes, was becoming a mere variety of the Southern or West Saxon. This last was the 'standard' dialect of English at the time, holding the same sort of position as the English which educated people now speak, and which we find in books—that is, it was the dialect used by the upper and educated classes in speaking, and the language of

---

[1] See especially Freeman's *Norman Conquest*; and Skeat, *Principles of English Etymology*, Second Series.

literature.¹ And it was a highly cultivated language. Though it appears that not very much had been written in it since the beginning of the eleventh century, this is only an instance of what we commonly find in literature—namely, that its progress is not steady, like the flow of a river, but in waves, as the tide comes in. And, no doubt, but for the coming of William the Conqueror, Old English would have had other great periods of literature, each probably in some respects showing an advance upon the last. But, taking the mass of writings in Old English as they existed at the Norman Conquest, inherited from different periods, including the poems of Cædmon, the other religious poems, such as the one on the finding of the True Cross, the metrical sermons of Ælfric, the Béowulf, whatever its age may be, the battle songs, such as the Song of Brunanburh, inserted in one of the Chronicles, and translated by Lord Tennyson, the Song of the Battle of Maldon, translated by Dr. Freeman in his *Old English History*, and the other lyric poems, and last but not least the Chronicles, which in some parts, such as the account of Alfred's reign, and even as late as the section where William the Conqueror's character is described, rise to the level of first-rate contemporary history, our literature was superior to that existing at the time in any one language spoken in Europe. And we must remember that, though probably on the whole the best works have been preserved, yet a very large part of Old English literature must have perished, in the neglect which it suffered for centuries, and in the merciless destruction at the Reformation of libraries in the monasteries, where most of the Old English books still surviving were preserved.

Now in any history of English after the Norman Conquest there are three questions which have to be considered.

---

¹ The later Mercian writings are a good deal coloured by it, just as modern writings in some English dialect almost always have a good deal of 'standard' English in them, besides what the dialect owns.

First, What effect did the Norman Conquest have upon the position of English in England as the language of the upper classes and of books, and for what reasons, and by what steps did English regain the position which it then lost, but which it plainly holds at present ?

Secondly, How did English change, whether through the Norman Conquest or from other causes, in the time during which it was in the shade, so to speak, overshadowed by French and Latin ?

Thirdly, Why was the dialect of English which became the 'standard' language in the fourteenth and fifteenth centuries a different one from the dialect which held that position before William the Conqueror came to England ?

It will be best to consider these questions separately, as far as possible. They may be more shortly stated thus—

(1) What are the facts as to the position of English in England from 1066 or 1100 [1] to 1366 or thereabouts, a period of about 300 years ?

(2) What changes took place in English, or in its different dialects, between those dates ?

(3) How did one dialect finally win a position superior to the rest ?

(1) In order to account for the predominance of French in England after the Norman Conquest, a theory grew up that William the Conqueror deliberately set himself to degrade, and, if possible, to root out the English language. Now there is nothing absurd or impossible in this idea in itself, for the Russians are at the present time engaged in a similar attempt to root out Polish in Poland, and German in the Baltic Provinces of Russia. But, as a matter of fact, William made no attempt of the kind. His wish was to represent himself not as the foreign conqueror but as the legitimate English king, the heir of Edward the Confessor, and of the English kings, 'my predecessors.' And any consistent attempt to

[1] When the generation born before the Conquest had mostly died out.

destroy the language of the country, to substitute French for it, for instance, in writs, proclamations, and other official documents, would plainly have given the lie to this claim. And, as a matter of fact, many of his writs and grants, as, for instance, his confirmation of the privileges of London, are in English; and it is said that he tried to learn English himself, though he found the language too hard for him, as has been the case with many foreigners since.[1] But after the battle of Hastings the estates of those immediately concerned in what he called the 'rebellion' against him (chiefly in Kent and the neighbouring parts) were confiscated and given to Normans and other foreigners who had come with him from France; and when the men of other districts of England rose, during the next few years, their lands were treated in the same way. These foreigners had to be rewarded for their support, and they were a garrison, though a rather mutinous one, to hold the conquered country. It was the great landowners, who held their lands directly from the king, who were to such a large extent either driven out of the country, or reduced to hold some part of their estates left to them as tenants of the new Norman owner. The lesser country-gentlemen, or farmers, were not nearly so much disturbed, and townspeople (in London, for instance), as well as the serfs or villeins, not at all. Besides this, William, with the consent and support of the Pope, in the course of a few years got rid of almost all the native English bishops and put foreigners in their place. And many Normans, especially merchants, migrated to England as a new field for enterprise, like the parents of Thomas à Becket.

The theory, then, that William deliberately tried to destroy the English language, besides being in point of fact untrue, as we have seen, is not in the least required to explain the facts. The great landowners, the bishops and abbots,—that is to say, the aristocracy,—now spoke French

[1] His writs, etc., would of course be put into English by his clerks.

naturally, as their native language, instead of English, and so did a certain number of merchants and others. For, though the Normans were of course 'Northmen,' Scandinavians, and not Frenchmen by origin, as any one can see to this day from their build and colour in those parts of Normandy where the breed is purest (such as the neighbourhood of Bayeux), yet Danish was nearly or quite extinct in Normandy, at any rate among the upper classes, in 1066. And, therefore, the Normans in England

> Spoke French as they did at home, and their children did also teach.[1]

But before we go any further, we ought to see what kind of French it was which the Normans brought into England. To begin with, it did not bear a very close resemblance to the language which we are accustomed to call 'French,' the modern form of the Central or Parisian dialect which is now established as the language of educated people in France, and of French books. Very many of the French words which came into our language early, in the 300 years which followed the Norman Conquest, cannot possibly be derived from the French to which we are accustomed. Obviously we cannot derive *espy* or *spy* from *épier*, *feast* from *fête*, *wage* from *gage*, or *assets* from *assez*,[2] with its Modern French pronunciation. As a matter of fact, the French which the Normans spoke in England was different from what we ordinarily mean by French, for two reasons, to which a third was afterwards added.

(*a*) It was a much more old-fashioned or archaic form of French. We know that French is a corrupted form of Latin,

---

[1] Robert of Gloucester (modernised), see p. 261.
[2] *i.e.* 'enough to meet claims' (Earle, *Philology of the English Tongue*). *Assets*, properly a collective noun, looks like a plural; consequently it has been treated as such, and a singular formed for it; thus we speak of 'a single *asset*.' The uneducated treat *chaise* ('shays') somewhat in the same way, speaking of 'a *shay*,' or sometimes giving it a plural verb, as in 'The chaise *are* at the door.' This is, of course, 'analogy' again.

and French as it was spoken in England is much nearer to Latin than modern literary French; the alteration had not gone so far, and it is often much easier to recognise the Latin original. Thus in *francs hom* the *s* shows the old termination of the masculine adjective; *habet* is *ad* (not *a*), and *habetis* is *avetz*; *ille homo* is *l'um* (not *l'on*); and in *apelum* it is easier to recognise the first person plural than in *apelons*; *erent* is almost and *fuissent* exactly the same as in Latin. And the nearer resemblance to Latin was not only in the spelling. Very many letters, especially terminations, were then pronounced which are now silent as a rule.

(*b*) But it was not even an older form of the same French dialect as that which is now the literary language of France. It was *Norman*-French. One characteristic of this form of the language was that it preserved a simple W in many words which in other Old French dialects had GU (pronounced GW), which again has become a simple G in Modern French, sometimes in spelling, always in pronunciation. Thus, Norman-French had *wages* for Modern French *gages*, *warene* for Modern French *garenne*, and *warant* for *garant*. Still Norman-French had many words beginning with GU as well, such as, for instance, *guerdon*, and *guise*, in which the U was once pronounced as W.

(*c*) Norman-French in England was to a great extent separated from its sister dialects on the Continent, especially after the loss of Normandy in 1204. It thus went a way of its own, and developed differently from other French dialects even of this earlier period. It is quite true that some words of Parisian French found their way into the Norman-French spoken in England, through intercourse with France and the study of French poems written on the Continent. Central French forms even took the place of words already in the language, as when *rei* became *roi*, and *lei*, *loi*; hence *reial* and *leial* (or *leal*, as in 'the land o' the leal') became respectively *royal* and *loyal*. But the enormous proportion of those French words which are a part of our daily life, and which we cannot do without, such words as *habit, damage, distance, honour, chief, oblige, suffer,* besides a mass of other words, come to us from Norman-French. And it was the presence of so many words in English taken from one French dialect which made it so easy to go on borrowing from Parisian French, as we have been doing ever since we ceased to borrow from Norman-French. The words did not sound or look strange in the language.

We have already seen that, besides the differences between French in the ordinary sense and Norman-French which are obvious in the spelling, there must have been differences in the pronunciation as well. For *assets* can only be derived from *assez* if this Z was pronounced as TS, which was the case at the end of words for some time after the Conquest. But the differences of pronunciation went further than this. J (written I), CH, G, QU[1] were not pronounced as in *juge, cheval, rouge, quinze,* but as they now are in English, as in the words *jolly, judge, juror; change, charge, check; gentle, gist, wage; quit, conquest*.[1] The vowels were of course different, like 'new pronunciation' Latin or Italian, just as the English vowels were at the time.[2] But our English pronunciation of the consonants will not be far wrong for Norman- or Anglo-French. It will be necessary to remember this when we come to the influence of the Norman Conquest on our spelling. But perhaps the greatest difference was that (almost always) all the letters were pronounced, such as the final *-s, -e, -es, -ent,* which are

[1] But QU was pronounced as a simple K in some words; *qui,* for instance, is constantly written *ki.*

[2] These Anglo-French words, having been fully adopted into English before the great changes took place in our way of pronouncing the English vowels, followed their fortunes, and have for the most part changed the sound of their vowels like them. It is in the French words introduced since about 1660 that we not unfrequently find the sound of French vowels (as well as consonants) retained more or less completely; in such words as *mirage, écarté, pique, coupon, mauve, bureau, connoisseur, prestige, croquet.* See Skeat, *Principles of English Etymology,* Second Series.

usually silent in Modern French, as well as letters inside the word, like the P in *corpse*, Modern French *corps* (*cor'*). Examples of this Norman-French will be found farther on. The piece of poetry at the end of the chapter (p. 172), written in Normandy, but before the two forms of Norman-French on opposite sides of the Channel had diverged to any great extent, will show us what Anglo-French was like to start with; this is followed by a bit of later Anglo-French prose; and a few sentences on pp. 279, 280, are an example of Anglo-French in its last stage.

Thus the language of the upper classes was now a dialect of French, and an entirely distinct language from English, not differing in some few points only, as Midland or Northumbrian differed from West Saxon, or even as Danish or Norse differed from English. It would plainly be impossible for two such distinct languages as French and English to make compromises, by combining their grammar and so on, so as to form a 'mixed language' in the strict sense of the words.[1]

At first, no doubt, none of the Normans would understand English, none of the English French. But very soon many of the Normans would learn some English, while a great many of the English would try to pick up some French. For they soon got to live on tolerably friendly terms with each other, and many even of those who came with William married English wives. A landowner who knew no English, besides having his society narrowed, would be very much at the mercy of clerks, bailiffs, and other subordinates in dealing with his tenants and serfs, if he could not understand what they said. And as the large majority of the people spoke English, a Norman would soon get familiar with the sound of the language, so as to be able to understand it, even if he spoke it with difficulty and incorrectly, or if he preferred not to

---

[1] The influence even of Danish upon English seems to have been mainly in the way of destroying or simplifying English grammar. Except in the pronouns, *they, their, them,* and *tenth, both,* it is very difficult to name points in which English grammar copied Danish (see p. 133, etc., and below). But the French plural in *-s* had, no doubt, some share in establishing this form as the ordinary English plural.

speak it at all, as being a vulgar language. And the Normans engaged in trade would, of course, from the first have to pick up as much English as they possibly could, for the purposes of their business. On the other hand, the lower, and more especially the middle classes of Englishmen, would find it convenient to be able to communicate with their superiors, and would also think it fine or refined to be able to talk French, and to interlard their English talk with French words and expressions. As John of Trevisa says,[1] even in 1387, when the predominance of French was becoming a thing of the past : 'Uplandish[2] men will liken themselves to gentlemen and contrive with great trouble to speak French, "for to be more y-told of."'[3] That is, that their friends might say, 'So-and-so is quite the gentleman; he can speak French.' Thus we can account for the large number of French words which have found their way into English, as will be seen later on.

Now, as Professor Freeman says,[4] nothing is more unusual in histories than any statement of the language in which people spoke on a particular occasion, the historian thinking it quite enough to give their meaning. But there are enough statements or hints in histories to show that even the heads of the aristocracy, who spoke French habitually, knew some English. Henry I. perhaps wrote a book in English. At any rate he had a wife of English descent, Edith (older form *Ead-gyth*, like *Ead-ward* and *Ead-gar*), also called Matilda, in order to suit the Norman taste in names; and 'Godric,'[5] as the King was nicknamed on account of his supposed partiality for the native English, could certainly speak and understand English. So too the wife of a man of the French-speaking class, Hugh de Morville, father of one of the murderers of

---

[1] Skeat's *Principles of English Etymology*, First Series, p. 31.
[2] Countrymen, uncultured men. The extract is modernised, except the last few words.   [3] Accounted of.
[4] *Norman Conquest*, vol. v. p. 528; a work to which I am very largely indebted in this part of my subject.
[5] That being a common English name at the time, though it has long been extinct, like most of the Anglo-Saxon Christian names.

Thomas à Becket (who lived therefore about 1140), addresses him in English thus: *Huge de Morevile, ware, ware, ware, Lithulf heth his swerd adrage.*[1] She would hardly have spoken to him in a language that he could not understand. Henry II. (1154-89) understood English, and Edward I. (1272-1307) could and sometimes did speak it. These facts, and many other hints that we get, show that the account given above of the relative position of English and French between 1066 and 1366 is correct.

The strange thing is that French should have lasted as a spoken language in England so long after the Normans and English had become one nation, when a writer of about 1180 says that it was then impossible to tell who were Normans and who were Englishmen.[2] But we must remember that until Normandy was lost in 1204, early in John's reign, many English landholders held estates in Normandy as well. When they went over there they would find French the universal language, and so keep their knowledge of it alive.

But when foreigners were brought into England, such as the Poitevins under John, and Provençals under Henry III., their coming was always resented by the men, even of foreign ancestry, who were already settled in the country, and who were, at least after the loss of Normandy in John's reign, to all intents and purposes Englishmen. Yet the custom of speaking Norman- or Anglo-French went on even when the nation was still more closely united at the time of De Montfort's government and the Barons' War (1258-65), in the reign of Henry III., when the nobles who usually spoke French, the

[1] *Materials for the History of Thomas à Becket*, edited by Canon Robertson, Rolls Series, 1875, p. 128. The story is good evidence for English having been spoken on the particular occasion, or perhaps rather for its being likely that a wife should use it to her husband, if the story is a slander; but the form of the English is, no doubt, that of 1170, or later. There was no antiquarian accuracy on such matters in those days. So another person has written in the margin what seemed to him better English: *Lyulph haveth his swerd ydrawen*; and in another manuscript it is *Hue of Morville, war, war, war, Lithulf haves his swerd idragen.* 'Haves' is the Northern form.

[2] 'Dialogus de Scaccario,' Stubbs's *Documents* (see note on next page).

lower classes in London and other towns who spoke English only, and the intermediate classes, many of whom must have known both French and English, were, for the most part, united to secure decent government.[1] It is remarkable that the different classes of a single nation should for a long time have spoken two different languages.

But, besides long habit, there was another cause which prevented French from going out of use in England. In fact, its supremacy was greatest in the last 150 years of its reign in England, from the time when, early in the thirteenth century, it took the place of Latin as the language of Government and of the Law Courts, as we shall see presently. It did not lose its position as a spoken language, for in the thirteenth century it became the fashion in most of the Courts of Europe to speak French,[2] just as at this day the Russians of the upper classes at St. Petersburg usually talk French, or as in Hungary down to the earlier part of this century Latin was the language used in Parliament, and to a large extent by the nobles in conversation as well. Still, from the beginning of the thirteenth century, when the English landowners no longer had possessions in Normandy, when it was no longer possible, without studying genealogies, to say whether a man were mainly of English or of Norman descent,[3] when the whole nation could and did combine to resist despotism and the intrusion of foreigners, who were almost always Frenchmen, it is quite plain that the habit of speaking French among the upper classes was a mere fashion, irrational and inconvenient. Even the poor

---

[1] Poems or political verses on the Barons' War still remain both in French, Latin, and English. And there is one proclamation by Henry III., of 1258, in English.

[2] This influence was all in favour of 'standard' French as distinct from the Norman dialect. Yet the 'standard' French merely coloured Anglo-French to some small extent and did not drive it out. Anglo-French was one kind of French after all.

[3] 'But now, from the English and Normans living together and marrying wives from among each other, the nations are so mixed, that at the present day (1177) it can scarcely be distinguished (I speak of freemen) who is an Englishman and who a Norman by descent.' The villeins are excepted, who would all be English.—'Dialogus de Scaccario,' Stubbs's *Documents*.

schoolboys suffered from it, being obliged to construe Latin into French, as being the more refined language, though some of them must have known very little of it. And this Anglo-French was a local and more or less artificial language, no longer like any dialect of French spoken on the Continent. Thus at Marlborough (where there was an important royal castle, in which Parliaments were sometimes held, as in Henry I.'s reign,) there was a spring, now no longer used, which was supposed to make people who drank it speak bad French.[1] And so too, at the very end of the ascendency of French, Chaucer says of his Prioress—

> And Frensh she spak ful faire and fetisly,[2]
> After the scole of Stratford atte Bowe,
> For Frensh of Paris was to hir unknowe.

Thus the habit of speaking French in England began naturally among the upper classes, since every man talks his mother-tongue, and children copy their parents. But to have two languages for one nation was certainly inconvenient, and in the latter half of the fourteenth century it had become little more than a mere fashion. On account of its great inconvenience and, one may say, its absurdity, it required but a small push to overthrow it. And this seems to have been given by the French wars of Edward III. (1337-74) which would bring home to numbers of Englishmen by actual experience the fact that French was, after all, a foreign language,[3] the language of their enemies whom they had so often beaten, and therefore an unnatural language for Englishmen to talk. If Anglo-French was French it was unnatural for Englishmen to talk it; as differing from 'standard' French it was a mere insular jargon.

[1] Freeman, *Norman Conquest*, vol. v. p. 891. *Nous giveons*, in a document of 1258, is an extreme example of *Anglo*-French.—Koch, *Historische Grammatik der Englischen Sprache.*

[2] =neatly, cleverly.—*Prologue to Canterbury Tales*, ll. 124-126 (after 1386 A.D.), edited by Morris and Skeat; and see Appendix D.

[3] *Norman Conquest*, vol. v. p. 535.

And when a blow had been given to the inconvenient fashion among the upper classes of talking and writing French, its downfall was tolerably rapid. Thus between 1350 and 1385 the custom in the schools of construing Latin into French died out. In 1362 the King's speech at the opening of Parliament was, by request of the Commons, made in English. In 1363, also on the request of the Commons, it was ordered that the business of the Law Courts should be conducted in English, since French was little understood. Still, French did not die out all at once. It was not entirely disused in Parliament for another century, and even now the words in which the King's or Queen's assent is given to a Bill, *Le Roi* (or, *la Reine*) *le veut*, are a relic of the time when all Parliamentary business and all the business of Government was conducted in French. So too the *Oh yes* of a town-crier (*oyez!* hear!) carries us back to the time when French was used in the humblest official acts. And the Law and Law Courts are full of French words, of which *plead* (*plaider*), *mortmain*, *justice*, and the terms ending in *-ee*, *payee*, *mortgagee*, and so on (where the ending represents French *-é* of the past participle), are familiar instances.[1]

The victory over English at and after the Conquest was not won by French only, Latin had a share in it. Now Latin was throughout the Middle Ages the learned, and, one might almost say, the universal language of Europe. Besides the books written in Latin, in England as well as abroad, about which something will be said presently, it had once been, even in England, the language used for grants of land and legal documents in general. And though these had got to be more and more written in English, still some were in Latin, either wholly or in part, down to the end of the Anglo-Saxon monarchy. And on the Continent Latin was the regular language of legal and Government documents. William the

---

[1] But it must be remembered that the use of French as the official language of Government and of the Law did not become at all complete for 150 years after the Conquest.

Conqueror had followed the ordinary custom in Normandy, and when he came to England he and his secretaries still retained it. It was the ordinary practice abroad; it was by no means unknown in England; and it was no insult to his new subjects, as the use of French would have been. Sometimes, indeed, in his character of native English king, as the heir of Edward the Confessor, he issued writs in English, as 'his predecessors' would have done. But the Latin continued to gain ground, and after Henry I.'s time very few of these documents are in English. Then in the year of Magna Charta (1215) they begin to be in French. This seems curious at first, but no doubt Professor Freeman's[1] explanation is the correct one. Until the Norman Conquest was practically forgotten it would have been a 'badge of conquest,' and therefore offensive to the mass of the nation, to use Norman-French, the speech of the conquerors, as the language of Government. But now that the Conquest was 'ancient history,' and all the inhabitants of the country were for practical purposes one English nation, one part of whom spoke a kind of French as a mere fashion, there was no harm in using that language, which was after all the usual speech of those who had most to do with the business of Government, while only the small class of learned men knew Latin.[2] How English in its turn drove out French has been already described.

So far nothing has been said of the literature of the country after the Norman Conquest. Now books plainly imply people to read them or hear them read, and so the languages in which they are written must, one would think, be those which are spoken in the country. Why then were so many books written in Latin during the Middle Ages? One reason is that, as the Church Service and the Bible were

---

[1] *Norman Conquest*, vol. v. pp. 529, 530.
[2] The clergy were not a very small class taken together; but a large number of the inferior clergy knew very little Latin.

in Latin, which was regarded as a sacred language, the clergy and monks were almost obliged to know something of it; and, in fact, it almost held the position of a vernacular or spoken language among the more learned members of the clerical and learned population of Europe.

And it was not only a sacred language but a cultivated language, with models in the Latin classics which could be more or less copied, and which invited imitation. We must remember, too, that in the early part of the Middle Ages French, and Provençal, and Italian, and the other Romance languages (see pp. 33, 55, 56), were mere vulgar dialects of Latin, and it was natural that books should be written rather in the cultivated than in the vulgar or popular dialects of the language. So that, while these dialects were developing into distinct languages, Latin had the chance of fixing itself as the learned language of Europe.

In Germany, Scandinavia, and England, on the other hand, Latin was from the first a foreign language, and owed its position to its use by the Church, to reverence for classical culture, and to the example of the rest of Europe.

But England had, as we have seen, to a large extent stood apart from the rest of Europe by using its own tongue for writing books. It is true that the books produced in Northumbria, such as the works of the Venerable Bede, were mostly written in Latin. Even later, after English prose had through Alfred's example come thoroughly into use as a cultivated language, some books, especially histories, written in England were in Latin, such as the life of Alfred, attributed to Asser, and the work of 'Patricius Consul Fabius Quæstor Ethelwerdus,' who in English was plain 'Æðelweard ealdormann.'

Still, on the whole, English literature was remarkable for being chiefly written in English. But, as has been said, William the Conqueror replaced the English bishops and abbots, as soon as he had the chance, by foreigners. These men, the natural heads of the learned class in England,

Foreign Ascendency

were not likely to encourage the barbarous insular custom of writing histories, for instance, in English.[1] Besides, the Norman Conquest increased the general intercourse of England with the Continent enormously, and brought England under Continental influence. And so we find that, though there was a great deal of English history written in England in the twelfth century,[2] its language (except in the Peterborough Chronicle) was Latin. And it is somewhat remarkable that the satires of the twelfth century on the Pope and the Clergy should also have been written in Latin.

But the upper classes of society did not, for the most part, understand Latin. For them there were the Romances, the Tales of Charlemagne, and, a little later, of Arthur and his Knights. Some of these were written in Normandy, some in other parts of France, some in England. But these last were in a French dialect as well as the others, though some of them were afterwards translated into English; they would naturally be written in the language of those who took most interest in the deeds of knights like themselves.

Besides this, there was during this period a literature in English: sermons, poems of various kinds, translations of French Romances, and one regular Chronicle, just like the Anglo-Saxon Chronicles before the Conquest, written at Peterborough, and carried down to the end of Stephen's reign, for those who spoke, and read, or listened to English by preference, or who understood no other language. The English between the Conquest and about 1450 is best called 'Middle English.'

[1] Professor Earle (*Two of the Saxon Chronicles*, introduction, p. xxiii.) thinks that Lanfranc caused one of the Anglo-Saxon Chronicles to be transferred from Winchester to Canterbury, and to be brought up to date (1070) there. But still this is not quite the same thing as encouraging the writing of fresh histories in English. And Lanfranc was a man of special enlightenment.

[2] By Florence of Worcester, Simeon of Durham, William of Malmesbury, Henry of Huntingdon.

Beginning of the 'Roman de Rou'

By Wace, a native of Jersey, and Canon of Bayeux in Normandy, who lived from about 1090 to 1180.

> Pur[1] remembrer des ancesurs
> Les feiz e les diz[2] e les murs,
> Les felunies des feluns
> E les barnages des baruns,
> Deit l'um les livres e les gestes
> E les estoires lire a festes.
> Si escripture ne fust feite
> E puis par clers litte e retraite
> Mult fussent choses ubliées
> Ki de viez tens sunt trespassées.

The French Chronicle of London[3]

Written about 1350.

xiij.[4] Henry Darcy, meir,
  William Pountfreit et Hughe Marberer, vicountes.

En cele an nostre joevene roy se apparila ove graunt poer des Engleis et de Gales, si passa la mer à Orewelle en Essex,

---

[1] Meyer, *Recueil d'Anciens Textes Bas-Latins Provençaux et Français*, 2ᵉ Partie, Ancien Français. Paris, 1877. 'In order to remember the acts and words and customs of our ancestors, the low crimes of the felons and the high deeds of the barons, one ought to read at feasts the books and the knightly tales and the histories. If writing had not been made, and then read and told by clerks, many things would have been forgotten which have passed away a long time ago.'

[2] Pronounced 'fei*ts*,' 'di*ts*.' All vowels and consonants are to be sounded (see above).

[3] Edited from a MS. in the Cottonian Library, by G. J. Aungier, Camden Society, 1844.

[4] 'Thirteenth (year of Edward III.) Henry Darcy, mayor, William Pountfreit and Hugh Marberer, sheriffs.

'In that year our young King prepared himself with a great power of Englishmen and of Wales, so he crossed the sea at Orwell in Essex, and came et ariva sus en Flaundres, et ses gentz passerent avant en le ysle de Cagent, et tuerent touz qe leinz porroyent estre trovez, et si avoyent illoqes graunt avoir, et puisse ardoient sus tot le dit isle. Et adonke nostre joevene roy prist son host, si s'en ala en Braban, et demorra pur long temps à Andwerp, et tint illoqes son parlement, et là furent jurez à luy tous ceux de Flaundres, de Braban, de Henaud, et de Alemaygne à nostre joevene roy, de vivere et morir ovesqe luy en sa querele vers le roy de Fraunce. Auxint nostre joevene roy graunta d'estre lour lige seignour, de vivere et morir ovesqe eux et lur defendre et meintenir vers totes gentz de mounde pur touz jours.

up to land in Flanders, and his people crossed before into the isle of Cagent (Cadsand), and killed all that therein could be found, and so had there great possessions (spoil), and then burnt up all the said isle. And then our young King took his host, so he went thence into Brabant, and stayed for a long time at Antwerp, and held there his parliament, and there were sworn to him all those of Flanders, of Brabant, of Hainault, and of Germany, to our young King, to live and die with him in his quarrel against the King of France. And so our young King consented to be their liege lord, to live and die with them and defend and maintain them against all people in the world for ever.'

CHAPTER XIV

EFFECTS OF THE NORMAN CONQUEST UPON ENGLISH

Loss of Old English poetical style—Dialects put on an equality—Simplification and shortening of inflexions—English spelt as French—French idioms — French words in English — Their first appearance — How they were introduced—Duplicate words—French words with English terminations—'Hybrid' words—Influx of French words about 1280—French words of Government, War, Architecture, Medicine, Sport, Religion—Words related in French and English—Pronunciation—French and English accent.[1]

WE have now seen that French was the ordinary speech of the upper classes in England for 300 years from the Norman Conquest; that during this time it divided the field of literature in England with Latin and English; and that for the second half of the period (about 1215-1362) French was, exclusively, the language of Government and Law. Being thus in contact with English, it could not fail to leave its mark upon it, which it did in four ways.

(1) The ascendency of French practically destroyed the cultivated or 'standard' West Saxon English, and especially the old-fashioned form of it used in poetry. It degraded the cultivated West Saxon dialect, putting all other dialects on a level with it, and helping on the tendency to pare down and obscure its terminations.

(2) It altered English spelling, so as to make it agree with Norman-French models.

(3) It introduced French idioms into English.

---

[1] Freeman, *Norman Conquest.* Kington Oliphant, *Old and Middle English.* Earle, *Philology of the English Tongue.* Sweet, *History of English Sounds.* Brachet, *Historical French Grammar,* translated by Kitchin. Skeat, *Principles of English Etymology,* First and Second Series.

Effects of Norman Conquest upon English 175

(4) A very large number of French words were brought into English, and, besides them, a good many words direct from Latin.

Of these changes (1) began at once, as soon, that is, as the generation born before the Conquest had died out; the change in spelling also began at the same time, and was completed by about 1400; both (3) and (4) begin soon after the Conquest, but the inroad of French words took place to a much greater extent towards the end of the period during which French was in the ascendant.

(1) We must remember that down to the Conquest cultivated West-Saxon English had been the literary language, besides being the speech of the Court of Winchester; and the English were still 'in touch' with their literature. English prose and poetry were not merely for the monks and clergy. The earls and thanes and other Englishmen, even if they could not read, would like to hear and learn the Béowulf, the Song of Brunanburh and of Maldon, and other battle-songs, such as were sung around the camp-fires in the night before the battle of Hastings; and the more devout among them would take pleasure in such poems as those ascribed to Cædmon, and that on the finding of the True Cross. And poetry of the old form was still a living art, besides the new style which was growing up. There is in one of the Anglo-Saxon Chronicles a short poem on the death of Edward the Confessor and the accession of Harold, evidently contemporary— that is, written in the earlier half of 1066 A.D. Here are the last six lines of it—

And se froda swa þeah · befæste þæt rice ·
the old man   yet   entrusted   the kingdom
heah ðungenum menn · Harolde sylfum ·
to-an-illustrious man (dat.) Harold (him-)self
æþelum eorle · se in ealle tíd ·
a noble   earl   who   all   time
hyrde holdlice · hærran sinum ·
served   loyally   lord   his

wordum and dædum · wihte ne agǽlde.
in-words   in-deeds   a whit not was-careless
þæs þe þearf wæs · þæs þeod kyninges.
about-what (the) need was of-the people's-king.

In this poem we find the characteristics of the Old English poetical style, not only a different order of the words from that used in prose, but the use of purely poetical words, such as *hærra, sin*. It is interesting as the last effort of 'classical' Anglo-Saxon poetry.

For after the Conquest English lost its educated patrons. The bishops and abbots were replaced by foreigners. The earls and thanes, the courtiers of the Court of Winchester, the cultured laymen, were mostly dead or in exile, or at least they had lost their commanding position. With them the cultivated English had lost its patrons and its ascendency; the patronage of the new upper class was given to French poetry. And as Anglo-Saxon poetry was to such a remarkable extent in an old-fashioned style artificially preserved, far removed from the ordinary talk of Englishmen, it could hardly survive the loss of its educated patrons. Thus we find that Henry of Huntingdon, who wrote about 1150 A.D., within a century of the Norman Conquest, though he is fond of the old songs in the Chronicles and translates them in his Latin history, makes many mistakes in rendering them, just as any one might do now who knew only Anglo-Saxon prose. In fact, the tradition of Old English poetry died at the Conquest.[1]

Henceforward, too, all dialects were on a level. West Saxon was no longer the Court language. Winchester was no longer the one capital of England. 'At Easter,' we are told, 'William wore his crown at Winchester, at Pentecost at Westminster, and at midwinter (Christmas) at Gloucester.'[2] And even if Winchester had still been the capital, this would have made little difference, for the language spoken at Court

---

[1] But its metre survived in some shape till 1500 and later.
[2] *Peterborough Chronicle*, 1086. Earle's *Anglo-Saxon Chronicles*.

was no longer any dialect of English, but Norman-French. All dialects therefore being equal, if any one wished to write an English book, he wrote it in that dialect of English which he himself spoke—in the West Saxon or Southern dialect, if he lived in the South; but in Northumbrian, or East or West Midland English, if his home was elsewhere. And with the loss of its rank as a 'standard' speech, West Saxon seems to have taken a step downwards, not only in its position as superior to other dialects, but in the character of the language itself. In the same way, if we could imagine French substituted for German in Germany as the chief language of books and of educated speech, there can be no doubt that the talk of those who still spoke German would become much nearer to the speech of the lower classes, and would no longer mark its inflexions so fully and clearly. And this would gradually extend to the written language, as it did in England. If English was a vulgar language, though practically useful, it did not much matter how it was spoken. And writers were bound to follow the spoken language, however slowly and reluctantly. Still, the effect on Southern English was, for the most part, to pare down the terminations which marked gender, case, and so on, but not to annihilate them. It is wonderful how long they survived in some shape or other; and this shows that they were a most natural and necessary part of Southern English (or West Saxon) before the Conquest. We must look elsewhere for the main causes which finally did away with them, first in the East Midlands and in Northumbria, where they died out, all but a very few, much earlier than in the South and West. It will make what has been said clearer, if we take two specimens—one of an English sermon, written not very long before the Conquest, and the second of the same sermon, re-written so as to be easily understood in the second half of the twelfth century.

THE DAY OF PENTECOST

ÆLFRIC

A Homily written in the beginning of the Eleventh Century.

1 Fram ðam halgan easterlican dæge sind getealde fiftig daga
   From   the   holy   Easter-   day   are   counted   fifty days
to þysum dæge, and þes dæg is geháten Pentecostes, þæt is,
  to this day and this day   called   that is,
se fifteogoða dæg þære easterlican tide. Þes dæg wæs on
  the fiftieth day of-the Easter- season. This day was in
ðære ealdan ǽ gesett and gehalgod. God bebead Moyse on
  the old law appointed   hallowed.   ordered   in
5 Egypta-lande þæt hé and eall Israhela folc sceoldon
  the-Egyptians'-land   all   Israel's people should
offrian æt ælcum hiwisce Gode an lamb anes geares and
  offer from each household to-God a   of-one year
mearcian mid þam blode rode-tacn on heora gedyrum and
  mark with the blood sign-of-the-Cross   their door-posts
oferslegum, ða on ðære nihte ferde Godes engel, and acwealde
  lintels, then   that   went   angel,   killed
on ælcum huse ðæs Egyptiscan folces þæt frumcennyde
  in each house of-the Egyptian people the   first-born
10 cild and þæt leofoste. And Israhela folc ferde on ðære
  child and the dearest.   went
ylcan nihte of þam leodscipe, and God hí lædde ofer ða
  same   from the country,   them led   over the
Readan sǽ mid drium fotum.[1]
  Red Sea with dry feet.

[1] Thorpe, *Ælfric's Homilies*, 1844.

The same adapted so as to be intelligible in the second half of the Twelfth Century.

(All words substituted by Ælfric's adapter, and these only, are translated.)

1 [F]ram þan halie hester dei ! boð italde . fifti daʒa¹
             are
to þisse deie and þes dei is ihaten pentecostes þet is

þe fiftuða dei fram þan ester tid. þes dei wes on
      from *the*
þere alde laʒe iset and ihalden. God het Moyses on
  law   *kept.*   *ordered*
5 egipte londe þet he and al þet israelisce folc² sculden
           the Israelitish people
offrien of elchan hiwscipe gode an lomb of ane ʒeres and
  from   *of*
merki mid þan blode hore duren . and hore ouersleaht.
       their doors.   *lintel*
þa on þere ilke nihte ! iwende godes engel to and acwalde
   same   *went*   *to*
on elche huse of þam egiptissen folche þet frumkenede
     of *the*
10 childe and þet lefeste ! and þet israelisce folc ferde on þere
         the Israelitish
ilca nihte of þam londe.³ and god hom ledde ofer þa
      land.   *them*
rede se ! mid druʒe fotan.⁴

¹ ʒ = '(h)y' or something of the kind. It comes from the softening of a G, see p. 183.
² Inserted (not in Ælfric), þet he þider iled hefde ! þet heo.
       that he thither led had; that they.
³ Inserted (not in Ælfric), forðon muchele wawen þet hi þer iðoleden.
      for the great woes that they there endured.
⁴ Morris, *Old English Homilies*, 1867.

It is really hardly necessary to lay stress on the change which had taken place in the language. First of all, some of the words had become obsolete—a process which is always going on in all language—and so the man who re-wrote the sermon found it advisable to change *sind* into *boð*, and *æ* into the Danish *laʒe*. Secondly, we see the process of softening C and G, which began before the Conquest, in *child* for *cild*, *elchan* for *ælcum*, and in *halie* for *hálgan*, *dei* for *dæg*, *iset* for *gesett* (see p. 214, etc.), as well as the loss of the old diphthongs. Thirdly, there is the 'levelling' of the vowel of the inflexions in *offrien* for *offrian*, *sculden* for *sceoldon*, to an E with no very distinct sound, as in German terminations at the present day. And sometimes there is a still greater loss, as we see in *halie*, *þisse*, *alde*, and other words, as compared with their older form. *Merki*[1] and *tid* have lost their terminations altogether. *Hom* (older form *heom*) for *hi* shows us the dative of *he* 'crowding out' the accusative (p. 114). On the other hand, there are plenty of inflexions left; *þa* (accusative singular feminine) at the end of the piece, *þere* (dative singular feminine), '*þet* . . . *folc*,' because *folc* is neuter, 'mid *þan* blode' (dative singular neuter). So too most of the other terminations are 'levelled' in their vowel and clipped, but few are gone altogether. We shall see the same state of things in Layamon, who wrote somewhat later (p. 245). No doubt many of these changes had begun, at least in popular English, before the Conquest.[2]

[1] The I is not a part of the termination but a connecting vowel, as it is in *mearc-i-an*, compared with *find-an*. It still survives in many words in the Somersetshire dialect.

[2] The vowels of '*daʒa*,' 'fiftuða,' 'elchan,' and 'fotan,' are probably due to the scribe copying those words without fully reducing them to his own language. This is also plain in 'of ane ʒeres.' Mr. Sweet (*History of English Sounds*, p. 155) says: 'Many twelfth century texts, such as the Hatton Manuscript of the Gospels, Morris's Old English Homilies, show a mixture of Old English and Middle English forms, which is the result of copying from Old English originals, and only partially modernising them. Such texts do not represent any actual language.' But this specimen hardly seems to stand on a level with the Gospels of about 1160, where whole verses have hardly been altered at all. The forms in general, with some exceptions, such as those referred to in the note, are supported by Layamon, *e.g.*, who certainly had no English original to copy.

(2) We have seen (p. 119, etc.) that English was originally written as if it had been Latin. It now gradually got to be written as if it had been Norman-French. We must remember that there was no fixed way of spelling words, though every one who copied a book was, of course, inclined to copy its spelling as well, and every one who was used to writing naturally tended to spell words as he had been used to see them. But there were no fixed rules as there are now, and the object of every one who wrote down a word was to write it as it sounded. When, therefore, a scribe was used to writing Norman-French books, and had the sound of Norman-French and the look of its words in his head, he naturally wrote English words more or less as a Norman would do who knew no English. We will take some of these changes in spelling, choosing those only which have survived in Modern English. It must always be remembered that English vowels were still pronounced like Latin ('new,' or correct pronunciation), Italian, or roughly like German, though some of the consonants were getting softened; also, that in Norman-French J, CH, QU, and soft G were pronounced, not as in Modern French, but as in English at present.

Ū was changed to OU (or OW); thus—

hús	became	hous
þú	,,	thou
út	,,	out
cúþ	,,	(un-)couth
hú	,,	hou, and how

U was used between vowels for F, which in Old English expressed the sound both of F and V. Thus we have *œure* (*œfre* in Anglo-Saxon) and *Lauerd* (Anglo-Saxon *Hláford*). U and V[1] were employed both as vowels and consonants, and so we find such curious-looking words as *vp* (*up*), *vuel*

---

[1] V is often a vowel at the beginning of words. U is generally employed between two vowels. So it was even in the Authorised Version, in its original spelling, *e.g.* St. John vii. 53 : 'And *euery* man went *vnto* his owne house.' —Earle, *Philology of the English Tongue.*

(*uvel* = *evil*). UU, VV, or W were written for the Old English Runic letter ᚹ, as in *uuerse and uuerse* on p. 228. But W was also used as a vowel with the sound of U, as in *how*, for the older *hú*, as explained above. There is a good deal of confusion in these modes of spelling, but it was only necessary to make V exclusively a consonant and U exclusively a vowel to get something like our modern spelling in most of these words and in others like them.

As C was in French pronounced soft (like S)[1] before E and I, the Old English hard C was turned into K before those vowels, since otherwise the spelling would, on French principles, have suggested that it should be pronounced soft. So we get *king* for *cyning* or *cyng*, and *kene* for *céne*.

On the other hand, as the hard sound was just the same before other vowels (A, O, U), K is sometimes used for C before them as well, as in *selkouth*.

And now that English C was no longer regarded as a hard letter before E, such French words as *face*, *vice*, on being introduced into English, could and did keep their French spelling. And such words have infected the spelling of native English words, such as *mice*, *once*, *twice* (for *mýs*, *ánes*, *twies*).

CW was changed to QU, thus—

cwén	became	*queen*
cwic	,,	*quic*, or *quick*.

H in the middle of a word was 'guttural' in Old English, like German CH, as in *liht, niht*; Lowland Scotch or Modern Northumbrian *licht, nicht*. The same fact is shown by the word *next*, which is the superlative of *nigh*, and was in Anglo-Saxon written *néhst*,[2] and by *buxom*, originally *búhsom*—that is to say, *bow-some*, 'pliable,' 'obedient,' according to its earliest sense. Now the French H had not this guttural

---

[1] Or (at first) like TS. [2] So too *soik't* is Lancashire for *sighed*.

sound. So the words were re-spelt *liȝt*,[1] *niȝt*, or *light, night* (implying the same sound), and the latter spelling has prevailed.

TH is often written for the old Runic letter Þ, and gradually drove it out altogether. We sometimes see them appearing together, as in þe, *the*, þu, *thu*, on pp. 228, 229. Þ left a relic till quite recent times in *yᵉ* for *the*, since þ got to be written precisely like *y*.

The compound letter Æ, æ, was dropped, not being used in French, and E or AI was written for it (*æfre, euere, ever*; *wǽgen, wǽn, wain*). Besides AI a number of fresh combinations of vowels appear, representing changes of pronunciation, or, at first, specially French sounds. But the examples given above will be sufficient to mark the general character of the change in our spelling, and we must remember that these did not involve any change of pronunciation. It was merely that the scribe, being used to the look and sound of French, and regarding it as the more refined language, wrote down English sounds as if they had occurred in French words. If phonetic spelling were to come into use in English now, and we began to write it thus—

on Lindən, wen dhə sən wəz lou,
aol blədles lei dh' əntrodn snou,[2]

it would look as if a great change had taken place in English pronunciation at the end of the nineteenth century, whereas the change would be only in our way of marking the sounds in writing.[3] Changes in pronunciation did take place as well, and were probably in part due to the position and influence of French, but these will be discussed in the next chapter.

[1] ȝ, originally a form of G, in the middle of a word = GH, or German CH; a sound which may be represented in English by HY (Y as a consonant, of course).

[2] Skeat, *Principles of English Etymology*, First Series, p. 339.

[3] There is, of course, a question whether this spelling represents the average pronunciation. In the text it is assumed that it does. The change would also be greater, because we should be making up arrears. The spelling has been getting more and more unlike the sound since 1400.

It is plain that, as the spelling of English was altered to accommodate it to French, French words, such as *face, vice, pais,* or *pees* (peace), could come into the language without alteration in their spelling, as we shall see that they did.[1]

(3) French idioms made their way into the language.

This must necessarily have been the case. People who usually spoke French would naturally introduce French idioms into their English talk, just as schoolmasters not unfrequently see English idioms in (manuscript) Latin prose, and as an Englishman is inclined to write and say '*Il a sorti*' for the correct French idiom '*Il est sorti.*' Besides this, people who translated a book from French into English would copy some of its turns of expression, to some extent unconsciously. But these idioms are rather hard to detect with certainty. For different languages often have the same phrase or turn of expression, not because the one has borrowed it from the other, but because men's minds are more or less the same in different countries. But the following are tolerably certain examples of the borrowing of French idioms.[2]

The use of *of* (preposition with the dative) for the genitive case, just as *de* is used in French. Thus in the *Peterborough Chronicle* for the year 1091 we get—

    wære se cyng yrfe numa of eallon Normandig;
{ *were* / *should-be* } *the*   *heir*   *all*

while in the next sentence the older English form is retained—

    yrfe numa ealles Engla landes.

So in the entry for the year 1085 we have

    Cnut cyng of Den mearcan,

and

    Will'm Engla landes cyng.

---

[1] As has been said above, the sounds of the vowels were mostly much the same in the two languages. Where they were not, English had been adapted to French. Thus English U was written OU because U to a Frenchman meant (in many words) Devonshire U, or German ü.

[2] From Kington Oliphant's *Old and Middle English.*

These are early examples; later on, in the *Ormulum*, written before 1200 A.D. (see p. 231), we get *gife off Godd*, as well as *Godess gife, burrh off ʒerrsalem*, instead of the two nouns being in apposition, and a number of expressions like 'the hope of,' 'need of,' 'loss of,' just as in Modern English, where Anglo-Saxon would have used the genitive.[1] This change is, no doubt, partly due to the 'analytical' tendency—the tendency to use phrases for inflexions, which was present in the language itself, that is, in the Englishmen who spoke it— but it must have been helped by the influence of French. The result is that in Modern English the old genitive is hardly used except to mark the possessor of a thing (for instance, 'my brother's dog'), while an expression like 'my brother's love,'[2] meaning 'love for my brother,' strikes one as unusual. The old genitive is now not always used even to show the possessor; we can say either 'the gardener's boots,' or, 'the boots *of* the gardener.' French had a share in causing this phrase to be used for the termination in English, and such was also the general tendency of its influence.

Another French idiom is the use of *ye* (now *you*) for *thou* in addressing a superior, or in polite and formal speech, which comes to the same thing.[3] This distinction is tolerably well marked in Shakespeare, and *thou* is used familiarly, even so late as 1775, by Mrs. Malaprop in Sheridan's play of *The Rivals*.[4] We are now so universally polite that *thou* is never heard except in country districts, and from the Quakers, who often show how unnatural the 2nd person singular now is by mangling the grammar, as in 'th*ee* knows.'[5]

For me, or *for myself*, meaning 'as far as concerns myself,' in such expressions as, 'You may go where you like *for me*,'

---

[1] Kington Oliphant, *Old and Middle English*, p. 234.
[2] Shakespeare, *Richard III.*, I. iv. 229, 230.
[3] Precisely as in French to this day.
[4] III. iii. ; also in *Evelina*.
[5] But both 'mistakes' are supported by various English dialects (see pp. 85, 86).

or, '*For myself*, I shouldn't do it,' seems to be the French *pour moi*. 'The *most high* Prince' (for *the highest*) is also probably from the same source, 'le *plus haut*,' 'le Roi *plus Chrétien*.'

'They knew not what *to do*' (for 'what *they should do*') is a French expression—'ils ne savaient *que faire*.' So too the use of *for to* with the infinitive is Norman-French, *por à*; and this idiom is found not only in Chaucer but in the Prayer-Book Version of the Psalms (1539 A.D.), 'Thou shalt make room enough under me *for to go*,'[1] and in the Authorised Version of the Bible, '*For to do* whatsoever thy hand and thy counsel determined before to be done.'[2] The phrase is now no longer correct English, but it is constantly to be heard from uneducated people, as, for instance, 'I didn't go *for to do* it.' All these are now (or have been) regular English idioms. They are not to be found before the Conquest, but examples of them all may be found within the 150 years after it, and show how French was influencing English modes of expression.

(4) And the same is the case with French words, only to a far greater extent, though it was towards the end of the period when French was in the ascendant in England that these came in not as 'single spies but in battalions.' However, the advance-guard made its appearance early. *Tresor, canceler, carited, prisun, iustise, rente, privilegie, miracle*, all occur in the entry for the one year 1137 in a Chronicle which represents East Midland English very nearly as it was spoken at the time. Now, with some of these words it is possible to find some justification for their coming into English. In the case of *canceler*, which describes a new office, introduced from abroad, it was natural to use a foreign word. *Iustise*, as describing the firm and rather brutal execution of the law among proud and restless nobles, and between two nations still distinct, the justice which Henry I. did and which

[1] Psalm xviii. 36.   [2] Acts iv. 28.

Stephen did not do, might fitly have a new word to express what was more or less a new idea. The *privilegies* which the Abbot of Peterborough gained for his monastery from the Pope were something not quite new, but at least more commonly granted after the Conquest than before. *Carited* has something like its special ecclesiastical sense of 'charity,' as representing the *caritas* of the Latin Bible.[1] *Rente* too, which was commonly paid to a French-speaking landlord, might naturally be called by the word that he would give to it. But for 'treasure,' 'prison,' and 'miracle,' we certainly had words of our own—*hord* (now spelt *hoard*), *cweartern*, and *wundor*, meaning precisely the same as the French words. For these then, and for *pais* (peace), Anglo-Saxon *friþ*, in the entry for 1135 it is more difficult to account. But we saw before (pp. 141, 143) that certain Latin words had made their way into English, such as *munt, cuppe, fǽmne*, without any apparent necessity. The fact is that, when the speakers of French and the speakers of English were so much mixed as they were, and when so many of the one class knew something at least of the language of the other, French words crept into English—

(*a*) Because the man who usually spoke French brought in French words into his English almost unconsciously.[2]

(*b*) Because the speaker of English used them, 'for-to-be-more y-told-of.'

(*c*) Because those who wrote books, or translated them from French, though they would mostly use only words in common use, as they do at present, would also sometimes

---

[1] But *carited* is from a form *cariteit*. In many cases words have really been adopted owing to their occurring in the Latin Bible or Vulgate, but have received a Norman-French form to bring them into line with the numerous Norman-French words in our language. See Skeat, *Principles of English Etymology*, Second Series, p. 253, etc.

[2] So in *The Newcomes*, vol. i. chap. xxxviii., the German waiter says: 'Her Excellency the Frau Gräfinn von Kew is even now *absteiging*;' *absteigen* being a German word.

give currency to a word, or get it accepted through their use of it, just as Sir Walter Scott brought in *following*, and Coleridge *reliable*.

Thus we can account for the many cases in English where we have two words with the same meaning, one derived from French, and one pure English, such as—

French.	*English.*
flower	blossom
commence	begin
safe	sound
pray	beg
language	speech
perform	do
cure	heal
tempest	storm
people	folk
continue	go on

and a host of others. But in the case of many of the pairs the meaning of the two words was either to begin with slightly different, or one or other word has been 'specialised' since. There are some lines of Chaucer which illustrate this well—

A knyght ther was, and that a worthy man,
That fro the tymë þat he first bigan
To ryden out, he loued chiualrye
Trouthe and honour, fredom and curteisye.

Here, as Professor Earle points out, the French word *honour* had, in the context, the same sense as *truth*, and *courtesy* as *freedom*.[1] But it was only in one of its meanings, in a particular context, that *truth* was identical with *honour*, and *freedom* with *courtesy*. And the difference between them has grown so that the last two at least could not be used as synonyms at all. Now it is a distinct gain to a language to have words with different shades of meaning. Thus the French

---

[1] *Philology of the English Tongue*, p. 83. Mr. Earle remarks that 'I plight thee my *troth*' (another form of *truth*), in the Marriage Service, is the same as saying, 'I pledge thee my *honour*.'

word *pay* has taken part of the work of Anglo-Saxon *gildan*, and left it to mean only *yield*. *Easy* discharges part of the former duties of *líht* (light), and the language is all the clearer for the additional word. And it is no loss to have two words meaning the same thing. But it is, perhaps, a loss, so far as our sentiment is concerned, that we should have finally parted with so many native English words—a loss which was certain often to occur when two words, one from each language, were contending for the mastery. We should be puzzled now to replace such words as *voice, please, peace, praise* by native Teutonic words. However, there is no need to distress ourselves about the exchange. It may have been foolish of our ancestors to adopt foreign words without any necessity, but these Norman-French words are now thoroughly naturalised; they have been in the language for more than 500 years, even the very youngest of them. Thus they occupy a different position from words like *brusque, prestige, machine, corps, bouquet,* which carry the marks of their foreign origin in their pronunciation, though they are now unquestionably part of the English language. Such words as *naïve, nom-de-plume, contretemps,* and many others, of course hold a still more doubtful position; they have hardly emerged from the stage where they must be written (apologetically) in italics. But we must make up our minds to the fact that, as Normans came to form a part of the English nation, so Norman-French words are a most essential part of the English language. These words, of course, when they were introduced into English, followed the rules of English grammar, just as we say, 'he telegraph*ed*,' and 'omnibus*es*,' and were also compounded with English prefixes, suffixes, and words. So while the prefix *ge-* of the past participle still survived, though in a mutilated shape, we had such forms of the verb as 'we bieþ[1] i-*entred*,' 'i-*armed*,' and so on. So too we find *defend*-en (present infinitive); *amend*-eþ (2nd person

---

[1] = are.

plural imperative, see p. 85); *acord*-edun (3rd person plural past tense); *suffr*-eþ; *sacr*-id, and *acord*-ad (past participles); and very many other such forms are to be found. The substantives for their plural naturally took -*s*, just as most of them did in their native land, since this was also a common plural termination in English; thus we have *bestes, iuglurs, figures*, quite early.[1] The recruits thus gained for the plural in -*s* must have helped to make it the ordinary English plural, as it already was in the Northern dialect (see p. 134), with which other words, which originally had a different termination, were made to agree by imitation or 'analogy.'[2] So too we have compound words, 'hybrid' words, as they are called, like the Chimæra, with a body from the one language and a tail from the other; *piteous* ly, *sudden*-ly, *deceit*-ful, un-*pardoned*, are familiar examples of this. But we also used the imported French suffixes, such as -*ment*, -*able*, -*ous*, -*ess*, -*ance*, to form English words. For the suffixes were to be found in many French words used in English; it was easy to distinguish the suffix from the rest of the word, and yet no one thought whether either part was English or foreign, so that by imitation of the words already in the language these suffixes were fastened on to English words where needed. So we get not only *pave-ment*, but fulfil-*ment, abomin-able* and lov-*able*, *peril-ous* and slumbr-*ous, count-ess* and godd-*ess, repent-ance* and hindr-*ance*.[3]

And just as, after the Danes had begun to settle in England, fresh swarms kept coming over to join them, so it has been with French words, and with words passing to us from

---

[1] Adjectives borrowed from French (and occasionally others) also have a plural in -*s*, as in *places delitables, causes resonables*. This is about the only piece of pure French grammar to be found in English.

[2] But the Southern dialect also 'levels' old plurals (in -*u*, *e.g.*) under -*en*. Hence we find *schipen* (ships). We have taken *children* (Anglo-Saxon *cildru*, Lancashire *childer*) as one of the Southern contributions to 'standard' English; *housen* is still to be heard in Wiltshire; *kine* (like *children*) is a double plural, the Northern *kye* (Anglo-Saxon *cý*) being already a plural.

[3] In the above paragraph the part borrowed from *French* is in italics.

Latin through French. The fresh words which people tried to introduce found other words looking and sounding like them already in the language, and consequently we have never ceased to borrow words from French ever since the Norman Conquest.[1] The easy reception of words like *mobilise* is due to our having received such words as *baptise* in the period when Norman-French and English were spoken side by side in England.

It has already been said that it is towards the end of the period during which French was spoken in England that most French words were adopted into our language. They began to come in 'in battalions' towards the end of the thirteenth century. The reason of this was as follows.[2] We have seen that early in the thirteenth century the speaking and writing of French received a new impulse, from its being the Court language all over Europe. French was now regarded in England not in the least as 'a badge of conquest,' but as the more refined language.[3] In consequence of this fashion, though throughout the time between the Norman Conquest and Magna Charta (1215 A.D.) many books had been written in the various English dialects, yet between 1220 and 1280 hardly any English was written; although, of course, it continued to be spoken, and there were now in all probability hardly any Englishmen who could not speak it if they chose. Now we know, if we think for a moment, that the words used in ordinary conversation are a small part of any language. At the present day the words used in ordinary English talk are from 3000 to 5000 in number, while Milton uses about 8000, and Shakespeare 15,000.[4] When English

---

[1] But now, when a word is fully naturalised, we usually go by the spelling, and sound it like English. In the twelfth to fifteenth centuries, as we have seen, the two languages were sounded pretty much alike.

[2] See Kington Oliphant, *Old and Middle English*.

[3] That this view was not confined to England is shown in Brachet, *Historical French Grammar*, p. 21. See also Freeman's *Norman Conquest*, vol. v. pp. 529, 530.

[4] Whitney, *Language and its Study*, edited by Morris, pp. 18, 23.

books began to be written once more, about 1280 A.D., those English words which did not occur in ordinary talk were obsolete. Few people were alive whose memories reached back to the time when English was commonly written and read. But the gap had to be supplied somehow. The taste for making or using compound words, especially those formed with prepositions, which exists in German at the present day, had died out, particularly in the East Midland dialect; we may say that the power had been lost by disuse, just as people's brains lose their vigour if they are not used.[1] But there was a language still existing side by side with English, which had never ceased to be a literary language. Many words borrowed from it were already thoroughly naturalised. Many more must have been occasionally introduced into English talk. And it was not unnatural, therefore, that more should be brought in from the spoken and written French to fill the gaps,[2] especially as there was then no such gulf between English and French pronunciation as there is now.

As to the parts of our language in which French words occur, there are hardly any subjects which can be talked or written about without using some French words. Even in those classes of terms which are usually most permanent (see pp. 19, 20), we have *uncle, aunt, nephew, niece, cousin,* as names of relations, and, among numerals, *other* has been turned out of the language in favour of *second,* except only in the phrase 'every *other* day.' But there are certain classes of terms in which French words actually predominate.

[1] This is really a metaphor; any one could make any number of compound English words now, but others would not adopt them, so that it would be useless. Compound words are strange to us, and 'do not sound right.' So the verbs *outspeak, outstep, instrike,* in Browning's *Hervé Riel,* draw our attention at once. *To*-break (Judges ix. 53) is a solitary survivor of the words formed with this prefix which once existed, and the formation is so unfamiliar that very few understand the word, which means 'break in pieces,' or 'smash.'

[2] Orm, about 1200 A.D., has only four or five French words in the whole of his very long poem. Robert of Gloucester, about 1300 A.D., has 100 in his first 500 verses. Robert Mannyng, about 1340 A.D., has 170 in the same number of lines. See Koch, *Historische Grammatik der Englischen Sprache.*

Effects of Norman Conquest upon English

(1) In titles, as is natural.

Here *King* and *Queen* are native English, but *sovereign, royal, royalty* are French; so too are *prince* and *princess*. *Knight* and *lady* are pure English; *earl* is English, though with its meaning altered by the Danish use of its sister-word *jarl*. But *countess* is French, and so are *duke, marquis, viscount, baron,* with their feminine forms, except *marchioness*;[1] so too is *esquire*. *Gentleman* is half French, half English; *mayor* is French; *sheriff* and *alderman* English; *clerk* and *bailiff* are French, while *beadle* is English.

So too with the terms of government. *Parliament* and *Privy Council* are French. *Lords* is an English word, but its synonym *peers* is French. So is also *Commons*. And in a most important part of the business of government, the administration of justice, we find (as we should expect from the law courts having used French so long) only a few words, such as *witness*, which are native English. *Law* is Danish, but *assizes, circuit, court, justice, judge, jury, defendant, prisoner, counsel, verdict, sentence*, are all French. And sometimes terms of law have so entirely kept their French shape that they can be recognised at a glance, as in *peine forte et dure*, and *trespass damage feasant (faisant)*.

(2) The terms of war are mostly French. This is true of words brought in in more modern times, as well as of words of earlier introduction. In the older class *fortress, fort, tower, moat, battlement, portcullis, warrior, lance*, are French, while the arms which ordinary soldiers would use have mostly English names, such as *bow, arrow, spear, sword, shield*. *Wall* was borrowed from Latin at a very early period (see p. 140), *gate* is a purely native word. But the improvements in the art of war, which were largely concerned with the fortification of castles, brought their own names with them from abroad.

In the same way in later times we have gone on borrowing military terms. For we have not been great inventors in this

---

[1] Taken straight from Latin *marchionissa*.

field, though we have shown some capacity for using the inventions. So *general, colonel, captain, sergeant, corporal, army, corps, regiment, battalion, camp, cannon, musket, carbine, bayonet, grenade, bomb*, have all come to us from French, though some of these words were borrowed by the French themselves from the Spaniards[1] or from the Italians,[2] both of which nations were at certain periods great in the art of war.

(3) Architecture is full of French words.

Edward the Confessor got foreign workmen to build the original Westminster Abbey, and later on Gothic architecture came to us from France. With the foreign style and workmen came foreign terms. *Wall*, as we have seen, and also *tile* are words borrowed from Latin at an early period; *stone* is pure English, and *window* Danish; but *arch, porch, pillar, brick, mortar, chisel, plumb, plummet, trowel, mason*, are all French.

(4) The Doctor's art is full of words borrowed from French. Many of the clergy studied it, who would be obliged to know some French (as also would the laymen who were doctors) for the purposes of their profession. And if the doctors knew both languages, French was the more 'refined' language to use, and the names of diseases especially sound brutal in the 'vulgar' tongue. The description of the Doctor in the Prologue to the *Canterbury Tales* is full of words which are French in form, such as *phisik, surgerye, pacient, practisour, humour, drogges* (drugs), *letuaries* (electuaries), *diete, pestilence, cordial*.[3]

(5) It is usually said that there are many French words in English connected with 'the chase.' And so no doubt there ought to be, considering the fondness of the Normans for that amusement and the pains taken by the upper classes, their descendants or successors who spoke French, to keep it to themselves. But though such words were once very numerous,

[1] e.g. *grenade*.   [2] e.g. *colonel*.
[3] Derived from Latin, as are the great mass of French words; but some of them (*phisik, surgerye*, e.g.) come ultimately from Greek.

Effects of Norman Conquest upon English 195

the character of sport has altered so much within the last three centuries that very many of them have become obsolete (like the expression 'the chase' referred to above); and the new sporting terms are mostly English. The changes in sport and in its terms are due mainly to the substitution of shooting for hawking, and to a change in the whole character of hunting.

Many of the words for the different kinds of hawks—*falcon, peregrine, tercel, merlin*—are French, and their *jesses, lures,* and *mews* also have French names. From the same language come the names for many of the birds at which they were flown, such as *heron, partridge, pheasant.* It is correct to speak of a *covey* (*couvée*, Old French *covee,* or brood) of partridges, and a *bevy* of quails. Though, on the other hand, some of the technical terms of hawking, such as *pitch,*[1] *stoop*, are not French, the number of French words connected with the sport was (and is) very large.

With the old-fashioned form of stag-hunting are connected such words as *quarry* (from *curée*, originally part of a slain animal given to the hounds),[2] *mort*, the notes on the bugle sounded when the deer was killed, and many others. *Kennel* is also Norman-French.[2] Many words connected with horses are also French, such as *amble, trot, gallop,* and *stable,* though horses were of course not exclusively used for hunting. But the proportion of French words to English in the technical terms of shooting is not greater than it is in the English language in general, and the terms used in fox-hunting, such as *hound, hunt, meet, find, run, death,* 'ware wheat,' are almost exclusively English. The reason is that shooting, and hunting in its modern form, are of much later invention than the time when speakers of French monopolised sport. As if to remind

---

[1] *e.g.* These growing feathers pluck'd from Cæsar's wing
Will make him fly an ordinary *pitch.*
Julius Cæsar, I. i. 77, 78.
It seems to be from this technical term that expressions like 'to reach such a *pitch*' are derived. [2] Skeat, *Etymological Dictionary.*

us of the old state of things, the word *battue* has come into English within the last fifty years, though it has a rival in the half-English word *cover(t)-shooting*. As was said above, *chase* is nearly obsolete as a sporting term. We speak of a *steeple-chase* and a *paper-chase*, but no longer of a *fox-chase* as our ancestors did.

(6) Our greatest loss at the time when English was borrowing so largely from French was in dropping our native religious terms, and adopting foreign words instead of them, whether these were French or borrowed direct from Latin. As long as a word is merely a name to mark a simple thing, it does not much matter whether a division of the country, for instance, is called *shire* (English), or *county* (French), whether its governor is called *earl* or *count*. But when we come to words for ideas difficult to grasp, it is a distinct gain that the word should of itself say what it means, without our having to learn its sense as in a foreign language. It is fortunate that we borrowed the verb *save* from French, as well as its derivative *Saviour*. Otherwise the latter word could not carry its meaning with it, as *Hǽlend*, the *Healer*, necessarily did. So *Redeemer* to any one ignorant of Latin conveys no distinct meaning unless he has been specially taught it, whereas *Again-buyer*[1] has its meaning written on its face. The same is the advantage of *godspellere* over *evangelist*, of *fullian*[2] (to wash, or clean) over *baptize*, of *þrynnes*[3] (*threeness*) over Trinity.

Even in 1340 (see p. 263) it was possible to have the Apostles' Creed in English without any foreign words except *general*, in *general-liche*, and one or two which had been part of the language for centuries, *y-pyned* (Latin *pœna*) and *cherche* (κυριακόν). But it was not very unnatural that the better educated among the clergy, who wrote the religious books, should bring in French and Latin words.

---

[1] Kington Oliphant, *Old and Middle English*, p. 526.
[2] Formed from Latin *fullo*, a fuller or cleaner of cloth.
[3] There is a book written in the Southern Dialect, in 1340, called *Ayenbite (Again-bite) of Inwyt*. We should now have to say 'Remorse of Conscience.'

They were obliged to know French, if only to hear the confessions of a large part of their flock. They were not above the idea that there was a certain refinement in using French words, and solemnity in using Latin ones. The use of the Latin Bible drew their language in the same direction, and some words, such as *scribe* for *writere*, were borrowed directly from it. And those who first took to using foreign religious terms set the fashion to the rest. Moreover, such ideas as *repentance, propitiation, regeneration*, could plainly not be expressed in English except by compound words, and these were going out of use soon after 1200, especially in the East Midlands, whence, for the most part, our modern 'standard' English comes. Fashion was against them; for some reason or another they 'did not sound well.' If, then, compound English words were not to be tolerated, it was necessary to borrow the words ready-made from French or Latin. These had the advantage of sounding learned and solemn; the disadvantage that they were, in themselves, unintelligible. Thus, though *húsel*, or, as it was now spelt in the French manner, *housel*, being a simple word, lived on for a long time, both as substantive and verb, and is used so late as by Shakespeare, its compounds *húsel-bearn, húsel-disc, húsel-gang*, were disused in favour of foreign words, and of phrases, and thus we now use instead of them *communicant, paten, going to the Communion.*

Such are some of the classes of words in which the inroad of French has been largest. But it extends more or less to the whole of the language, except the definite and indefinite articles (*the, a, an*), the pronouns, and the auxiliary verbs (*be, have, may, shall*, and so on). In our ordinary talk we could hardly get on without such words as *pay, money, wages, habit, beauty, part.* Agriculture is tolerably free. It has already been noticed by Trench[1] that the words for the live animals

---

[1] *Study of Words*, twelfth edition, pp. 98-100. Quoted in Earle, *Philology of the English Tongue.*

(which are eventually eaten) are pure English, but that, when they are served up at table, *ox* becomes *beef*; *sheep*, *mutton*; *pig*, *pork*; and *calf*, *veal*. This can hardly be altogether due to the fact that the English serf or villein fed them, and the French-speaking landowner ate them. Many persons who spoke English habitually must have been in a position to eat meat. It is rather that the way of speaking at table followed the custom of the upper classes. It did not matter what the animal was called in the field or the farmyard. At table it would have been 'vulgar' to call the meat by its English name.

As to the ultimate source of these French words, most of them are from Latin, since the bulk of the French language is derived from 'Low' or popular Latin. Some, such as many of the medical terms used in the description of Chaucer's Doctor, came to Latin from Greek. But French contains also many Teutonic words, which the Franks brought into the language, just as the Normans brought French words into English. And some of these found sister-words already in English, so that it is impossible in some cases to say whether the French term would seem to those who adopted it into English to be a new word, or merely a different pronunciation or form of a word which they already had.[1] In some cases we still have both forms, as—

English.	*French.*
rich	riches (richesse)
hard	hardy
(other-)wise	guise
ward	guard
mark, march	marqu-(is)

Sometimes a word came back through French which was a still more distant relation of a corresponding English word. Thus the French *neveu* is derived from Latin *nepos*, and,

---

[1] So we saw (p. 143) that Old English *calic* gave way to the French form *chalice*, as *regol* did to *reule*, or *riule* (rule). These are ultimately from Latin *calic(-em)* and *regul(-am)*, respectively.

according to Grimm's Law, *nepos* is the same word as Anglo-Saxon *nefa*. The French form of this word finally prevailed.[1]

Now the only sound way to find out the derivation of a word is to trace its history carefully, or to consult the books of those who have done so. Still, we shall in most cases be right if, when we find the same identical word both in English and French, we consider that English is the borrower, for French has borrowed comparatively very few words from English, mostly in modern times.[2] But both may have borrowed the word independently from Latin. In many cases, however, it is quite clear that English has taken the word from French, and not directly from Latin, by the form of the word. Thus *voice* is plainly derived from Anglo-French *voice* and not from *vox*; honour from Anglo-French *honour*, as the U shows, and not from Latin *honor*. So too *estate* cannot be taken straight from Latin *statum*,[3] but comes from Norman-French *estat*, the E having been put on at the beginning to make the word easier to say, ST being to a Frenchman or Norman a hard combination of letters to pronounce at once. In the same way *esquire* comes ultimately from *scutarium* (= shield-bearer), but directly from Old French *escuyer*. So too *hour, honest* still retain a trace of their French origin by their H being dropped, as in French, and *herb, hospital, humble,* and *humour* were, till almost our own time, pronounced in the same way.[4] But the history of many words

---

[1] We must always remember that the resemblance of an English to a French word is in some cases due merely to the fact that Latin and Teutonic are related. Thus *one* is not derived from French *un*, Latin *unus*, since (besides other reasons) its earlier form is *án* (Lowland Scotch *ane*). Both are derived from a word in the Indo-European language (see p. 137).

[2] Connected with politics, *e.g. budget, bill*; industrial improvements, *e.g. drainage, wagon, rail*; sporting-terms, *e.g. turf, jockey, boxe, dogue.*—Brachet, *Historical French Grammar*, translated by Kitchin, p. 39. In a recent French work on Training and Training Stables the boys employed are spoken of as *les lads*.

[3] French substantives are nearly always taken from the Latin *accusative*, not from the nominative.

[4] The words in which the H was dropped early are words derived from Latin, in which language the H was weak to begin with.

has been made more difficult to trace by changes in spelling, and especially by the anxiety of people in the sixteenth century to mark the ultimate source of the word by the spelling; as, for instance, to show that *doubt* is derived from *dubito*. If the word were spelt *doute* (as it used to be) and as it is pronounced, without the B, it would be clear that the word is taken from French (as it is), and it would not be hard to trace it further to Latin. So *fault*[1] was *faute*; *debt*, *dette*, both in French and English,[2] and our English words are not derived directly from *fallo* and *debitum*. In trying to mark the ultimate source of the words these improvers of our spelling have obscured their history.

The form in which French words were adopted into English shows that we were right in saying that English vowels were still pronounced in general like those in Italian or Latin ('new' pronunciation). If *hound* (English) and *found-our* (Anglo-French *found-our*) were spelt in the same way, it was because they were pronounced alike, with OU as in *uncouth*. If *face* was adopted into English without change, it was because A suggested to an Englishman the sound which it now has in *are*, *father*. For those who wrote then had no objection to changing the spelling of a word to express its sound, and French words were taken into English from a living language spoken in the country.[3] We have already seen that English spelling had been adapted to French models, and this again proves what English pronunciation was like. *Ût* would not have been spelt *out*, for the benefit of persons used to French, if it was to give them a totally wrong idea of the sound. The rhymes prove the same thing; in the extract from Chaucer

---

[1] Here the spelling has at last influenced the sound as well. But in Pope, e.g. *Essay on Criticism*, ll. 169, 170, *faults* rhymes to *thoughts*.

[2] Our re-spelling was mainly copied from a reform (?) of French spelling in the sixteenth century, which did not last.

[3] Of course there is the alternative that French vowels were then pronounced as English vowels are now. Among other reasons why this is impossible there is the fact that the sister-languages derived from Latin (Italian, Spanish, and so on) agree in the main with French in the pronunciation of their vowels.—Skeat, *Principles of English Etymology*, Second Series, p. 133, etc.

Effects of Norman Conquest upon English

(p. 270, ll. 5, 6) the English word *aboute* rhymes to the French word *doute*. So too (ll. 11, 12) the English *lyte* rhymes to the French *visyte*. The standard of spelling was French, and therefore these words were pronounced as 'viseete' and 'leete' would be pronounced in English now. Thus the Lancashire pronunciation *leet* (light), *neet* (night), *deein'* (dying), as well as the Somersetshire *rhine* ('reen'), and the sound in *Ouse* and un*couth* are relics of the old sound of English vowels.

A word or two must finally be said about the accent of French words in English;[1] the principles on which our native words have been accented have hardly varied from the earliest times. Now in French of the present day, as it is usually pronounced by Frenchmen, it is exceedingly hard to detect an accent on any one syllable more than on another. But this was certainly not the case in the earliest French, while that language was forming itself out of popular Latin, for the Latin accent always preserved the syllable on which it fell, however the others might be clipped, as in '*mo*bilis,' '*meu*ble'; '*cal'*dus,' *chaud*; 'na*vi*gare,' 'na*ger*.' And the rule given for the accent in Modern French is that all words are accented on the last syllable, except when this syllable is mute E, when it goes back one place, and thus it agrees, in words naturally formed,[2] with the Latin accent out of which it sprang. Only, as has been said, the accent is now so slight that it can scarcely be heard. But since it was strong enough to give its character to the language while it was forming, and retained its full power till the eleventh century, and since it is still the accent of French words so far as they possess one, it is only reasonable to suppose that in the eleventh century, when Norman-French was brought into English, it was much more distinctly heard than it is at present.[3]

---

[1] Brachet, *Historical French Grammar*, translated by Kitchin. The accented syllable will be for the rest of this chapter in italics.

[2] Words like '*mobile*,' '*portique*' (Latin '*porticus*'), were introduced much later from Latin by learned men, who paid no regard to the Latin accent.

[3] Germans in pronouncing French often give the correct accent (according to the above rule) very distinctly, *e.g.* 'Avez-vous quelque chose à décla*rer*?'

Accordingly French words in English, for a considerable time after the date of their introduction into our language, mostly kept the French accent, as we can easily see when they occur in poetry. So in Chaucer's Prologue to the *Canterbury Tales*, written shortly before 1400 A.D., we find, for instance—

> And bathed every veyne in swich licour,
> Of which vertu engendred is the flour.[1]

But now, as we know, these words are pronounced '*virtue*,' '*liquor*.'[2] Why has the accent changed?

The rule of English as regards the accent is roughly to throw it back as far as possible,[3] or farther, according to the notions of a German trying to learn the language. Such words as '*com*fortable,' '*ap*plicable,' are strong instances of the tendency. These are not, of course, native words, but they are thoroughly naturalised with the English accent. On the other hand, in *The Nut-brown Maid* (about 1500), we still find the French accent in 'comfortable' and 'variable.'

> Here may ye see that wymen be in loue meke, kinde, and stable,
> Late neuer man repreue them than, or calle them variable ;
> But rather prey god that we may to them be comfortable.[4]

The fact is, that French words introduced into English were at first pronounced with the French accent, which, as-

'La grande nation.' They do this, no doubt, partly from conscientiously exaggerating the rule which they have been taught, partly because accents in German are very distinctly pronounced. But their pronunciation will probably give us a correct idea of the way in which French accents were formerly sounded.

[1] Lines 3, 4, as edited by Morris and Skeat.

[2] '*Liqueur*,' adopted into English from Modern French, still has the French accent.

[3] In compound words, especially verbs or participles, the accent often falls on the main part of the word, and not on the adverb prefixed, as in 'ever*last*ing,' 'fore*go*ing,' 'out*do*.' In substantives, on the other hand, it often falls on the prefix, *e.g.* '*ever*green,' '*fore*mast,' '*out*come.' This distinction is as old as Anglo-Saxon, and was in early times more regularly applied. But if the first part is a substantive, this usually takes the accent, as in '*awe*-inspiring,' '*soap*-boiler.' There are, of course, rules about the accent in detail, but practically the rough rule given in the text carries us a long way.

[4] Skeat's *Specimens of English Literature*, 1394 A.D.—1579 A.D., p. 107. U is to be read as V ; see above, p. 181.

we saw, comes as nearly as possible at the end of the word. But the English accent made its way even into Anglo-French. And still more when words had been adopted into English, since no one thinks of the derivation of a word when he is using it, there was a constant tendency to pronounce them like ordinary English words, with the accent thrown back. Some people with correct ears liked to hear the word pronounced as they had been used to hear it, with the French accent; others tended naturally to copy the ordinary sound of English words, to give the word the English accent by 'analogy.' Of these conflicting tendencies the last mostly prevailed, either soon or in the course of centuries. But numerous words still keep the French accent, such as 'di*vine*,' 'pay*ee*,' 're*ply*,' 'ac*cord*,' 'o*blige*,' though these have been naturalised for more than five centuries.[1]

Even in Chaucer a very large number of French words have already acquired the English accent, such as '*pro*cesse,' '*mor*tal,' '*gen*til,' '*se*soun,' and yet we cannot read far into the *Canterbury Tales* without coming across such lines as—

   So priketh hem na*ture* in hir co*rages*—
   Than longen folk to goon on pilgri*mages*;[2]

or—

   Me thinketh it acordaunt to re*soun*,
   To tellë 3ow al the condici*oun*.[3]

And there is no mistake about the lesson to be learnt from Chaucer's lines, for his metre is very accurate and musical, if only it is correctly read, which means for the most part pronouncing such final E's as are the relics of

[1] Of course the verbs could not keep the French accent exactly, where it fell on the termination, as in the infinitive. For French verbs when taken into English were conjugated as English verbs. Thus, 'acor*der*' became 'a*cor*den'; the English termination could not take the accent, which, however, at first remained as near as possible to the end of the word. Words of later introduction keep the French accent more than the earlier ones, such words, *e.g.*, as 'dra*goon*,' 'ca*det*,' 'fa*tigue*,' 'ha*rangue*.'

[2] *Hir* = their, 'co*rage*' = heart, now '*cour*age,' with the later French spelling and English accent, and an altered sense.—*Prologue*, ll. 11, 12.

[3] *Prologue*, ll. 37, 38.

Old English terminations. Sometimes the same word is accented both ways in different passages, since, no dcubt, usage varied. The two tendencies were still fighting it out, and the accent of the word was not yet fixed (just as some people now say 'oc*to*pus,' and some '*oct*opus'), so that neither the English nor the French way of accenting it would sound strange. Thus we have seen 'ver*tu*' accented on the last syllable, but we also have the line—

>Sowninge in moral *v*ertu was his speche.[1]

Thus too we get in one place—

>And elles certein werë thei to blame.
>It is ful fair to been y-clept ma*d*ame.[2]

And in another—

>And she was cleped *m*adame Eglentyne.[3]

So too there is '*b*ataille' and 'bata*i*lle,' '*te*mpest' and 'tem*pest*,' '*p*itous' and 'pit*ous*' (now *p*iteous), and other examples of the accent varying.

Thus too we find in Spenser, in Shakespeare occasionally, and in Milton many words retaining their old French accent, which have wholly lost it now. In fact, this explains the metre of many lines in these poets where it seems strange to us, of such lines as—

>And all sixe brethren, borne of one pa*re*nt.[4]

>Throwne out by angry Jove in his ven*ge*ance.[5]

>Is it upon re*c*ord, or else reported
>Successively from age to age he built it?[6]

>By policy and long pro*c*ess of time.[7]

>Beyond all past example and fu*ture*.[8]

---

[1] *Prologue*, l. 307.
[2] *Ibid.*, ll. 375, 376.
[3] *Ibid.*, l. 121.
[4] Spenser, *Faery Queene*, III. i. 44.
[5] *Ibid.*, IV. vi. 14.
[6] Shakespeare, *Richard III.*, III. i. 72, 73.
[7] Milton, *Paradise Lost*, II. 297.
[8] *Ibid.*, X. 840.

And even in Scott, in an imitation of an old ballad—

> There are twenty of Roslin's barons bold,
> Lie buried within that proud cha*pelle*.

In many of these later instances the poets are, no doubt, consciously introducing an old-fashioned pronunciation, as is the way of poets, and not using the pronunciation of their own time. But we have words, just like some of those quoted above, which still keep their French accent. Such words as 'ad*vice*,' 'de*gree*,' 'ex*cess*,' 'ac*cord*,' as well as 'se*cure*,' and 'ma*ture*,' borrowed from Latin, keep the Latin accent, which, as we saw, the French language retained.[1] It is often impossible to say why, among similar words, some have changed their accent and some have not.

It is curious that in many cases this variety of accent distinguishes substantives from verbs which are exactly like them apart from the accent. Thus *dis*count is a substantive, but a banker dis*counts* a bill. So we re*cord* an event (keeping the French accent which, as we have seen, the substantive also has in Shakespeare), but the result is a *re*cord of what happened. Missionaries con*vert* the heathen and make *con*verts of them. A burglar is con*victed*, and becomes a *con*vict.[2] This may, perhaps, be partly explained by a rule which we find in Old English, by which many compound substantives were accented on the prefix, while the corresponding verbs have the accent on the main part of the word.[3] So we still say, 'to out*do*,' and 'the *out*come.' But a reason which has doubtless had more to do with causing the distinction in French or Latin words is this: even in the period before our inflexions were almost annihilated, those of the

---

[1] So too 'as*pect*,' 'ab*ject*,' in Shakespeare keep the Latin accent ('as*pect*us,' 'ab*ject*us').

[2] Some of these words come to us straight from Latin. But this makes no practical difference, since the French accent is, as we have seen, the Latin one. The rules for the two are not the same, but practically produce the same result.

[3] Sweet, *History of English Sounds*, p. 105, and Schipper, *Englische Metrik*. See above, p. 202, note.

verb were on the whole heavier than those of the substantive. And since about 1500 the difference has been still greater in favour of the terminations of the verb, -*ing*, and in some cases -*ed*, being fully pronounced, while the substantive had usually no inflexion beyond a mere -*s*, which, of course, did not make an extra syllable. Now it is plain that if the verb, at first 'con*vert*-en,' then 'con*vert*,' started with the accent on the second syllable (as it would do [1]), the forms 'con*vert*-ed,' 'con*vert*-ing,' would tend to keep it near the end of the verb in those forms, and, of course, no one would divorce parts of the same verb by accenting them in different ways; analogy would forbid this. On the other hand, '*con*vert' (the substantive) easily followed the accentuation of pure English two-syllabled words, such as '*gir*dle' and '*spi*der.' [2]

Besides, the distinction is so useful practically that it must have found ready acceptance, though some words, such as '*account*,' 're*pair*,' 're*lease*' (both verb and substantive), have never been brought under the rule.[3]

From what has been said above, it is quite plain that the English accent is a very strong and masterful thing. And it has not only prevailed over the foreign accent, as we have seen, in many French words, but it has also affected the pronunciation of a mass of words, both English and French, in various ways. Sometimes this change is marked in the spelling, sometimes not, according as the alteration took place before or after our spelling became fixed. In this influence on the form of words it is like the Latin accent, which has to a very large extent determined the form of words in French. For instance, a word in passing from Low Latin to French [4] not only (as a rule) lost its last syllable (which was unaccented), as in '*clav*(em),' 'clef'; '*fact*(um),' 'fait,' but also,

[1] See p. 203, note, p. 205, note.
[2] Skeat, *Principles of English Etymology*, Second Series, p. 60.
[3] It is, of course, possible for the substantive to infect the verb if it is older, or in more common use.
[4] The accent in Low Latin was generally the same as in classical Latin, but not quite always.

Effects of Norman Conquest upon English

if a word was accented on the last syllable but two in Latin, the vowel after this always disappeared, as in '*hu*milem,' '*hu*mle' or '*u*mble'; '*cu*bitum,' '*cou*de.' And other unaccented syllables fall out according to other rules. The work of the English accent[1] has been very similar, only that while the accent in French has long since spent its force, and is now almost inaudible, the English accent has kept its full vigour from the earliest times down to the present day. The English accented syllable seems to be always trying to take up the whole life of the word. The syllables, both before and after it, tend to become obscured and even to disappear, though, as has been said before, if this has happened since our spelling has become more or less fixed, the word as written does not show it; we must think of its pronunciation.

Thus, to begin with, some words have lost their first syllable when this has been unaccented. 'E*pi*scop(us)' has become '*bi*scop' and '*bi*shop,' and 'e*pi*stol(a)' and 'a*po*stol(us)' are to be found in Anglo-Saxon as '*pi*stol' and '*po*stol' respectively, though from the French and Latin forms the two last have now been restored to their correct Latin shape. Thus too 'ger*é*fa' has become *reeve*, and 'ened-*ra*ke' (duck-king) is now *drake*. In the same way many Norman-French words have lost their first and unaccented syllable. In a number of cases the fuller form has been preserved as well, so that we can easily see what has happened. Thus there is *mend* and '*a*mend,' *spy* and 'e*spy*,' '*sa*mple' and 'en*sa*mple.'

Where the accent falls on the first syllable (according to the usual English rule), it has often led to the loss of a following syllable or syllables. Thus '*mó*naðͦ' was sometimes written *món*ðͦ, even before the Conquest, and '*mu*nec' is now *monk*. In much the same way, among the French words which had taken the English accent, '*cha*pelein' became '*cha*plain'; '*chi*menee,' '*chi*mney'; and '*pe*rilus,' '*pa*rlous.'

[1] It would, perhaps, be more correct to say, 'the main accent.' There is a secondary accent in long words, as *e.g.* on the first syllable of 'unpatriotic'; but, except in poetry, it may be left out of the account.

So we now clip '*medicine*,' '*venison*,' into '*med'*cine,' '*ven'*son,' though the spelling may not be altered. And the same thing has happened in such proper names as Gloucester ('Glo'ster'). So too in '*cox*swain,' '*boat*swain,' '*cup*board' ('cox'n,' 'bo's'n,' 'cubbud'), the last syllable has been weakened as much as it could be without being lost altogether. And, in general, the vowels following the accented syllable have very often been thus weakened, as in '*de*cade,' '*magi*strate.' In '*com*fortable,' for instance, the accented syllable is the only one that is quite distinctly heard as written. The word is generally not much more than '*comf't'b'l*.' And if we think of it, this powerful English accent must have had a great influence in sapping the inflexions. If it can have made the following syllables indistinct in '*comf*ortable' and '*cup*board,' it must have helped to make the -*a*, and -*u*, and -*an* of Anglo-Saxon sink to the indistinct -*e* and -*en*, as in '*nama*,' '*namĕ*'; '*scipu*,' '*scipe*'; '*oxan*,' '*oxen*.' If it could wipe out whole syllables, changing '*mold*warp' into *mole*, it must have helped to throw off the terminations altogether, as with '*nama*,' '*namĕ*,' '*nam*(e).' So the Latin accent did in French as we have seen. And at the present day in German, a language in which the accent is strong, it is sometimes very hard to hear whether the -*e* is pronounced or not, as in 'Ich neh*me*,' 'der *Kna*be'; and thus this -*e* is constantly clipped in German verse. Again, in the same way as the English accent has reduced '*munec*' to one syllable, *monk*, so it has helped to make '*wordĕs*' into *words*, '*comĕs*' into *com(e)s*, and '*pourĕd*' into *pour'd*. There were other causes at work, as we have seen and shall see, which made these changes happen when they did. But the English accent must have been throughout their most useful ally.[1]

[1] See p. 180, etc.

For the accent in English, see Skeat, *Principles of English Etymology*, First and Second Series; and Koch, *Historische Grammatik*. For general information upon the influence of French on English, see Skeat, *Principles of English Etymology*, Second Series, and Earle, *Philology of the English Tongue*.

CHAPTER XV

CHANGES IN THE SOUNDS OF ENGLISH

Changes in English sounds—Not directly traceable to French influence—Changes of long A—of C—of SC—of G—ȝ and þ lost.[1]

THERE were other changes going on in the English language, most of which at any rate were only remotely due to the influence of those who spoke French. We have already seen (p. 177, etc.) that the Norman Conquest put on the hands of the clock, so to speak, by clearing away the obstacles to changes in the inflexions—that is to say, by doing away with a 'standard' dialect of English, and an English-speaking upper class who were careful how they talked, just as educated people are careful now. For the same reason the changes which took place in the sounds of English came on faster, at all events, than if there had been no Norman Conquest. It is probable too that some of these changes may have been helped on by imitation of the sounds of French words, which, of course, were constantly to be heard. But, on the whole, it seems that they would mostly have occurred sooner or later in any case.

Now these changes in sounds are not an easy subject to deal with. First of all, we must be quite sure what the letters mean. For instance, *-ment* implies very different sounds in English and Modern French respectively; and, as

[1] Sweet, *History of English Sounds*. Skeat, *Principles of English Etymology*, First Series, and *Man of Lawes Tale*.

P

we have already seen, the English vowels before the Norman Conquest, and for centuries after it, did not represent the same sounds as they do now. Secondly, there are questions about some of the sounds which have not yet been settled with certainty. And thirdly, vowels are so liable to be affected by the consonants which come just before and just after them (especially R), that the rules about their changes leave a considerable number of exceptions. So that instead of attempting to describe all the changes which took place in English sounds between 1066 and 1400, only four sets will be taken as a sample—namely, the changes of long A (Old English or Anglo-Saxon A'), C, SC, and G. Fortunately, spelling was still 'phonetic'; those who wrote tried to represent the sounds by their spelling, so that the letters nearly always changed with the sounds. There has been a greater shifting of English sounds since 1400 than between 1066 and 1400, and yet the changes are not obvious, since the spelling has remained to such a large extent unaltered.

And first, as to the fact that the sounds really did change. Look at the extract from the Gospels in Anglo-Saxon on p. 154. There we find *sower* written *sáwere*, and *sooth*, *good* appearing as *sóþ* (in *sóþ-lice*), and *gód*. *Shrunk* was then (*for*)*scruncon*, and *fowls*, *fuglas*. These are specimens of the changes about which something will now be said.

(1) Old English Á or Ā was written O or OO in Middle English, with the sound of OA in *broad*, *roar*.

Try the experiment of saying A (as in *are*), then OA, as in *broad*, and then O. It will be found that OA comes half-way between the other two.[1] We sometimes, in the country, hear 'roäd,' 'oäts,' pronounced almost as two syllables, and they then come very near the sound of OA in *broad*, which proves the same thing. Even in Old English we find O written for

---

[1] Or we may put it in this way. If one says A, and then, while moving one's mouth and tongue into the right position for saying O, checks them half-way, the result is OA, as in *broad*.

A, as in 'on *londe*' (p. 99), *monig*. In both cases we have kept or returned to the A, and write *land*, *many*, though we do not now give the words the old pronunciation of A.

We will now try to follow the gradual changes of this long A, and see the traces which they have left in the language, like the gravel which a river leaves behind it when it changes its course, or like fossil animals preserved from past ages.

First of all, the sound OA in *broad* is not so very far removed from the sound of A, as in *father*, *are*. It is even now found written as A in *wrath*,[1] where the R before it has tended to preserve the sound. So too in *naught* (Old English *náht*) the GH has protected the Middle English sound, seeing it safely settled in the language before it died itself.[2]

In Middle English the sound of *broad*, coming from an Old English long A, is (except sometimes in the thirteenth century) spelt with O or OO. So that, for instance, Anglo-Saxon *brád*, *rád*, *fá* (now *broad*, *road*, *foe*), were written *brood*, *rode*, *foo*, and pronounced *broad*, *raud*, *fau*. *Cloth* still represents this sound by O. Neither its spelling nor its sound has changed since 1300 A.D.[3]

Thus OA was rarely written in Middle English, though the sound was very common. But some of these words moved on further and got the sound of O, much as it is pronounced in Modern English. When the combination of letters OA was revived in the sixteenth century to express the sound in *broad*, those words which retained this sound were so spelt, for instance, *broad*, *roar*, *hoar* (where the R is probably the cause of the Middle English sound being preserved), and so were other words such as *road*, *oath*, which were then

[1] The adjective is spelt with an O, but has (usually) the same sound. Both adjective and substantive are derived from the Old English adjective *wráþ*.

[2] Thus these words have changed their sound once, but have had no further change. We find this same change in Low German or Platt-Deutsch, the English that stayed at home on the Continent. There *Ja* (=yes) is pronounced pretty nearly as 'yaw,' and the O in *ol* (=old, High German *alt*) has a very similar sound.

[3] That is, if it is pronounced nearly like *clorth*; some people pronounce it otherwise, in deference to the spelling.

pronounced in the same way, but have since altered their pronunciation, though not their spelling. Those words which had got to a simple O sound (much as we pronounce that vowel) were still spelt with O, such as *foe, roe,* to *clothe.*

Finally, since the sixteenth century, most of those words which had lagged behind and were still pronounced like *broad,* took the sound of a Modern English long O, such as *road,* and *oath.*[1]

Thus English of the present day keeps samples of all these spellings with their sound unchanged.

The sound OA is still represented by A in the word *wrath,* which carries us back to Anglo-Saxon *wrāð.*

The Middle English spelling, O, appears in *cloth.* The sixteenth-century spelling in *broad, roar, hoar.* While *road, toad, oath,* and other words have come to be pronounced as if they were spelt with a simple long O, though their spelling shows what their former pronunciation was. If, however, Old English long A[2] was, through these stages, turned into a long O, it would seem that there could be no long A's in Modern English. But English long A's[3] chiefly come—

(*a*) From French words, such as *face, dame.*

(*b*) From various diphthongs; for instance, *hale* is from Danish *heill,*[4] and not from Anglo-Saxon *hál,* which has become (*w*)*hole*; *day* is from *dæg, gray* from *græg.*[5]

(*c*) From the lengthening of what was short A in Anglo-Saxon before a single consonant which was followed by a

---

[1] But O is now (since about 1800) pronounced with a suspicion of a W after it, *i.e.* with the lips rounded.

[2] *Short* A's are constantly preserved as A, though with some change of pronunciation, e.g. *can,* Anglo-Saxon *can*; *lamb,* Anglo-Saxon *lamb,* etc.

[3] The *sound* of A, as in *face,* dates from the seventeenth century. This is the ordinary English pronunciation of long A, and it is really equivalent to the Old English long E.

[4] Icelandic, probably representing *the old Norse form introduced into England,* which is what is meant by 'Danish' throughout the book. The diphthongs of Old English also became merged in simple vowels, see p. 180.

[5] G becoming Y and coalescing with the A as a vowel, see below, p. 220.

vowel, such as *name* (Anglo-Saxon *năma*), *shāme* (Anglo-Saxon *scămu*). This change took place in the thirteenth century. But in the Northumbrian dialect the change of Ā to OA and O did not often take place. So in Lowland Scotch, a modern form of Northumbrian, *who* is still *wha* (Anglo-Saxon *hwá*), as in

    Scots *wha* hae wi' Wallace bled.

Often this A has the modern sound of long A in English (as in *lame*, Latin Ē). *Thae* (= those), *ane* (= one), *nane* (= none), *laith* (= loth), represent the Old English words þá, án, nán, láþ. The spelling *stǽnas* (for *stánas*) and some similar instances in the Northumbrian Gospels seem to show that this process had already begun in the tenth century.[1]

It is plain from what has been said above that in the Middle English period the letter O represented two sounds— OA from Old English long A, and O from Anglo-Saxon long O. That they were two sounds is shown by their different fate. Most of the original O's, though still spelt with O or OO, have moved on their sound to U (as in *rue*); for instance, *sooth* from Anglo-Saxon *sóþ*, *good* from *gód*, *do* from *dó*, *doom* from *dóm*. On the other hand, R has sometimes preserved something like the old sound of the vowel, as in *door, floor*, though the R itself is usually no longer pronounced.

These changes are certainly not due in any direct way to the Norman Conquest.

We now come to the most obvious and important changes in the consonants.

Before we look further into these changes it is necessary to remind ourselves that Middle English consisted of more dialects than one, and that the changes which took place in one dialect did not necessarily occur in another, just as we saw that A was kept in Northumbrian, while it was altered in the more Southern dialects. In the same way the softening

---

[1] Kington Oliphant, *Old and Middle English*, p. 107.

of C took place most in the South. So what is the *Church* in England is the *Kirk*[1] in Scotland, Lowland Scotch being Modern Northumbrian. The East Midland dialect (from which 'standard' English mostly comes) is midway between North and South, in dialect as in position, and it is of this dialect that we are now going to speak.

(2) The C of Old English before E and I[2] became CH (as in *chick*) in Middle English.

In order to understand this change we must remember that C (*hard* C or K) can be pronounced either in the back or in the front of the mouth. If any one says first *cart* and then *king*, the sound is in both cases that of hard C (or K), but the first is made in the back, the second nearer the front of the mouth. For A (as in *cart*) is pronounced in the back of the mouth, E (Latin or German E, or as in *break*) and I (as in *pique*) further forward. And consequently the tongue naturally tries to make the C in the place where it has to be in order to form the vowel, without travelling to different parts of the room, so to speak, and thus we get the slightly different sounds of C in *cart* and K in *king*.[3]

So far there is no great difference in the sounds. But when the C (or K) is once made in the front of the mouth, it is liable to get further altered. We all know the slip in pronunciation where people say '*ky̨ind*' and '*sky̨y*,' and if we listen attentively we shall find some trace of this not at all uncommon, even with people who would 'scorn the imputation.' It comes from sliding the tongue forward too soon in preparation for the I or Y. In much the same way, if we do not take the trouble to bring the tongue up to the palate, when we are trying to say a C or K forward in the mouth, we shall get German CH (as in *ich*). So *ic* or *ik*[4] is the original form

---

[1] There is a Danish form *kirkja* which probably influenced the sound, see below, p. 216.
[2] Also Æ, e.g. *cæster*, Chester.
[3] The principle is much the same as in the 'mutation' of vowels, see p. 104, etc.
[4] A sister-word to *ego*, see p. 29.

Changes in the Sounds of English 215

of the pronoun 'I' in the Teutonic languages, as is shown by the Old English and Gothic form, but in Southern Middle English and in German this became *ich.*

The softening of the C gives many signs of its presence even in Old English writing,[1] and probably in the popular speech at least, if not in all speaking, the softening of this letter was carried out to a considerable extent before the Conquest, first and most extensively in the South, less in the East Midlands, least in Northumbria. But it is from the East Midland dialect that our Modern English mostly comes, and so we will confine ourselves chiefly to the change which took place in this dialect.

Through this German CH then (as in *ich*) comes the later Middle English CH (as in *check*). It is a very small change, involving only a slight raising of the tongue, and is a more distinctly audible sound. And it is quite possible that the sound of CH in Norman- or Anglo-French, which was constantly heard, and which, as we saw, was the same as in Modern English, may have helped to fix what had once been C in English to this particular sound, the sound which CH had (and has) in such words as *change* and *charge*.

Thus, then, if we take the 'front' vowels E, I,[2] in Old English (whether by themselves, or as the first part of a diphthong), we shall expect C to become CH before them, and we shall not be disappointed. A good instance is the word *kitchen* from *cycene*. Y is not properly the same letter as I (though they became much confused), but a 'modified' U (German ü, French and Devonshire U). So the C remains hard before it (*ki-*) but becomes soft before the E (*-tchen*).

What shall we say then about *church*? Here the Y in *cyrice* had passed into I (just as we find *cirice, circe,* in Old English), and it was this form that prevailed. But the fact that what is now I was Y in Anglo-Saxon has often preserved

---

[1] *e.g.* there are the double forms *cald* and *ceald, secan* and *secean,* þencan and þencean, in Old English (*ce-*, as in '*ky*ind,' see above). [2] Also Æ.

the hard sound, as in *kin* (Anglo-Saxon *cyn*), *kith* (Anglo-Saxon *cýð*). So we have *calf, can, cool, cow, king,* from Anglo-Saxon *calf, can, cól, cú, cyng;* but *chapman, churl* (formerly spelt *cherl*), *cheese, child,* from *céapman, ceorl, cése, cild.* Many of the words which still have K (hard C) before E and I come from Danish, a language in which the K was not pronounced right in the front of the mouth, whatever vowel followed it. For instance, *keel, keg, kid, kill, kilt.*[1]

Sometimes a 'front' vowel seems to affect a C coming after it as well. But the change in nouns (and sometimes in verbs) is probably helped by the inflexion[2] coming after, for this often in Old English, and always in Middle English, had E for its vowel. Sometimes too the nominative of a substantive ended in E. So we get *þæc, thatch; líc* (a dead body), *lich-* or *lych-*, as in *lych-*gate; *flicce, flitch; birce, birch.* Ich (the southern word for 'I'), which has no inflected form in the least like it (for instance, its genitive was *min*), is supposed to be a form pronounced with less emphasis than *ic*, and therefore not so clearly.[3] The Norman-French words beginning with CH of course came in ready-made and without alteration. Whether the Norman-French sound influenced the development of the sound of the English C much or little, at all events the spelling of it as CH is due to Norman or Anglo-French.

(3) The SC of Old English usually became SCH or SH in Middle English.

Here the C was naturally pronounced in the front of the mouth, in the same place as the S, which cannot be pronounced anywhere else, so that the vowel coming after or before it does not matter. The C seems to have become first a sort of Y. If the tendency was to pronounce the C imperfectly, like a German CH (as in the case of C alone before E or I), this CH, coming immediately after S, is practically a Y. For German CH

[1] For their spelling with K see above, p. 182.
[2] See Skeat, *Principles of English Etymology*, First Series, p. 354, etc.
[3] By the rule, C does not change before another consonant, e.g. *crib*, Old English *crib*; *cringe*, Old English *cringan*.

is very much like 'a hissed Y,'[1] and as the S supplies the hissing, there is scarcely any difference between S + CH and S + Y. This SY then passed to SH (as we sound it) just as the S in *sure* or *sugar* has done. An English U is not like a Latin or German U but YU. And now *s(y)ure* has slipped on into *s(h)ure*.[2] So SC seems to have passed through SCH, or SY, to SH in most English words.

Thus we have *disc, dish; fisc, fish; asce, ash; æsc, ash* (-tree); *scamu, shame; scip, ship,* and so on.

But there are a good number of words in English still beginning with SC (or SK, as many of them are written). Some of these (e.g. *science*) are from Latin directly or through French. But most of them come from Danish. The Danes did not pronounce their C's very far forward in the mouth, so that there was less chance of their getting softened.[3] Among these Danish words are *skill, skull, skin, sky.*

Some words too, whether Danish or English originally, seem to owe their preservation of SC (or SK) to the tendency that there was in the North, and to some extent in the East Midlands, to keep the C hard, just as we saw in *Kirk.* This keeping the hard C may be due to the practice and example of the Danes. On the other hand, in the South, and to some extent in the East Midlands, the SC was softened to SH. Thus there are often two forms of the same word—one with the SC (or SK), and the other with SH; and it seems likely that the first came from the North, the second from the South. The East Midlands, where the language that we now speak was mostly formed, was a sort of meeting-place for words and forms of words from the other two dialects. Thus in Old English we have *sceran* (to cut), *scearu, scor.* These are now

---

[1] Skeat, *Man of Lawes Tale*, introduction, p. xiv. The only difference is that Y is 'voiced,' (German) CH 'breathed.' See p. 4.

[2] Sweet, *History of English Sounds*, pp. 192, 267.

[3] Sweet, *History of English Sounds*, p. 194. But now SK is pronounced SH in Norse in some cases at least. *Sky* (shoes), for instance, sounds like English *shee*. This change has taken place since the Danes settled in England. The change is exactly similar in the two languages.

to *shear, share* (a part cut off), *score* (a cut, in a stick for instance, like Robinson Crusoe's calendar). Again, there is the expression 'to pay your *shot*' (a contribution '*shot* in'), and '*scot*-free,' meaning, to begin with, 'free from payment.' This is an example like the last; *shoot* is a native English word. But, on the other hand, from the Danish word *skyrta*, both *skirt* and *shirt* come. And the Danish word *skrœkja* has more forms still. First, there is the pure Northern form *skrike*, with neither C-sound softened, and *shriek* and *screech* are each of them a kind of compromise.[1] Thus Danish words are modified by English pronunciation, and also English words by Danish. Many of the words beginning with SC (or SK) which are English, have Danish words exactly corresponding to them, e.g. *skor, skot*. While Danish was still spoken in England, or while its pronunciation had left traces in certain parts of the country, this must have done much to fix the 'hard' forms.

To sum up, then, SC usually changed to SH. But there are a good number of exceptions, some being Latin or French words, a larger number distinctly Danish words. As to the native English words, we know that the North had a tendency to keep C's hard, as the Danes did too. If there was a Danish sister-word, of course with a hard C (or K), this, considering the mixture of the two races in the East and North, would in many cases keep the C of the English word hard. On the other hand, the English of the South were inclined to soften SC (or SK) wherever the word came from. The working of these various conflicting tendencies has produced the variety of English forms.[2]

(4) G at the beginning of a word before E and I changed

---

[1] For the words see Skeat's *Etymological Dictionary*.

[2] *Ask*, from *áscian*, seems to have a history of its own, and to have been kept hard by the analogy of *ácsian* ('axe'), used by King Alfred and Chaucer, though it is now 'vulgar' to say, 'I *axed* him to do it.' *Axe* (*aks*) and *ask* are plainly alternative forms, like *birdes* and *briddes* (Chaucer), *yrn* (Old English and Somersetshire), and *run*. But to say *ash* and *axe* would be to divorce the pair altogether.

to (ʒ, ʒ, or) Y; in the middle, or at the end of a word, to Y or GH or W.

The changes of G had at least begun in Old English, as we saw *iung* (*young*) and *ioc* (*yoke*) before the Conquest, and *hig* (for *hí*, they) certainly does not rhyme to *pig*.[1] The change was much the same as is heard in some German dialects; for instance, 'sa*j*en'[2] for 'sa*g*en,' 'guten mor*j*en' for 'guten mor*g*en,' just as the people of Berlin are said to speak of 'Eine *j*ute *j*ebratene *j*anze.' A G changes to something like the sound of German CH, or what is much the same thing, to Y if we begin to pronounce the letter in the front of the mouth and do not bring the tongue far enough upwards to touch the palate, and a G is sometimes pronounced just like Y by people speaking carelessly in Modern English. As in the case of C, we may say that the change of G at the beginning of a word only took place in English[3] before vowels pronounced in the front of the mouth—that is, before E and I.

Thus we have *géar, year*; *geolu, yellow*; *geolca, yolk*; *gieldan, yield*; *ge, ye*; *git, yet*, and so on.

On the other hand, G remains before A, O, U, Y,[4] and long Æ, as in *gást, ghost*; *gold, gold*; *gós, goose*; *gyldan, gild*; *gut, gut*; *gǽs, geese*. But to this rule there are many exceptions. Some of these come from Danish, whose G was not pronounced right in the front of the mouth any more than its C or K was; for instance, *girth, gills* (of fish). *Give* may be explained by its having a past tense *gave*. It would have been too absurd to say '*y*ive, *g*af, *y*iven.'[5] *Gift* would follow the sound of its verb. The same may have been the case with 'be*g*in, be*g*an, be*g*un,' the G of the present being

---

[1] It would be pronounced more as in German *König, traurig*.

[2] German J = English Y, see p. 217, note.

[3] That is to say, in one form of the language, East Midland, which eventually became the 'standard' dialect.

[4] = ü as before, see p. 107.

[5] On the other hand, Chaucer has past tense *yaf* (or *ʒaf*) as well as *yive* and *yiven*. These are Southern forms. See Sweet, *History of English Sounds*, p. 196, etc.

preserved by the 'analogy' of the other parts of the verb. But in many words the G's at the beginning cannot be so explained. Now in the South, soon after the Conquest, all initial G's seem to have been Y's, or on the way to becoming so. Possibly, therefore, it was again the influence of the Danes, with their hard pronunciation of G, that helped to keep the G hard, even in English words, in the North and in the East Midlands. And at any rate it is probable that the hard G's in *get, giddy, gear*, and so on, are cases where the Northern and East Midland form of the word prevailed, while the Y's came from the South.

Ge-, the prefix of the past participle in Old English, as in *ge-clepod* (called), *ge-boren* (*borne* and *born*), was not only weakened to *ye-* (like the 'vulgar' German '*j*enug' for '*g*enug,' '*j*ebraten' for '*g*ebraten'), but took a slight step further, and became a simple Y or I, or, as it is sometimes written, E. Hence come '*y*-clept,' '*i*-wiss' (*ge*-wis), and '*e*-nough' (*ge*-nóh).

In the middle or at the end of a word G often became Y as in 'dæ*g*,' 'da*y*'; or GH,[1] as in 'we*g*an,' 'wei*gh*'; or soft G (pronounced like our J), as in 'crin*g*an,' 'crin*ge*'; or W, as in 'dra*g*an,'[2] 'dra*w*,' 'fu*g*ol,' 'fo*wl*.' After changing to Y or W this weak and changeable consonant usually lost its independent existence altogether by combining with the preceding vowel, as in *day, slain* (*slegen*). In NG and CG the NY, GY, developed into the sound of NJ, J, or, as we write them, *-nge, -dge*. For instance, *sengan, singe; brycg, bridge; secg, sedge*. Sometimes CG has acted as if it had been simple G and coalesced with a vowel, as in *licgan, lie*. Northumbrian, in the shape of Lowland Scotch, still preserves some of these G's intact, as in *lig* for lie, *brigg* for bridge, as in the Brigg of Turk[3] and Bothwell Brigg.[4]

---

[1] Nearly the same sound, see pp. 217, 219.
[2] *Draw, dray*, from *dragan, dræge*, illustrate two of the changes of G; *drag* is from the sister-word in Danish.
[3] Scott, *Lady of the Lake*, I. vi.
[4] Scott, *Old Mortality*. The keeping of the G and C hard may be also

Then, of course, there are the Norman-French G's, sounded hard before A, O, U, soft (like J) before E, I, as in *gallon, gorge, gules*; and, on the other hand, *general, gentle, gin* (a trap), *ginger* — all these being French words adopted into English. GU was later on pronounced simply as hard G in English; hence from the words *guerdon, guise*, this mode of spelling has been transferred to some English words, merely to mark the G as hard, for instance in *guest, guilt, tongue* (Anglo-Saxon *tunge*). Thus the soft Norman-French G, as in *gentle*, had a sound identical with the Middle English GG in *brigge, segge* (*bridge, sedge*). It may have had something to do with making the English sound take the shape that it did.

Now it is plain that the letter G had to stand for a great many sounds. Fortunately, the form of the French G differed somewhat from the English way of writing it. This English G (ȝ, ȝ) was used in Middle English to express the sounds which had developed out of the English G—that is to say, Y at the beginning of a word, as in ȝelu, *yellow*; ȝer, *year*; and Y or GH at the middle or end, as in daȝ, *day*; slaȝe, *slay*; niȝt, *night*. French G, on the other hand, much the same in form as our present *g*, was used to express French sounds, either in French or English words, the hard G in *gallon, good*, the soft G in *change, singe*. ȝ, ȝ went out of use in the fifteenth century, Y and GH being used for it, as is shown above. But the Scotch still used it, writing it as Z, which it resembled in form before; as, for instance, 'the zier of God, 1568 Zeirs,'[1] as the date to a proclamation, and it is still found in this form in *capercailzie*—that is, *capercailȝe* or *capercailye*.[2] A trace of it also remains in some

---

due to the early loss in Northumbrian of most of the cases of the nouns, which, ending in E, tended to soften the G before them (see p. 216). This will be spoken of later on. See Skeat, *Principles of English Etymology*, First Series, p. 365.

[1] Earle, *Philology of the English Tongue*, p. 131.
[2] Skeat, *Principles of English Etymology*, First Series, pp. 317, 446.

Scotch surnames. In 1890 a Scotch gentleman's death was recorded in one newspaper under the name of Dalzell, while in another it was spelt Dalyell. ȝ, ȝ is the link between the two. The Z is due to the form of the letter; the Y to its pronunciation. The final disuse of ȝ and þ was due to the fact that the types for printing, made abroad, did not contain these English letters. Consequently they did not appear in books and died.[1] Another reason for the disuse of þ was that it had already got to be written almost or exactly like y. And for this reason y^e and y^t were often printed for *the* and *that*, even down to the present century, because y in shape resembled the lost þ in its latest form, just as z (as written in manuscript) resembled the lost ȝ and was used for it.[2]

[1] Article 'English Language,' in *Encyclopædia Britannica*, Ninth Edition.
[2] Skeat, *Principles of English Etymology*, First Series, p. 318.

CHAPTER XVI

DIALECTS OF ENGLISH AFTER THE CONQUEST, ESPECIALLY THE EAST MIDLAND

The four main dialects of English—Where spoken—All have contributed to Modern English—But especially East Midland—First appearance of that dialect—The *Peterborough Chronicle*—Inflexions dying out—Orm—His grammar—Danish influence on English—Contrast of the Southern dialect—Northumbrian the parent of Lowland Scotch.[1]

WE have now seen something of the effect of the Norman Conquest on English, and of the changes which took place in the sounds of the language chiefly after that event. We will now look at that dialect of English from which our present 'standard' English is chiefly derived, and trace it down from its first appearance as a local dialect till it became the language of all educated Englishmen.

The time between the Norman Conquest and the end of the fourteenth century was the period when English dialects were in their glory. Their position was then quite different from what it is at the present day, when dialects are spoken in different parts of England but are seldom written. About 1100, or soon after, the generation died out which had known West Saxon as the literary language of England without a rival, as that dialect was down to the Norman Conquest. After that, one dialect was as good as another; all were alike

---

[1] Morris, *Specimens of Early English*, Part I. Earle, *Two of the Saxon Chronicles*. Kington Oliphant, *Old and Middle English*. Sweet, *Middle English Primer*, etc.

'vulgar,' overshadowed by French, the language of the upper classes, whether of clergy or laity. But English was still the language of the bulk of the laity, and most of the monks and clergy, though not at first their bishops and abbots, were English, and spoke English as a rule, so that there were plenty of people to read or listen to English books, and also to write them. But each man wrote the dialect of his own district, the English which he himself talked. The number of these dialects must have been almost infinite. Just as at the present time people say that in Lancashire, for instance, a distinct difference of dialect can be sometimes detected in two adjoining villages, and as there is more than one variety of the Somersetshire dialect, so it must have been in the time after the Norman Conquest, only that, as the means of communication and intercourse were so much less, these differences must then have been far greater. Still, for practical purposes these dialects fall into four main divisions.[1]

(1) The Southern dialect, south of the Thames, and reaching over it to the north,[2] and in the counties of Worcester, Gloucester, and Hereford (p. 131, etc.). This dialect is the direct successor of West Saxon. Kentish may now be considered as one variety of it.

(2) East Midland, north of this, and bounded (roughly speaking) by the Humber on the north, on the north-west by the eastern boundaries of Lancashire and Cheshire, and then by a line drawn south-east to Bedford, and then nearly east to Colchester. East Anglian is a strongly-marked variety of it.

(3) West Midland to the north-west of (2), including Southern Lancashire, the whole of Shropshire, Cheshire, and Staffordshire, with part of Derbyshire.

---

[1] Kington Oliphant, *Old and Middle English*, p. 140, etc. Skeat, *Principles of English Etymology*, First Series, p. 39.

[2] The East Midland had encroached upon the Southern dialect before Chaucer's time, see Map, p. 256.

(4) Northumbrian, reaching roughly from the Humber to beyond Edinburgh, and spreading, or destined to spread, over the South-West Lowlands, and along the east coast to the very north of Scotland.

The difference between East and West Midland is chiefly due to the settlement of Danes in the eastern but not (to any considerable extent) in the western part of Mercia (p. 123, etc.) Both in the East Midlands and in Northumbria it was the popular speech, coloured by Danish both in grammar and vocabulary, which gave these dialects the form in which we now find them written (p. 125, etc., p. 135).

Of course the people who lived near the boundaries of one of these dialects spoke a mixed speech. In this way all of the dialects influenced each other where they touched, and this influence often spread further. Thus all have more or less affected our 'standard' English. For instance, *such* (Anglo-Saxon *swylc* = *swa-lik*, Gothic *swa-leiks*, 'so like') is a distinctly southern form, U being employed for Y in the South.[1] So too the present participle in *-ing*, in 'I was writ*ing*,' for instance (for the Anglo-Saxon writ-*ende*, later writ-*inde*), first appears in Layamon, a Worcestershire poet, Southern, so far as his dialect is concerned.[2] To Northumbria we owe the termination of the 3rd person singular of verbs in *-es* and *-s*, instead of *-eth* (p. 85), and perhaps much of our peculiar pronunciation of vowels, the Modern English Ā (as in *lane*), and of Ē (as in *creep*), just as before the Conquest *scép* was written *scip* ('sceep,' as we should now write it), and *stánas*, *sténas* (Lowland Scotch *stanes*) in Northumbria[3] (p. 213). But the dialect to which Modern English owes

---

[1] At first probably because the French U = German ü, often implied the same sound as Y; see pp. 107, 184, note.

[2] Mr. Sweet (*History of English Sounds*, p. 155) says West Midland. At all events he lived near the junction of the two dialects.

[3] It must be constantly borne in mind that the English vowels had their Latin, Italian, or German pronunciation then. Therefore, if a man wrote *scip*, *stánas*, he meant the sounds which we should now write, 'sceep,' 'stainas.' These words are in Modern 'standard' English *sheep* and *stones*.

incomparably more than to any other is the East Midland. Even now, the dialect of these counties, and especially of South Lincolnshire, Northamptonshire, and Cambridgeshire, is far less marked—that is, it resembles 'standard' English far more closely—than that of the South, or West, or North.[1] In fact, Modern 'standard' English is practically Modern East Midland, with such peculiarities of the other dialects as succeeded in establishing themselves in that dialect. It would be impossible to derive English in its present form directly from the Southern dialect (West Saxon) or from Northumbrian. But if we take the earliest writings in the East Midland dialect, not only do they bear a considerable resemblance to our Modern English, but we can trace this infant 'standard' English down through writings in that dialect, till East Midland becomes established as the literary dialect of all England.

Now we have seen already that the Midland dialect was nearer to Modern English than the Southern or West Saxon dialect, and East Midland is of course one variety of Mercian or Midland English. But the East Midland of the twelfth and thirteenth centuries had altered a good deal from the language that is found even in the Rushworth Gospels[2] (pp. 132, 155), and had got much nearer to the English with which we are familiar. This change, as has been already said, and as will be clear shortly, was mainly due to contact with the Danes.

It is interesting to see the first appearance in writing of what was to become 'standard' English. Something like it had of course been spoken long before.

In 1116 A.D.[3] a great fire took place at the Abbey of

---

[1] See *Transactions of the Philological Society*, 1875-76, paper on English Dialects, by Prince Louis Lucien Bonaparte; and Kington Oliphant, *Old and Middle English*, p. 449.

[2] We must bear in mind that any Mercian writings after Alfred's time, and before the Conquest, are almost sure to be coloured more or less by the literary West Saxon, just as writings in a dialect, *e.g.* Barnes's poems, now are by Modern 'standard' English.

[3] See Earle, *Two of the Saxon Chronicles Parallel*, p. xliii. etc. Kington Oliphant, *Old and Middle English*, p. 142, etc., p. 163, etc.

Peterborough, and probably all, or the greater part of its books were lost. It appears to have been this which caused the *Peterborough Chronicle* to be written. No doubt the monks had had one or more Chronicles in their library before; and though it was now the prevailing custom to write history in Latin, yet, as other monastic libraries had English Chronicles, and as Peterborough had possessed them before, it was only natural that they should wish to be on a level with other monasteries in this respect. Besides, the early glories of the abbey might be incidentally brought out in the work. So a monk was set to compile a Chronicle, which, after a short account of the nations who inhabit the island, begins with the landing of Julius Caesar in Britain. There were then many Old English Chronicles to draw from, far more than have survived; and in some parts it can be seen what Chronicle is the source of the Peterborough history, and in others what the part of England was in which the writer of the original Chronicle was specially interested—that is to say, where it was written. The greater part of the *Peterborough Chronicle* is not in Peterborough English. The monk who compiled it copied the language of his authorities, though he modified the spelling to some extent. In the later part we find later English, which the compiler probably found in the late Chronicles which he copied, and sometimes a sentence occurs which is doubtless original, being something quite different from the language of the rest, and, no doubt, much nearer to the English which the monk himself spoke. Besides this, there are inserted at intervals long accounts of the early glories of Peterborough, and of the distinctions conferred on it by English kings.[1] These are evidently intended to be in an old-fashioned style, as if the records had been actually preserved at Peterborough. There are plenty of inflexions in these documents, but they are not always the right ones, just as some people now think that Middle English can be

[1] Written by another hand, Earle, see above.

reproduced by merely putting a final E at the end of nearly every word, or as manuscript Latin Prose, in spite of the best intentions, is not always free from mistakes in grammar. Thus we even find *seo kyning* for 'the king' in an entry which is supposed to date from 656. This is as correct as ἡ βασιλεύς would be in Greek, or *die König* in German. However, at any rate this shows that the old inflexions were now for the most part dead at Peterborough, since even the average monk could not write the old literary English, and doubtless no one else was likely to detect his mistakes. With 1121 the first writer stops, and the monk who took up his work carried it on as an original Chronicle in something like his own spoken language, though with some imitation of the language of the earlier prose. From the entry of the year 1132 a third hand appears in the manuscript, and here the language is extremely near what the monk himself spoke and heard spoken at Peterborough. This latest part was probably written about the year 1160. We will now let it speak for itself.

PETERBOROUGH CHRONICLE

OF THE YEAR 1137 (WRITTEN ABOUT 1160)

J ne can ne í ne mai tellen alle þe wunder ne alle þe
I not   nor   not   wonders
pines ð hi diden wrecce men on þis land . J ð lastede
tortures that they   (to) wretched   and that
þa xix wintre wile Stephne was king J æure it was uuerse
the xix winters while   ever   worse
J uuerse. Hi læiden gæildes o[n] the tunes æure umwile
             laid contributions   towns ever at (all) times
J clepeden it tenserie.[1]   þa þe uurecce men ne hadden
  called   rent.   When   wretched

---

[1] Probably for *censerie*, see note in Morris.

Dialects of English after the Conquest

nan more to gyuen. þa ræueden hi ⁊ brendon alle the
none   then   robbed   burned
tunes. ð wel þu myhtes faren all a dæis fare sculdest
thou   journey   journey
thu neure finden man in tune sittende . ne land tiled.
dwelling
Þa was corn dære ⁊ fle[s]c ⁊ cæse ⁊ butere . for nan ne
Then   cheese
wæs o þe land. Wrecce men sturuen of hungær . sume
on   starved
ieden on ælmes þe waren sum wile rice men . sume
went on alms (begging) who were   rich
flugen ut of lande.[1]
fled   out

In this extract we ought to notice first of all the French influence on the spelling 'æure,' 'gyuen,' where U is employed for the Old English F · (pronounced as V between vowels, *cǽfre, gifan*), and UU in '*uurecce*,' '*uuerse*,' for the Old English W (Þ). In another part of this last section of the Chronicle we find '*quartern*,' which in Old English would have begun with CW. The French mode of spelling is gaining ground, though it is not yet thoroughly established (see p. 181, etc.) The C's, as in '*cæse*,' are left, though it is not likely that they were all of them still pronounced as K.

Secondly, though there are several inflexions which we have now dropped, such as the *-en* of the plural '*diden*,' '*læiden*,' and so on, and the *-en* of the infinitive, as in '*tellen*,' '*gyuen*,' both of which bits of grammar were to last for some centuries longer, yet the inflexions are very limited indeed compared with those in 'classical' Old English. '*Wrecce*,' '*sume*,' are the plural of adjectives—any case, for '*wrecce*' stands for the dative. '*Lande*' at the end of the extract is, no doubt, a dative, but as we find '*of þe land*' earlier in this part of the

---

[1] Earle, *Anglo-Saxon Chronicles.* Morris, *Specimens of Early English,* Part I.

Chronicle, we cannot suppose that this -*e* of the dative was a very essential part of the language.¹ The same is the case with the definite article. In the South, as we shall see, its cases were used occasionally in something like their old shape for two centuries more, though the one form þe is also used for most of them. Here, though we have 'þa xix wintre,' two lines lower down we get ' þe uurecce men.'

Now we have said before that English was an 'inflexional' language before the Norman Conquest. This is a question of degree, of more or less inflexions. English is certainly not an inflexional language now, and yet no one would think it correct to say, ' he come ' for ' he comes,' or 'three boy.' The question is, does the correct understanding of the language depend upon our taking notice of the inflexions, or not? In 'classical' Old English, the older Chronicles, for instance, and still more in the poetry, it does. We should frequently be liable to go wrong if we did not recognise the force of a termination. But in this East Midland English of 1160 the inflexions are not nearly of the same importance. Much of the spelling is unfamiliar to us, and a few of the words. The first difficulty is easily got over, and if we learn the meaning of the few strange words, we can easily make it out by the light of nature without troubling ourselves about the few inflexions left. These, then, are no longer essential; this East Midland English is not an inflexional language. And any one can judge for himself how much nearer it is altogether to Modern English than the specimen given before on p. 179, or than the examples of Southern English to be found on pp. 261-263.

There are some Northern forms which had filtered in; J² (= I, Southern *ich*), and *til* in another part of the Chronicle. There are also Danish words, *fra* ³ for *fram*, the proper English

---

¹ Just as it is put in or left out in German datives of the present day.
² J at this period is merely I with an ornamental tail.
³ Kington Oliphant, *Old and Middle English*, p. 167.

Dialects of English after the Conquest 231

form; also *bathe* (both) for Old English *begen, bá*, the first of which also appears in this section of the Chronicle in the form *beien*. The Danish word quickly spread over the whole of England. *Take*, which is also a Danish word, is frequently used in various senses. The past participles, such as *tiled*, have no *ge-* prefixed, a bit of inflexion which lasted very long in the South in a weakened form as *i-* or *y-*. This loss is probably due to the example of the Danes, who had no *ge-* to their past participles.[1] And in general it looks already as if it were the contact with the Danes (which comes out clearly, as in the examples given above) that caused the English inflexions to be clipped. But this will be more evident from our next example.

Somewhere about the year 1200, or perhaps earlier, a certain Orm or Ormin wrote a series of homilies or sermons in verse, containing a sort of history of Christianity, beginning with the religion of the Jews, which was the type of it. His metre is probably modelled on some Latin poem,[2] one of those written by accent, and not by quantity like 'classical' Latin verse. As has been said already, there are hardly any French words in it—four or five in 32,000 lines.[3] The book was named *Ormulum*, as the author himself tells us, because Orm made it.[4] There is nothing but the dialect to tell us where it was written, and so the authorities are not agreed upon this point. Dr. Morris says that it was probably written near Lincoln; Mr. Kington Oliphant[5] is inclined to place it in the neighbourhood of Derby; but it is quite enough for our purpose to know that it is in the East Midland dialect. This

---
[1] See p. 133, note.
[2] Morris, *Specimens of Early English*, Part I., p. 39.
[3] We saw (p. 186) that there were more French words than this in the entry for one year in the *Peterborough Chronicle*. Orm seems to have had a dislike to them, and to have avoided them.
[4] Þiss boc iss nemmnedd Orrmulum
    Forrþi þatt Orrm itt wrohhte.
        wrought.
[5] Morris, *Specimens of Early English*, Part I., p. 39. Kington Oliphant, *Old and Middle English*, p. 212.

poem is most valuable for many reasons. First of all, the manuscript is believed to be in the actual handwriting of the author of the poem; it has not been copied out by a scribe who was sure to write the words more or less as they were pronounced in his own day, and in his own part of the country. Secondly, the author himself was a very careful and accurate man. He means to express the pronunciation of the English of his day as exactly as possible, and adjures all who copy his poem to copy its spelling as well. So that we can lay stress on it as a specimen of what a man of accurate habits of mind thought that the English of his day was and ought to be. Let us look at a sample of it. To understand the metre we must pronounce every letter (except the second of doubled consonants), unless an E at the end of a word comes just before a word beginning with a vowel, in which case it is cut off, as in Chaucer, and in Latin verses.

ORM

East Midland

(About 1200)

1. & nu icc wile shæwenn ʒuw
And now I will shew you
Summ del wiþþ Godess hellpe
Some part with God's help
3. Off þatt Judisskenn follkess lac
Of that Jewish people's sacrifice
Þatt Drihhtin wass full cweme,
That to-the-Lord was pleasant,
5. & mikell hellpe to þe follc,
much
To læredd & to læwedd,
learned lay (unlearned),

Dialects of English after the Conquest

7. Biforenn þatt te Laferrd Crist
   Before   the   Lord
   Wass borenn her to manne.
   here as
9. Acc nu ne geȝȝneþþ itt hemm nohht
   But now   gaineth (helps)   them nought
   To winnenn eche blisse,
   eternal
11. Þohh þatt teȝȝ standenn daȝȝ & nihht
    Though   they
    To þeowwtenn Godd & lakenn ;
    serve   sacrifice
13. For all itt iss onnȝæness Godd,
    against
    Þohh þatt teȝȝ swa ne wenenn,
    so (do-) not ween,
15. Forrþi þatt teȝȝ ne kepenn nohht
    Because   take-thought
    Noff Crist, noff Cristess moderr.
    Neither-of   nor-of   mother.
17. & tohh-swa-þehh nu wile icc ȝuw
    nevertheless
    Off þeȝȝre lakess awwnenn,
    their sacrifices make clear
19. Hu mikell god teȝȝ tacnenn uss
    How   good   (be-)token to-us
    Off ure sawle nede ;
    our soul's
21. Forr all þatt lac wass sett þurrh Godd
    sacrifice   through
    Forr þatt itt shollde tacnenn,
    should
23. Hu Cristess þeoww birrþ lakenn Crist
    servant it-becomes to-sacrifice to Christ

Gastlike i gode þæwess,
Spiritually in good ways-of-living,
25. Wiþþ all þatt tatt bitacnedd wass
that
Þurrh alle þeʒʒre lakess.¹

Now one result of Orm's extreme desire for accuracy is to make this poem at first sight seem less like our Modern English than it really is. We must, of course, remember that the vowels were still pronounced pretty nearly as in 'new pronunciation' Latin, or in Italian, or in German. The change from this was not to begin in the Midlands and in the South for more than two centuries. So that, to listen to, this English would have been less like our Modern English than it looks. But, for its appearance in writing, what seems most strange to us is the constant doubling of consonants, 'icc,' 'shæwenn,' 'hellpe.'² Now there is no doubt that, to begin with, a doubled consonant meant a doubled consonant—that is to say, that the letter was pronounced twice, as in 'unnecessary,' 'pen-(k)nife.' These doubled consonants had a tendency to make the vowel before them short, as in *fēdan, fĕdde* (*feed, fed*). Then, as a double consonant often came after a short vowel, this rule was made general, and a double consonant in the *Ormulum* is only a device of Orm's to show that the vowel coming before is short. It is his favourite way of marking quantities. And we have kept this sign in many words. 'Penny,' as opposed to 'penal,' 'ratting,' as opposed to 'rating,' are instances. But we make no attempt to use it consistently, any more than the other rules of Modern English spelling, and very seldom double consonants at the end of words, as Orm does. We see much the same process

---

¹ The *Ormulum*, edited by Dr. R. M. White, re-edited by Rev. Robert Holt, 1878 ; also in *Specimens of Early English*, Part I., Morris, 1884 ; and in Sweet's *First Middle English Primer*, 1884.

² As a matter of fact, when we remember what it means, it often gives us something like our modern pronunciation (if we allow for the change of vowel sounds), *e.g.* wĭth, hĕlp, hēre (see lines 2, 5, and 8).

in the history of the final E's. In two-syllabled words like *name*, the A, for instance, was originally short.[1] By the beginning of the fourteenth century it came to be pronounced long. Therefore a long vowel now often came before a short E; and when, not very long after, this E ceased to be sounded at all, the writing of it looked like a mere trick of spelling, a sign of quantity; and a silent E was adopted generally (not quite consistently, of course, in English spelling),[2] to show that the vowel before it was long.

Another thing in the *Ormulum* that looks strange is the change of þ (TH) to T when it comes after a D or T; for instance, *te33* for *þe33* in lines 11 and 14 of the extract. This occurs too in the *Peterborough Chronicle* and elsewhere. It was, no doubt, easier to pronounce, though we find no difficulty in saying 'that they,' or, 'and they.'

We see an instance of the change of A to O (p. 210, etc.) in *nohht* (Old English *náht = náwiht*, 'no whit'). C (= K) is softened to CH (p. 214, etc.) in *eche* (line 10), of which the Old English form is *éce*; SC to SH (p. 216, etc.) in *shæwenn*, Old English *scéawian*, and *shollde*, Old English *sceolde*; and G to ȝ (p. 218, etc.) in *daȝȝ*, Old English *dæg*, and in *onnȝæness* from *ongéan*, though this G still remains hard in Modern English, *against* and *(a)gain-say*. On the other hand, Orm keeps many C's hard which we have softened; for instance, *asskess* (*ashes*), *bisscopp* (*bishop*); and A's which we have changed to O, such as *tacnenn* (line 19), corresponding to *(be-)token*. These two peculiarities he shares with Northumbrian English (of which Lowland Scotch is the best modern example). He seems to have lived not far from the southern borders of that dialect.

---

[1] Anglo-Saxon *náma*. The second A, like the other vowels at the end of words, was weakened to an indistinct E.

[2] e.g. *live*, *love* are exceptions. V is not now allowed to end a word. The lengthening of the vowel also had a good deal to do with causing the final *-e* of inflexions to be dropped. It hardly sounded in the predominance of the long syllable. See article 'English Language,' *Encyclopædia Britannica*, Ninth Edition. But see also Skeat, *Principles of English Etymology*, First Series, p. 309, etc. The accent also must have been sapping the terminations steadily.

As to his spelling, though he will not have French words, we see that he cannot avoid French spelling (p. 181, etc.). This comes out clearly in his use of K in *Judisskenn, mikell* (Anglo-Saxon *Iudéiscan, micel*), and of C as equivalent to S[1] in *milcenn* (Anglo-Saxon *miltsian*) in another part of his work. On the other hand, the process is not complete. We have *nu* in line 1, *ure* in line 20, for *nou, our*, as they were spelt later on. These points are worth noticing; but after all, the main thing is Orm's grammar, in which we shall find him advanced at least half-way on the road from Old to Modern English.

It has been said before that Anglo-Saxon had a very elaborate stock of grammatical forms, more marked and distinct than German grammar, for instance. But the grammar of the *Ormulum* is not very difficult to master. Let us take the points in which it differs from Modern English, first stating that we may expect the vowel of all the terminations to be E, whatever it may have been in Old English, and that all the letters are pronounced except in the case of doubled consonants. E mute was not yet invented, and -*es*, for instance, and -*ed* were distinct syllables, just as they still are in 'fish-*es*,' 'rent-*ed*.' It will be convenient to begin with the adjective.

Now, we have already seen (p. 108) that there was a special 'weak' form of the adjective in Old English, used after the article, demonstrative pronouns (*this, that*), and possessives (*his*, and so on), as in German.[2] Of this we have an instance in *Judisskenn*, line 3 (Old English *Iudéiscan*). But so old-fashioned a form is rare; the weak form of the adjective generally has to be content with -*e*, for instance—

<blockquote>
Wiþþ all þatt Judewisshe lac.
Jewish sacrifice.
</blockquote>

Then there is an -*e* for the plural of the adjective, and we have done with its inflexions.

As to substantives, Orm has some 'irregularities,' as they

---

[1] Or to TS. And the spelling CH is probably copied from French, see p. 216.
[2] Also in the vocative case.

appear to us, correct or less corrupted forms as they would have appeared to an educated Englishman of the time before the Conquest.[1] *Ure sawle nede*, in line 20, is an instance of these, for *sáwol* (*soul*) was a feminine substantive, and its genitive was *sáwle*. But we also find

till ȝure sawless hellpe.
   to

In fact, this 'regular' declension (like that of *day* in Modern English) was rapidly swallowing up the others. Words otherwise declined are rare in the *Ormulum*, though commoner than in Modern English. There is also sometimes an -*e* for the dative in Orm's declension; for instance, *to manne* in line 8. But as *lac* in line 3, *Drihhtin* in line 4, and *follc* in line 5, have an equally good right to it, this dative inflexion cannot be considered a very essential part of the grammar.[2] We saw this variation before in the *Peterborough Chronicle*. As the uniformity and simplicity of declension gained ground the old distinctions of gender were bound to perish. We no longer have it marked by the terminations, in substantive and adjective, and it is on the way to becoming purely rational, just as now *man* and *boy* are masculine, both in fact and in grammar, *woman* and *girl* feminine, and *chair* neuter. We have seen that in English before the Norman Conquest certain words for *woman* and *child*[3] were neuter. But our ancestors did not think any less of them on that account;[4]

---

[1] From the point of view of Anglo-Saxon grammar Orm's *menness*, our *men's*, is an absolutely stupendous form. The change of vowel in the plural belongs to the nominative and accusative only, and to add the inflexion of the genitive singular on to this is like making the genitive plural of *homo*, *hominesis*, or of *regnum*, *regnæ*.

[2] The -*e* of the dative in German substantives is in just the same position at the present day.

[3] *Childer*, the Lancashire plural of 'child,' represents *cild-ru*, a distinctly neuter form of the plural. 'Childer' is also to be found in the 1549 Prayer-Book in the words 'child*ers* children.' 'Child*ren*' is a plural twice over.

[4] Though the gender may have originated in some such feeling. But we cannot enter sufficiently into the feelings of our very remote savage ancestors to explain the genders which are attached to words in Old English.

this gender was a matter of grammar only, of terminations in the substantive and its adjective, and, with the loss of special inflexions to mark it, it passed away as a matter of course.

In the verb, the singular of the present indicative is (except for the *-e* in the 1st person) declined much as in the Bible and Prayer-Book—we can hardly say 'as in Modern English,' though these forms are still used in poetry.

    icc, i telle
    þu tellesst
    he telleþþ

The plural of both tenses and moods ends in *-enn*, or, as any one but Orm would have written it, *-en*. We have already seen this inflexion in the Rushworth Gospels (*doan*, see p. 86), and it is to be found more or less till Henry VII.'s time. But where does this form come from? It is not the termination of the present indicative in West Saxon, the 'classical' Old English. There, as we have seen, the termination is *-aþ*, and it was still *-eþ* in the South when the *Ormulum* was written, and for a long time afterwards (see p. 261, 'lowe men holdeþ'). But in the subjunctive present and past, and in the past indicative, it was *-en* or *-on*, in the earliest West Saxon that we have. And this seems to be the explanation of its getting into the present tense as well; that it was due to imitation or 'analogy,'[1] just as we have learnt to say *eyes* instead of *eyne;* though the plural of the word was originally *éagan*. It is just the sort of levelling, or 'grammar made easy,' which the bad example of the Danes would be likely to encourage. Why should the present indicative be conjugated differently from its subjunctive, and from the past tense? They were not likely to trouble themselves with such niceties. The *ge-* before past participles is dropped by Orm, just as it was by the Peterborough chronicler; so in line 8 we have *borenn*, which in Anglo-Saxon would be *ge-boren*. Danish did not have this prefix for its past participles.

[1] Article 'English Language,' *Encyclopædia Britannica*, Ninth Edition.

Dialects of English after the Conquest 239

We may notice that Orm makes verbs which were '.strong,' or 'irregular,' 'weak'; for instance, *sleppte* (Anglo-Saxon *slép*), *weppte* (Anglo-Saxon *wéop*), and *hæfedd* (*heaved*) as the past participle, as well as *hofenn* (Anglo-Saxon *hafen*).[1] This is a process which had begun much earlier, was continued, and is still going on at the present day. 'It *winded* about,' and 'he *beseeched* him,' are among the 'weak' perfects now trying to gain admission into literary English. Popular or 'vulgar' English makes 'weak' perfects freely; 'he *catched* it' (or, '*cotched* it'), and 'I *seed* him,' are two of the common ones.

The definite article was in Anglo-Saxon fully declined. We cannot say that this was still the case even in the southern dialect of the twelfth and thirteenth centuries, since þe is often found standing for a good many cases of different genders and numbers; still, many of the old forms of the cases were alive, and crop up long after the date of the *Ormulum* in a shape which is wonderfully suggestive of Anglo-Saxon. Thus, in 1340, we find 'þane þridde day,' like Anglo-Saxon '$\begin{cases} \text{þone} \\ \text{þane} \end{cases}$ þriddan dæg.' But in the *Ormulum* we have nothing but þe, plural þa and þe,[2] for all genders and cases, much as in Modern English. The neuter of þe, namely þatt (Anglo-Saxon þæt), had been adopted as a demonstrative and relative pronoun, undeclined, for all genders, just as we use it now. As was said before (p. 111, etc.), to use the article as a demonstrative or as a relative was not a very violent change, but to use one gender of a pronoun for one part of speech, and another gender for another, does certainly seem a curious contrivance, and shows how the old grammatical system was breaking up. Þi in *forrþi* (line 15) is the old instrumental case, preserved in

---

[1] We still use a 'strong' past tense for this verb occasionally, as in 'He *hove* him a rope.' For the verbs quoted above see Kington Oliphant, *Old and Middle English*, p. 229, to whom I am in general much indebted in this part of my subject.

[2] *e.g.* þa goddspelless; te posstless; *te* being used for þe after a D or T.
        gospels   the apostles

one or two expressions only, as *for why* (because), which is still to be heard in the country, and occurs in the 'Old Hundredth.'

As to the personal pronouns, it is worth while to give Orm's declension of them, which can be compared with the 'classical' Anglo-Saxon forms (p. 113). The parts of them which are now obsolete are in italics.

Singular

	I	*Thou*
Nom.	*icc*, i	*þu*
Gen.	*min*[1]	*þin*
Dat.	me	*þe*
Acc.	me	*þe*

Dual

	We two	*You two*
Nom.	*witt*	*ȝitt*
Gen.	*unnkerr*	*ȝunnkerr*
Dat.	*unnc*	*ȝunnc*
Acc.	*unnc*	*ȝunnc*

Plural

	We	*You*
Nom.	we	*ȝe*
Gen.	ure[2]	*ȝure*[2]
Dat.	uss	*ȝuw*
Acc.	uss	*ȝuw*

Singular

	He	*She*	*It*
Nom.	he	*ȝho*	itt
Gen.	hiss	hire	*hiss*
Dat.	*himm*	hire	*himm*
Acc.	*himm*	hire	itt

Plural

Nom.	þeȝȝ[3]
Gen.	þeȝȝre, *heore, here*
Dat.	þeȝȝm, *hemm*
Acc.	þeȝȝm, *hemm*[4]

---

[1] The genitive of these pronouns is usually the possessive case (or possessive adjective) only, as in Modern English.

[2] U was later written OU in French spelling, at first without any change of pronunciation, see p. 181.

[3] See pp. 220, 221, ȝ has become a vowel, and eȝȝ = ei.

[4] Koch, *Historische Grammatik.* Sweet, *Middle English Primer.*

Dialects of English after the Conquest 241

Many of these are to be found in the extract.

Thus the personal pronouns (except the dual, now lost) are in Orm's dialect mostly the same as at present, if we allow for the great change that has taken place in the pronunciation of English vowels, and remember that Orm's doubled consonants are merely a sign that the vowel before them is short. As we shall see, they are nearer to our present personal pronouns than the forms used in the South at the time. The dative has in all of them 'crowded out' the accusative. The H has been dropped in (*h*)*it*. This is probably the less emphatic form,[1] and therefore less carefully pronounced, just as we frequently hear educated people say, 'I told '*im* so.' The genitive is rapidly becoming a 'possessive'[2] only, as it is in Modern English. *His*, as the genitive or 'possessive' of *it*, is the form used even in the 'Authorised Version' of the Bible; for instance, 'The fruit tree yielding fruit after *his* kind;'[3] 'And it (the rock) shall give forth *his* water.'[4]

On the other hand, we have dropped Orm's favourite form *icc*. ȝho (from *heo*) is now only to be heard in the Lancashire *hoo* (= she). We use instead the form first found in the *Peterborough Chronicle*, *scæ* (from *séo*, feminine of the definite article in West Saxon)—'god wimman *scæ*[5] wæs.' The dual lived on for nearly another century. It is last found in the poem of Havelok the Dane, about 1280.[6] *Heore*, or *here*, and *hemm* come directly from the Old English forms, and are still found in Chaucer, as *here*, *hir*, and *hem*. The last must be the origin of '*em*, in a sentence like 'Give it '*em*.' But þeȝȝ, þeȝȝre, þeȝȝm (*they, their, them*), though they seem familiar enough to us now, cannot well be traced to Old English. The

---

[1] Sweet, *History of English Sounds*, p. 189.
[2] Orm declines these genitives as possessive adjectives, *e.g.* hise; 'And wessh himm *hise* claþess.'
washed   clothes.   [3] Genesis i. 11.   [4] Numbers xx. 8.
[5] This writer never uses SH or SCH, but puts C's in general accordance with the old way of spelling English, and it is pretty certain that *scæ* was pronounced like *she* at present, except of course its vowel, which was more like A in *lane*.
[6] Kington Oliphant, *Old and Middle English*, p. 355.

R

plural of the definite article (þá, þǽra, þǽm) comes nearest, and we might imagine that this had passed into a personal pronoun. Both these are originally demonstratives, just as *il* and *le* in French both come from the Latin *ille*, so that it would not be a very violent change. But why should English have developed a second personal pronoun, þeʒʒm, for instance, when it had *hemm* already? Let us then look at the corresponding pronoun[1] in Danish, and compare it with the forms in the *Ormulum*.

	Danish.[2]	*Ormulum.*
Nom.	þeir	þeʒʒ
Gen.	þeira	þeʒʒre
Dat.	þeim	þeʒʒm

It is plain that the English plural *they, their, them*, is derived from Danish, though, as the Old English article (*sometimes* used also as a demonstrative and personal pronoun [3]) was so much like it, it was all the more easily adopted by the East Midland Englishmen. It must have seemed as if it were merely altering the pronunciation of an English word, and using it in a slightly different way from what was customary, though they also had *some* examples of this use in their own language.

And yet this is a very striking example of the influence of Danish on the East Midland dialect, and through that on 'standard' English. For, as we saw on p. 19, a personal pronoun is a sort of word to which a language holds most strongly, and for English to have received a pronoun from Danish shows something that comes very near to a mixture of the two languages. And this instance does not stand alone. *Both* (Danish *báðir*) had already begun to drive out the Old English forms *begen, bá, bú*, and this is another word which would not readily be

---

[1] It is also a demonstrative = 'that,' and is, of course, own-brother to *þá, þǽra, þǽm*.

[2] Icelandic. As has been said before, this old-fashioned language closely represents the language spoken by the Norsemen and Danes who settled in England, who were called indifferently 'Danes' by our ancestors. The word 'Dane' is used in this wide sense here, and 'Danish' usually means Icelandic, since that language best represents Norse and Danish in their old form.

[3] See p. 154, where *ǽton þá* is exactly 'ate them.'

Dialects of English after the Conquest 243

adopted from a foreign language. Danish has invaded the numerals as well. 'Tenth' is in Old English *teoða*, the modern form of which is *tithe*. In Danish it is *tiundi*. Our modern form *tenth* is a compromise between Old English and Danish. To pass to less striking instances, *fra* is the Danish form of the English *fram*, now *from*; Orm uses it as an ordinary preposition ('*fra þe chaff*,' 'from the chaff'), and we still keep it in the phrase 'to and *fro*.'[1] And of ordinary Danish words—substantives, adjectives, and verbs (the same classes of words in which we have borrowed so largely from French)—Orm's English is full. To take some of these which are still in constant use, he has *anger, clip, die, ill, kid, raise, scare, thrive*,[2] all superseding quite different Old English words. We have already seen (p. 216, etc.) that many words which keep the hard C and G are derived from Danish. Fresh Danish words kept making their way into East Midland and Northumbrian English, and spreading into the other dialects. Besides the instances given, Orm has many Danish words, forms of words, and idioms which have not survived. Orm's very name is Danish, and his English has a very strong dash of Danish indeed. But, taking even ordinary 'standard' English, we have seen that Danish has made its way to some extent even into the very grammar of our language, thus affecting it more deeply than French has done.

And if Danish came so closely into contact with English as this, it is surely probable that the great loss and simplifying of inflexions which we find in the *Ormulum* as compared with Old English is due to the imperfect attempts of the Danes to speak the language, which the English themselves imitated, especially as this view has already been shown to be reasonable (see p. 125, etc.).

In the matter of inflexions, then, Orm has advanced a long way towards Modern English. The language which he writes

---

[1] A changing to O in the South, and to a large extent also in East Midland (as in *báðir, both*). Lowland Scotch keeps *fra* in its original form.

[2] Kington Oliphant, *Old and Middle English*, p. 239.

is at all events not more inflected than Chaucer's 200 years later; but then Chaucer's dialect, though it is a kind of East Midland, has much more in common with Southern English, which was a far more conservative dialect. Thus with Orm we have got considerably nearer to Modern English. What makes his language look so strange is—

(1) His peculiar trick of spelling, which is, after all, nothing but marks of quantity, just as if he had written *tc, shœwĕn, ŏf.*

(2) The very large number of Old English words in his poem for which we have now substituted Norman-French words, as the 'glosses' to our examples show.

The old theory of the development of Modern English was that its inflexions were worn down by contact with French after the Norman Conquest. We have already seen that the Conquest did affect them, by giving the popular careless speech an open field, because it destroyed the position of English as a cultivated and literary language. But if it had been the main cause of the loss of our inflexions, these would have been worn down as much in Worcestershire as at Peterborough, Lincoln, or Derby. Let us look at a specimen of the Southern dialect from a poem written about 1205, certainly not earlier than the *Ormulum*, by Layamon, a priest living at Areley, in Worcestershire. It is a translation, very free indeed, of a poem by Wace in Norman-French. This part describes the coming of Hengest and Horsa to Kent.

LAYAMON
Southern Dialect
About 1205 A.D.

1. Sone swa heo hine   imetten ⋮ [1]
    Soon   as   they him (acc.)   *met*
 fæire heo hine igrætten.
    fairly   greeted.

---

[1] *Heo = hi* (they), *i.e.* Hengest and Horsa. A full stop marks the end of the couplet (or line) ⋮ the end of the line (or half-line), not necessarily a pause in the sense.

3. & seiden þat heo him   wolden ͵
                 him (dat.)
   hæren i þisse londe.
   obey in   land.
5. ȝif he heom wolde ͵
   if   them
   mid rihten at-halden.
   with right   keep.
7. Þa andswerede Vortiger ͵
   Then answered Vortigern
   of elchen vuele he wes war.
   each   evil   ware.
9. An alle mine iliue ͵
   In   life
   þe   ich iluued habbe.
   which I lived have.
11. bi dæie no bi nihtes ͵
              nor
    ne sæh ich nauere ær swulche cnihtes.[1]
    not saw I never ere such

We can see at once that this dialect is more inflected than the *Ormulum*. First, there is the prefix *ge-*, corrupted to *i-*, which Orm nearly always drops, both in past participles and in the other words which once had it.[2] Secondly, there is *hine*, the old accusative of *he*, though Layamon also uses *him* for the accusative. Then the termination of 'elch*en*' (line 8) represents *-um* of Anglo-Saxon. Þe (in line 10) is the old relative (see p. 113), where Orm would use *þatt* as we now do,[3] as for instance in the line—

'He *that* will not when he may—'

---

[1] From Morris, *Specimens of Early English*, Part I., p. 66.
[2] e.g. *cweme*, line 4, which in Old English was *ge-cweme*.
[3] We also, of course, now use *who* and *which*, originally interrogative pronouns, as relatives. 'Which, whose, whom, occur as relatives as early as the end of the twelfth century, but *who* not until the fourteenth century, and was not in common use before the sixteenth century.'—Morris, *Historical Outlines of English Accidence*, p. 130. Which appears in the Prayer-Book of 1549, in Collects where we have *who*, e.g. 'O God, *which* art author of

Layamon's grammar is not very regular or consistent. He has forms closely resembling those in Old English for the different cases and genders and numbers of the definite article, or sometimes simply þe for most of them. So too in other words he has 'correct' and also weakened forms for the same case, and the weakened form is a final -e, which later on stood for most inflexions in English. But there are large relics of Old English grammar in his language. Sometimes lines occur which are not very different from what they would be in Anglo-Saxon. For instance—

Anglo-Saxon. to sécenne under lyfte { land / lond } and gódne hláford.
Layamon. to sechen vnder lufte lond and godne lauerd.
Modern English. to seek under heaven land and a good lord.

Anglo-Saxon. hé hæfde ǽnne wisne { mann / monn }.
Layamon. he hæfden ænne wisne mon.
Modern English. he had a wise man.

Anglo-Saxon. fægrest ealra þinga.
Layamon. fairest alre þinge.
Modern English. fairest of-all things.

Anglo-Saxon. { on / in } Englena { lánde / londe }.
Layamon. in Ænglene londe.
Modern English. in the land of-(the-) English.

We see that Layamon uses E as the vowel of his terminations; but his grammar is evidently nothing but degraded Anglo-Saxon.[1] Orm's is Anglo-Saxon greatly altered by contact with another language.

peace,' '*whiche* haste safelye brought us to the beginning of this day,' in the order for Morning Prayer. And even in the Authorised Version of the Bible (1611) *who* (nominative) is rare as a relative, *which* or *that* being usually found instead, as in the Lord's Prayer.

[1] It is, however, often impossible to say of an author, and especially of a poet, how far he copies old-fashioned forms to be found in old books, but which were no longer in actual use. We must make some allowance for this, but it will not seriously affect the main argument. Some of Layamon's most archaic forms are to be found much later in the South.

Layamon is, from his dialect being Southern, fonder of CH for C, and of O for A than Orm is (see p. 213, etc.).

We now come to another great English dialect which must be contrasted with the East Midland—namely, Northumbrian. This, like East Midland, is coloured by Danish, but the basis of it is the older Northumbrian English, and it is a dialect with very distinct characteristics. The relations of these two dialects might be expressed as follows—

Old Mercian English + Danish influence = East Midland.
Old Northumbrian English + Danish influence = the later Northumbrian.

The specimen given below is from a translation of the Psalms, made in the latter half of the thirteenth century, though the copy of it which we possess is not earlier than the reign of Edward II. (1307-1327).[1] It is, of course, made from the Latin version of the Bible, called the Vulgate.

PSALM CVII. (CVI. IN THE LATIN VERSION)[2]

NORTHUMBRIAN (ABOUT 1280)

1. Schriues[3] to Lauerd, for gode he is ;
 For in werld[4] es merci his.

2. Saie þai with gode wille and thoght,
 Whilk[5] þat of Lauerd ere boght ;
 Wham he boght of hand of faa,[6]
 Fra rikes[7] samened[8] he þa.[9]

3. Fra sun-spring to setel-gang,[10]
 Fra north, fra þe see swa[11] lang.

4. Þai dweled in an-nes[12] in drihede[13] wai ;
 Of cite of woning-stede[14] noght fand þai.

---

[1] *Specimens of Early English*, Morris and Skeat, Part II., p. 23.
[2] *Anglo-Saxon and Early English Psalter*, published by the Surtees Society, 1843-47. [3] Confess to, praise (*confiteor*).
[4] Latin, *in sœculum* = for ever. [5] Which. [6] Foe.
[7] From kingdoms ; Latin *regionibus*, perhaps confused with *regnis*.
[8] Gathered. [9] Them. [10] From sun-rising to setting.
[11] So. [12] Wilderness. [13] Dry. [14] Habitation.

> 5. Hungrand[1] and thristand als-swa,[2]
> Þe saule of þam[3] waned in þa.[3]
>
> 6. And þai cried to God when droued[4] þai ware,
> And of þar[5] nedinges[6] he out-nam[7] þam þare.[8]
>
> 7. And he led þam in right wai,
> In cite of woning-stede þat ga suld þai.[9]

Now the first thing that strikes one about this specimen of English is that it is hardly more inflected than our Modern English. There is, indeed, *schriues* in verse 1, the Northumbrian plural of the imperative, which in the Southern dialect would be *schriueth*; and if we looked in other parts of these Psalms we should find an indicative plural corresponding to this, as in the line

> Vpsteg*hes* hilles and feldes dounga*s*.[10]
> Up-mount   -go.

Hungrand keeps nearer to the old form of the present participle *-ende* than 'hunger*ing*,' which we now have, and which is the form used by Chaucer, though this is after all only putting one inflexion instead of another. But in Southern or in East Midland English of the thirteenth or fourteenth century the past tenses *dweled, fand* (verse 4), *suld* (verse 7), would have the plural marked by a termination, either *-en* or a sounded *-e*.[11] The *-e* in *ere* (verse 2) had no doubt once been pronounced; probably it is meant to be pronounced here, as appears from the metre; but, if so, it is a solitary survivor, an 'archaism' or old-fashioned form, or else copied from the other dialects for the purposes of the metre. In other places it is simply *er*. In fact, we may say that by the beginning of the fourteenth century the verb in Northumbrian was almost as little inflected as in our Modern English. The other final

---

[1] Hunger*ing*. [2] Also. [3] Them. [4] Troubled.
[5] Their. [6] Necessities. [7] Took out. [8] There.
[9] Other words will be easily identified if we remember that 'standard' English often has an O for Old English and Northumbrian A, or from the Bible.
[10] *Specimens of Early English*, Part II., p. 32.
[11] Nearly always, even in the fourteenth century.

Dialects of English after the Conquest 249

-*e*'s too were not pronounced at this time.[1] *Gode* in the first verse is a clear example of this, for even in Old English, before the Norman Conquest, the nominative singular masculine of the adjective had no termination. Why, then, were these final -*e*'s written if they were not intended to be pronounced? The fact is that the scribe, or person who copied out books, did not copy out one English dialect, or even one language only. This would have been specialising with a vengeance, and such a one-sided scribe would have been comparatively useless.[2] We have already seen that scribes used to French spelling naturally employed it in English books, and that they did this to such an extent that it gradually coloured all our English spelling.[3] So too it was to some extent with the different English dialects. A scribe who spoke Southern, or East or West Midland English, or who was used to copying books in those dialects, when he came to write out a piece of Northumbrian English, though he might try to copy it accurately, would naturally write some of the words as they sounded to him or as he had seen them written. We must remember that there was then no fixed standard of spelling, such as we have now.[4] But, besides this reproducing of the sounds in the scribe's head, he would also try (unconsciously) to make the page look as he was accustomed to see it. Now English writing, except in Northumbrian, abounded in final -*e*'s, and thus he wrote them carelessly in *saule* and other words, in order to make the writing look as he was accustomed to see it.[5] It is

[1] This of course does not apply to *cite*, which is a French word.
[2] It would have been almost like the Butcher in the 'Hunting of the Snark' who could only kill beavers.
[3] No doubt there was also the idea that French spelling ought to be the standard.
[4] The metre and the rhyme sometimes make it possible to see what the word really was. Thus, in these Psalms, *brade* (*broad*, plural) rhymes to *mykelhede*. Now *mykelhede*, by its history, cannot have had its final -*e* pronounced. Therefore the -*e* in *brade* was also merely ornamental.
[5] Nouns in the dative properly had an -*e* in Southern and Midland English at this time, but this was not always sounded. Consequently a careless scribe would often write a word with an -*e* without thinking whether it were in the dative or not. This is another element of confusion in many manu-

partly this trick of writing final -*e*'s for the sake of appearances which caused them to be retained in Modern English where they are no longer sounded, though they have now got to act as marks of quantity.

Well then, if Northumbrian is in 1300 A.D. already so much like Modern English in having dropped most of its terminations, why should we not say that Modern English sprang from it ?

In the first place, because it is not historically correct. 'Standard' English, what is now the one literary dialect for the whole of England, made its first appearance farther south, in the district of which London was a part, and in that city, as we shall see presently.

Secondly, there are some points in this Northern English which have nothing in our Modern English answering to them. The most striking of these are (1) the keeping of A instead of its being changed to O, as it is in Midland English of the same period, as well as in Modern English;[1] for instance, in the words *wham* (*whom*), *faa* (*foe*), *fra* (*fro* or from), *lang* (*long*), *ga* (*go*); and (2) the use of S for SH, as in *sal*, *suld*.[2]

And if we look carefully at these points we shall see what Northumbrian really developed into. Its most distinguished child is Lowland Scotch,[3] that dialect of English which was the standard or literary dialect of the Scotch Court and of Scotland till after the union of the crowns at the accession of James I., and which is the ordinary speech of the Scotch Lowlands at the present day. Thus the poems of Burns are in Modern Northumbrian, and we can find many instances of it in Scott's novels, as, for instance, in *The Fortunes of Nigel*,[4]

scripts even where a Southern or Midland scribe was writing his own dialect.

[1] But the O has changed its sound somewhat in tolerably recent times (p. 212, note). [2] For the hard C's retained in Northumbrian see chap. xv. [3] Sweet's *History of English Sounds*, p. 201.
[4] He breaks his word and oath *baith*.
Banishment *frae* our Court, my lord, said the king.
My back is *sair*.
There go *twa* words to that bargain.

Dialects of English after the Conquest

where James I. speaks Modern Northumbrian, in the mouth of the Baron of Bradwardine in *Waverley*, from Mause and Cuddie Headrigg and others in *Old Mortality*,[1] and also in some of Mr. Stevenson's novels. Though the dialects of Northern Yorkshire, Durham, Westmoreland, and Northumberland are also founded on Northumbrian, Lowland Scotch is the best example of its modern form, since this has been preserved as a *literary* dialect, we may say, down to the present day.

We have seen (p. 134, etc.) that the decay of Northumbrian inflexions began even before the Norman Conquest. And now the question arises, Why did it lose its inflexions earlier than East Midland English, which was about equally liable to be influenced by the Danes? Now very many of the variations in language cannot have causes assigned to them; we can only say what they are, and give other instances of like changes. But there are some facts in the history of the North which seem to account for this change, in part at any rate. We have seen that, after inflexions began to be less accurately used, after their time of ascendency was past, when the 'tendency of the age' was against them, it was education which tended to preserve them, and the careful utterance of educated, or at least of cultivated people; not the careless speech of the vulgar who are not particular as to how they speak so long as they are understood. We have also seen that Northumbria was, to begin with, the most educated, literary, and cultivated part of England. How much Northumbrian writings did to give a model of style for the works of Alfred, for instance, we shall never know, since almost all this Northern literature has perished, at least in its original form. But literature does not start into life full-grown, like Athena. A rustic's letter is about the height of style to which its prose could reach.

---

[1] I'se be silent or thou *sall* come to harm.
Ye *suld* ken.
Like *wha* but him.

The West Saxon literature must have been largely formed on Northumbrian models.[1]

But this peaceful and enlightened period soon passed. Northumbria had fallen into great confusion even before the Danes came. And when the Danish invasion took place, though this was shared by the East Midlands, the disorder lasted far longer in Northumbria. Even just before the Norman Conquest we can see how uncivilised Northumbria was. Siward, its earl, who conquered Macbeth, though he was a fine fellow in his way, was a regular barbarian. Tostig, Harold's brother, Earl of Northumbria, seems to have thought that he could govern the savage Northumbrians only by taking a leaf out of their book and murdering some of their chief men by treachery. The Northumbrians very inconsistently resented this, and invaded the centre of England treating it like an enemy's country, until Edward the Confessor agreed to banish Tostig, and to appoint as their earl the man whom they wished to have.[2] Then came the invasion from Norway by Harold Hardrada, the rebellion of the Northumbrians against William the Conqueror, and the ravaging of the country between the Humber and the Tees by him, from which, as is seen in Domesday Book, the country had hardly even begun to recover fifteen years later. Nor was it left at peace even then. It was near the Scotch border; and such troubles as the laying waste of the country by the Scotch before the Battle of the Standard in Stephen's reign (1138 A.D.) were not likely to restore its prosperity. And the country which had been ceded to Scotland, and in which Northumbrian was also spoken, was almost as much troubled as Northern England. It had shared the miseries of the Danish invasions. It was invaded by Siward, and again and again by the Norman kings.

It is plain that in the midst of this disorder and misery learning and education could have no chance. And so, while

---

[1] Earle, *Philology of the English Tongue*, p. 29, and see chap. x.
[2] See Freeman, *Old English History*.

Dialects of English after the Conquest 253

the decay of the elaborate literary language was delayed in the East Midlands (down to the Norman Conquest) by the influence of the Anglo-Saxon literature, by the near neighbourhood of Wessex, where nothing but the inflected West Saxon or Southern English was spoken, and by the careful speech of educated Mercians, in Northumbria this decay went on unchecked. It was natural, therefore, that Northumbrian should be ahead of East Midland in its loss of inflexions. The three main dialects after the Norman Conquest are in this respect like three regiments marching in *échelon*, one in flank of another and to its rear, but not stepping over quite the same ground. First comes Northumbrian, then East Midland, the Southern dialect last. Each has its own peculiarities; all are on the way to getting rid of the mass of their inflexions; but one is more advanced on the road than another. And yet Northumbrian (as represented by Lowland Scotch), which changed most rapidly once, now looks a most old-fashioned dialect. For in some of its innovations 'standard' English has caught it up; in its loss of inflexions, and in its *pronunciation* of A (see p. 225). On the other hand, Northumbrian has kept the Old English A, in writing at least, in many words where we have altered it to O, and some of its words, such as *wha*, *twa*, and also *oot*, *hoo* (*out*, *how*), sound just as they did at Alfred the Great's Court.[1] This dialect then is like a man who, having been a Radical in his youth, has seen the world move on and realise his pet ideas, and in his old age becomes conservative, as having no more changes to wish for.

Lowland Scotch also differs largely from 'standard' English in the words which it uses. The nations were for centuries under separate governments, and consequently the dialects, besides their original differences, developed independently. The points in which the Lowland Scotch vocabulary differs from 'standard' English fall mainly under three heads.

[1] In *die* (pronounced 'dee' rhyming to 'free' in the poem—'Scots wha hae wi' Wallace bled') as well as in *chield* or *chiel* and other words I keeps its old pronunciation. *Necht* (night) exactly represents *neht*, a parallel form to *niht* in Old English.

(1) 'Modern Northumbrian' owns a good many Norse words which we do not use, such as *levin* (lightning), *fra* (from), *gar* (make, oblige), *tod* (fox). As we have seen, the Norse element was very strong in the Northumbrian dialect.[1]

(2) 'Modern Northumbrian' retains a great many Old English words which, in 'standard' English, have been 'crowded out,' either by other English words or by French words. Among these are—

Lowland Scotch.	Old English.	English.
dree	dréogan	suffer
eme	ćam	uncle
ferlie	fǽrlíc	terrible (sudden)
halse	hals	neck
speir	spyrian	inquire
wud	wód	mad

(3) On the other hand, owing to the friendship between the Scotch and French, which lasted from the War of Independence down to the time of Mary Queen of Scots, a good many French words have been introduced into Lowland Scotch, besides those from Norman-French brought in by the Normans (as, for instance, the Bruces and Balliols), who had almost as much influence in the Lowlands of Scotland as they had in England. Among these later French words are—

Lowland Scotch.	Modern French.	English.
ashet	assiette	plate
dishabill	déshabillé	déshabille, *treated as a foreign word.*
douce	doux, douce	pleasant
fash, fashous	fâcher, fâcheux	vex, vexatious
jigot	gigot	leg of mutton

And now we may leave Northumbrian to develop into Lowland Scotch, and turn once more to the sources of our 'standard' English.

---

[1] One of the strongest instances of this is the use of *at* for *to* with the infinitive, as in Icelandic. So in the Northumbrian Psalter, quoted above, we find Þat leres mi hend at fight nou (Ps. xviii. 34).
 teachest hands to
So we can speak of 'making a great ado' ('*at* do'=to-do).

CHAPTER XVII

ENGLISH DIALECTS IN THE FOURTEENTH CENTURY

East Midland English in the first half of the fourteenth century—The ancestor of 'standard' English—Robert of Brunne—The Southern dialect of Gloucestershire, and of Kent—The West Midland dialect.[1]

WE saw in the last chapter that the first specimens which we possess of the East Midland dialect—that is, of 'standard' English in its infancy — were written at Peterborough. Orm, whose language contains so many prophecies of what Modern English was to be, very probably lived in or near Lincolnshire (p. 231). And even now the same dialect runs down from north to south, from Lincolnshire, to the neighbourhood of London,[2] and is nearer than any other popular dialect to our 'standard' English, the English of books and of educated people. Consequently, if we take a specimen of this dialect of English in the first half of the fourteenth century, we shall be on the right line for tracing the origin of our 'standard' English. The poem, a part of which will be quoted, was written by Robert Manning of Brunne, or Bourn, in Lincolnshire, who was a monk or Canon of Sempringham. It was compiled from various authors—Bede, Peter of Langtoft, and from Wace (who wrote the *Roman de Rou*)—in 1338 A.D.

[1] Morris and Skeat, *Specimens of Early English*, Part II. Skeat, *Principles of English Etymology*, First Series. Kington Oliphant, *Old and Middle English*; *The New English.* Furnivall, *Chronicle of Robert Manning*.

[2] London itself, like most large English cities, now has a special dialect of its own.

I

INCIPIT PROLOGUS DE HISTORIA BRITANNIE TRANSUMPTA
PER ROBERTUM IN MATERNA LINGUA

1. Lordynges,[1] [tha]t be now here,
   if ȝe wille listene and lere [2]
3. All [þ]e story of Inglande
   als [3] Robert Mannyng wryten it fand,[4]
5. & on Inglysch has it schewed,
   not for þe lerid bot for þe lewed,[5]
7. ffor þo [6] þat in þis land[e] * wone [7]
   þat þe Latyn no [8] Frankys [9] cone,[10]
9. ffor to haf solace and gamen [11]
   In felawschip when þai sitt samen.[12]
11. And it is wisdom for to wytten [13]
    þe state of þe land, and haf it wryten,
13. what manere of folk first it wan,[14]
    & of what kynde [15] it first began;
15. And gude it is for many thynges
    for to here þe dedis of kynges,
17. whilk [16] were foles, and whilk were wyse,
    & whilk of þam couthe [17] most quantyse,[18]
19. and whilk did wrong, and whilk ryght
    & whilk maynten[e]d pes & fyght.[19]

The part quoted above is taken from a Manuscript which shows traces of having been written by a scribe who spoke a more Northern dialect than that of Lincolnshire.[20] It is

---

[1] Sirs. [2] Learn. [3] As. [4] Found. [5] Unlearned.
[6] Them, those. [7] Dwell. [8] Nor. [9] French. [10] Know.
[11] Amusement (*gammon* and *game* both come from the word).
[12] Together. [13] Know. [14] Won. [15] Race. [16] Which.
[17] Knew (=could). [18] Cunning, from Old French *cointise*.
[19] From Furnivall's Edition in the Rolls Series.
* It appears that the Northern copyist cut out an E (sign of the dative) as an inflexion which was not familiar to him. The line will not scan without it. [20] e.g. þam (line 18) is distinctly a Northern form.

S

chosen because it is an original part of the poem, and also because the difference in language is not very great. The other Manuscript, which is supposed to represent Robert's own dialect with tolerable exactness,[1] has lost this introduction, but a bit which comes later on will now be given. It is almost or altogether free from incorrect or unpronounced -*e*'s, but -*e* is elided before a vowel and sometimes before an H.

II

1. Bretons of Walys herde wel how
   Þat þe Englische þe monkes slow ;[2]
3. Þey gadered þem to consail[3]
   How to venge þat tyrpayl.[4]
5. Þre noble men were in þat cite,
   Þo þre made a gret semble ;[5]
7. Þo þre weren alle kynges,
   & of þe Bretons lordynges :
9. Bledryk, of Cornewaille was sire,
   & lord ouer al Deueneschire,
11. Als þe water of Ex rennes[6]
    ffro þe hed,—þer[7] men hit kennes,[8]—
13. Vnto þe se þer hit gos yn ;
    Longe helden hit þe Bretons kyn,
15. Euere til Adelston[9] cam ;
    He dide þat kynde[10] mykel scham.[11]

In the *Peterborough Chronicle* and in Orm's poem we saw a language which had started on the way to becoming Modern English. In Robert of Brunne the change is near completion so far as the inflexions are concerned, and the proportion of French words used by him is nearly the same as in the least

---

[1] Furnivall, Introduction. The extract is from the same edition.
[2] Slew, that is, the Monks of Bangor, in 607 A.D.
[3] Counsel.   [4] Slaughter, infamous deed.   [5] Assembly.   [6] Runs.
[7] Where.   [8] *Kennes* is not the Northern plural, as on p. 85. The indefinite *man* (like *man* in German), or *men*, or *me*, constantly takes a singular verb.
[9] Athelstan, or Æthelstan.   [10] Race.   [11] Disgrace, shame.

English Dialects in Fourteenth Century 259

stilted English writings of modern times. In fact, he is more modern than Chaucer and Wycliffe half a century later, but then they wrote in a more Southern, and therefore more conservative form of the East Midland dialect, as we shall see. The influence of the almost uninflected Northumbrian dialect, which bordered on Lincolnshire, must have been strong in that county.

Let us now see quite shortly what are the points to be noticed in Robert Manning's English.

First, as to the spelling, both þ and *th* are used in the first example. We have seen how and why the latter finally drove out its rival. U is written for V between vowels, as it was for another three centuries, and V for U at the beginning of words.

To pass to the grammar, þem (as well as *hem*) is already used for the dative and accusative plural of *he*, as it was in *The Ormulum*, and as it is now, though in Chaucer and Wycliffe we shall find only *hem* and *her*, like the Old English forms, for *them* and *their*. It took 150 years after Robert Manning's time to establish our modern forms, derived from Danish, in the predominant dialect of English. Þey is equally a Danish form, but this is also used by Chaucer and Wycliffe.

Hit, the neuter of *he*, still keeps the H, which is found much later than this, even in Tyndale's *New Testament* (1526).

In *allë* (ii. 7) the *-e* marks the plural of the adjective; in 'monkës' (ii. 2) the termination is an extra syllable, not a mere S added, as at present. *Dedis* (i. 16) shows this still more clearly.

Then, as to the inflexions of the verb. The infinitive has two forms—'wytten' (i. 11) and 'vengë' (ii. 4), just as we shall find them in Chaucer. And we get all three forms of the plural—'weren,'[1] 'helden' (ii. 7, ii. 14); 'herdë' (ii. 1); and 'gadered,' without any termination to mark the number. *Gos, rennës* (instead of *goeth, renneth*) are the Northern form of

---

[1] These are, of course, past tenses. But the termination of the present is just the same in the Midland dialect, *e.g.* in another work of Robert's,

the 3rd person singular, which had, as we see, begun to make its way southwards, though it did not become the correct form in 'standard' English for some time after the more Southern East Midland became established in that position. Robert Manning's language is, as we shall see presently, nearer to Modern English than Chaucer's is.

It is very important to keep well in mind that it is the East Midland only that we have been speaking of. Northumbrian we have already seen developing into Lowland Scotch. Southern English is very distinct from both of these and seems to us much more old-fashioned. West Midland, on the other hand, is, as might be expected, nearer to the East Midland dialect. To prove this we will take three specimens of them, two Southern and one West Midland. But, first of all, it will help to give us a clear idea of the difference between them if we look at the present indicative of the verb in the three main dialects.

Southern.		East Midland.		Northern.	
ich	sende	ich, i,	sende	ic, i,	sende, send
þou	sendest	þou	sendest	þou	sendes
he	sendeþ	he	sendeþ, sendes[1]	he	sendes
we	sendeþ	we	senden	we	send, sendes
ȝe	sendeþ	ȝe	senden	ȝe	send, sendes
hi	sendeþ	þei	senden	þai	send, sendes

These forms would enable us roughly to identify the dialect of the extracts. But the West Midland (and to a less extent the East Midland) has both Northern and Southern grammatical forms.

To begin with, we will take an extract from the *Metrical Chronicle* of Robert of Gloucester,[2] written in 1298, a part which is interesting for its meaning, as well as for its language. Gloucester, as we have seen, belonged to the South in dialect.

Men clepyn þe boke 'Handlyng Synne.'—Kington Oliphant, *Old and Middle*
   call
English, p. 473.   [1] Originally a Northern form.
   [2] Edited by Aldis Wright. Rolls Series.

ROBERT OF GLOUCESTER

Southern

1298

1. Þus com lo engelond · in to normandies hond.
    came   *hand*
   & þe normans ne couþe speke þo · bote hor owe speche,
              not could   *then*   *but their own*

3. & speke french as hii dude atom · and hor children dude
    spoke   *they did at home*
   also teche.
   So þat heie men of þis lond · þat of hor blod come·
       high   *came*

5. Holdeþ alle þulke speche · þat hii of hom nome.
       the same   *took*
   Vor bote a man conne frenss · me telþ of him lute.
              know   *one reckons*   *little*

7. Ac lowe men holdeþ to engliss · & to hor owe speche ȝute.
   But   *yet*
   Ich wene þer ne beþ in al þe world · contreyes none··
    think   *are*

9. Þat ne holdeþ to hor owe speche · bote engelond one·
                                                     only
   Ac wel me wot uor to conne · boþe wel it is·
   one knows for

11. Vor þe more þat a mon can · þe more wurþe he is.
                  knows

Every letter here has its force; there are no silent *-e*'s, though *-e* is cut off, as usual, before a vowel. The dots in the middle of the line show the division of the verse; it might equally well be written in two halves. Bearing these two facts in mind, we shall be able to scan it, though the metre is rough. There will be four accents in the first half-line, three in the second. It is like Sam Weller's song in *Pickwick*—

{ Bold Turpin once on Hounslow Heath
  His bold mare Bess bestrode-a ;
{ When there he see the Bishop's coach
  A-coming along the road-a.

In the language the chief things to notice are—

(1) He keeps to the Old English forms of the 3rd personal pronoun, instead of the Danish forms *they, their, them*, thus—

       Nominative plural *hii* (l. 3)   Anglo-Saxon *hí*
       Genitive   plural *hor* (l. 2)   Anglo-Saxon *heora*

(2) The plural of the present indicative of verbs ends in *-eþ*, as in *holdeþ* (l. 5), *beþ* (l. 8), which is the proper Southern termination, inherited directly from the West Saxon *-aþ*, as in *healdaþ, beoþ*.

(3) We have already seen that the final *-e*'s are real parts of the language. For instance, in *couþe* (l. 2), *come* (l. 4), *nome* (l. 5), *-e* marks the plural of past tenses, in Anglo-Saxon *cúþon, cómon, námon*. In *speke* (l. 2) it marks the infinitive, Anglo-Saxon *spǽcan*. *Conne* (l. 6) is 3rd person singular present subjunctive. *None* (l. 8) is the plural of the adjective.

(4) Besides this Robert of Gloucester keeps the prefix *ge-* of the past participle in a mutilated form—

       þis bataile was *ido* (*ge-dón*, done, fought),

and

       he was *aslawe* (*ge-slagen*, slain).

We will next take another specimen of the Southern dialect, later in date, but still more old-fashioned, archaic, or conservative in language, though, as it is a translation of the Apostles' Creed, it will not be so hard to make out. It is by Dan Michel of Northgate in Kent,[1] a monk of St. Augustine's, Canterbury, and was written about 1340.[2]

---

[1] ? Northgate in Canterbury. I can find no other Northgate in Kent. *Dan* is for *dominus*, a title of monks, and of priests who were not Masters of Arts.

[2] From *Specimens of Early English*, Morris and Skeat, Part II., p. 106.

THE APOSTLES' CREED

KENTISH (SOUTHERN)

1340

Ich leue ine god / uader almiȝti. makere of heuene / and of erþe. And ine iesu crist / his zone on-lepi¹ / oure lhord. þet y-kend is / of þe holy gost.   y-bore of Marie Mayde. y-pyned onder pouns pilate. y-nayled a rode.²   dyad. and be-bered. yede doun to helle. þane þridde day a-ros uram þe dyade. Steaȝ to heuenes. zit aþe riȝt half of god þe uader al-miȝti. þannes to comene he is / to deme þe quike / and þe dyade. Ich y-leue ine þe holy gost. holy cherche generalliche.³   Mennesse of halȝen. Lesnesse of zennes. of ulesse arizinge. and lyf eurelestinde. zuo by hyt.⁴

This extract is, as has been said already, still more old-fashioned than the last, but we need only notice the more striking points in the language. There is the prefix *y-* (the corruption of *ge-*) to a swarm of past participles. In '*þane þridde day*' the article has the same form for the accusative singular masculine as it sometimes has in Anglo-Saxon. 'To com*en*e' is the Anglo-Saxon *to cumenne*, the gerund or dative of the infinitive, like *to sáwenne* in the Parable of the Sower on p. 154.

The Z for S in *zone, zuo* is the Southern pronunciation (as in 'Zummerzet'), and so is U or V for F, as in *uader, uram* (from). This last we have already had in Robert of Gloucester, in *uor, Vor* (ll. 10, 11); and the other grammatical forms are much the same as in his poem, *-e* being an essential part of the grammar. Kent has even now a dialect distinct from that of the shires to the north of London, but it has been too much in touch with London for centuries to have kept

¹ Only.   ² On cross (rood).   ³ Universal, catholic.
⁴ So be it (amen). The rest can easily be made out from the Prayer-Book.

anything like its position of the fourteenth century as the most conservative in language of all English counties.

As a specimen of the West Midland dialect we will take part of the 'Instructions for Parish Priests,' composed at the end of the fourteenth or beginning of the fifteenth century,[1] by Myrc, Canon of Lilleshall in Shropshire.

WEST MIDLAND

About 1400 (?)

1. God seyth hym self, as wryten we fynde,
That whenne þe blynde ledeth þe blynde,
3. In to þe dyche þey fallen boo,[2]
For þey ne sen whare by to go.
5. So faren prestes now by dawe;[3]
They beth blynde in goddes lawe,
7. That whenne þey scholde þe pepul rede[4]
In to synne þey do hem lede.
9. Thus þey haue do now fulle ȝore,[5]
And alle ys for defawte of lore,[6]
11. Wherefore þou preste curatoure[7]
ȝef[8] þou plese thy sauyoure,
13. ȝef thow be not grete clerk,[9]
Loke thow moste on thys werk;
15. For here thow myȝte fynde and rede[10]
That þe behoueth to conne[11] nede.[12]

Now this seems tolerably easy at first sight, and a good deal like Modern English. But it is not its direct ancestor,

---

[1] Kington Oliphant, *The New English*, vol. i. p. 104. The book has been edited by Peacock for the Early English Text Society, and the extract is taken from that edition. The MS. is of about 1450, the language older; Professor Skeat says about 1420.

[2] Both; Anglo-Saxon *bá*.   [3] Nowadays.   [4] Advise.
[5] Done now full long ago.   [6] Want of teaching.
[7] With a cure of souls.   [8] If.   [9] Very learned.
[10] Read.   [11] Know.   [12] Of necessity.

for modern 'standard' English did not as a matter of fact arise out of the West Midland but from the East Midland dialect. There is, indeed, a considerable resemblance between the two. Here, in l. 8, we have þey (nominative), but *hem*[1] (dative and accusative), just as Chaucer uses them, though later the Danish form (*their, them*) prevailed in the oblique cases as well, the form which we have seen in Orm and in Robert of Brunne. Again we have *sen* (l. 4), and *faren* (l. 5), the Midland form of the plural, though in line 6 there is *beth*, which is the Southern plural. Just in the same way we have both the Southern and the Northern 3rd person singular in a line of another poem by Robert of Brunne—

>Þe holy man telleþ vs and sey*s*
>Þat þe lofe made euen peys,[2]
>*weight,*

which is just like Shakespeare's line—

>It bless*eth* him that give*s* and him that take*s*.[3]

So far the West Midland dialect bears a considerable resemblance to the East Midland. And we shall find some instances of the Southern plural in 'standard' English, even in Shakespeare. But West Midland is a mixture of Northern and Southern forms[4] to a still greater extent. For instance, in the part about the priest's hearing confessions—

>Fyrst þow moste þys mynne,[5]
>What he ys þat doth þe synne,
>Wheþer hyt be *heo* or he,
>ʒonge or olde, bonde or fre.

and

>*Scho* may that wepen euer more.

---

[1] But Myrc also uses *them*.
[2] *Specimens of Early English*, Morris and Skeat, Part II., p. 53. I have preferred to take the longer extracts from the other poem, as the 'Handlyng Synne' seems to have been a good deal altered by a Southern scribe. But this point might be illustrated from the MS. (quoted above), which is believed to represent his own dialect best.
[3] *Merchant of Venice*, IV. i. 187.
[4] See Kington Oliphant, *The New English*, vol. i. p. 104.   [5] Remember.

Here we have the Northern *scho* for 'she,' as well as the old Southern form *heo*. This *heo*, the proper feminine of *he*, is still used in the dialects of Cheshire and Lancashire (branches of the West Midland) in the form *hoo* or *'oo*. So too we get in Myrc the Southern form *chylderen*, and the Northern *chyldere* ('childer').

And besides this West Midland has some forms peculiar to it, such as *vche*, for 'each,' which do not appear in 'standard' English. On the whole, then, we may conclude that, though West Midland is the dialect most nearly resembling East Midland, yet it is not identical with it, and that, judging both from history and from the character of the dialects, it is East and not West Midland that is the parent of 'standard' English.[1]

[1] The *-e*'s, as written in the extract, cannot be pressed. The poem was *written down* about 1450, when *-e* had become merely ornamental. But the *-e* in *rede* (l. 15), and *conne* (l. 16), for instance, appears to be sounded as a sign of the infinitive, and in *nede* as a sign of the dative. In *grete* (l. 13), on the other hand, it must be a mere ornament.

The versions of *Piers Plowman*, though it is a most interesting work, appear to be too mixed in dialect (as we possess them) to be usefully quoted for our present purpose. This is partly owing to those who copied them out.

CHAPTER XVIII

THE BEGINNINGS OF 'STANDARD' ENGLISH

No fixed 'standard' English in Chaucer's time—Chaucer's dialect—His grammar—Wycliffe and Purvey—Contemporary letter-writing—Southern English still written.[1]

WE have now seen how great a variety of dialects there was in England in the fourteenth century. We have seen that 'standard' English cannot be derived from Northumbrian, and it is clear that the East Midland dialect of Robert of Brunne is nearer to Modern English than any of the others. Now, at the middle of the fourteenth century we are approaching the time when one dialect was to become the standard dialect of English. This was certain to happen after French lost its ascendency. So far we might say that the standard language in England had been French. But we have already seen (p. 167, etc.) that soon after the middle of the fourteenth century French began to go out of use, and it was to be expected that, as has happened in other countries, some one dialect of English should, sooner or later, establish itself in a position superior to the rest.

It is sometimes said that this 'standard' English begins with Chaucer. In a sense, perhaps, this is true. Chaucer was 'the father of English poetry,' since all later poets owe

---

[1] Morris, Chaucer's *Prologue and Knightes Tale.* The same re-edited by Skeat. Kington Oliphant, *Old and Middle English, The New English. The New Testament,* Wycliffe and Purvey, edited by Forshall and Madden, re-edited by Skeat. Eadie, *The English Bible.* Article, 'The English Bible,' *Encyclopædia Britannica,* Ninth Edition.

something to him. This is partly because later English poetry is to a very considerable extent modelled on Spenser, and Spenser's debt to Chaucer is very large indeed. Then too Chaucer is the oldest English poet who is at all commonly read at the present day for the sake of his poetry (just as people read Tennyson), and not merely to learn what our language was like at a particular time. But then, as we can see by this time, Chaucer owes his language (as well as his metre, in the main) to the writers of Middle English who preceded him. There is no break in the chain. A standard dialect of English could not suddenly spring into life ready made, nor could any one dialect at once gain supremacy over the others. In Chaucer's lifetime (about 1340-1400) English gained the victory over French, as we have seen before. But English writing might still be in any one of many dialects. Chaucer died in 1400, leaving his *Canterbury Tales* still unfinished. Now, in 1387, John of Trevisa, Vicar of Berkeley, in Gloucestershire, translated Higden's *Polychronicon* into Southern Engglish.[1] The *Legend of St. Edith* was written in the Wiltshire (Southern) dialect about 1420.[2] And there are other examples of the same kind. These show clearly, what is probable to begin with, that there was as yet no one form of English in which authors were bound to write. One dialect of English was coming to the front, but it had not yet established its position. So in Germany, Luther's translation of the Bible, which eventually settled the question as to which of the German dialects should be the dialect of literature and of polite conversation, was published in 1534. And yet well on in the seventeenth century Low German was still used for all purposes in Hamburg and Lübeck, as may be seen from the texts written up in the Lübeck churches. 'Standard' English took less time to establish itself than this; but, when

---

[1] Kington Oliphant, *The New English*, vol. i. pp. 150, 151. *Specimens of Early English*, Morris and Skeat, Part II., p. 235.
[2] Kington Oliphant, *The New English*, vol. i. p. 224.

Chaucer began to write, there was as yet no one dialect in that position at all.

Chaucer, then, must have written some one dialect of English, and not 'standard' English, since there was as yet no such thing. What dialect, then, did he write in?

Chaucer was an out-and-out Londoner. He was born in London. He spent nearly the whole of his life in London, except when he was serving in the French Wars, or on embassies to Italy and other parts.[1] Under these circumstances he must have spoken and written the dialect of London.

The next question, then, is, What was this London dialect? Now, London must have spoken a Southern or Saxon dialect to begin with.[2] London is in Middlesex, the country of the Middle Saxons. And even within a century or so of Chaucer's birth, Londoners spoke a dialect which would certainly be called Southern.[3] But they were near the borders of the East Midland dialect, and that variety of English was extending its domain. It was, for one thing, a sort of acceptable compromise, without the strong characteristics, which we should now call 'provincialisms,' of the Northern and the Southern dialects. Besides, London was on the north bank of the Thames, open to invasion, so to speak, by the East Midland speech, cut off to some extent, in spite of London Bridge, from the support of the Southern dialect of Surrey and Kent.[4] And so in the latter half of the fourteenth century the dialect spoken in London was in the main East Midland, though with a strong dash of the South about it still remaining. This appears in Chaucer, for instance, by his using only the true English forms *here* or *hir*,[5] and *hem*,[6]

[1] See Morris, Chaucer's *Prologue and Knightes Tale*, Introduction.
[2] *Encyclopædia Britannica*, Ninth Edition, Article 'English Language.'
[3] See specimen of it in Kington Oliphant's *Old and Middle English*, pp. 300, 301.   [4] Skeat, *Principles of English Etymology*, First Series, p. 29.
[5] *e.g.* And eek *hir* wyves wolde it wel assente.—*Canterbury Tales, Prologue*, l. 374. Edited by Morris and Skeat, from which edition the subsequent quotations are made.
[6] But sore weep she if oon of *hem* were deed.—*Prologue*, l. 148.

where Orm mostly used *their* and *them*, as we now do. Yet Chaucer uses *they* for the nominative, not *hi*, like Robert of Gloucester. He is also fond of the prefix *y-* (from *ge-*) to past participles (for instance, *y-shrive* = *shriven*[1]), which, as we have seen, was usually dropped farther north. There are still a good many traces of the Southern dialect left in 'standard' English. *Vixen*, for instance, is a distinctly Southern form, corresponding to the masculine *vox*, just as we saw *uor* in Robert of Gloucester, and *uram* in Dan Michel of Northgate. So too is *vat*, corresponding to the Northern (wine-)*fat*, which is the form used in the English Bible.[2] But the more Northern form of the East Midland, the dialect of Orm and of Robert of Brunne, did not cease its influence, and thus many of these Southern characteristics of Chaucer's language have disappeared in 'standard' English.

It is not necessary to give more than a slight sketch of Chaucer's language. It may be studied in those parts of his works which have been edited by Dr. Morris and Professor Skeat. On the whole it is not unlike the extract given above from Robert of Brunne, only more Southern, as has been said. This will be made clearer by taking a short specimen of it. It is part of Chaucer's description of the 'Parson.'[3]

(The words derived from French are here printed in italics.)

1. *Benigne* he was, and wonder[4] *diligent*,
   And in *aduersitee* ful *pacient*;
3. And swich[5] he was y-*preued*[6] ofte sythes.[7]
   Ful looth were him to cursen[8] for his tythes,
5. But rather wolde he yeuen,[9] out of *doute*,
   Vn-to his *poure parisshens* aboute

---

[1] *Prologue*, l. 226. [2] *e.g.* Isaiah lxiii. 2.
[3] *Canterbury Tales, Prologue*, l. 483, etc. In this extract I have altered the U's and V's into conformity with the MSS. (as given in Furnivall's Six-Text Edition) and with the practice of Chaucer's time. The smaller quotations are left just as in Morris and Skeat's Edition of the *Prologue*, etc.
[4] Wonderfully. [5] Such. [6] Proved. [7] Often-times.
[8] *i.e.* excommunicate. [9] Give.

7. Of his offring,¹ and eek of his *substaunce*.
   He coude in litel thing han *suffisaunce*.²
9. Wyd was his *parisshe*, and houses fer a-sonder,
   But he ne lafte³ nat, for reyn ne⁴ thonder,
11. In siknes nor in *meschief*⁵ to *visyte*
    The ferreste in his *parisshe*, moche and lyte,⁶
13. Vp-on his feet, and in his hand a staf.
    This *noble ensample* to his sheep he yaf,
15. That first he wroghte, and afterward he taughte;
    Out of the gospel he tho⁷ wordes caughte.

This English is not very difficult to make out. But in lines 3, 6, 10, 16, it seems as if the metre were faulty, and so it would be if we read it like Modern English. But, as a matter of fact, *ofte, poure, lafte, wordes* are each of them two-syllabled, though a final -*e* is cut off before a vowel or H,⁸ as *wer(e), wold(e)*, in lines 4 and 5. Having taken notice of the fact that final -*e*'s are a part of Chaucer's grammar, we shall now be able to look further into it.

(1) *Cursen, yeuen, han* (ll. 4, 5, 8) are infinitives. For the -*en* we sometimes have a simple -*e*, as *visytë* (l. 11), or in the line—
   To make him *livë* by his propre good.⁹

(2) The plural of the verb is marked by -*en* (or -*n*), -*e*, or (very rarely) not at all, as in the lines—

   His eyen *twinkled* in his heed aright,
   As *doon* the sterrës in the frosty night.¹⁰

   And specially, from every shires endë
   Of Engelond, to Caunterbury they *wendë*.¹¹

---

¹ *e.g.* Easter-offerings. The verb is found in Anglo-Saxon, derived from Latin.—Skeat. ² Have (*infin.*) sufficient. ³ Ceased.
⁴ Nor. ⁵ Misfortune. ⁶ Great and little.
⁷ The, *plural* (Anglo-Saxon þá, p. 108).
⁸ Only before certain weak H's. The -*e* is sometimes saved by the 'cæsura,' or pause in the line. ⁹ *Prologue*, l. 581.
¹⁰ *Ibid.*, ll. 267, 268. We may imagine the -*e* of *twinkled* cut off before the *in*. But the -*e* is then usually written.—Of *hem* that *yaf* him wher-with to scoleye (l. 302) is a similar instance.
study ¹¹ *Ibid.*, ll. 15, 16.

(3) The singular of the subjunctive is -*e* throughout (not -*e*, -*est*, -*eth*)—

>That if gold rustë, what shal yren do?[1]

(4) The plural and the genitive singular of nouns is an extra syllable if they are one-syllabled words in the nominative,[2] as, for instance, *wordës* in l. 16 of the extract, and, as an example of the genitive—

>But-if a mannës soule were in his purs.[3]

(5) Final -*e* marks the plural of the adjective, as in *lytë* (l. 12); *moche* has the *e* cut off.

(6) It marks also the 'definite' form of the adjective, that declension of it which we find in German as well, when it is joined to the definite article, or to a demonstrative or possessive pronoun (pp. 108, 236). This is nearly its last appearance in English literature.[4]

These are the points of most common occurrence in which Chaucer's grammar differs from Modern English, but they do not, of course, at all exhaust the list. For instance, -*e* marks the dative of a substantive, as in the lines—

>But sore weep she if oon of hem were deed,
>   *wept*
>Or if men smoot it with a *yerdë* smertë,[5]
>   *rod*   *smartly*

where the -*e* in *yerde* is certainly pronounced; it also marks the adverb in *smerte*. Chaucer also sometimes uses the imperative plural in -*eth* (Anglo-Saxon -*aþ*), as in the line—

>And seyde; 'Lordinges, herkn*eth* if yow leste.'[6]
>   *hearken (ye)*   *list*

---

[1] *Prologue*, l. 500.
[2] Not quite always; *e.g. armes* is a single syllable in *Knightes Tale*, l. 2033.—Schipper, *Englische Metrik*.   [3] *Prologue*, l. 656.
[4] *e.g.* Anon he yaf the *sekë* man his bote.—*Prologue*, l. 424.
    sick   *remedy*
And eek hir *yongë* suster Emelye.—*Knightes Tale*, l. 13.
[5] *Prologue*, ll. 148, 149.   [6] *Prologue*, l. 828.

The Beginnings of 'Standard' English

Then there are more or less isolated relics of the older grammar, such as *aller*, *alder*[1] (from *ealra*, *alra*), the genitive plural of 'all.' On the whole, Chaucer's grammar is very much the same as that used by Robert of Brunne, but rather more Southern and conservative. It is distinctly more elaborate than in Modern English, but, as we see from the terminations being sometimes dropped (as in *twinkled*, for instance), having already a tendency towards dissolution.

We must not fail to notice the G softened to ȝ or Y, as in *yeven*, *yaf* (ll. 5, 14). The tendency to this was strongest in the South, but there is a good deal of it also in the East Midland dialect. It was the influence of the North and of Norfolk and Suffolk which reversed the process, when the Y seemed almost fixed in 'standard' English.

But there is another book which was perhaps of greater importance even than Chaucer's poems in establishing East Midland English as the 'standard' language of the country. Chaucer was a great poet, and his works were widely read, and other poetry was largely modelled on him, but a translation of the Bible was likely to have a still wider influence in raising the dialect in which it was written, and establishing its position.[2] Now, as we know, Wycliffe and his friends translated the whole Bible from the Latin Vulgate into English, the Gospels at least being the work of Wycliffe himself. This was towards the end of the fourteenth century, just about the time that *The Canterbury Tales* were written. Parts of the Bible had been translated before, as in the Northumbrian Psalter quoted above, not to speak of the Anglo-Saxon Gospels, or they had been paraphrased. But the earliest translation of the Bible as a whole is due to Wycliffe. However, a very few years later, the whole was revised by John Purvey. This later version, though it still contains some turns of expression which are close renderings

---

[1] *Prologue*, ll. 586, 710, and see p. 109.
[2] See Koch, *Historische Grammatik der Englischen Sprache*, vol. i. p. 19.

of the Latin,[1] but are certainly not English, is far smoother than Wycliffe's own version, more like what ordinary East Midland English was then, and certainly more like what 'standard' English was to be, especially the English of the Bible. The Authorised Version of 1611, which is still in use, owes a great deal to John Purvey's version of Wycliffe's translation, at any rate in its language. That is, the language of our Bible would have been different from what it is if Wycliffe and Purvey had never made their translations. This is true of the language in general, but especially of particular words and expressions used in our Bible. For instance, a great many of our Latin religious terms (coming for the most part from the Vulgate)[2]—such words as *testament, tribulation, persecution, revelation, reconcile, edify, confound*[3] —are due to the influence of these versions. Whoever first brought the words into English, their appearing in our present translation of the Bible is mainly due to the influence of Wycliffe and Purvey's translation. As a sample of Purvey's language we will look first of all at the Parable of the Sower (which may be compared with the Old English translations on pp. 154, 155), and then speak of certain points in his language which are not covered by the longer example.

[1] *e.g. Vulgate.* Dixit autem princeps sacerdotum, si hæc ita se habent ?
Purvey. And the prynce of prestis seide to Steuene, Whethir these thingis han hem so ?—Acts vii. 1.
Vulgate. Visum est et mihi . . . tibi scribere.
Purvey. It is seen also to me . . . to write to thee.—St. Luke i. 3.
Or, in the example below—
Vulgate. Qui habet aures audiendi.
Purvey. He that hath eris of heryng.

[2] Some of them came into the English language through French ; more were adapted to a French form. But the great majority come ultimately from the Vulgate, and their appearance in Wycliffe is very largely due to the fact that he translated from that Latin Version.

[3] On the other hand, there are some traces of the older plan of forming pure English compounds instead of using foreign words (see pp. 145, 196, 197), *e.g.*—
Purvey. He made vs saaf, bi waischyng of aȝen-bigetyng, and aȝen-newyng of the Hooli Goost.
Authorised Version. He saved us, by the washing of regeneration, and renewing of the Holy Ghost.—Titus iii. 5.

ST. MATTHEW xiii. 3-9

Purvey's Version, 1388[1]

3. And he spac to hem many thingis in parablis, and seide, Lo! he that sowith, ȝede out to sowe his seed.

4. And while he sowith, summe *seedis* felden bisidis the weie, and briddis of the eir camen, and eeten hem.

5. But othere *seedis* felden in to stony places, where thei hadden not myche erthe; and anoon thei sprongen vp, for thei hadden not depnesse of erthe.

6. But whanne the sonne was risun, thei swaliden,[2] and for thei hadden not roote, thei drieden vp.

7. And other *seedis* felden among thornes; and thornes woxen vp, and strangeleden hem.

8. But othere *seedis* felden in to good lond, and ȝauen fruyt; summe an hundrid foold, an othir sixti foold, an othir thritti foold.

9. He that hath eris of heryng, here he.

Now it will at once be plain that this is something very much like our Modern English, just as Chaucer's language is. Only two words (ȝede, 'went,' and *swaliden*, 'withered') are quite obsolete. But the words were still a good deal more declined and conjugated than they are at present, and the grammar is nearly the same as in Chaucer.

First, there can be no doubt that the plural and genitive termination adds a syllable to the word (as in Chaucer so far as one-syllabled words are concerned). This is obvious when we find *thingis, parablis* (v. 3), *seedis, briddis* (v. 4), and *mannus sone* (the Son of man). The letters I and U were certainly not written merely for ornament.

---

[1] Edition by Forshall and Madden, re-edited by Skeat. In this edition the old letter þ is always altered to *th*. The italics mean (as in our Bible) that the word is implied, but not expressed in the original.

[2] Withered.

Secondly, the *-e* has much the same functions as in Chaucer. It marks the plural of an adjective, *summe seedis* (v. 4), *othere seedis* (v. 5). It also marks the infinitive (*to sowe*, v. 3),[1] and sometimes a dative.[2] In *erthe, sonne*, the word was, to begin with, one of two syllables, as in Anglo-Saxon. On p. 154 they appear as *eorþan, sunnan*, the nominatives being *eorþe, sunne*. The *-e* is not used to mark the 'definite' adjective[2] (p. 272). But though the *-e* is still an important part of the grammar, it is occasionally put in where it has no business, and in verse 7 we see it omitted in *other*. This is the case too in other Manuscripts of the time, and is a sign of its approaching dissolution.

Thirdly, the plural of the verb is usually marked by *-en*, but sometimes by *-e*, just as in Chaucer. There are plenty of examples in the extract of the fuller termination, such as *felden, camen*.

Fourthly, the declension of *he* in the plural is just as in Chaucer.

Nom. thei
Gen. her
Dat.
Accus. } hem

There is an instance of the accusative in verse 4, and of the genitive in the following verse:—

Thanne he touchide *her* iȝen, and seide, Aftir ȝoure feith be it doon to ȝou.[3]

The imperative plural (in *-eth*) is not used, nor the *y-*, as a prefix to the past participle. Purvey's grammar, then, is in the main the same as Chaucer's. In the points as to which

---

[1] Properly, the gerund, *to sáwenne*, but this had long been confused with the infinitive in most dialects (see Appendix E).

[2] See Skeat's Introduction to Forshall and Madden as above. In *depnesse* (v. 5) it is difficult to say whether the *-e* is ornamental or not. It was (as long as genders survived) a feminine word, and most of its cases ended in *-e*. (The ungrammatical use of the various cases (especially dative for nominative) did much to bring in the ornamental *-e* at the end of words.)

[3] St. Matt. ix. 29.

they differ Purvey is nearer to Modern English. There are, of course, other isolated relics of the old grammar in this version of the Bible, just as there are in Chaucer, such as *thou were* (Anglo-Saxon þú wǽre), *the tothir* (Anglo-Saxon þæt óþere), a use of the neuter of *the*, which is still preserved in 'vulgar' English. So too 'ʒe *witen*'[1] is the plural, while 'ʒour fadir *woot*' (knoweth)[2] is the singular. In Tyndale and in our version[3] *wot* is both singular and plural. Such changes as this which were taking place in the 'strong' verbs will be spoken of later on.

Besides these points of grammar Purvey has many soft G's (or Y's) which are now pronounced hard, such as ʒauen in the extract, ʒouun (*given*), aʒen (*again*). Something more will be said on this point presently.

We may just notice that *brid* (*bird*), *no but* (*except*), *axe* (*ask*), are found in Purvey's version, though they are now banished to 'provincial' English.

It will now perhaps be interesting to give one or two more specimens of the East Midland dialect, soon to become 'standard' English. It will be hardly necessary to draw attention any more to the main points in the grammar; any one can pick them out for himself. Finally, a specimen of the Southern dialect will be given which is interesting evidence as to the position of English dialects at the end of the fourteenth century, and which will also show that the East Midland was still only one of the dialects in which an English book might be written.

[1] St. Matt. xx. 25. [2] St. Matt. vi. 8. [3] Acts vii. 40.

THE VOIAGE AND TRAVAILE OF SIR JOHN MANDEVILLE, KNIGHT [1]

EAST MIDLAND

About 1390

In Ethiope ben [2] many dyverse folk: and Ethiope is clept [3] Cusis. In that Contree ben folk, that han but o [4] foot: and thei gon so fast, that it is marvaylle: and the foot is so large that it schadewethe [5] alle the body aȝen the Sonne, whanne thei wole lye and reste hem. In Ethiope whan the Children ben ȝonge and lytille, thei ben all ȝelowe: and whan that thei wexen of Age, that ȝalownesse turnethe to ben alle blak. In Ethiope is the Cytee of Saba; and the Lond, of the whiche on [4] of the iii Kynges, that presented oure Lord in Bethleem, was Kyng offe.

. . . . . .

And beȝonde theise Yles, there is another Yle, that is clept Pytan. The folk of that Contree ne tyle not, ne laboure not the Erthe: for thei eten no manere thing: and thei ben of gode colour, and of faire schap, aftre hire gretnesse: [6] but the smale ben as Dwerghes; [7] but not so lityll as ben the Pigmeyes. Theise men lyven be the smelle of wylde Apples: and whan thei gon ony fer weye, [8] thei beren the Apples with hem. For ȝif [9] thei hadde lost the savour of the Apples, thei scholde dyen anon. Thei ne ben not fulle resonable: but thei ben symple and bestyalle.[10]

---

[1] Halliwell's Edition, reprinted 1866. The U's and V's have no doubt been reduced to modern usage, as also in the letter following. The book is merely a compilation, and is not really an account of any one man's travels. See Kington Oliphant, *The New English*, vol. i. p. 160, and Article 'Sir John Mandeville,' *Encyclopædia Britannica*, Ninth Edition.

[2] Are.   [3] Called ('y-clept' in Milton).   [4] One.

[5] The E is ornamental; as it also is in *turnethe, oure, offe*. In *lye, reste*, it represents the infinitive, in *wote* the plural, in the words derived from French too (e.g. *marvaylle*) it might be pronounced.

[6] In proportion to, considering their size.   [7] Dwarfs.

[8] Any distant journey.   [9] If.   [10] Like animals.

It will be interesting to compare with this literary prose part of a letter written in 1403, one of the earliest specimens of letter-writing that is in English, and not in French or Latin. The earlier part even of this is all in French. It is from the Dean of Windsor (who was also Archdeacon of Hereford) to Henry IV., on the subject of a Welsh raid into Herefordshire. The Dean asks for reinforcements, and that the King will hasten his coming there. The part in French may serve as a specimen of what Anglo-French was like in its last days; it is very evident that it is a long way removed from 'standard' French.

War fore for Goddesake, thinketh on ȝour beste Frende God, and thanke Hym as He hath deserved to ȝowe; and leveth nought that ȝe ne come[1] for no man that may counsaille ȝowe the contrarie; for by the trouthe that I schal be to ȝowe[2] ȝet, this day the Walshmen supposen and trusten that ȝe shulle nought come there, and there fore for Goddeslove make them fals men. And that hit plese ȝowe of ȝour hegh Lordeship for to have me excused of my comynge to ȝowe, for, yn god fey,[3] I have nought ylafte with me over two men, that they beon sende[4] oute with Sherref and other gentils of oure Schire for to with stande the malice of the Rebelles this day.

Tresexcellent, trespuissant, et tresredoute Seignour, autrement say a present nieez.[5]

Jeo[6] prie a la Benoit[7] Trinite que vous ottroie[8] bone vie ove tresentier sauntee[9] a treslonge durre,[10] and sende ȝowe sone to ows in help and prosperitee; for, in god fey, I hope to Al Mighty God that, ȝef[11] ȝe come ȝoure owne persone, ȝe schulle have the victorie of alle ȝoure enemyes.

[1] Fail not (so as not) to come, a double negative, as in Greek; *nought* is only a fuller form of *not*.
[2] As I shall show myself trustworthy to you.
[3] In good faith.   [4] In that they are sent.
[5] I know nothing besides at present.
[6] I (*Je, ego*).   [7] Blessed.   [8] To give you.
[9] With very complete health.   [10] For very-long lasting.   [11] If.

And for salvation of ȝoure Schire and Marches al aboute, treste¹ ȝe nought to no Leutenaunt.

Escript a Hereford, en tresgraunte haste, a trois de la clocke apres noone, le tierce jour de Septembre.

Vostre humble creatoure et continuelle oratour,²

RICHARD KYNGESTONE,
Deane de Wyndesore.³

This letter is in much the same dialect as Chaucer and Purvey, and shows that the language in which they wrote was much like the common speech and not any artificial literary dialect, for a letter is the nearest written representation of ordinary talk. But here there is very great confusion about the *-e* at the end of words. It must often have been dropped in speaking; if it had been an absolutely essential part of English grammar, Richard Kyngestone would have written it in the right places instinctively. No doubt there were persons who prided themselves on their correct pronunciation, and these would add their *-e*'s correctly. But it must have been already in a precarious condition, on the way to becoming a mere ornament of writing, or the Dean could not have dropped it in *fals* (plural of the adjective), and inserted it in 'your beste frende,' ȝowe, and other words, where it meant nothing. *Them* makes almost its first appearance in the Southern form of East Midland, which was so soon to take the position of 'classical' or 'standard' English. It is interesting to see in *thinketh* that the plural imperative (here a polite plural addressed to a superior) was still alive in ordinary speech; there is also the *y-* in *ylafte*. Purvey in language seems to have been almost ahead of his age, and to have kept clear of old-fashioned forms.

We will now conclude this sketch of English in Chaucer's time with a specimen of Southern English, in order to show

---

¹ Trust.   ² Creature, who constantly prays for you.
³ *Royal and Historical Letters during the Reign of Henry the Fourth*, edited by Hingeston, Rolls Series, 1860.

The Beginnings of 'Standard' English

that a writer who did not happen to be a Midland man had still liberty to write in his own native dialect. The fact of the extract being in Southern English shows this, and it is also implied in the part to be quoted. It is from the translation of Higden's *Polychronicon* (with additions), made in 1387 by John of Trevisa, Vicar of Berkeley, in Gloucestershire, which county, as we saw, spoke the Southern dialect. It certainly does not look at first sight as if he were Chaucer's contemporary.

After saying that the practice of learning French had much decreased in England, he goes on to speak of English.

Hyt[1] semeth a gret wondur houʒ[2] Englysch, þat ys þe burþ-tonge of Englysch men & here oune[3] longage and tonge, ys so dyuers of soun[4] in þis ylond; and þe longage of Normandy ys comlyng[5] of a-noþer lond, and haþ on maner soun among al men þat spekeþ[6] hyt aryʒt[7] in Engelond. Noþeles[8] þer ys as meny dyuers maner Frensch yn þe rem[9] of Fraunce as ys dyuers manere Englysch in þe rem of Engelond.

Also, of þe forseyde Saxon tonge þat ys deled a þre,[10] and ys abyde scarslych wiþ feaw vplondysch men,[11] and ys gret wondur;[12] for men of þe est wiþ men of þe west, as hyt were vndur þe same party[13] of heuene, acordeþ[6] more in

---

[1] It, neuter of *he*.   [2] How.
[3] Their own; the nominative of *here* is *hy*, in Southern English.
[4] Sound.   [5] A stranger.   [6] The Southern plural.   [7] Aright.
[8] Nevertheless, *no-the-less, ná-the-les*, *i.e.* not less *on that account* (see p. 109).
[9] Realm, Old French (*not* Norman-French) *reaume*.
[10] 'Dealed on three,' *i.e.* divided into three.
[11] Is left sparingly with few country people. The statement is much too strong.—Skeat. We have a different view in *Richard Coer de Lion* (fourteenth century)—

> In Frenssche bookys this rym is wrought,
> Lewede menne knowe it nought,
> Lewede menne cunne French non ;
> Among an hondryd unnethis on.
>   Schipper, *Englische Metrik*.

lewed = unlearned ; *cunne* = know ; *unnethis on* = scarcely one.

[12] And the state of things about it is very strange.
[13] Part, line from east to west, parallel of longitude.

sounyng of speche þan men of þe norþ wiþ men of þe souþ; þer-fore hyt ys þat Mercij,¹ þat buþ² men of myddel Engelond, as hyt were parteners of³ þe endes, vnderstondeþ⁴ betre þe syde longages,⁵ Norþeron & Souþeron, þan Norþeron & Souþeron vndurstondeþ⁴ eyþer oþer.⁶ Al þe longage of þe Norþhumbres, & specialych at ӡork, ys so scharp, slyttyng & frotyng,⁷ & vnschape,⁸ þat we Souþeron men may þat longage vnnethe⁹ vndurstonde.¹⁰

[1] Mercii, Mercians, the J being merely an I with an ornamental tag, afterwards specialised for the consonant, while I was confined to the vowel.
[2] Are, Southern form. [3] Partners with.
[4] The Southern plural. [5] Side languages. [6] Each other.
[7] Grating. [8] Unshapen, rough. [9] Uneasily, with difficulty.
[10] Infinitive after the auxiliary, may, *i.e.* 'are able.' There is no instance of the prefix *y-* in the extract. Most of the past participles have a prefix already in the verb, e.g. *for-seyde, a-byde,* and these never had the *ge-* or *y-*; but it is dropped in *deled.* However, it is in general common in Trevisa, e.g. *y-knowe (known), y-tauӡt (taught), y-rokked (rocked),* and also with words derived from French, as *y-turnd* (p. 189).—*Specimens of Early English,* Morris and Skeat, Part II., p. 242. See also Skeat, *Principles of English Etymology,* First Series, p. 32; to both of whom I am largely indebted in the above notes.

CHAPTER XIX

EARLY 'STANDARD' ENGLISH

The changes of the fifteenth century—East Midland becomes 'standard' English—Causes of this—Changes in the language itself—Confusion and loss of final -e's—Other terminations dropped or compressed—their, them, displace her, hem—give or yeve—that—those—y-(clept)—Caxton's English.[1]

CHAUCER died in 1400, so that we now come to the fifteenth century—a most important period in our language, since it was during this time that

(1) The East Midland dialect became established as the literary dialect of England, and the speech of educated Englishmen.

(2) English, so far as its *written* appearance is concerned, settled practically into its present form, though the *sound* of the vowels was to a large extent different from what it is at present, and several consonant-sounds, such as K in '*k*nave,' GH in 'ni*gh*t,' were still sounded, though they are now silent.

We will take these two points separately.

(1) Already before Chaucer's time the East Midland dialect was encroaching upon the others. In the early part of the thirteenth century Oxford was beyond the border of the East Midland, and the London dialect was still Southern. But Wycliffe in 1380 wrote something like the speech of Oxford, and

---

[1] Kington Oliphant, *The New English.* Skeat, *Principles of English Etymology*, First Series. *Encyclopædia Britannica*, Ninth Edition, Article 'The English Language.'

yet his dialect would be classed as East Midland. Purvey, as we have seen, revised this into what is completely East Midland, to which Wycliffe's language was near already.[1] Chaucer, too, who died in 1400, wrote London English, but this London dialect was now also a form of East Midland. On the other hand, the extract from Trevisa shows that this East Midland dialect was not yet fully established as 'standard' English. Still, by the end of the fourteenth century it was well on the way to becoming the language of books and of educated speakers as it is at present.

The main causes of this were as follows—

(a) First, it was intelligible to those who spoke the other dialects; they could read books written in it with ease, and could understand those who spoke it. When we look at Northern English of the thirteenth century (pp. 247, 248) it seems in many ways so like our own language of the present day, that it is hard to realise how strange the speech of Yorkshire sounded to other Englishmen in Chaucer's time.[2] But we have in several respects got nearer to the Northern dialect (for instance, in the pronunciation of A in *lame*; 'he goes,' for 'he g*oeth*'), and yet a Scotchman or even a Yorkshireman, speaking his own dialect, is not always easy to understand. East Midland English, on the other hand, being a sort of half-way house between Northern and Southern, could be understood, learnt, and copied with tolerable ease by those who spoke either of these

---

[1] There is an element of the Northern dialect, Wycliffe's native Yorkshire speech, in his own translation. Hereford, who translated most of the Old Testament for Wycliffe, was a Southerner, and wrote accordingly.—Kington Oliphant, *The New English*, vol. i. p. 137, etc. Skeat, Introduction to Wycliffe and Purvey's New Testament.

[2] Chaucer thus mimics the Northern clerks living at Oxford—
 A wilde fyr upon thair bodyes falle !
 Wha herkned ever swilk a ferly thing ?
  such strange
 Ye, thei sul have the flour of ille endyng !
 This lange night ther tydes me na rest.
     The Canterbury Tales, Aldine Edition,
where *thair*, *tydes*, are ridiculed as part of the Northern dialect, as well as *sul*, *wha*, *na*, and *lange*, which are to be found at the present day in Lowland Scotch, and some of them in the Craven dialect of Yorkshire.

dialects.¹ The West Midland was also a sort of compromise of the kind. But then it had not these further advantages.

(b) London, Oxford, and Cambridge all spoke East Midland English, though not exactly the same variety of it. Now London as the largest town, and the place where the King and his Court mostly were, has had an immense influence on English. Winchester, which was the capital before the Norman Conquest, had a somewhat similar influence then, though it was not the largest place in the kingdom. As to those counties which lie near London, the influence of the capital has almost driven out their peculiar dialects by constant sapping. Kent, for example, where in Chaucer's time, and later, as we can well believe if we look at Dan Michel's language (p. 263), was spoken 'as brode and rude englissh as is in ony place of englond,'² has now not a very strongly-marked dialect of its own. And though the infection of the London dialect was less in more distant counties, still it affected the upper classes throughout the country, just as at the present day the speech of an *educated* Londoner is the standard of 'standard' English.

Then the language of the University towns would plainly infect all their students more or less, who in the fifteenth century were more numerous in proportion to the population of the country, and were drawn from more varied classes.

(c) Chaucer wrote in East Midland. And as his poetry was superior to anything written in English between the Conquest and a period long after his death,³ his influence on literature was naturally immense. Besides this, his

---

¹ Trevisa states the converse of this, p. 282.
² Caxton, quoted by Kington Oliphant, *The New English*, vol. i. p. 328.
³ *The Owl and the Nightingale* (Morris, *Specimens of Early English*, Part I., p. 171), written in Southern English about 1250, may perhaps rank with Chaucer's poems. *Piers Plowman*, by Langland, a contemporary of Chaucer, is perhaps almost equally strong, though in a different way from Chaucer's works. After him there is hardly anything to compare with him till we come to Spenser (1579), or perhaps to Thomas Sackville, Lord Buckhurst, who preceded Spenser by about fifteen years. What Chaucer's influence was is shown by the fact that even his grammar is imitated so late as by Spenser, in such forms as '*y*-cladd,' 'she bad him tell*en*,' 'so forth they march*en*,' all of which forms were quite obsolete in Spenser's time.

contemporary Gower, though he was a Kentish man, wrote in East Midland English like Chaucer's, and his successors, Hoccleve and Lydgate, were East Midland men.[1] Their poetry and their influence were far inferior to Chaucer's, but at least they pulled in the same direction. By about 1450, if any one expected his poetry to be generally read, he would write East Midland English.

(*d*) Wycliffe's translation of the New Testament[2] in the main, and Purvey's completely, were in East Midland English. This book would affect all classes. When we think of the enormous influence that the 'Authorised Version' of the Bible has had throughout England, and even in Scotland, not only colouring the style of writers, but affecting speech as well, we can understand that Wycliffe and Purvey must have done much towards spreading and establishing the position of the dialect in which their translation was made. Of course Wycliffe's Bible was not nearly so widely spread as our present translation. Few people could read, there was as yet no printing,[3] and the clergy were against it as a heretical version. And it was then as much as a man's life was worth to fall under suspicion of heresy. But, in spite of all this, the number of copies that there were in England is shown by the very large number of Manuscripts that have survived down to our own time.

The position of the East Midland dialect was confirmed by the introduction of printing. The printers used that dialect, which was by this time established as the 'standard' form of English; and the printed books spread it more widely than Manuscripts could ever have done.

---

[1] Sweet, *History of English Sounds*, pp. 200, 201.

[2] The translation of the Old Testament was mainly written by Hereford in his own Southern dialect.

[3] And a New Testament written out was worth as much as £40 in the money of our day. In 1519 Roger Parker, of Hitchenden, said to John Phip, that 'for burning his books he was foul to blame, for they were worth a hundred marks.' To whom John answered ' that he had rather burn his books than that his books should burn him.'—Eadie's *English Bible*, vol. i. pp. 91, 93.

(2) The second change, which took place in the fifteenth century, was the dropping of many terminations which still existed, so that English grammar was brought very nearly to its present condition—that is, having very few inflexions indeed.[1]

If we look at the English of Chaucer (p. 270, etc.), written at the end of the fourteenth century, we shall find final -e standing for many of the older inflexions—for instance, the plural of adjectives (*lytë*), the plural of the tenses of the verb (*wendë*), and the infinitive (*visytë*). The two last are also marked by the fuller form in -*en*. Final -e is also sometimes used for the dative of a noun (*yerdë*).

Its use in the definite form of the adjective may be dismissed, as we have seen that Purvey does not use it. This is not the whole list of the final -*e*'s, but these are enough to refer to for our present purpose.

Now the first thing to notice is that in Chaucer's time final *e*'s are found written which are not justified by the grammar, just as we saw them in Mandeville and the Dean of Windsor's letter. On the other hand, though a final -*e* in Chaucer which is a part of the grammar is nearly always sounded, there are cases in which this is not so.[2] For instance, the -*e*, marking the plural of a verb, is sometimes silent, as—

That from the tyme of king William *wer(e)* falle.[3]

Also, in the infinitive—

Men moot *yev(e)* silver to the povre freres.[4]

---

[1] It must be remembered that these terminations were constantly being sapped by the influence of the accent (see p. 206, etc.).
[2] This of course does not refer to its being cut off before another vowel, which is quite a different thing.
[3] *Prologue*, l. 324. These are from the edition by Morris, re-edited by Skeat, where the Manuscript chiefly followed (the Ellesmere MS.) is unusually correct. In the earlier edition, which follows another MS., the instances of an -*e* written but silent are more common. [4] *Prologue*, l. 232.

The -*e* of the dative was more frequently dropped than kept, and we have already seen plural verbs without any termination (*twinkled, yaf*, p. 271).

From these instances, as well as those in Mandeville and the letter (pp. 278-280), we conclude that in Chaucer's time—

(*a*) Final -*e* was sometimes dropped, both in conversation and in writing, where it should, strictly speaking, have been pronounced.

(*b*) Final -*e* was sometimes written 'for ornament,' where the grammar did not justify it.

(*a*) It was 'uncertain,' and this was due to the constant opposition between those who try to speak correctly, and as they have heard their fathers speak, and those who do not care how they talk so long as they are understood, and consequently from laziness clip their words. In an age like Chaucer's, when there was as yet no 'standard' dialect of English to act as a pattern of speech and writing, when educated people were few, and when even the books did not always bring home to their readers the fact that E, if written, was to be sounded like other letters, it was quite certain that final -*e* would disappear, according to the process which had already begun.

The position of final -*e* in German at the present day is much as it was in Chaucer's time. In the dative of nouns it is as often dropped as retained, in speaking at all events. And in general it is 'uncertain,' being not only constantly dropped by uneducated speakers, who say, for instance, *a Pfeif'* for *eine Pfeife*, but it is also often left out in poetry, for instance—

Ein(e) feste Burg ist unser Gott,

or in Heine's song—

Da weinten zusammen die Grenadier(e),

a line which rhymes to *mir*. Why, then, has it not suffered the same fate as its English brother? The reason is partly that educated Germans are far more particular about their talk, and talk more 'like books' than Englishmen do now or did in Chaucer's time, but much more that the final *-e* in German was practically alive till a later date, when the language became more or less fixed by printing. But in England during the fourteenth century and the beginning of the fifteenth the Northern form of English was constantly setting an example of dropping the final *-e*, and the laziness of mankind worked in the same direction. Now, as we have already seen, the East Midland dialect, which to some extent retained this *-e* (especially in its more Southern form as spoken in London), was not the one 'standard' dialect of England in Chaucer's time, though it was on the way to becoming so. And by the time that it had fully gained that position the final *-e* was dead. 'Already by 1420, in Chaucer's disciple Hoccleve, final *-e* was quite uncertain; in Lydgate it was practically gone.'[1] So that by the time that the East Midland of London had established itself as the 'standard' dialect of English, it had no final *-e* to make all educated Englishmen copy. If East Midland English had ousted Norman-French a century earlier, before the inflexions had been worn down so much, or if printing had been introduced by 1350 or 1400, English would probably have been a good deal more inflected than it is, through becoming fixed at an earlier stage.

(*b*) As to the *-e*'s being put in for ornament in writing, this almost follows from their being 'uncertain' and unnecessary in conversation, so that the scribe constantly heard them dropped in talking. He was conscious that *-e*'s were constantly written in Manuscripts (so that he ought to write them as well), and that they were sometimes pronounced. And yet the average scribe might not be very certain as to the right place for introducing them; and at any rate would not have

---

[1] *Encyclopædia Britannica*, Ninth Edition, article 'English Language.' This, of course, means that Hoccleve's style is more old-fashioned than Lydgate's, since they were contemporaries.

clear enough ideas on the subject to prevent him from making mistakes through carelessness in the weary labour of writing out some long work.[1]

Of course when the final -*e* was dead, those who wrote out the books would follow the old fashion by writing -*e*'s at the end of words occasionally, without a notion of what they had once meant.

The fuller inflexions, -*eþ* of the imperative plural (*herkneth*, p. 272), -*en* of the infinitive (*to cursen*, p. 270), and -*en* of the plural verb (*doon* for *doen*, p. 271), perished too. We have already seen that Purvey does not use the first, and it died out before the end of the fifteenth century.[2] So also did the -*en* of the infinitive, and the -*en* of the verb in the plural was alive but little longer than the other two. We have seen that the N was not always left in Chaucer; the termination might be either -*en* or -*e*; for instance, in the lines—

> I dorste swere they weyeden ten pound
> That on a Sonday *were* upon hir heed.
> Hir hosen *weren* of fyn scarlet reed.[3]

The same was the case with the infinitive—

> Wel coude he *singe* and *pleyen* on a rote.[4]

If, then, the infinitive and the plural of the verb could be just as correctly marked with the final -*e* as with -*en*, and the final -*e* was dropped, they could be pronounced either with a termination or with none at all. And if either was correct, the

---

[1] We must remember that the scribe had no grammatical training in English; he did not learn a Middle English grammar. All depended on his carefulness and correctness of ear. A great source of confusion in substantives was the dative. Here the -*e* had long been dropped at pleasure, so that the dative and nominative were confused. But if they were 'for practical purposes' the same, then the nominative might have an -*e* as the dative had had. For the reason why -*e* got to be a sign of the length of a vowel before it, see p. 235.

[2] Caxton reproduces it in reprinting the *Book of Curtesye*. The book was written in 1450, printed by Caxton about 1477. But in 1483 he will not have this form, or the *y*-, in printing Chaucer's *House of Fame*. They were already obsolete forms.—Kington Oliphant, *The New English*, vol. i. pp. 332, 337.

[3] *Prologue*, ll. 454-456. 'They' are the Wyf of Bathe's kerchiefs.

[4] *Prologue*, l. 236. *Rote* = a kind of guitar, or fiddle.

general decision was sure to be in favour of the shorter form. But the *-en* of the plural lived longest of these inflexions. It is found as an alternative to our modern uninflected form throughout the fifteenth century. Caxton uses it at times, especially in his earlier works,[1] and *ben* (are) to the end. Ben Jonson (died 1637) says—

'The persons plural keep the termination of the first person singular. In former times, till about the reign of King Henry the Eighth, they were wont to be formed by adding *en*; thus—

'lov*en*, say*en*, complain*en*.

But now, whatsoever is the cause, it hath quite grown out of use.'[2]

In general we may say that those grammatical forms which are found in Chaucer, and are now quite extinct in poetry as well as prose, died out in the fifteenth century.

The clipping of the N was not confined to these plural forms. It extended to strong past participles as well, in which we now usually retain it. Thus Chaucer says of the Knight—

At many a noble aryve hadde he *be*.[3]

And there are many similar instances in his poems, sometimes with the *i-* or *y-* prefixed, as *y-falle*[4] for *fallen*. The longer form was mostly retained or restored through the influence of more Northern English, which kept the N, probably through the influence of Danish, in which it was sounded distinctly. Still there are many words in which the N has gone, and the E which it protected along with it; for instance, 'he has

---

[1] *Encyclopædia Britannica*, Ninth Edition, article 'English Language.'
[2] Ben Jonson, *The English Grammar*.
[3] *Prologue*, l. 60. *Aryve* = arrival, or disembarkation of troops.—Morris and Skeat.
[4] *Prologue*, l. 25. We saw that Robert of Gloucester clips his N's—*i-do*, *a-slawe*, and so on (p. 262). This seems to have been characteristic of Southern English.

run, found,' and in the alternative forms, *bid, forgot,* instead of *bidden, forgotten.*[1]

And now a word or two must be said of the cases where an E has been dropped inside a word, where the termination is retained, but now consists merely of a consonant, and does not add a syllable to the word, as, for instance, in 'fowl*s*,' 'man'*s*,' 'he run*s*.' This is a process which had begun long before the Conquest, and is not quite completed now.[2] In Anglo-Saxon there is both *hireð* and *hirð* (*heareth*), both *séceð* and *sécð*,[3] and so on. So in Robert of Brunne (p. 258) we had 'rennës' and 'gos.' And in Chaucer nouns of more than one syllable are usually inflected with a mere -*s*, as in Modern English, not with *es*. Even if the E is written in these words, we can tell by the metre that it was not pronounced, as, for instance, in the line—

Grehoundes he hadde, as swifte as fowel in flight.[4]

And -*ed* is sometimes clipped in the same way in pronunciation, as in the line—

This worthy limitour was *cleped* Huberd.[5]

In the genitive and plural of nouns, in the 3rd person singular of the present tense, and in the termination -*ed* of the past participle we now always cut out the E in speaking, unless it would leave the word unpronounceable, as in *fox's, horses,* 'he *rises,' knighted, founded*. Of course it would be a mistake to say that we 'insert an E' under those circumstances, the fact being that it is the old E of the inflexion left there, because to take it away would make the word impossible to

---

[1] Milton's line—

New presbyter is but old priest *writ* large

(*Sonnets*)—is another instance. But this form has not established itself.

[2] Under the influence of laziness (pp. 4, 288), and of the English accent (p. 208).

[3] We saw that the termination at a still earlier time was -*ið*, not -*eð*. This I affected the vowel of the stem in the contracted forms, e.g. *stent* from *standið*. See p. 103, etc., and Sweet's *Anglo-Saxon Primer*, pp. lix. and lx.

[4] *Prologue*, l. 190.   [5] *Ibid.*, l. 269.

pronounce.¹ But this E inside the word did not go so soon or so easily as the -*eþ* of the imperative, -*en* and -*e* in the infinitive and plural of the verb. Even now many people pronounce the -*ed*, as in *lovëd*, when they read the Lessons in church, an old-fashioned pronunciation suited to the old-fashioned language of the Bible, and it not unfrequently has to be so pronounced in poetry, as, for instance—

To his heart
He pressed his son, he kissëd him and wept.²

But poetry is more archaic, or old-fashioned, than prose, and even this -*ed*, which is one of the last survivors of the terminations formed by a syllable and not by a mere consonant, cannot be said to be a part of our living language at the present day. This, however, was not the case in the fifteenth century. These terminations, though they were sometimes clipped, were sometimes also pronounced in full. This is evident if we look at the extract from Caxton below, where we have 'by *goddys* grace' (genitive), *bookys, yerys, scolis*, and *eggys* (plural), as well as *vsid* and *axyd*. I and Y were not silent letters, and when Caxton writes the terminations with them we cannot doubt that he meant them to have the extra syllable, and often so pronounced them himself.

(*c*) We may now speak shortly of some other changes which took place in the fifteenth century. One of these was the final victory of the Danish forms of the 3rd personal pronoun, *they, their, them*, over *hi, her, hem*. We saw (p. 240, etc.) that Orm (about 1200 A.D.) was the first writer to use these Northern and Danish forms. But in the South, in Orm's time and long after, the Old English cases kept their place. So in Robert of Gloucester (1298) the French

Speke french as *hii* dude atom.

---

¹ In such forms as *speaketh* we do not try to clip the E. But this is an old-fashioned form, and not a part of living 'standard' English. If we go out of our way to use it at all, it may as well be pronounced in the old-fashioned way. ² Wordsworth, *Michael*.

Robert of Brunne,[1] on the other hand (1338), uses both forms for the genitive and dative, but not *hi*. In Chaucer too (died 1400) the Northern declension has gained ground; *they* is the only nominative, but he keeps to *her* and *hem* respectively for the genitive and for the dative and accusative. *Hi*, then, as the nominative, is dead, and so is *heo* for *she* in 'standard' English.[2] During the fifteenth century either the Northern *their*, *them*, or the Southern *her*, *hem*, can be used in 'standard' English. The following verse of a Christmas Carol about the Three Kings is a curious example of the mixture of the two sets of pronouns—

> As *thei* ȝedyn[3] with *her* offeryng,
> *Thei* met Herowd, that mody[4] kyng;
> He askyd *hem* of *her* comyng,
> That tym,
> And thus to *them* gun[5] say.[6]

Of course a Northern or Southern writer of what was becoming 'standard' English prefers his own form. But by the end of the century *they*, *their*, *them* were enthroned as 'standard' English, and the Southern forms were banished.[7]

The triumph of the Northern forms was partly due to Caxton, though he also uses *her*, *hem* sometimes. When he translated from French the *Recuyell of the Historyes of Troye*, he was living in the Netherlands (which then belonged to the Duke of Burgundy), and the Duchess of Burgundy, who was sister to Edward IV., was his patroness. When she looked over his translation, 'anon she found defaute[8] in mine English, which she commanded me to amend.' No doubt

---

[1] Robert of Brunne writes a more Northern form of the East Midland dialect than Chaucer.

[2] Piers Plowman has *he* for *they*, and so has a Carol in a MS. of the fifteenth century in the British Museum; *he* (*heo*) is constantly used for 'she' in a Wiltshire poem of about 1420, just as *hoo*, *'oo* (also for *heo*) still is in Lancashire and Cheshire. [3] Went. [4] Haughty. [5] Began to, or did (say).

[6] T. Wright, *Songs and Carols*, Percy Society, 1847.

[7] So far as 'standard' written English is concerned. In colloquial English *hem* still survives in such expressions as 'give it 'em.' *Hem* has now lost its H, like (*h*)*it*. [8] Fault.

it was not Northern enough for a lady of the House of York. Under this influence Caxton turned the scale in favour of *their, them*.[1] He also 'tightened up' certain G's which had come to be pronounced as Y (p. 273) everywhere, except in the North and more especially in Norfolk and Suffolk,[2] so that *again* had been written and pronounced as *ayein, give* as *yeve*, and these softer forms seemed to have already fixed themselves in 'standard' English.

That, originally the neuter of the definite article (as in *the tother*, þæt óþer), was, as we saw (p. 239), used by Orm as a relative and demonstrative pronoun, just as it now is, and this use of it spread further. It had already, before Chaucer's time, superseded the old þe as a relative pronoun. In the course of the fifteenth century it also finally drove out *thilke* as a demonstrative pronoun.

Those also came into 'standard' English from the North.[3] The history of the word is curious. *This*, in Middle English, had two plurals, þes and þás. The þás became þos (as in *fá, foe*, see p. 210, etc.). Þá, the plural of the definite article, had in the same way become þo, and this was often used as a demonstrative in the same sense in which we use *those*. *Those* sounded like þo, and consequently was used in the same sense without any recollection of its having originally meant the same as *these*.[4]

---

[1] Kington Oliphant, *The New English*, vol. i. p. 328. Caxton was a Southerner, from 'Kent in the weeld.' He would, at his date, naturally write 'standard' English, though, of course, with a tendency to use Southern forms where they were still possible.

[2] In the *Paston Letters* the hard G is generally found in these doubtful words, where the letter is by a native of one of these two counties. This Y was originally written ȝ, the Old English form of the letter G; and it is found so written to the very end of the fifteenth century. The ȝ or Y in *give* and *against* (*yeve* and *ayenst*) died hard. We shall see them in Tyndale, and *yeven* is found for *given* in a letter of Queen Elizabeth.—Kington Oliphant, *The New English*, vol. i. p. 578.

[3] Kington Oliphant, *The New English*, vol. i. p. 109, etc. It was thus one of the words which did not keep the old long A in Northumbrian.

[4] Skeat, *Etymological Dictionary*. Stratmann, *Dictionary of the Old English Language*.

Y- (or i-), as a prefix to past participles, was also lost in the fifteenth century.[1] We have seen that Orm, about 1200, uses it very rarely. His dialect, in its more modern form, is becoming victorious all along the line.

We will now look at a specimen of Caxton's English, part of the preface to one of his last works, the *Eneydos*, printed in 1490.

CAXTON (1490)[2]

1   After dyuerse werkes made / translated and achieued / hauyng noo werke in hande. ,I sittyng in my studye where as laye many dyuerse paunflettis[3] and bookys. happened that to my hande cam a lytyl booke in frenshe. whiche late
5   was translated oute of latyn by some noble clerke of fraūce[4] whiche booke is named Eneydos / made in latyn by that noble poete & grete clerke vyrgyle / whiche booke I sawe ouer and redde therin. How after the generall destruccyon of the grete Troye, Eneas departed berynge his olde fader
10 anchises vpon his sholdres / his lityl son yolus on his honde. his wyfe wyth moche other people folowynge / and how he shypped and departed wyth alle thystorye of his aduentures that he had er he cam to the achieuement of his conquest of ytalye as all a longe shall be shewed in this present boke.
15 In whiche booke I had grete playsyr. by cause of the fayr and honest termes & wordes in frenshe / Whyche I neuer sawe to fore lyke. ne[5] none so playsaunt ne so wel ordred. whiche booke as me semed sholde be moche requysyte to noble men to see as wel for the eloquence
20 as the historyes / How wel that many honderd yerys passed was the sayd booke of eneydos wyth other werkes

---

[1] It occurs two or three times in Shakespeare, frequently in Spenser. But both there and in Milton's 'y-clept' it is a mere imitation of older English, such as all poets allow themselves more or less.

[2] Caxton does not discriminate in the length of his stops as we do now. Both the dots and / are sometimes equivalent to a comma sometimes to a longer stop. The end of a line also makes a stop unnecessary.   [3] Pamphlets.

[4] The – over the *u* means an *n* after it, as in the MSS.   [5] Nor.

made and lerned dayly in scolis specyally in ytalye &
other places / whiche historye the sayd vyrgyle made in
metre / And whā I had aduysed me in this sayd boke.
I delyvered [1] and concluded to translate it in to englysshe 25
And forthwyth toke a penne & ynke and wrote a leef or
tweyne / whyche I ouersawe agayn to corecte it / And whā
I sawe the fayr and straunge termes therin / I doubted that
it sholde not please some gentylmen whiche late blamed
me. sayeng þ̇[2] in my translacyons I had ouer curyous 30
termes whiche coude not be vnderstande[3] of comyn peple /
and desired me to vse olde and homely termes in my
translacyons. and fayn wolde I satysfye euery man / and
so to doo toke an olde booke and redde therin / and
certaynly the englysshe was so rude and brood that I coude 35
not wele vnderstande it. And also my lorde abbot of
westmynster ded do[4] shewe to me late certayn euydences
wryton in olde englysshe for to reduce it in to our
englysshe now vsid / And certaynly it was wreton in
suche wyse that it was more lyke to dutche than englysshe 40
I coude not reduce ne brynge it to be vnderstonden /
And certaynly our langage now vsed varyeth ferre from
that. whiche was vsed and spoken whan I was borne /
For we englysshe men / ben borne vnder the domy-
nacyon of the mone. whiche is neuer stedfaste / but 45
euer wauerynge / wexynge one season / and waneth &
dycreaseth another season / And that comyn englysshe
that is spoken in one shyre varyeth from a nother.
In so moche that in my dayes happened that certayn
marchaūtes were in a ship in tamyse for to haue sayled 50
ouer the see into zelande / and for lacke of wynde thei
taryed atte forlǫnd.[5] and wente to land for to refreshe them
And one of theym named sheffelde a mercer cam in to an
hows and axed for mete. and specyally he axyd after eggys

---

[1] Settled.   [2] That.   The þ is a good deal like a y, but not the same.
[3] Understood.   [4] Cause people to.   [5] At the Foreland.

55 And the goode wyf answerde. that she coude speke
no frenshe. And the marchaūt was angry. for he also
coude speke no frenshe. but wolde haue hadde egges / and
she vnderstode hym not / And thenne at laste a nother sayd
that he wolde haue eyren [1] / then the good wyf sayd that she
60 vnderstod hym wel / Loo what sholde a man in thyse dayes
now wryte. egges or eyren / certaynly it is harde to playse
euery man / by cause of dyuersite & chaūge of langage.
For in these dayes euery man that is in ony reputacyon in
his coūtre. wyll vtter his comynycacyon and maters in
65 suche maners & termes / that fewe men shall vnderstonde
theym / And som honest and grete clerkes haue ben wyth me
and desired me to wryte the moste curyous termes that I
coude fynde / And thus bytwene playn rude & curyous I
stande abasshed. but in my Iudgemente / the comyn termes
70 that be dayli vsed ben lyghter to be vnderstonde than the
olde and aūcyent englysshe / And for as moche as this
present booke is not for a rude vplondyssh man [2] to laboure
therin / ne rede it / but onely for a clerke & a noble gentyl-
man that feleth and vnderstondeth in faytes [3] of armes in
75 loue & in noble chyualrye / Therfor in a meane bytwene
bothe I haue reduced & translated this sayd booke in to our
englysshe not ouer rude ne curyous but in suche termes as
shall be vnderstanden by goddys grace accordynge to my copye.[4]

This extract in many respects speaks for itself. We can
see from what Caxton says that although it was already
settled that the 'standard' dialect of England was to be the
East Midland, yet that in many points the way which literary
English was to follow was not yet fixed. In fact, Caxton

---

[1] Eggs. The plural of *æg* in Anglo-Saxon was *ægru*. This, like many other words, was in the South made to conform to the declension whose plural was in *-en*. But the R was left, so that it is a sort of double plural, exactly like *child-r-en* (Anglo-Saxon *cildru*).
[2] Country-man.   [3] Feats.
[4] From a copy printed by Caxton, in the British Museum.

himself contributed a great deal to settle many points in it, as, for instance, by his adopting *their, them*, instead of *her, hem*, and of a hard G in *agayn, given*, and some other words, instead of Y. But this last change, like so many changes in language, took a long time to establish itself completely.

In looking at his language we see no differences in grammar from our present ordinary English except his use of the 3rd person singular in *-eth*, instead of the Northern form in *-es* or *-s*; the isolated plural 'they *ben*,' as well as 'they *be*,'[1] and the 'strong' past participle *understanden* or *understonden*, or with its final N dropped in the Southern manner, *understande* and *understonde*.[2] We now use the past tense *understood* for the past participle as well.

It might appear at first sight that the numerous cases of final *-e* also mark a difference of grammar. But, as a matter of fact, the *-e*'s are mere ornaments. We have seen that the final *-e*, pronounced, was gone before Caxton's time. And the same thing can be shown from Caxton himself. In Chaucer the final *-e* is added to an adjective when it is in the plural, to a verb when it is in the infinitive mood, or when the tense is in the plural number, and so on. But Caxton's E's at the end of words can be reduced to no principle. *Booke* (l. 34) has certainly no business with an E, nor has *oute* (l. 5), and in line 58 we find 'she *vnderstode*,' and two lines afterwards 'she *vnderstod*.' This last instance by itself is almost enough to prove that the *-e* in Caxton is merely ornamental, though this use of it is due to a habit inherited from a time when it was a real part of English grammar.

And there are many other examples of the unsettled character of our spelling, a variety which does not correspond to a difference in the pronunciation. For instance, *booke* (l. 15) and *boke* (l. 14) were certainly pronounced the same. So too we have *them* (l. 52) and *theym* (l. 53). Spelling, as we saw, had in earlier times aimed at expressing the sound of

---

[1] L. 70. [2] Ll. 78, 41, 31, 70.

the word, though the writer was more or less influenced by his recollection of the look of it in other books. In the fourteenth and fifteenth centuries this latter tendency increased,[1] and spelling became less 'phonetic,' though much was still left to the taste of the individual writer, who was not obliged even to be consistent with himself. Caxton, the first English printer, naturally spelt his words as if he had been writing them. But his art gradually stereotyped English spelling.[2] The printers naturally tended to spell a word as they usually saw it spelt, and, if only for the sake of speed in putting the letters together, always in the same way. Thus, except in some few particulars, of which the most important is the present curious arrangement by which the final -e is used to mark a long vowel in the syllable coming before it,[3] and, as a rule, not otherwise,[4] our spelling is practically the same as in Elizabeth's time, and in very many words as it was in the time of Caxton or earlier. Since language cannot be made to stand still, the consequence is that the spelling does anything but express the present pronunciation in very many English words. In one word, indeed, Caxton's two ways of spelling it show us how differently it was pronounced in his time. We find both *please* (l. 29) and *playse* (l. 61). Now *ay* was certainly never pronounced as E now is, and hence we conclude that *please* was in Caxton's time pronounced according to its present sound in Ireland. The Irish have kept the Old English pronunciation while we have changed. More will be said on this subject presently. Only it is well to remember that most of the English vowels and diphthongs were in Caxton's time pronounced very differently from their present

---

[1] Skeat, *Principles of English Etymology*, First Series, p. 331, etc.

[2] *Encyclopædia Britannica*, Ninth Edition, article 'English Language.' Skeat, *Principles of English Etymology*, First Series, p. 321.

[3] Also the distinction between U and V, that U should be a vowel and V a consonant, and the use of the form of I which had a tail to it (see p. 282, *Mercij*) as a sign of the consonant J.

[4] For an explanation of this see p. 235, etc. But E is also put after a V. For the reasons of this see Skeat, *Principles of English Etymology*, First Series, p. 317.

sound. His use of U and V is not mere variety but founded on a principle, though quite a different one from that which guides writers and printers at the present day. Now V is the consonant, and U the vowel. Then each was both consonant and vowel, but V was generally used at the beginning of words, and U between two vowels, as in *vsed* (l. 42), *haue* (l. 76). This had long been the practice, and in the 'Authorised Version' of 1611 and later it was still continued. Caxton, at least in his later works, may be fairly considered the first writer of Modern English. With the sixteenth century we shall come to works which still more unmistakably belong to the modern period of our language.

CHAPTER XX

ADDITIONS TO THE ENGLISH VOCABULARY DOWN TO 1625

French words—French words Latinised—New Latin words—'Doublets' — Latin words in Shakespeare — Dutch words, how they were borrowed, and how they are to be recognised—Spanish and Portuguese words—Italian words—Celtic words—Hebrew and Aramaic words — Words from Arabic — American and Indian words — How words pass from one language to another — Why English is not swamped with foreign words.[1]

BEFORE we pass to the principal changes which took place in English during the sixteenth century, it will be as well to say something of some further additions to our vocabulary or stock of words. And since some of the sources from which new words were derived in and before the fifteenth century were still drawn upon in the sixteenth century and later, we will anticipate a little and carry on this part of the subject into the seventeenth century.

First, as to French. When the Norman or Anglo-French died out and thus ceased to supply fresh words, we borrowed words from central or literary French instead. Caxton, for instance, introduced *resist* and *playsir* (*pleasure*).[2] Thus fresh words kept coming in from that language and have never ceased to do so. But ever since French ceased to be a language spoken in England, and still more when the sound of our

---

[1] Skeat, *Etymological Dictionary*, *Principles of English Etymology*, First and Second Series. Kington Oliphant, *The New English*. Eadie, *The English Bible*.
[2] See Skeat, *Principles of English Etymology*, Second Series, p. 155.

vowels began to get farther off from their French pronunciation, they have not been adopted into the language in the same half-unconscious way as they were down to Chaucer's time.

In the fifteenth century and shortly before that time there was a tendency to change some of the French words already in the language so as to make them more like the Latin from which they originally came, and these attempts went on in the sixteenth century. The revival of learning which began in the fourteenth century caused Latin to be more studied; learned people became more 'classical' in their tastes, and were offended at finding many words, both in French and English, which were obviously derived from Latin, so shamefully corrupted. Some of these were brought nearer to Latin, in spelling at all events. For instance, Chaucer has the form *parfit*, this word was brought back to the Latin form *perfect*;[1] so too *delitable* became *delectable*. *Vitaille* has become *victuals*[2] like *victualia*, just as we have already seen that *dette* was changed to *debt* to agree with *debitum*, in spelling at all events, though no doubt few people were sufficiently conscientious to pronounce the two last words as they spelt them. But in *fault*, the earlier form of which is *faute*, the sound has now been altered as well, and brought nearer to the Latin *fallo*, from which the word ultimately comes.[3] *Receipt* for the older *receit* is a compromise, the completely 'classical' form is, of course, *recept*; and in the same way *deceipt* is found, though that spelling did not survive. These alterations of course imply that the words were derived straight from Latin (which they were not) and are absurd pieces of pedantry and ignorance. The study of Latin at the same time introduced a good many duplicate words from that language, very distinct in shape from

---

[1] But *perfite* is found still surviving in the Geneva Bible, 1560, and *perfit* in the Authorised Version as it was at first printed.—Eadie, *The English Bible*, vol. ii. p. 258.
[2] See Kington Oliphant, *The New English*, vol. i. p. 167, etc.
[3] See Shakespeare, *Love's Labour's Lost*, V. i. 21; Skeat, *Principles of English Etymology*, First Series, p. 324, etc.; and above, p. 200.

the form that they had assumed in French. The new word did not usually turn out the old one as a sham, but, as distinct words, they lived on together, usually acquiring different senses when naturalised, if they had not got them already. Among these pairs are—

Natural French Form.	'Learned' Form.	Latin.
pursue [1]	prosecute	prosecutum
feat	fact	factum
purvey	provide	providere
nephew	nepotism	nepotem

The borrowing of words direct from Latin went on and increased. We have already seen (pp. 196, 274) how many of our religious terms come from Latin, especially through the influence of what was the 'Authorised Version' of the Bible in the Middle Ages, the Latin Vulgate. But sometimes a word which seems to be derived directly from Latin has really gone through French almost unaltered—that is to say, it has been taken into French from Latin books, and has not passed through colloquial Latin into the French language. In this case it is often impossible to say from the mere look of the word whether it has passed through French or not. The words which we borrow straight from Latin take just such a form as they would have if they had been 'learned' words in French. Sometimes we have borrowed a word from French in both its forms; for instance, the English words—

'Colloquial' Form (through Low Latin).	'Learned' Form.	Classical Latin.
obeisance	obedience	obedientiam
penance	penitence	poenitentiam
ransom (*Anglo-French* ransoun)	redemption	redemptionem

The number of words taken from Latin nearly in their Latin form, whether directly or through French, received constant additions. The sixteenth century, for instance,

---

[1] Still a law term in Scotland, where the prosecutor is called 'the pursuer.'

introduced multitudes of them. Shakespeare is full of such words, and these often show that they have not left Latin long by their meaning being as it is in that language, though it has since his time been worn down and altered. For instance, in the lines from *Julius Cæsar*—

> For, I believe, they are *portentous* things
> Unto the climate that they point upon,[1]—

portentous retains the original meaning of *portent*, 'that which portends or forebodes.' It has now lost its exact meaning, and is nothing but a strong word for 'very extraordinary.'

Again, in this passage from *Richard III.*—

> Madam, and you, my mother, will you go
> To give your *censures* in this weighty business?[2]—

censure merely means 'opinion,' or the expression of it, like the Latin *censura*. It has now been specialised, and means 'the expression of an adverse opinion.'

Some of these words too still show their origin by their accent being on the syllable which has it in Latin, or at least by its not falling so far back as in English words generally. Of course the tendency has since been to level the naturalised strangers under the rules of accent to which native words submit. But this, like all processes in language, requires time to work itself out. Thus in Shakespeare we find as*pect*, ab*ject*,[3] and other instances, as the metre shows.

Most of the words with which Greek supplied us came through Latin; some of these passing through French as well. A few, such as *dynasty*, *tactics*, were derived directly from Greek, which, early in the sixteenth century, began to be studied in England once more.

---

[1] I. iii. 31, 32. *Portentous* has passed through French.—Skeat, *Etymological Dictionary*. [2] II. ii. 143, 144.
[3] 'Whose ugly and unnatural as*pect*.'—*Richard III.*, I. ii. 23. 'We are the queen's ab*jects*, and must obey.'—*Ibid.*, I. i. 106 (see Abbott, *Shakespearian Grammar*, p. 388, etc.). These two lines will not scan with the accent thrown back by the ordinary English rule (see p. 202, etc.).

English has also borrowed a considerable number of words from Dutch, though of course nothing approaching the number which we owe to Latin, directly or through French. These seem not to have arrived in any quantity before the sixteenth century, but they began to come in the fourteenth and even earlier. There was plenty of intercourse between the two countries to give them an introduction. England was not then a manufacturing country; the raw wool which was our chief source of wealth was taken to the Netherlands (now Belgium and Holland) to be manufactured there. Henry VII., when his throne was endangered through the support given to Perkin Warbeck by the Yorkist Duchess of Burgundy, whom we have already seen as Caxton's patroness, stopped the export of wool to the Netherlands, which then belonged to the Dukes of Burgundy. This had its effect; they 'desired peace, because their country was nourished by the king's country.' So too Chaucer says of his merchant—

> He wolde the see were kept for any thing
> Bitwixe Middelburgh and Orewelle.[1]

It is therefore very natural that some Dutch words should have found their way into English then, as they also did in Elizabeth's time, chiefly through the Englishmen who went to help the Netherlanders in their revolt against the Spaniards. Besides, when the Duke of Parma took Antwerp,[2] it is said that a third of the merchants and manufacturers took refuge in London.[3] It is therefore only natural that some Dutch words should have come into English in the fourteenth or fifteenth, and more in the sixteenth century; but they are not very easy to identify. For English and Dutch are both of them Low

---

[1] *Prologue*, ll. 276, 277. Middelburgh is in Holland, close to Flushing. The Orwell runs out in Suffolk, near Harwich. 'For any thing'=whatever happened, 'kept'=guarded from pirates, and so on.

[2] Where Flemish, a Low German dialect akin to Dutch, was then spoken, as it still is to some considerable extent.

[3] See Skeat, *Principles of English Etymology*, First Series, p. 483, and the whole chapter. See also Appendix B.

German languages, and consequently it is often impossible to tell by the form of the words to which language they originally belong. Sometimes, indeed, it is possible to decide with certainty. *Deck*, for instance, is a Dutch word. It is own brother to *thatch*, or *thack* (both being related to Latin *tego*), but it has been affected by one of those changes or 'shiftings' of consonants which spread over Germany after the ancestors of the English had crossed the sea (p. 40). Most of them were confined to High German, and it is these which have had a large share in making that language as different from English as it now is. But this change (which also shows its effects in '*das*,' Low German '*dat*,' English '*that*') extended right down to the sea, and has left its mark on the Dutch word *deck*. As a rule, however, it is not possible to distinguish Dutch from English words by their shape alone.[1] Often the only proof available is, 'this word is found in Dutch, it appears in English in the fifteenth century (for instance) and not before, therefore it is derived from Dutch.' But, in the first place, a large quantity of Old English literature has perished. Secondly, some books which still remain have as yet been neither edited nor studied. Thirdly, a word may live in speech for centuries without getting admitted into literature, just as Scandinavian (or Danish) words sometimes crop up for the first time in the Southern dialect, which had no direct intercourse with the Danes, and Celtic words in the east of England far away from any Celtic people. They have lived and travelled underground, so to speak, passed from mouth to mouth, but disregarded by literature. So too many words which were used in Anglo-Saxon writings are to be found in people's mouths at the present day, but are not used in books.[2] Thus it is

[1] Or from Scandinavian words, for that matter, Danish and its sister-languages being also related to Dutch and English, though not quite so closely as these are to each other. It may be noticed that *-kin* in *manikin*, *minikin*, is a Dutch (double) diminutive, and affords a mark for identifying some Dutch words.

[2] Of course, if a book is written to represent a particular dialect, such words

plain that a word may be in the language without appearing in literature, and so the fact that a word is not found in earlier writings, even if we had them all, would be no certain proof that it had come into English at a particular time. Therefore some words in English, which are supposed to be Dutch because they are found in that language and not in Old English, may, after all, be part of the stock common to the two languages. But, so far as can be judged, the following are among those which came in from Dutch into Middle English:— *huckster, spool, tub.*

The number of these Dutch words in English was, as we have said, very largely increased in the sixteenth century, through the connection between England and Holland in Elizabeth's time. A large number of these are nautical terms. The Dutch were then and for a century afterwards fonder of the sea and more experienced sailors than any other nation. As examples of these words we may take *to hoist, hull, hoy, to moor, rover*,[1] and there are many more Dutch nautical terms now used in English. As examples of other words derived from Dutch at this early period and still in common use among us there are *beleaguer, boor, to foist, fop, frolic, to loiter, mope, toy, trick, uproar.*[2]

A good many words came to us from Spanish, some quite early, as, for instance, *capstan, cork,* and *pint,* along with a certain number which are really Arabic, being derived from the Moors who were settled in Spain; this last class will be spoken of presently. But in Elizabeth's time Spanish words came to us in larger numbers, when we were in contact

reappear in writing. As a few examples of them we may take *carl-cat* (tom-cat), which is good Anglo-Saxon, and is preserved in the Northern dialect, as also is the verb *fang*, which in East Midland, and therefore in 'standard' English, was superseded by the Danish verb *take* and the French verb *seize*. —Morris, *On the Survival of Early English Words in our Present Dialects*. *Nobbut* (only) is common in Wycliffe, and is still used in the Midlands and in Lancashire. 'To *lark*' (p. 87), 'to *swipe*,' 'to *rile*,' and 'to *snub*,' have all been 'classical' English at one time or another.

[1] Skeat, *Principles of English Etymology*, First Series, p. 482.
[2] *Ibid.* p. 485.

with the Spaniards, generally on unfriendly terms, in the Netherlands, and in America in the sort of way described in *Westward Ho!* Some also reached us through that universal medium—French. Among the Spanish words which had made their way into English before 1625 are *alligator, armada, bastinado, paragon, punctilio, renegade*.

From Portuguese came *apricot, cash, negro*, and some other words.

Our debt to Italian is very considerable. Besides those words which came through French, we borrowed a good many directly. The oldest of these is *pilgrim*, found in Layamon (about 1200), of which word Professor Skeat says, 'the English *pilgrim* obtained the Italian word by the actual process of going to Rome and fetching it thence.'[1] But the time when most Italian words came into English was the sixteenth and seventeenth centuries, when Italy was a model to the rest of Europe in literature, and to some extent in other branches of civilisation. And in the latter part of the sixteenth century many Englishmen travelled there. Besides these reasons for the presence of Italian words in English, it must be added that many Italian military terms were introduced into French by the wars which France carried on there, in the sixteenth century for instance, and from French these have passed to English. Among the Italian words which had made their way into English before 1625 are *alarm* and *alarum*,[2] *cavalry, citadel*, a *corporal, infantry, musket; sonnet, stanza, madrigal; duel, junket, monkey, motto, nuncio*.

The great majority of the French and Italian words come ultimately from Latin, while the Dutch words strengthened the Teutonic element in our language.

Celtic words were still making their way into English,

[1] *Principles of English Etymology*, Second Series, p. 295, and see the various chapters of the same book for the Italian element, etc.
[2] The same word as *alarm*, the extra syllable merely expressing 'the strong trilling of the preceding R.'—The word came through French, and is found so early as in *Piers Plowman*.—See Skeat, *Etymological Dictionary*. So an Irishman's pronunciation of *arm* is often written 'arrum.'

though in small numbers. Among these were *bard, brogue* (a kind of shoe), *gallowglass*, all probably from Irish; while *crag, creel, glen, loch, spate* came from Gaelic through Lowland Scotch;[1] and from Welsh, *flannel* and one or two others. The number of these words has been considerably increased in recent times. For instance, many are due to Sir Walter Scott (died 1832). However, considering the close contact of the English with nations speaking Celtic languages, it is surprising that the number is not larger.[2]

But our borrowing was not confined to languages of our own Indo-European family. We also added some words from the Semitic languages, Hebrew, Aramaic, and Arabic. The Hebrew words have mostly come to us through translations of the Bible, and some reached us quite early through the Vulgate and the Latin service, such as *cherub, jubilee*. Our English translations have of course brought in many more, such as *behemoth, Pharisee, cinnamon*, besides words derived from proper names. And we have also a certain number of Hebrew words which have first been thoroughly naturalised in some other language, such as Greek. Among these is *alphabet*, the Greek letters and their names having been borrowed from Hebrew. *Elephant, camel, sapphire* have passed through Latin and French as well, and came in during the Middle English period. So also did *cider*, and by the same route, being derived from a Hebrew word meaning any strong drink. Aramaic had contributed a few words quite early through Greek and Latin and sometimes French as well,—*abbot, abbess*, and *abbey*—all from *Abba*, father or head of the community.[3] From our present translation of the Bible come *mammon* and *Messiah*.

The Arabic words in English are fairly numerous, and this seems curious at first, for of course words cannot leap across

---

[1] Not always quite in their present shape. And many of the Gaelic words had not made their way beyond the Lowlands of Scotland at present.

[2] Skeat, *Principles of English Etymology*, First Series, chap. xxii.

[3] See Romans viii. 15.

from Arabia to England. They have come partly through trade. An article of commerce usually carries its name with it, and thus we had taken the words *myrrh, saffron*, and *cotton* into the language before the fifteenth century. Then too the Moors, who spoke Arabic, held various parts of Spain for nearly 800 years before 1492, and thus very many of their words found their way into Spanish, and afterwards to us, either directly or through the medium of French. This Arabic had a literature, and among the Moors especially there were many men who studied Greek science, as, for instance, the works of Aristotle, and made further discoveries for themselves. Thus sometimes Arabic words are derived from Greek; for instance, *al-chemy* is χημεία, with the Arabic article prefixed (as in *algebra, alcohol*). *Alchemy, alembic, nadir*, and *zenith* are among the Arabic words found in English in Chaucer's time, and *cipher* about the same period.

Artichoke, civet, garbage, garble, nitre, syrup, also reached us before 1625. So too did *racquet*, derived from an Arabic word meaning the palm of the hand, so that Racquets developed itself out of Fives.[1]

The discovery of America brought in some native American words, of which *potato, maize, cocoa, canoe, cannibal* are early instances.[2] These were soon followed by the word *tobacco*. Increased intercourse with Asia introduced the words *rajah* and *indigo*.[3] This is a foretaste of the selection of words which English traders and travellers were to bring into English from almost every language under the sun. Many of the

---

[1] *Raket* is found in Chaucer.

[2] About 1555. Kington Oliphant, *The New English*, vol. i. p. 536. Most of these words did not appear originally in quite their present form.

[3] There are some other sources from which we had picked up a few words indirectly. Thus the Sanskrit words *hemp* and *pepper* had already found their way through Greek and Latin into Anglo-Saxon. *Beryl* and *nard* followed by the same route before 1400. *Sugar* is found in Chaucer, having come from Sanskrit through Persian, Arabic, Spanish, and French. From Persian came (indirectly) *chess*, and its derivatives *check* and *chequer* or *exchequer* (all from *shah*, a king), besides other words. —See Skeat, *Etymological Dictionary* and *Principles of English Etymology*, Second Series.

words mentioned did not come to us direct but through Spanish.

We ought by this time to be able to see how words pass from one language into another. They cannot take a jump, but can only pass by contact of some kind or other, like an infectious disease, such as measles. The two languages may touch, either by both being spoken in the same country, as Welsh and Danish and Norman-French were spoken in the same country as English, or from literature, by which means Latin and Greek words have passed into English, or by commerce, as Arabic words have come to England with the things for which they were names, or by travellers bringing the words home, as *rajah*, *horde*, and other words have been introduced into English from the East. Of course, when one language has 'caught' a word, it can pass it on to another, and thus many words have come to us through several stages, French very often being the last. Our debt to French is so large as it is, partly because we have been in contact with it so long in all these ways, partly because, ever since the great infusion of French into our English vocabulary, which took place while Norman-French was spoken in England, the form of French words did not look strange in English, and thus they were easily naturalised.

All the words instanced above are to be found in English by 1625. Since that time, though we have made large additions to our vocabulary, no new source of any great importance has been opened for the supply of fresh words. It is true that in more recent times we have derived words much more freely from Greek, such as *anomaly, archaic, chorus, electricity*, which, like our earlier borrowings from that language, are often in a Latinised form. But, on the whole, we have now got a view, in outline, of all the main sources from which our stock of words in English is derived, though the vocabulary has received great additions in the last 250 years. At the same time many words have been lost, foreign as well as

Additions to the Vocabulary

native English.[1] For instance, a good many of the French words to be found in Chaucer have become obsolete,[2] as well as words which have come to us directly from Latin, or through French unaltered.[3] And so our language has not become overloaded with foreign words, constant as the invasion has been. It is quite possible to write English (on any ordinary subject) without using more words of foreign origin than were used by Robert of Brunne in 1338.

[1] *e.g.* (including Danish words) in the Authorised Version—*scrip, ear* (plough), *swaddle, leasing* (lying), *mete, gazing-stock, to-break* (Judges ix. 53), 'Woe *worth* the day!' (Ezek. xxx. 2; see p. 96), and many other words are not now used in the same sense, e.g. *bunches* (humps) of camels (Isa. xxx. 6), *fowl, meat*.—See Eadie, *The English Bible*, vol. ii. p. 246, etc.

[2] e.g. *delivere* (quick, nimble), *pricasour* (hard rider), *purfiled* (embroidered), *farsed* (stuffed), *poraille* (poor people), etc.

[3] There are a good many of these in the headings to the chapters of the Authorised Version, e.g. *to dehort, to mure* (build in), *to ruinate, inconsideration, prelation.* Also many in Shakespeare, e.g. *antre, attent, cautelous, composture, crescive, facinorous, ostent, prompture*, etc. And in other works of the sixteenth and early seventeenth centuries, *amplexed, precordial, funest, cœcity, placation, assubtiling*.—See Eadie, *The English Bible*, vol. ii. pp. 238-241.

CHAPTER XXI

SIXTEENTH-CENTURY ENGLISH

Character of sixteenth-century English—Some of its literature—Translations of the Bible in the sixteenth century—Our present Bible a revision of these, hence its language was old-fashioned in 1611—Prayer-Book of 1549—Latimer—Spenser—Shakespeare—Specimens of sixteenth-century English—Differences of sixteenth-century English from our own: the Verb, Substantives, Adjectives, Pronouns; Soft G or Y; 'ax'—Idioms—Freedom of sixteenth-century English—Dialects which have contributed to form 'standard' English.[1]

IN the fifteenth century, as we have seen, English parted with most of those inflexions which distinguish Middle English from the language that we now speak, and at the same time the East Midland dialect gained the position of 'standard' English, which it has ever since retained. At first this literary dialect, as belonging to London and its neighbourhood, had a strong Southern tinge, some signs of which are still visible in the English which we now speak and write. But we saw it drawing nearer to the more Northern form of the East Midland during the fifteenth century, and by about 1500 it had in the main assumed the form, though not the pronunciation, of our present English.

Thus in the sixteenth century English was much as it is now in shape, and was at the same time getting nearer to our

---

[1] Koch, *Historische Grammatik der Englischen Sprache*. Eadie, *The English Bible*. Abbott, *Shakespearian Grammar*. Morris, *Historical Outlines of English Accidence*. Kington Oliphant, *The New English*. *Encyclopædia Britannica*, Ninth Edition, article 'The English Bible.'

present pronunciation. The former statement we can easily recognise as true. Tyndale's translation of the New Testament (1526) has supplied a great deal of our present English Bible, in many passages almost without alteration. The Prayer-Book Version of the Psalms was made in 1539, and has since been altered only in spelling, with the exception of a few words here and there. The Prayer-Book of 1549 is reproduced, almost without alteration, in very many parts of our present Prayer-Book. Towards the end of the century Shakespeare's first play was written, and though some 'irregularities' in his grammar have been smoothed down in modern editions, and the spelling altered, his works are, on the whole, left very much as he wrote them, as may be seen by the specimen from the original edition which is given below. Then in 1611 we come to our present 'Authorised Version' of the Bible, which has since been changed only in spelling and in the form of a few words. Now the Prayer-Book Version of the Psalms, Shakespeare, and the 'Authorised Version' are what we should call merely old-fashioned Modern English. Their language is, in all essentials, the same as that which we use at present, and does not include such differences running all through it as we find even in Chaucer. Thus with the sixteenth century [1] we bring our language down almost to its present state.

In order to avoid the necessity of continually turning away from our main subject in order to explain the date or character of some book or translation, a short sketch will first be given of the works which will be referred to, and then specimens of some of them.

In 1526 Tyndale published his New Testament, the first translation into English made from the original Greek. This was printed abroad, at Worms. It was not safe to have it printed in England; the bishops were still too much opposed

---

[1] Shakespeare's earlier plays belong to the sixteenth century, and so does the language of the Authorised Version ; see below.

to any such thing; but large numbers of its successive editions were imported. Tyndale also began to translate the Old Testament, published the Pentateuch, and seems to have got as far as 2 Chronicles before he was put to death. But this last part was not published. It was left by him in manuscript.

In 1535 Coverdale translated the whole Bible 'out of Douche (German) and Latyn.' The 'Douche' versions were Luther's Bible, and some other translations which are now less well known. The 'Latyn' was not only the Vulgate, but also a new translation recently made. Then in 1537 'Matthew's' Bible was published. This was really compiled by John Rogers,[1] who was afterwards burnt in Mary's reign, 'Thomas Matthew,' to whom the book ascribes itself, being merely an assumed name. The New Testament in it is Tyndale's translation, with a few alterations, and so probably is the Old Testament down to the end of 2 Chronicles; the rest is from Coverdale's Bible. This was the first English translation of the Bible authorised to be used in England.

It was followed in 1539[2] by the 'Great Bible.' This was 'Matthew's' Bible, revised by Coverdale,[3] who was helped to make it more correct in the Old Testament by a Latin translation recently made from the Hebrew, and in the New Testament by the Latin translation of Erasmus from the Greek. The Prayer-Book Version of the Psalms which we now use is taken from the 'Great Bible,' and so were the Epistles and Gospels in the first English Prayer-Book, made in 1549.

Next, some of those Englishmen who had fled to the Continent early in Mary's reign set to work at Geneva on an

---

[1] Eadie, *The English Bible*, vol. i. p. 309, etc., which is also my authority for nearly all the part just following.

[2] In the same year 'Matthew's' Bible was also revised by Taverner. The word 'passover' in our version, instead of 'pasch' (besides some other renderings), is due to this version.

[3] Thus the Old Testament, except Genesis—2 Chronicles, was Coverdale, revised by himself.

improved translation, or rather a revision of Tyndale's version and of the 'Great Bible.' They improved on both to a considerable extent, using not only their own knowledge, but also other translations recently made in Latin and other languages, such as that by Beza. This version is commonly known as the Geneva Bible, as it was made and first printed there. It was completed and published at the beginning of Elizabeth's reign, in 1560, and held its ground for more than half a century as the best known and most popular translation both in England and Scotland. It even continued to be printed for thirty years after our present version of the Bible was made in 1611, and this is very largely indebted to it both for renderings, and for turns of expression in its English.

In 1568, and again in 1572, the 'Great Bible' was revised by some of the bishops and other scholars. This version is therefore known as the 'Bishops' Bible.' It formed the groundwork of the Authorised Version, but itself never acquired any great amount of popularity.

A translation of the Bible into English from the Vulgate was also made by some of the Roman Catholics who had fled from England in Elizabeth's reign. It is commonly known as the Douai Bible. The New Testament was published at Rheims in 1582, the Old Testament at Douai in 1609. The Authorised Version owes some turns of expression to it. But there is an enormous amount of Anglicised Latin in it, for instance, 'every knee bow of the celestials, terrestrials, and infernals' (Phil. ii. 9). It has since by many revisions been brought near to our own Bible.[1]

Finally, in 1604, immediately after James I.'s accession, the project was started of a new translation of the Bible, which should supersede all others. It seems to have arisen out of some remarks made by one of the Puritan representatives at the Hampton Court Conference. The King took up the plan and urged it. Accordingly the best Hebrew and

---

[1] See Eadie, *The English Bible*, vol. ii. pp. 114 *sqq.*

Greek scholars in England were set to work. The Bible was divided into parts, each part being assigned to a kind of committee, or division of the whole body, and then the work of each of these was revised by some others of the translators. Most of its renderings and expressions are to be found in one or other of the earlier versions mentioned above. These were not bad translations, by any means. A mere selection from them would give a very good translation. And where the translators thought that an improvement could be made upon all of them, they of course gave their own rendering. The result, whether it is regarded as a translation of the Hebrew and Greek, or as a piece of English, is, we know, excellent.

Thus the Authorised Version was really much such a revision of former translations as the Revised Version recently made, except that in the latter case one translation only was to be amended, while in the Bible of 1611 it was 'the former translations' that were 'diligently compared and revised.'[1] Hence the English is not exactly such as was spoken or even written at the time when it was published. The 'diction,' the mode of expression appropriate to the Bible, had been already to a great extent fixed by Tyndale and Coverdale, and partly too by Wycliffe and Purvey (p. 274). The language is in some points more modern than that of the versions made in the sixteenth century, for some old forms had become impossible in the meantime, such as *hit* (*it*), *tho* (the, those), *yeve* (*give*), *bryd* (*bird*), *lewgh* (*laughed*), which are found in Tyndale; and *braste* (*burst*), *stale* (*stole*), *holpe* (*helped*), which occur in the Geneva version. But its language was more old-fashioned than that ordinarily written by the translators themselves.

It is very hard to know how much Wycliffe's and Purvey's versions contributed to it. There is no doubt that these had given many religious words a settled place in English, but it

[1] Title of Authorised Version.

is difficult to say how much influence they had besides. Tyndale must have known them, and though his translation was certainly original and not a revision of any earlier one, his mode of expression was probably coloured by the earlier translations. The first part of the fourteenth chapter of St. John, for instance, is very much alike in both Purvey and Tyndale.[1] And the revisers after Tyndale seem to have looked at the Wycliffite versions. For instance, here are some expressions from Purvey which are found in practically the same form in our present Bible, but are different in Tyndale—

Sone of perdicioun.[2]
It is good vs to be here.[3]
Thou sauerist not tho thingis.[4]

This account of the translations of the Bible shows us that we must not take our present version as an exact specimen of the ordinary English of 1611. Its language is rather that of the earlier versions partially modernised. In the same way the Revised Version is not a specimen of the English of 1870-80. But the English which the revisers of 1611 wrote, if it was slightly antiquated, was perfect of its kind and thoroughly adapted to its purpose. This can hardly be said of some of the variations brought in in the latest revision.

We will now place some other works which will be mentioned later on.

In 1549 the first English Prayer-Book was compiled, much of it being simply translated from the Latin Service-Books. And a large part of this Prayer-Book (besides its version of the Psalms taken from the 'Great Bible') is retained in our present Prayer-Book almost unaltered. To the same year belong some sermons of Latimer which give us

---

[1] It is also much the same in the Authorised Version, which is usually not very different from Tyndale.
[2] St. John xvii. 12.   [3] St. Matt. xvii. 4.
[4] St. Matt. xvi. 23.—See Kington Oliphant, *The New English*, vol. i. pp. 139, 140 ; see also pp. 408, 409.

something near the English ordinarily spoken by an educated man at that time.

In 1590 the first three books of Spenser's *Faery Queene* were published;[1] he cannot be appealed to to establish any point in our subject, though he illustrates many. Ben Jonson says of him, 'Spenser writ no language,' though he certainly wrote splendid poetry.

He has frequent instances of forms of grammar which were obsolete in his day, such as past participles with *y*- prefixed, '*y*-cladd,'[2] '*y*-mounted';[3] infinitives in -*en*, 'to vew*en*,'[4] 'she could tell*en*';[5] plurals of verbs in -*en*, as 'they be*en*,'[6] 'all hurtl*en* forth,'[7] as well as other archaisms. This is what all poets do more or less, though hardly any to the same extent as Spenser. The frequency of these obsolete forms of grammar in his works is probably largely due to his imitating Chaucer.

Shakespeare's plays were written between 1590 and 1616. The earliest collected edition of them, the 'First Folio,' was published in 1623.[8] The parts of these plays which are in verse represent the ordinary English of his time as nearly as poetry can be expected to do; the parts of them which are in prose of course bear a very close resemblance to the English then spoken.

We will now look at some specimens of sixteenth-century English, the Parable of the Sower, from Tyndale's New Testament, part of the Prayer-Book of 1549, an extract from a sermon of Latimer preached (and printed) in the same year, a bit of Shakespeare, and the Parable of the Sower in the Authorised Version, all in their original form.

---

[1] Article VI. of the XXXIX.
[2] I. i. 1.   [3] I. ii. 29.   [4] I. i. 23.
[5] I. iii. 24. [6] I. i. 10.   [7] I. iv. 16.
[8] Many of the plays were written before 1600, and, as no distinction can be made between the English of the earlier and later ones, I have quoted from them indifferently.

TYNDALE[1]

St. Matthew xiii.

1526

And he spake many thynges to them in similitudes / sayinge: beholde / the sower went forth to sowe / and as he sowed / some fell by the wayes syde / and the fowlles cam / and devoured it vppe. Some fell apon stony grounde where it had nott moche erth / and a non it spronge vppe / be cause it had no depht of erth: and when the sun was vppe / hit cauth heet / and for lake of rotynge wyddred awaye. Some fell amonge thornes / and the thornes arose and chooked it. Parte fell in goode grunde / and broght forth good frute: some an hundred fold / some fyfty fold[2] / some thyrty folde. Whosoever hath eares to heare / let him heare.

THE PREFACE TO THE PRAYER-BOOK OF 1549

Now called
'Concerning the Service of the Church'

There was neuer any thing by the wit of man so well deuised, or so surely established, which (in continuāce[3] of time) hath not been corrupted: as (emong other thinges) it may plainly appere by the common prayers in the Churche, commonly called diuine seruice: the firste originall and grounde whereof, if a manne woulde searche out by the auncient fathers, he shall finde that the same was not ordeyned, but of a good purpose, and for a great aduauncement of godlines: For they so ordred the matter, that all the whole Bible (or the greatest parte thereof) should be read ouer once in the yeare, intendyng thereby, that the Cleargie, and specially

---

[1] From the facsimile of the first edition, edited by Arber.
[2] A mistake in this version.
[3] The − over the *a* means an *n* (or sometimes an *m*) after it, just as had generally been written in Manuscripts.

suche as were Ministers of the congregacion, should (by often readyng and meditacion of Gods worde) be stirred vp to godlines themselfes, and be more able also to exhorte other [1] by wholsome doctrine, and to confute them that were aduersaries to the trueth. And further, that the people (by daily hearyng of holy scripture read in the Churche) should continuallye profite more and more in the knowlege of God, and bee the more inflamed with the loue of his true religion. But these many yeares passed this Godly and decent ordre of the aunciēt fathers, hath bee [2] so altered, broken, and neglected, by planting in vncertein stories, Legēdes, Respondes, Verses, vaine repeticions, Commemoracions and Synodalles, that commonly when any boke of the Bible was begon : before three or foure Chapiters were read out, all the rest were vnread. And in this sorte, the boke of Esaie was begon in Aduent, and the booke of Genesis in Septuagesima : but they were onely begon, and neuer read thorow. After a like sorte wer other bokes of holy scripture vsed.

. . . . . .

Moreouer, the nōbre & hardnes of the rules called the pie, and the manifolde chaunginges of the seruice, was the cause, yt [3] to turne the boke onlye, was so hard and intricate a matter, that many times, there was more busines to fynd out what should be read, than to read it when it was founde out.

These inconueniences therfore considered : here is set furth suche an ordre, whereby thesame shal be redressed. And for a readines in this matter, here is drawen out a Kalendar for that purpose, whiche is plaine and easy to be vnderstanded,[4] wherin (so muche as maie be) the readyng of holy

---

[1] Plural of the adjective, by dropping the -e at the end ; see below, p. 338.

[2] The n dropped, in the Southern manner ; see pp. 291, 299.

[3] See pp. 222, 297.

[4] A 'strong' past participle made regular, the old form having been *understanden* (p. 299). This particular normalising of the language did not last. *Understanded* is also found in the XXIVth Article at the end of the Prayer-Book.

scripture is so set furthe, that all thynges shall bee doen in ordre, without breakyng one piece therof from another. For this cause be cut of [1] Anthemes, Respondes, Inuitatories, and suche like thynges, as did breake the continuall course of the readyng of the scripture.

. . . .

IN THE MARRIAGE SERVICE

(Taken from the 'Great Bible,' which is, in the Psalms, Coverdale's translation; see p. 316)

Deus miseriatur nostri. (Psalm LXVII) God be mercifull vnto vs, and blesse vs, and shewe vs the lighte of his countenaunce: and be merciful vnto vs.

That thy waye may bee knowen vpon yearth, thy sauing health emong all nacions.

Leate the people prayse thee (o God) yea leat all people prayse thee.

O leate the nacions reioyce and bee glad, for thou shalte iudge the folke righteously, and gouerne the nacions vpon yearth.

Leat the people prayse thee (o God) leat al people prayse thee.

Then shal the yearth bring foorthe her increase: and god, euen our owne God, shal geue vs his blessyng.

God shall blesse vs, and all the endes of the worlde shall feare him.

Glorye be to the father &c.

As it was in the beginning &c.

---

[1] *Of* and *off* were not yet distinguished. Tyndale uses both indifferently.

MATINS

¶ The Second Collect: for Peace

O God, which art author of peace, and louer of concorde, in knowledge of whom standeth our eternall lyfe, whose seruice is perfecte fredome: defende vs thy humble seruautes, in al assaultes of our enemies, that we surely trustyng in thy defence, may not feare the power of any aduersaries: through the might of Jesu Christ our Lorde. Amen.[1]

THE FIFTE SERMON OF MAYSTER HUGHE LATIMER

whyche he prached before the kynges Maiestye wythin hys Graces Palaice at Westminster the fyft. daye of Aprill [2]

(1549)

It is a daungerous thynge to be in offyce for . *qui attingit picem coinquinabitur ab ea,* He y^t medleth wyth pitch is like to be spotted with it. Bribes may be assembled [3] to pitch, for euen as pytche dothe pollute theyr handes that medle with it: so brybes wyl brynge you to peruertynge of iustyce. Beware of pytch, you iudges of the worlde, brybes wyl make you peruert iustice. Why you wil say We touche none. No mary.[4] But my Mystres your wyfe hath a fyne fynger

---

[1] From a copy in the British Museum. This Prayer-Book is also published in *The Ancient and Modern Library of Theological Literature*, but the U's and V's are to some extent reduced to modern usage.

[2] From a copy in the British Museum, printed in the same year, 1549; also reprinted by Arber.

[3] Compared. Anglo-French *assembler,* Latin *assimulare.*

[4] = by the Virgin Mary, usually written *marry.*

she toucheth it for you or els you haue a seruaunt a Muneribus* he wyl say yf you wyl come to my master and offer him a yoke of oxen, you shal spede neuer the worsse but I thincke my Mayster[1] wil take none, when he hath offered them to y^e maister, then commes another seruaunt and sayes. If you wylbring them to the clarke of the kichen you shallbe remembred the better. Thys is a fryerly fassion that wyll receyue no monye in theyr handes but wyll haue it put vpon theyr sleues. A goodly rag of popyshe religion. They be lyke graye fryers, they wyll not[2] be sene to receyue no[2] brybes them selues but haue other to receiue for them.[3]

* Anglice a receyuer of his masters brybes.

SHAKESPEARE

REPRODUCTION OF 'FIRST FOLIO' EDITION OF 1623[4]
Edited by H. Staunton, 1866

Merchant of Venice, IV. i. 184

The quality of mercy is not strain'd,
It droppeth as the gentle raine from heauen
Vpon the place beneath. It is twice blest,
It blesseth him that giues, and him that takes,
'Tis mightiest in the mightiest, it becomes
The throned Monarch better than his Crowne.
His Scepter shewes the force of temporall power
The attribute to awe and Maiestie,
Wherein doth sit the dread and feare of Kings:
But mercy is aboue this sceptred sway,
It is enthroned in the hearts of Kings,
It is an attribute to God himselfe;

---

[1] Often pronounced so still by people in the country. Anglo-French *maistre*, Latin *magistrum*.
[2] The double negative was still a thoroughly good English idiom.
[3] The Grey Friars or Franciscans were, by their rule, not allowed to touch money. But ways had been invented to evade the rule by others receiving it for them as trustees, and so on.
[4] This play was written in or before 1598. The shorter passages are quoted from the 'Globe' edition, unless otherwise stated.

And earthly power doth then shew likest Gods
When mercie seasons Iustice. Therefore Iew,
Though Iustice be thy plea, consider this,
That in the course of Iustice, none of vs
Should see saluation : we do pray for mercie,
And that same prayer, doth teach vs all to render
The deeds of mercie. I haue spoke thus much
To mittigate the iustice of thy plea :
Which if thou follow, this strict course of Venice
Must needes giue sentence 'gainst the Merchant there.

AUTHORISED VERSION
First Edition, 1611[1]
St. Matthew xiii. 3-9

3. And hee spake many things vnto them in parables, saying, Behold a sower went foorth to sow.

4. And when he sowed, some *seedes* fell by the wayes side, and the foules came, and deuoured them vp.

5. Some fell vpon stony places, where they had not much earth : and foorthwith they sprung vp, because they had no deepenesse of earth.

6. And when the Sunne was vp, they were scorched : and because they had not root, they withered away.

7. And some fell among thorns : and the thornes sprung vp, & choked them.

8. But other fell into good ground, and brought foorth fruit, some an hundred folde, some sixtie folde, some thirty folde.

9. Who hath eares to heare, let him heare.

These extracts will give us a general idea of what English was like in the sixteenth century, but of course they will not supply instances of all the points to be noticed in it. A short

---

[1] The shorter passages are quoted from the latest editions, unless otherwise stated.

sketch will therefore be given of those points which mark the progress of the language towards its present state. First of all, the differences in the spelling may be briefly dismissed. Enough has been said before on the use of I where we now use J,[1] on the difference of principle in the use of U and V,[2] and about the final E, which was now a kind of fossil in the language.[3]

English spelling did not settle down quite into its present state till about 1700.[4] That it did become fixed is due to the printers (p. 300), though even recently some few changes of spelling have taken place, such as the writing of S for Z in such words as *canonize*. But such changes are now very rare.

We come then to changes in the grammar during the sixteenth century, and we will begin with the verb.

(1) Here the main difference between the English of the sixteenth century and our own is that then, in prose, the 3rd person singular (present tense) usually ended in *-eth*. The Northern termination in *-s* or *-es* was still more or less colloquial. It is found in Latimer's sermons (p. 325)—'then commes another seruaunt and sayes,'—but these are more or less colloquial English. It is also very common in Shakespeare. In his prose this is not surprising; here the English is near to what was spoken in his own time. As to his poetry, other poets, and even Spenser, very frequently use the form, no doubt on account of its convenience as an alternative to the form in *-eth* for the metre. But it is not found at all in the Authorised Version of 1611. Otherwise the tenses of the verb were in the main conjugated as at present.

But we find occasionally in the sixteenth century—
(*a*) The Southern plural in *-eth* or *-th*.
(*b*) The Northern plural in *-s*.
(*c*) The Midland plural in *-en* (see p. 260).

---

[1] P. 282, note 1.   [2] P. 300.   [3] P. 287, etc., p. 299, etc.   It was for a time put in or left out by printers to make their lines even.
[4] Skeat, *Principles of English Etymology*, First Series, p. 329.

(a) We have seen this plural in *-eth* before (the Southern dialect having inherited it from Anglo-Saxon *-aþ*), as in Robert of Gloucester (p. 261) and in Trevisa (p. 282). In the sixteenth century it is found in Tyndale's *Obedience of a Christian Man*, thus—

And the propirties of the hebrue tonge *agreth* a thousande tymes moare with the english then [1] with the latyne.[2]

There is a plain instance also in the Prayer-Book of 1549—

Almightie God, whose prayse thys day the young innocentes thy witnesses *hath* confessed, and shewed foorthe, not in speakyng, but in dying.

It is found also in the 'First Folio' of Shakespeare, though it has usually been altered in modern editions; for instance—

Where men enforced *doth* speak anything.[3]

But it is not nearly so common in Shakespeare as

(b) The Northern plural in *-s*.

This must have been not uncommonly used in Shakespeare's time by North-country people, in speaking at all events. There are many instances of it in the 'First Folio,' most of which have been altered in later editions. Here, however, is one which on account of the rhyme cannot be got rid of, and which cannot be explained away—

Whiles I threat, he lives :
Words to the heat of deeds too cold breath *gives*.[4]

(c) The Midland plural in *-en*.

This, as we saw (p. 290, etc.), was practically extinct in 'standard' English by about the beginning of the sixteenth century, though it is still used in Lancashire, Cheshire, and

---

[1] *Than* is originally the same word as *then* = 'agreeth more with the English, then (in the next place) with the Latin.'
[2] Skeat, *Specimens of English Literature*, 1394-1579, p. 172; quoted also by Kington Oliphant, *The New English*, and by Eadie, *The English Bible*.
[3] *Merchant of Venice*, III. ii. 33. Abbott's *Shakespearian Grammar*, p. 237.
[4] *Macbeth*, II. i. 60, 61. Abbott's *Shakespearian Grammar*, p. 235, etc.; see also *Romeo and Juliet*, II. iii. 51, 52.

Shropshire. It had been definitely discarded in Modern English, and so Shakespeare uses it a very few times only, for instance—

> And then the whole quire hold their hips and laugh,
> And *waxen* in their mirth and neeze and swear
> A merrier hour was never wasted there.[1]

Perhaps the more exact view is that the plural in *-s* is in Shakespeare an inaccuracy of grammar, a levelling of the inflexions contrary to usage (as when an uneducated man, in the south of England, says, 'I knows it,' or 'we knows it'), but that it was justified and supported by the usage of the North. The same principle may explain the Southern plural in *-eth*. But after all, it comes to much the same thing. In the passage quoted above the *-en* comes in curiously in the middle of a mass of uninflected plurals. It was really dead in Shakespeare's time, so far as 'standard' English is concerned; but it is used by other sixteenth-century poets, and especially by Spenser, who was particularly fond of old-fashioned forms of language.

There are also in Shakespeare one or two instances of *y*-prefixed to past participles; for instance, *y-clad*,[2] and *y-cliped*[3] (for *ycleped*), and of course many more in Spenser. But this addition was quite disused in ordinary talk and in prose writing.

As to the past tenses of verbs, there were some ways of writing 'regular' or weak past participles, such as *pluckt* and *fetcht* in the Bible of 1611, which differed from our present use. But this is really a better spelling than our *plucked* and *fetched*, since it expresses the ordinary sound of the word. These and a few other forms in the 'weak' verbs differing from what we now use, such as *ought* for *owed*, *builded*, where we now use *built*,[4] do not, taken together, make any very great difference in the language. Points which are worth more

---

[1] *Midsummer-Night's Dream*, II. i. 55-57. Abbott's *Shakespearian Grammar*, p. 235.   [2] *Second Part of Henry VI.*, I. i. 33
[3] *Love's Labour's Lost*, V. ii. 602.
[4] Eadie, *The English Bible*, vol. ii. p. 255, etc.

attention are that in the sixteenth century the termination of the past participle of weak verbs was still often a separate syllable, and that Latin participles were often left as they stood, without the English inflexion being added. For instance, in a proclamation which, in 1530, was ordered to be read out by preachers—

The kings highnes and the prelats in soo doing, not suffering the Scripture to be *divulgid* and *communicate* in the English tonge vnto the people at this tyme, doth well.[1]

We should expect that the *-ed* of 'regular' past participles was still sometimes sounded in ordinary speaking from the frequency with which it has to be so read, in Shakespeare for instance. The spelling here proves the pronunciation; I not being a silent letter whatever E might be. As to the Latin participle, without further inflexion, there is an instance in our Bible—

O thou that art *situate* at the entry of the sea,[2]

and many similar examples in Shakespeare, such as

If he, *compact* of jars, grow musical,
We shall have shortly discord in the spheres.[3]

In the past tenses and past participles of 'strong' or 'irregular' verbs changes were still going on in the sixteenth century as they had been before. They would no doubt move at the same rate now if the educated classes were not so firmly opposed to any change in the language, especially in its grammar. These alterations are all on the same principle; they aim at levelling 'irregularities' in some way or another, but this is done in various ways.

(*a*) Some 'strong' verbs had been or were being made 'regular' throughout, reduced by analogy to the conjugation

---

[1] Eadie, *The English Bible*, vol. i. p. 260; *doth* is probably another instance of the Southern plural. But it is some distance from its subject, and might refer to the King especially.
[2] Ezekiel xxvii. 3. Eadie, *The English Bible*, vol. ii. p. 259.
[3] *As You Like It*, II. vii. 5, 6.

of the majority of verbs in English, of such verbs as *to hope*.

Present.	Past Tense or Perfect.	Past Participle.
hope	hoped	hoped

Thus *wash* had a past tense, *wessh*, so late as in Chaucer, but in the sixteenth century it had become 'weak' (or 'regular') as it is now. *Laugh* too was originally a 'strong' verb. In Tyndale the past tense is *lewgh*. But to the translators (or revisers) of 1611 this seemed obsolete English, and so we find in our Bible 'they *laughed* him to scorn.'[1] This process has always been going on. As we pass from one century to the next the 'strong' verbs drop off, like stragglers on a march.

(*b*) Sometimes the past participle alone remained 'strong' while the past tense had been made like the ordinary verb. For instance, *shapen*,[2] *shaven*,[3] *waxen*,[4] occur in the Bible, though the past tenses (or perfects) of these verbs are always regular—*shaped*, *shaved*, *waxed*, and not *shoop*, *shoof*, and *wex*, which are found in Chaucer or Wycliffe.[5] In the case of the verb *help* we can see the change in its past tense taking place during the sixteenth century.[6] For instance, *holpe* occurs in the Geneva Bible and in Shakespeare; but in our version the past tense is only *helped*,[7] though the past participle is often *holpen*, as, for instance, in St. Luke i. 54. Now the verb has become wholly regular. In the same way we can still talk of '*molten* lead,' but we should hardly say, 'he *molt*.'

---

[1] St. Luke viii. 53. But some changes of this kind made in the sixteenth century have not been maintained, e.g. *rived* for *riven*.
[2] Psalm li. 5.   [3] 1 Corinthians xi. 6.   [4] Jeremiah v. 28.
[5] The 'weak' or 'regular' forms too are found in Wycliffe, or in Purvey's revision of his translation.
[6] The 'weak' form is first found in the fourteenth century, so that the sixteenth century really saw the end of the struggle. Many of these new forms in the language took centuries to become established.
[7] *e.g.* Acts xviii. 27.

(c) There is further confusion in these strong verbs. They have been affected not only by the example of the weak verbs but by each other, and, what is more important, by parts of themselves. What has happened to them cannot be understood without looking back to the account of the conjugation of 'strong' verbs in Anglo-Saxon to be found on p. 86, etc.

But, first of all, in order to clear the ground, it must be pointed out that the *-en* of the past participle has been dropped in many of these verbs. We saw it in process of dissolution in Caxton's *vnderstande* for *vnderstanden* (p. 299). So too in Tyndale we find, 'have ye *vnderstonde* all these thynges?'[1] The *-en* had been weakened to *-e* in the South long before Caxton, but in earlier times this *-e* had still been pronounced. In Caxton's time it had no real meaning, and consequently the (now obsolete) past participle *understande*, as well as Milton's

New presbyter is but old priest *writ* large,[2]

exactly illustrate the way in which the past participles *bound*, *slung*, *swum*, and so on, have been formed. In some cases we still have both forms, as in *trod* and *trodden*, *got* and (*for*)*gotten*. We may now try to make out something about the workings of analogy on the 'strong' verbs.

First of all we see on pages 90, 91, that in some of these conjugations the past tense has a different vowel in the plural[3] from what it has in the singular, as in *ic band, wé bundon; ic scán, wé scinon*. In some other verbs the difference is merely one of quantity, and in others there is no difference at all. There were, therefore, plenty of examples to follow in the very natural process of simplifying the grammar of the verb by giving every past tense the same vowel throughout, and the vowel which prevailed was the vowel of the singular. In Wycliffe and Chaucer we still find

---

[1] St. Matt. xiii. 51.   [2] Also in Shakespeare, *Richard II.*, II. i. 14.
[3] And in the 2nd person singular. This had now in all strong verbs taken the ordinary personal ending which it had not had before, e.g., *sat-est, spak-est*.

traces of the distinction, as in 'I *woot*,' 'thei *witen*' (*wát, woot, wot* being originally a perfect like οἶδα, p. 23), and 'he *rood*,' 'thei *riden*';[1] but the simplification had been fully carried out by the sixteenth century. The conjugation of *fall, give,* and *shake* has been little altered since the Conquest; the doubled O in *shook* (p. 211) having originally been merely a mark of length, like the *-e* at the end of *woke*. The past tenses of *ride, shine, write* have had the A altered into O, as has nearly always been the case where A was long, and sometimes when it was short.

So far the development of the 'strong' verbs has been simple, now we come to the complications. These are chiefly due to the vowel of the past participle intruding itself into the past tense; sometimes the change of A to O in the past tense has helped this. In the conjugation of *bind* and *shine* the vowel of the past participle was the same as the vowel of the past tense in the plural, and this may have been some help as an analogy.[2] But in the main the notion which (unconsciously) influenced those who, by their speaking, altered and confused our 'strong' verbs seems to have been that one change of vowel was enough in the verb.

In *tore, spoke, broke,* from *torn, spoken,*[3] *broken,* the influence of the past participle is very clear, and it had been exerted between the time of Wycliffe and the sixteenth century. And even then the process was not complete, for we find *tare*,[4] *spake*,[5] *brake*,[6] the correct perfects, in the Bible of 1611, which, for the most part, represents sixteenth-century English (p. 318). But these were becoming old-fashioned when the

---

[1] See Morris and Skeat, *Prologue and Knightes Tale*, Introduction, p. xxxix.
[2] See Skeat, *Principles of English Etymology*, Second Series, pp. 458-460. In the verb *find*, *e.g.*, the past tense is singular *fond*, plural *fonde*, and *founde*, in Robert of Gloucester, and the past participle *y-fonde* and *y-founde*. It was no very great change from one to the other; *win*, past tense *wan*, then *won*, shows the change to O clearly.
[3] The past participle was at first *sprecen*, then *speken*. This verb seems to have been influenced by the analogy of *broken*, and then the new past participle coloured the past tense.
[4] 2 Kings ii. 24. [5] Genesis xlii. 22. [6] Judges ix. 53.

Bible was published. The vowel of the past participle was gaining the victory.

We have already seen that the -*en* or -*n* of the past participle was often dropped. When this was the case in a verb which had already adapted the vowel of its perfect to that of its past participle, there was of course no longer any difference between the two parts of the verb. *Spoke* was the same as *spoke(n)*, *begun* as *begunn(en)*. Hence we find in Shakespeare—

> And five years since there was some speech of marriage
> Betwixt myself and her, which was *broke* off.[1]

So too Ben Jonson says, 'Spenser *writ* no language,' using the past tense with the vowel of the past participle. Many of these perfects with the vowel of the past participle remained as alternative forms till very recent times. Sir Walter Scott, for instance, has *shrunk*, *sunk*, *rung*, *sprung*, as past tenses. Some of the alternative forms in A are gone past recall. For instance, there are no other forms existing besides *bound*, *found*, for the perfect, nor were there in the sixteenth century. We could not now say, 'I *slang*,'[2] 'I *tare*,' 'I *brake*,' though these are all found in the Bible. But quite recently there has been a reaction, and, where it is still possible English, the form which is different from the past participle is now preferred; in fact, it would not now be correct English to say, 'I *swum*,' 'I *rung*.' But it is no doubt owing to the fact that the past participle is like the past tense in all weak verbs and in some strong ones that we hear people say, 'I *seen* 'im,' ''E *done* it.'

And this resemblance of the clipped past participle to the past tense in so many 'strong' verbs, as well as their apparent identity in the 'weak' verbs (pp. 91, 92), led to a further piece of confusion or 'false analogy.'

If the past tense and past participle were 'for practical

---

[1] *Measure for Measure*, V. i. 217, 218.
[2] 1 Sam. xvii. 49.

purposes' the same, then the past tense could be used for the past participle. Instances of this are by no means uncommon in Shakespeare; for instance—

> The king himself is *rode* to view their battle.[1]
>
> Then, Brutus, I have much *mistook* your passion.[2]
>
> I will scarce think you have *swam* in a gondola.[3]

And some past tenses have in this way established themselves as past participles. *Held* has turned out the proper past participle *holden*, to be found in the Bible,[4] and preserved in 'be*holden*.' *Sat* had already driven out *sitten*, and *stood standen*, by the sixteenth century. In their nature, 'I have *stood*,' 'I have *held* it,' are no more correct than 'I have *shook*,' or '*ate* it.'

Thus throughout the whole progress of the English language the 'strong' verbs have been constantly passing into 'weak' verbs, or getting corrupted in various ways till their history becomes most difficult to trace. The 'strong' verbs, as we have them at present, are a sort of monument to the power of analogy in language.

(*d*) On the other hand, in a few cases where some 'weak' verb bore a close resemblance to a particular 'strong' verb, the analogy has been sufficient to make the weak verb strong. We have already seen that the past tense of *wear*, which in Chaucer is *werëd*, has become *wore*, from the analogy of *tear, bear, swear*. *Shown* probably follows the analogy of *grown, thrown, known, mown*; and *sewn* is due to these past participles and also to *sown*, which was confused with it. *Dug*[5] is not so easy to explain. We will now leave this very confusing subject.

The subjunctive was much more extensively used in the

---

[1] *Henry V.*, IV. iii. 2. See Abbott's *Shakespearian Grammar*, p. 244, etc.
[2] *Julius Cæsar*, I. ii. 48.   [3] *As You Like It*, IV. i. 37.
[4] Acts ii. 24.   [5] *Digged* only, in the Bible of 1611.

sixteenth century than it is now. For instance, in a conditional sentence, as in the following example from Shakespeare:—

Hold out my horse, and I will first be there,[1]

meaning 'if my horse holds (or hold) out.'
So too in *Hamlet*—

If it *be* now, 'tis not to come.[2]

It is also used in 'reported speech,' where a doubtful statement or thought is expressed—

I think he *be* transform'd into a beast;
For I can no where find him like a man.[3]

There are many other uses of the subjunctive in Shakespeare. Most of them are found also in the Bible of 1611, and these have been spoken of before (p. 100). 'If I *were*' is now almost the sole surviving representative of the subjunctive, in spoken English at all events.

(2) Next we come to the substantives. The plural already ends almost universally in *-es* or *-s*. *Egges* has got the better of *eyren* (p. 298). But *eyne* is found in Shakespeare—

Show me thy chink, to blink through with mine *eyne*,[4]

and there is *hosen* as the plural of hose in the Bible—

Then these men were bound in their coats, their *hosen*, and their hats.[5]

Again, we have already had an instance of *horse* as a plural in the sixteenth century (p. 107), and this form occurs in Shakespeare too—

But a team of *horse* shall not pluck that from me.[6]

---

[1] *Richard II.*, II. i. 300.   Abbott's *Shakespearian Grammar*, p. 265.
[2] V. ii. 231.   [3] *As You Like It*, II. vii. 1, 2.
[4] *Midsummer-Night's Dream*, V. i. 178.   [5] Daniel iii. 21.
[6] *Two Gentlemen of Verona*, III. i. 265.   Koch, *Historische Grammatik*.

The form *horses* had long existed by the side of it and has now entirely displaced it. *Sheep, deer* are still in use as plurals, just as they have been from the earliest times. So too *year* for *years* is found in Shakespeare,[1] though Caxton had *yerys*. These changes in language take a long time to become thoroughly fixed.

Thus the almost universal form of the plural was in -*s* or -*es*. But was this -*es* still ever pronounced as a separate syllable? We have seen (p. 292) that in Chaucer, who died in 1400, it is sometimes so pronounced and sometimes not. In Caxton it must sometimes have been an extra syllable (p. 293). And in the sixteenth century we find signs of its being sometimes a separate syllable still, though it was, no doubt, more commonly a mere -*s*. Thus in a document drawn up by Archbishop Warham in 1530 we find *sidys, tongis*, just like *yerys* in Caxton, and Coverdale has *bookys*.[2] Now I and Y were not silent letters in English, though E often was. And as -*is* or -*ys* is a substitute for -*es*, this -*es* must have been fully pronounced sometimes. Spenser gives us several instances of this -*ës* as a separate syllable,[3] but, as was said before, we cannot prove anything about sixteenth-century English from his usage. On the whole, it is evident that -*ës* as an additional syllable in the plural lingered on into the sixteenth century, but that the termination was usually slurred and equivalent to a simple S.

The same is true of the genitive or possessive case. Palsgrave[4] in 1530 says: "We put 'is' or 's' to a substantive when we wyll express 'possessyon.'" Tyndale has at least

---

[1] 'I know that Deformed; a' has been a vile thief this seven *year*.'—*Much Ado about Nothing*, III. iii. 132. Koch, *Historische Grammatik*. It was to be found too in the Bible of 1611, as it stood originally, *e.g.* 'threescore and two *yeere* old.'—Daniel v. 31. Eadie, *The English Bible*, vol. ii. p. 261.
[2] Eadie, *The English Bible*, vol. i. pp. 258, 259.
[3] *e.g.* 'That vanisht into smoke and *cloudës* swift.'—*Faery Queene*, I. xi. 54; also in I. v. 17, *woundës*.
[4] 'Lesclarcissement de la Langue Francoyse,' quoted by Eadie, *The English Bible*, vol. ii. p. 257.

one instance of it ending in -*is*, and Shakespeare scans some few lines on this principle; for instance—

To show his teeth as white as *whalës* bone.[1]

We may couple the genitive and the plural, and add to them the past participle in -*ed*, saying that all their terminations were sometimes extra syllables, but that usually the consonant only was pronounced, except indeed where necessity has preserved the full termination down to our own time, as in *races, race's, fated* (see pp. 292, 293).

(3) As to the adjective little need be said. *Other* is sometimes plural (just as *some* is still), the final -*e*, which it would have in Chaucer's time, being dropped; for instance—

And some said, What will this babbler say ? *other some*, He seemeth to be a setter forth of strange gods.[2]

Here *other* is an adjective used without a substantive, undeclined like other adjectives. And there is at least one instance in Shakespeare of the French plural of the adjective in -*s*—

And yet my letters-*patents* give me leave.[3]

(4) There is more to notice in the pronouns.

(*a*) To begin with, the H still lingered in (*h*)*it*, the neuter of *he*, until Tyndale's time, though it was frequently dropped much earlier, as in Robert of Gloucester, 1298 (p. 261).[4] On the other hand, the sixteenth century saw the birth of the new genitive of (*h*)*it*, namely *its*. If we look back at the original declension of *hé, héo, hit* (p. 113), we shall find *his*

---

[1] *Love's Labour's Lost*, V. ii. 332. And in Spenser, 'That like would not for all this *worldës* wealth.'—I. ix. 31. Koch, *Historische Grammatik*.
[2] Acts xvii. 18.
[3] *Richard II.*, II. iii. 130. Abbott, *Shakespearian Grammar*, p. 241. In a book published in 1600 by a Scotch Roman Catholic exile we find 'al thing*is* necessaires.' But this is Lowland Scotch, or Northumbrian. Eadie, *The English Bible*, vol. ii. p. 55.
[4] The H seems to have been lost from the word being usually unemphatic, just as people say, 'I told 'er so.'

the genitive in the neuter as it still is in the masculine. Of course this would cause ambiguity sometimes, and *it* was occasionally used for the genitive of the neuter, as early as the middle of the fourteenth century.¹ But this is plainly most awkward. *It* does not look like a genitive at all. On the other hand, when the H was so frequently dropped in (*h*)*it*, *his* hardly seemed to be a case of that word at all. There was also the word *itself*, which, though it is really *it self*, like *him self*, seemed on the analogy of *myself*, *herself*,² *ourselves*, *yourselves*, to be for *its self*. And so *its* was formed, on the analogy of substantives, like *man's*, *bird's*. The genitive of *it* therefore at the end of the sixteenth century was—

his, or *it*, or *its*,

the first being the most 'classical.'

We may now illustrate this account. In Tyndale's New Testament we find *hit* frequently, as well as *it* ; for instance—

Whatt shall *hit* proffet a man yf he shulde wyn all the hoole worlde : so he loose hys owne soule ?³

In Shakespeare we have all three forms of the genitive—*his*, *it*, and *its*—

His.   Last night of all,
When yond same star that's westward from the pole
Had made *his* course to illume that part of heaven
Where now *it* burns,—⁴

It.   The hedge-sparrow fed the cuckoo so long,
That it had *it* head bit off by *it* young.⁵

Its.   This music crept by me upon the waters,
Allaying both their fury and my passion
With *its* sweet air.⁶

---

¹ See Skeat, *Etymological Dictionary*. Morris, *Historical Outlines of English Accidence*, p. 124.
² Here again *her* is really dative and accusative.
³ St. Matthew xvi. 26.
⁴ *Hamlet*, I. i. 35-38. Quoted by Koch, *Historische Grammatik*.
⁵ *King Lear*, I. iv. 235, 236. Quoted by Koch, *Historische Grammatik*.
⁶ *Tempest*, I. ii. 391-393. Quoted by Koch, *Historische Grammatik*.

But the Authorised Version of the Bible refuses *its*, which was hardly established as 'standard' English in the early part of the seventeenth century. Ben Jonson does not mention it in his Grammar, though he uses it himself.[1] In Leviticus xxv. 5, what was written by the translators (or revisers) of 1611, was—

> That which groweth of *it* own accord,[2]

its being substituted in later editions. Otherwise, our Bible uses what was then the most correct form, *his*; as, for instance—

> The fruit tree yielding fruit after *his* kind, whose seed is in *it*self.[3]

However, *its* was gaining ground, and from the clearness and usefulness of the form supplanted *his* and *it* as the possessive case of the neuter.

(*b*) *Thou* was still a part of living English as much as *You*. It was used very much like *tu* in French and *du* in German, in speaking to persons with whom one was familiar, sometimes too in contempt. The plural *Ye* or *You* was a form of polite address, just as when a king uses *We* and *Our* of himself. For instance—

> Farewell to *you*; and *you*; and *you*, Volumnius.
> . . . . .
> Farewell to *thee* too, Strato,[4]

Volumnius and the other *you*'s being his friends, Strato his slave.[5]

We have seen that *thou* was alive till about a century ago, being found in Sheridan's play of *The Rivals*. It is now only used in the country, in poetry, and in prayers.

As for the distinction between *ye* and *you*, *ye* is properly

---

[1] Quoted by Koch, *Historische Grammatik*.
[2] Even Milton (died 1674) uses it only two or three times. Koch, *Historische Grammatik*.
[3] Genesis i. 11.   [4] *Julius Cæsar*, V. v. 31, 33.
[5] Abbott's *Shakespearian Grammar*, p. 156, etc., where apparent exceptions to the rule are accounted for.

the nominative, *you* the dative and accusative (p. 114). But in the sixteenth century [1] they were getting to be used indifferently. For instance, the Prayer-Book of 1549, though it usually observes the distinction, does not always do so. Thus, in the Catechism, we have—

You sayd that your Godfathers and Godmothers dyd promise for you that *ye* should kepe Goddes commaundementes.

In Shakespeare *ye* is used for *you* and *you* for *ye* indifferently, even in the same line—

I do beseech *ye*, if *you* bear me hard.[2]

The Authorised Version, in this as in many other points, kept to the old grammar, using *ye* for the nominative, *you* for the accusative, consistently, with but few exceptions.[3] But it was behind the ordinary English of the time. The general practice by the end of the sixteenth century certainly was to use both *ye* and *you* indifferently, and *you* more frequently than *ye*, which has now practically died out, being only used in poetry and in prayers, so far as 'standard' English is concerned. The use of *ye* as accusative (or dative) survived until lately in 'thankye,' or 'thanky,' which is now practically obsolete as well.[4]

(c) In the relative too a change was in progress.

We have seen that the undeclined relative in Anglo-Saxon, þe, was superseded by þat, properly the neuter of the definite article,[5] but used first by Orm (about 1200 A.D.) as a relative both singular and plural, of all cases and genders (p. 239). This spread to the South, and we had an instance of it in Robert of Gloucester (1298 A.D., see p. 261). But interrogative

---

[1] The confusion began in the fifteenth century.
[2] *Julius Cæsar*, III. i. 157. Abbott, *Shakespearian Grammar*, p. 159; and Koch, *Historische Grammatik*.
[3] Eadie, *The English Bible*, vol. ii. p. 259.
[4] See Koch, *Historische Grammatik*, vol. ii., sec. 299, on the whole point.
[5] The definite article, se, séo, þæt, was also sometimes used as a relative in Anglo-Saxon, but then it agreed with its antecedent, so that þæt was only used of neuters.

pronouns appear to have a tendency (as in Greek and Latin and German) to become relatives. Accordingly, the genitive and dative-and-accusative of *who*, namely *whose* and *whom* (as we now write them), got to be used as relatives. The 'oblique' cases of *who*, and also the neuter *what*, are first thus used by Orm, *which* rather later. But *who* in the nominative was still an interrogative pronoun only.[1] And this was still the common usage in the early part of the sixteenth century. Thus the relatives were—

> *Nom.* that, which, what.[2]
> *Gen.* whose.
> *Dat.* whom.
> *Acc.* whom, that, which, what.[2]

Accordingly, the Prayer-Book of 1549 usually has *which* for the nominative; as, for instance, in the Collect for Michaelmas Day—

> Euerlasting God, *whiche* haste ordained and constituted the seruices of all Angels and men in a wonderfull ordre.

And so usually in the Collects and other parts of this Prayer-Book,[3] though *who* does occur a few times as a relative. *Whose* and *whom* are used as at present. We have now specialised *who* to be used of persons, *which* of things.[4] This distinction was certainly not observed by Shakespeare, who seems to use *who, which,* and *that* almost indifferently.[5] Thus, in

---

[1] See Skeat, *Etymological Dictionary*.

[2] Used where there is no antecedent coming before it. The cases supplied by phrases, *of which*, etc., are not put down.

[3] Our Prayer-Book was brought into its present state in 1662.

[4] It is curious that *who* was not thus specialised earlier, as it has a distinct neuter *what*. It is sometimes used to personify things in Shakespeare, which is a step in the direction of our present use. *Whose* and *whom* (which are by origin as much cases of the neuter *what* as of *who*, which is properly the masculine and feminine nominative) are still occasionally used of things, just as they are in Genesis i. 11.

[5] Certain rules have been laid down, according to which each is *generally* used, by Abbott, *Shakespearian Grammar*, p. 176. They are not easy to master, have many exceptions, and are now obsolete.

the *Merchant of Venice*, the Prince of Morocco, in speaking of the caskets, says—

> The first, of gold, *who* this inscription bears,
> 'Who chooseth me shall gain what many men desire;'
> The second, silver, *which* this promise carries,
> 'Who chooseth me shall get as much as he deserves.'[1]

The Authorised Version in its use of the relatives is more like the 1549 Prayer-Book than Shakespeare. It uses *which, whose, whom* frequently, and sometimes, but less often, *who*,[2] as in Acts xviii. 27. *Which* is still used of persons, for instance—

How is it that thou, being a Jew, askest drink of me, *which* am a woman of Samaria?[3]

(*d*) *Mine, my; thine, thy.*

Mine and *thine* were the oldest forms, used originally both before a consonant and before a vowel. As early as Layamon and Orm (about 1200) *mi, thi* began to be used, but before consonants only. There is a curious survival of the old universal use of *thine* in Tyndale, '*thyne* neghbour.' The general practice in our translation of the Bible is for *thine* to be used before a vowel, and it is sometimes used before an H. *Thy* is used before consonants, but also sometimes before a vowel or H, for instance—

Why doth *thine* heart carry thee away? and what do *thy* eyes wink at?[4]

Mine and *my* are used in the same way. Shakespeare too makes use of the alternative forms before vowels almost indifferently.[5]

(*e*) *Tho* (þá, pp. 271, 295) is used almost for the last time by Tyndale—

> But none of *tho* thinges move me.[6]

It was superseded by the Northern *those*.

---

[1] II. vii. 4-7. Quoted by Abbott, *Shakespearian Grammar*, p. 181.
[2] As also does the *Great Bible*, see Psalm lxv. 6, 7.
[3] St. John iv. 9.   [4] Job xv. 12.
[5] But see Abbott, *Shakespearian Grammar*, p. 160.
[6] Acts xx. 24.

(*f*) It is curious to find the Southern substitute for *he*, namely *a*, still used in Shakespeare.

Ha or *a* had been in use ever since the twelfth century for *he, she, it,* and *they,* and is found in almost the latest piece of distinctly Southern literature — namely, Trevisa's work (1387 A.D.), for instance—

Also gentil-men children buþ ytauȝt for to speke Freynsch fram tyme þat *a* buþ yrokked in here cradel.[1]

It occurs not unfrequently in Shakespeare, for instance—

I know that Deformed ; *a* has been a vile thief this seven year ; *a* goes up and down like a gentleman : I remember his name.[2]

These are the Watchman's words, but it is not confined to the lower classes in Shakespeare. A gentleman uses it four lines further on. It is, of course, still alive in provincial English, especially that of the South-West, in such remarks as—

'*A* comes to me and *a* says, says he.'

But it certainly has no longer a place in our literature.

We will now leave the grammar of the sixteenth century, and look at some other points in the language of that time.

The soft form of G, ȝ, or Y finally lost its place during this century in *give, again, against*—words in which at one time it seemed as much established as in *yelp* or *yield* (pp. 273, 277, 295).

Tyndale has it frequently, for instance—

I wyll *yeve* vnto the the keyes of the kyngdom of heven.[3]

But in the same chapter he has *geve*. So too in the ninth chapter of St. Matthew we find—

Thy sinnes are *foryeven* the.
To *foryeve* synnes.

---

[1] Skeat, *Principles of English Etymology*, First Series, p. 30 ; and Morris and Skeat, *Specimens of Early English*, Part II. p. 241—*a* buþ = they are.
[2] *Much Ado about Nothing*, III. iii. 133.   [3] St. Matthew xvi. 19.

though sometimes the word has a hard G as at present. So too he writes—

Nether shall eny cite or housholde devyded *ayenst* it sylfe contynue. So yf satan cast out satan then ys he devyded *ayenst* him sylfe.[1]

But in other passages he has *againe* and *agaynst*. On the whole the form with Y is almost at its last gasp, though, as was said before, *yeven* is found in a letter written by Queen Elizabeth.

Ax is used by Tyndale instead of *ask*—

And the chefe preste *axed* them sayinge : Dyd not we straytely commaunde you that ye shuld not teache in this name ?[2]

This form of the word had been classical English in Alfred's time, classical English in Chaucer. It now appears for nearly the last time in literature, though our less-educated countrymen still hold fast to this time-honoured form.

Finally, we may notice, among the mass of idioms to be found in the sixteenth century which we do not now use, three which are especially striking—the double comparative and superlative, and the double negative. These are merely intended to make the comparative or superlative or negation stronger, and are most natural idioms. We find the double superlative in the Bible—

After the *most straitest* sect of our religion.[3]

So too in Shakespeare—

This was the *most unkindest* cut of all.[4]

Of the double comparative there are many examples in Shakespeare—

How much *more elder* art thou than thy looks ![5]

and *more better* in the *Tempest*.[6]

---

[1] St. Matthew xii. 25, 26. [2] Acts v. 27, 28.
[3] Acts xxvi. 5. Eadie, *The English Bible*, vol. ii. p. 262.
[4] *Julius Cæsar*, III. ii. 187 ; also *Cymbeline*, II. iii. 2.
[5] *Merchant of Venice*, IV. i. 251. [6] I. ii. 19.

The double (or treble) negative is a thoroughly English idiom, in use from the earliest times.

In Anglo-Saxon—

Ne nán ne dorste of ðám dæge hyne *nán* þing máre axigean.
Nor none not durst from that day him no thing more ask.[1]

In Chaucer—
>He *nevere* yet *no* vileinye *ne* sayde
>In al his lyf, un-to *no* maner wight.[2]

In Shakespeare—
>I have one heart, one bosom and one truth,
>And that no woman has ; *nor never none*
>Shall mistress be of it, save I alone.[3]

In the Authorised Version—

And shall *not* leave to my husband *neither* name nor remainder upon the earth.[4]

This idiom is now only represented by such 'illiterate' expressions as—
>I never said nothing to nobody.

All these forms of expression perished partly from excessive love of correctness (since they seem to say the same thing twice over), partly, and the double negative more especially, from imitating the Latin style and idiom, which has had a very large influence upon English. *For to*, with the infinitive, as, for instance—

>Thou shalt make room enough under me *for to* go,[5]

is another of these idioms which were common in the sixteenth century, and have now disappeared from literary English.

And besides the phrases and idioms in the Bible which are

---

[1] *Anglo-Saxon Gospels*, about 1000 A.D. St. Matthew xxii. 46. Koch, *Historische Grammatik*. [2] *Prologue*, ll. 70, 71.
[3] *Twelfth Night*, III. i. 170-172. Koch, *Historische Grammatik*.
[4] 2 Samuel xiv. 7. Eadie, *The English Bible*, vol. ii. p. 260.
[5] Psalm xviii. 36, Prayer-Book Version ; and in Authorised Version, Acts iv. 28.

now obsolete,[1] there is a mass of expressions in Shakespeare which we do not now use—some due to the earlier English (like the idioms spoken of above), some which seem to be experiments in language. For the age of Elizabeth saw the first great outburst of literature in England since the language had lost most of its inflexions. There was now little to show whether a word was adjective or adverb, a distinction which had been marked by a final -e (p. 272), whether it was verb or noun. This want is now supplied by usage, by the custom of the language as shown in its writings. But in the Elizabethan age there was little literature to copy, except in obsolete English. Therefore, as there was no fixed custom to follow, and since the words no longer had marked on them, so to speak, what parts of speech they were, the field was open for experiments in language, and there were bold and original men to make them. As Dr. Abbott says, in Elizabethan English "any noun, adjective, or neuter verb can be used as an active verb. You can 'happy'[2] your friend, 'malice'[3] or 'foot'[4] your enemy, or 'fall'[5] an axe upon his neck." So too you can *character* (carve) your thoughts on trees;[6] and a *she* is a woman (or her name) in the lines—

> Run, run, Orlando; carve on every tree
> The fair, the chaste and unexpressive *she*.[7]

There is a good deal of this freedom still in English. We still make no distinction between adjective and adverb in 'he does it right,' 'go slow.' We use verbs as nouns, for instance, 'a run,' 'a downpour.' 'To fall an axe' is only the

---

[1] *e.g.* Whereof every one bear twins, Song of Solomon, iv. 2. Asa his heart was perfect, 1 Kings xv. 14 (as it stood in 1611). Even to the mercy seatward, Exod. xxxvii. 9. See Eadie, *The English Bible*, vol. ii. p. 253, etc.
[2] Make happy, *Sonnets*, vi.
[3] Bear malice against, North's *Plutarch*.
[4] = kick, *Cymbeline*, III. v. 148. To 'toe' is now used in the same way, but this is slang.
[5] = let fall, cause to fall, *As You Like It*, III. v. 5. Abbott's *Shakespearian Grammar*, Introduction, and p. 199, etc.
[6] *As You Like It*, III. ii. 6.   [7] *Ibid.*, 9, 10.

same kind of change as when we speak of 'breathing' a horse or 'rising' a fish. To 'violent'[1] (act violently) is not a more startling expression than when people who have to do with horses speak of one horse 'savaging' another. But there are now some limits to what is possible in the language. Usage has to some extent settled how we must write English, and a good many of the experiments of Shakespeare's time are too bold for the English of the present day.

We may, in conclusion, sum up roughly the share which the different dialects have had in forming this 'standard' English, which in the sixteenth century is nearly complete. The bulk of it is East Midland, and the Southern colouring which this had on its first assuming the character of the one literary dialect has been taken out of it to a large extent, so that 'standard' English is, and was in Shakespeare's time, very much the same as the ordinary spoken dialect of Northamptonshire, for instance, or of Southern Lincolnshire, the country of Robert of Brunne, and perhaps of Orm. Still the Southern speech has left its traces in clipped past participles (pp. 291, 334), such as *bound*, *swung*, as well as in the form of certain words, such as *vat* (Northern *fat*, in *wine-fat*[2]), *vixen* (the feminine of *fox*), and also in *children*, which has the favourite Southern plural in *-en*, added to the remains of the old plural of the word 'child*er*.' Coverdale is thoroughly impartial between the two, writing 'thou shalt see thy child*ers* child*ren*.'[3] The most important contribution of the North has been the 3rd person singular in *-s*; it has also given us *hers*, *ours*, *yours*, and *those*, and each dialect has supplied some words which had been peculiar to itself,[4] and, no doubt, has contributed something towards our present pronunciation, though the share of each is not often easy to assign with certainty.

---

[1] *Troilus and Cressida*, IV. iv. 4.   Abbott, *Shakespearian Grammar*, p. 202.   [2] St. Mark xii. 1.   [3] Psalm cxxviii. 6.
[4] *Raid* is a very distinct instance of a Northern word.' It is another (Danish) form of *road*, which is used in the sense of 'raid' or 'foray' in 1 Samuel xxvii. 10. See Skeat, *Etymological Dictionary*.

CHAPTER XXII

CHANGES IN 'STANDARD' ENGLISH SINCE 1625

Changes in English mostly small since 1625—Changes in pronunciation since Chaucer—Not marked by spelling—How the former pronunciation is ascertained—Traces of it in English dialects—Changes of English vowel-sounds—Changes of EA, OI proved — Dropping and changes of consonants—Changes in grammar—Additions to vocabulary—Latin and Greek words—French words—Words from European languages other than French — Words from distant countries — Changes in style—What style is—Latin influence on English prose—The choice of words—The Johnsonian style—French words and idioms dragged into English—German intruders—English poetical style—Specimens of English prose — Hooker, Bacon, Milton, Addison, Johnson, Scott, Thackeray, the Modern Johnsonian style, Macaulay.[1]

WE have now begun to go over old ground. In Chapter I. something was said about recent changes in English, and so the end of the book has been joined on to the beginning, like a snake with its tail in its mouth. On that occasion, however, what was aimed at was merely to illustrate the changes of language in general. And so, to complete our sketch of English in the right order, something will now be said of the main changes which have taken place in the language since the early part of the seventeenth century, since Shakespeare and our present version of the Bible. But as a good many of these have been mentioned incidentally, and since, except

---

[1] Sweet, *History of English Sounds.* Earle, *English Prose.* Kington Oliphant, *The New English.* Skeat, *Etymological Dictionary; Principles of English Etymology*, First Series.

the changes in pronunciation and style, they are mostly small compared with those which have been described already, the sketch of them will be in outline only.

These changes in our language may be grouped under four heads: changes in pronunciation, in grammar, in the stock of words or vocabulary, and in style, which last, of course, includes as an important part of it the selection of words which an author uses. In speaking of pronunciation and style we shall have to look back beyond 1625.

(1) Changes in pronunciation.[1]

These, unlike the other changes, cannot be said to be slight. And, besides, we have some arrears to make up under this head, since nothing or next to nothing has been said of the sounds of English since Chaucer, who died in 1400 A.D. (see pp. 200, 201). We have seen that English altered its pronunciation before 1400, as it has done since that date. For instance, long A changed to O, as in *twá, two*, where Northumbrian or Lowland Scotch still keeps the A (p. 253). Thus the spelling changed as well as the sound. Our ancestors did not write *twá*, and say *two*, as on our modern principle of having an unalterable spelling for each word we should probably have done. For, since the change from A to O was made, we have come to pronounce the word 'tu'[2] or 'too,' though we still spell it T, W, O.

Thus, until about the sixteenth century, the spelling changed more or less with the sound, though it was not always up to date. And this plan seems reasonable, since the object of writing a word is, one would think, to express its sound. Our principle of spelling at present (due to the printers) is this. A certain collection of letters is taken to denote a particular word, but we do not trouble ourselves whether these

---

[1] See Sweet, *History of English Sounds*. Skeat, *Principles of English Etymology*, First Series, and *Man of Lawes Tale*.
[2] From the influence of the W (as in *who* = 'hu'), which is a sort of consonantal U.

letters represent the present sound of the word correctly or not. For instance, in *knight* exactly half of the letters are silent. Our present spelling in most words represents their sound in the fifteenth or the sixteenth century. The date at which this change of principle took effect cannot of course be accurately assigned. It was in progress from the fifteenth to the end of the seventeenth century. The writing of final -*e* (unpronounced) in the fifteenth century is a sort of foretaste of the new system; it is just the same as our now writing W in *write*, GH in *light*, and so on.

Of course the question how the language was pronounced is a very important one. It is English, as spoken, which is the actual language. Writing is, or ought to be, merely a set of symbols to express its sounds. And it is possible to find out with some considerable approach to accuracy what the pronunciation of English at particular periods was. If any one were asked how this could be discovered, he would probably say, 'By the spelling, and by rhymes in poetry.' Of these the first tells us a great deal up to the fifteenth century, and a certain amount after that. For instance, we learnt something from Caxton's two ways of spelling *please* (p. 300). But from the fifteenth century spelling fails us more and more. Printing began to fix or crystallise it. As to rhymes, these will tell us something about final syllables. But they will not necessarily give us much information. If in a poem we find that *say* rhymes to *may*, this does not let us know how AY was pronounced in English at that particular time. Of course if *say* frequently rhymes to *convey*, we should conclude that AY and EY were then at all events nearly alike in sound, but we may or may not be able to find out from this how both were pronounced. Then we must make allowance for what are called 'printers' rhymes,' where the two words are spelt the same, but are now pronounced differently, *love* rhyming to *move*, for instance, or *wood* to *flood*. These satisfy the eye in reading a poem, but sound imperfect when they are read aloud. So that we cannot find out everything from the spelling, and from rhymes.

But there are other ways in which information has been gained about the pronunciation of English in former times. For instance, there is an English Hymn to the Virgin, *written as* Welsh (not *translated into* Welsh),[1] just as we saw that English got to be written as if it were French (p. 181, etc.) The date of this is about 1500. And, from the sixteenth century downwards, there are French grammars, which of course say what English sounds correspond to particular sounds in French, as well as treatises on English itself, describing the sounds of the letters, at the time when the writer lived, by comparison with other languages, Italian for instance, and also the way of forming them in the mouth. From all these sources of information the authorities on the subject, such as Mr. Sweet, have been able to discover a great deal about the pronunciation of English at particular periods. We will not go through these changes in detail, but give a mere sketch to show the sort of changes which were taking place.

Now we saw that in the time of Chaucer (died 1400) the English vowels still had much the same sounds as in Latin ('new' or correct pronunciation), or in Italian, nearly as in German at present, nearly as in the French of Chaucer's time. There are a good many traces of this older pronunciation of our language in the various English dialects at the present day. Thus the short A in the fourteenth century was sounded nearly as it is very commonly pronounced in the country, in the word *man*,[2] for instance, what we should call 'broad' but not like Lowland Scotch 'mon.' The old sound of the long E is kept in the Somersetshire *ai* (*he*), *thaiz* (*these*),

---

[1] A language which has hardly altered its sounds since then.—Sweet, *History of English Sounds*, p. 203.

[2] It is very much like the German A in *mann*, like the A in *father*, only short.

bai-ŭnt (*been't*, am not), *raint* (rent).¹ The old I is preserved in Lowland Scotch *chiel* (*child*), in Somersetshire *eez* (*his*), *leedl* (*little*), and in Suffolk *deek* (*dyke* or *ditch*). One sound of O was as it is still constantly pronounced in the country, in Wiltshire for instance, like OA in *broad*. The Old English U keeps its old spelling and sound in the word *rune*; but this is a 'learned' word.² It was generally written OU (as the sound would have been expressed in French), and the old sound has been preserved in 'standard' English in the word *uncouth*, and also in the name of the river *Ouse* (in Anglo-Saxon *Use*). *House* in Chaucer's time would have rhymed to this.

The instances given above are chiefly of long vowels. In Chaucer's time there was no difference between long and short vowels, except that long A, for instance, had a longer or fuller sound than short A. Since then long and short vowels have gone each its own way; the short having been much more stationary than the long ones. Short E has not altered in sound since the time before the Conquest. *Send*, for instance, has not changed, so far as the first syllable is concerned, from Anglo-Saxon *sendan*. It is pronounced as it was in Alfred's time. The same is the case with short I, as in *bit*. But the long letters corresponding to these have moved away from them. The sound of long E is now what a Roman, if he could be revived, would call long I, and long I is nearly what he would write as AI. At any rate it is a diphthong. Long A too, as in *name*, has moved up into the place of long E.³

Now these changes have been in progress almost ever since

¹ 'The Dialect of West Somerset,' by Frederic Thomas Elworthy, *Transactions of the Philological Society*, 1875-76. In the writing of all these words the sound is given as much as possible according to ordinary English spelling. ² In Shakespeare, *King John*, II. i. 566, it is *roun(d)*.
³ It is impossible to pronounce an English long I, as in *site*, without moving the tongue *during* the pronunciation of it—that is to say, without two different positions of the tongue. On the other hand, in an English long E, as in *seed*, for instance, we put our tongue in the right position and keep it still while we are making the sound.—The general tendency of the vowels in English has been to get pronounced further forward in the mouth, also with the tongue more raised.—*Encyclopædia Britannica*, Ninth Edition, article 'The English Language.'

2 A

Chaucer's time. We can see the start of them in different dialects in the fifteenth century, while the letters for the vowels still suggested their old sound. Thus *declare* is spelt 'declair'; *leeks* is written 'lykys'; *here* 'hyr'; *feel* 'fyle.'[1] All these are found in Norfolk writings, and look as if the Northern pronunciation of long A and E (p. 225) was working its way South, as was the case with Northern words, such as *ours, those*. And the Wars of the Roses, when so many armies from the North marched to the South, and Southern armies into the North, may have tended to spread the Northern pronunciation of these vowels. At any rate they assumed something like their present pronunciation in the English of the sixteenth century.

So far, then, these are the facts, that the short vowels E and I have remained the same throughout the history of the language. That short A came to be pronounced as at present in the sixteenth century. And that in the same century the long E was pronounced much as it is now (as in *tree*, for instance), and long A was about half-way towards our present pronunciation of it (as in *name*), like a lengthened form of the A in *hath*.[2] The sound of the other vowels, and of most of the diphthongs, was more or less different. The consonants, such as K in *knead*, which are now silent were then pronounced. Therefore the pronunciation of Shakespeare and of the translators of our Bible was still very unlike the sound which their writings now suggest to us, though the language was moving in this direction.

We will not work our way through the seventeenth, eighteenth, and nineteenth centuries, noticing the pronunciation of each vowel or diphthong at each particular time. This

---

[1] Even in the fourteenth century there are words showing a change in the modern direction. *Brē* (*brae*) in Robert of Brunne shows the Northern pronunciation of long A. Besides this there are such words as *geme* (*game*), *pire* (*peer*).—Kington Oliphant, *The New English*, vol. i., from which work all the above words are taken.

[2] The sound is to be heard in some people's pronunciation of *path*, for instance, which nearly rhymes to *hath*, but is longer.

would, for one thing, be impossible to do accurately without learning a set of symbols not quite the same as the ordinary English alphabet. But we will take as specimens two combinations of letters, EA and OI, and we shall see from them that English did not settle down into its present pronunciation all at once, at the beginning or end of the seventeenth century for instance, but that, though its written form has long been the same, its sounds have been changing, as sounds in a language do. Our fixed spelling has been only a drag on the progress of the language. It may have made the waggon go slower, but it has not stopped it.[1]

We have already seen how EA was sounded by Caxton, namely like AY, or rather perhaps like E in *there*, when the word is very fully pronounced. It was a combination of letters revived in his time, but not common until considerably later, when it was used to express this 'open' sound of E. But this distinction of 'open' E and 'close' E (as in *mêlée*) did not last; in the seventeenth century EA was used for both.[2] EA still often has this same value of a French É in Somersetshire English, and also in the English spoken in Ireland, which represents an older form of the language, not having moved on in the same way as the speech of England itself. But in 'standard' English as well, down to the middle of the eighteenth century at any rate,[3] EA stood for this same sound. This is not only learnt from the old books on English mentioned above, but we can test it by rhymes. As has been said above, a rhyme is much better evidence of sounds corresponding when the spelling of the two words is not the same.

A clear example is to be found in Cowper's poem on

---

[1] It has sometimes restored a sound lost or changed, see below, p. 357.
[2] Much as it still is in *bear* and *break* respectively.
[3] Mr. Sweet (*History of English Sounds*, p. 235) says that the change to a long E (as we pronounce it now) took place 'towards the middle of the eighteenth century.' But the rhymes carry it on later. Either then the poets kept to an old-fashioned use, founded on the practice of their predecessors, but not justified by contemporary pronunciation, or the EA was still pronounced as AY by some people. Probably the fact is due to both causes.

Alexander Selkirk, written towards the end of the eighteenth century (1780-85)—

> I am monarch of all I sur*vey*,
> My right there is none to dispute,
> From the centre all round to the *sea*
> I am lord of the fowl and the brute.

This is a very late instance of a rhyme depending on the old pronunciation of EA. Again, the word *tea* is *té* in the dialect of Chinese from which we derive the word. Pope, in a poem of 1712, makes it rhyme to *obey* and *away*,[1] as the French *thé* would still do. In a hymn by Dr. Watts of 1719 there is another example—

> The busy tribes of flesh and blood,
> With all their lives and *cares*,
> Are carried downwards by Thy flood
> And lost in following *years*.

And in other hymns or psalms of the eighteenth century, or the very end of the seventeenth, we have *sea* rhyming to *away*, *seas* rhyming to *graze*,[2] *lead* to *made*, and *fear* to *care*. In fact, there are too many instances of it for its former pronunciation to be doubtful, on the ground of rhymes alone, though in some words, especially before a D, as in *head*, EA was already shortened to Ë, as at present.[3] 'To *tear*,' 'to *wear*,' *break*, *great*, *yea* are fossils in the language of the present day, relics of the older pronunciation. The R probably has something to do with this, except of course in *yea*, which is an old-fashioned word with an old-fashioned pronunciation.

Next, as to OI. In the seventeenth century this got to be pronounced like Modern English I, as it still is in the country and in vulgar English; as, for instance, in the advice about the fish—

Don't have them *biled*, Sir, but *briled*. If they're *biled* they're *spiled*.

---

[1] Skeat, *Etymological Dictionary*.
[2] Long A having by that time acquired very nearly its present sound.
[3] Sweet. *History of English Sounds*, p. 236.

So at the end of the seventeenth century we get such rhymes as—

> I'll mention Rahab with due praise,
> In Babylon's applauses *join*,
> The fame of Ethiopia raise,
> With that of Tyre and Pale*stine*.[1]

But the spelling caused the sound to be altered back in the latter half of the eighteenth century.

This temporary change in the pronunciation of OI accounts for the present form of the verb 'to *rile.*' It occurs as early as the fourteenth century, and was once spelt *roil*, at the time when it was a 'classical' English word. Then it suffered a reverse of fortune, and was for a long time unrecognised in literature, and consequently had no fixed spelling of its own. It is even now hardly more than slang. While it was in this reduced condition its OI changed to I, just as *boil* became *bile*. But no one thought of altering back its pronunciation afterwards; it had no spelling to redeem it, as it was seldom written. And so it has remained as *rile* ever since it changed, a monument of the time when OI was pronounced like I in English generally.

The changes in the consonants consist chiefly in the dropping of many letters which were still pronounced in Chaucer's time, and even much later. Our keeping signs for sounds after they had become meaningless is a still stranger piece of conservatism than our not having shifted the vowels when their sounds changed.[2] An A, an E, or an I, if they do not imply the same sound as they once did, at all events signify some sound, while our silent consonants either merely show that the vowel before them is long, as GH usually does, or are reduced to an obscure vowel-sound, like R in many places, or they mean nothing at all, like the W in *write*, K in *knot*, or G in

---

[1] Ps. lxxxvii., New Version of the Psalms. Tate and Brady, 1696.

[2] Still in French silent letters occur even more frequently than in English, and H in the middle of German words, *e.g. lahm, nehmen*, means nothing but that the preceding vowel is long, like GH or silent E in Modern English.

gnash. But these sounds were not commonly, or at any rate universally dropped until it was becoming fixed as a law that such and such a word should be spelt in such and such a way, however it might be pronounced.

GH, which had implied a sound like German CH, was, by the sixteenth century, weakened to a sort of mere breath, like an H, and almost universally dropped in the seventeenth century. In *cough, laugh, tough,* and other words it had already acquired the sound of an F.

The K in *knife, knave, knee* was plainly once pronounced, since *canif* is the same word as *knife,* being borrowed from Frankish, a Teutonic language. And it was still fully pronounced in the sixteenth century.[1] In the latter part of the seventeenth century, and early in the eighteenth, it was like an H—'*h*nife,' '*h*nave,' '*h*nee.' Now it has vanished altogether in pronunciation. The history of G in *gnaw, gnash* seems to have been very similar.

R was pronounced wherever it is written in Chaucer's time and much later. It has been getting weaker ever since the end of the sixteenth century, and now has its own proper sound only if it comes immediately before a vowel in the same word, or in one following without a pause; as, for instance, in *rich, hearing, there it is.* Otherwise it is never more than a vowel of the most obscure kind, as in *here they are,* in which sentence *here* is something like *hee-a,* only less distinct, while in *are* the R has no sound at all.

The W in *write, wretched,* and so on, was not, as is sometimes thought, impossible to pronounce. It means that the lips were to be rounded in pronouncing the R, much as in the French word *roi.* Its sound was dropped in the seventeenth century.

WH in *what, where* is really the 'breathed' form of W, which is a 'voiced' letter [2] (see p. 4, note). It has had a

---

[1] As it still is in the sister-language, German, e.g. *knabe, knie.*

[2] The H was probably more distinctly pronounced at a very early period. —See Sweet, *History of English Sounds,* p. 135, from which work this part of the chapter is mainly drawn.

chequered career in the language. In the *Peterborough Chronicle* for the years 1135 and 1137 we find *wua* for *hwa* (*who*), and *wile* for *hwile*, '*witte* sunne dei'[1] for *Whitsunday* in the *Old English Homilies* of the twelfth century, and *wat* for *what* in Robert of Gloucester (1298). But the WH was, for the most part, kept distinct from W by careful speakers until about 1770, when it began to be generally pronounced the same as its 'voiced' brother, and in the first half of the present century was universally sounded in that way. Quite recently, perhaps since 1865 or 1870, a reaction has set in, partly from the spelling, partly through the Scotch and Irish having retained the sound. The WH is now struggling with W in the pronunciation of words like *which, when*, and the victory is still uncertain.

As regards the letter H itself, a struggle has been going on for a still longer time. As we know, among uneducated people, in London especially, H is dropped under ordinary circumstances, but put in where it is required for emphasis, regardless of the spelling. Now an H is made by forcibly breathing out air from the lungs just before the rest of the word is begun. Emphasis is laid on a word in the same way by a jerk of the lungs *on* the accented syllable. If this is done too soon, 'us' becomes '*h*us,' the emphasis coming out before the word. Putting in an H, then, is an instance of 'misplaced emphasis.'[2] A good example is—

Well, if a *h*aitch and a *h*o and a *h*ar and a *h*ess and a *h*e don't spell 'orse, my name ain't 'Enry 'Olmes.

Here the emphatic syllables have the H. The name of each letter is a part of the crushing proof, the climax of which is

---

[1] In Morris's *Old English Homilies*. This, which is not a piece of ignorance in the writer, ought to remind us that *Whit*sunday is for *White*sunday, and has not any mysterious connection with the German word *Pfingsten*, which must have assumed its present form *after* the English had left the Continent. Besides, being heathens, they would not have used the word then at all.

[2] Sweet, *History of English Sounds*, p. 32 ; and *Handbook of Phonetics*.

past before "'orse,' and the last clause is said in a tone of quiet confidence.

Now these tendencies, both to drop H where there was no emphasis, as well as to insert it wrongly, date from a very early period in our language. Thus we meet with examples of H-dropping in Orm, who uses *it* for *hit*, as also does Robert of Gloucester, and in this word the H is now entirely lost. Robert of Gloucester also drops it in ȝe abbeþ (*ye have*), *ys* (*his*). But the H was also wrongly inserted; for instance—

He bring *hus* ut of this wo,

in a poem of about 1230.[1] The most terrible example is at the end of the Apostles' Creed, in the East Midland dialect of English (about 1250), namely, 'life with-*h*utin *h*end.'[2] The insertion of the H, though it is very common among uneducated people, has never had a chance of taking a recognised place in 'standard' English. But it appears that in the latter part of last century H at the beginning of words was being generally dropped,[3] until this came to be thought 'vulgar.' It is now, as we know, very carefully pronounced by educated persons, except in such sentences as 'Did 'e?' 'Tell 'im,' where it has absolutely no emphasis. The spelling, and the horror of dropping it, has also given it to words like *hospital*, *herb*, *humble*, in which it had always been silent in English—that is, for 500 years at least, just as it was in their French originals.

(2) In grammar the changes have been slight since 1625, and most of them have been mentioned already. The 3rd person singular of the verb, present tense, no longer ends in -*eth*, except in prayers and hymns, modelled on the language of the Bible, and occasionally in secular poetry, poetry being always old-fashioned in its language to a greater or less degree. The use of the subjunctive has become greatly restricted. And we noticed in the last chapter some forms of words, especially verbs, which were current English in the

---

[1] Kington Oliphant, *Old and Middle English*, p. 301. [2] *Ibid.*, p. 317.
[3] Sweet, *History of English Sounds*, p. 259.

sixteenth century and later, but are now obsolete. In recent years the tendency has been to be extremely accurate, and so we have given up such forms as 'I have *took*,' or *shook*, or *drank*, which were incorrect according to the history of the word, and never quite established themselves, though they are in themselves no worse than 'I have *held*,' or 'I have *sat*' (the perfect being used for the past participle in both cases), and were very commonly written. Again, such past tenses as 'I *sprung*,' 'it *rung*,' 'he *begun*,' which were common so lately as in Sir Walter Scott, are no longer thought right. *Thou* is practically obsolete, with the person of the verb belonging to it, though it lasted till about a century ago. *Thy, thine* have gone with it, and so has *mine* (except where it stands alone), so far as our ordinary language, both spoken and written, is concerned. And *an* is not used for *a* before an H.

(3) Next we come to the additions to our vocabulary, or stock of words, made since 1625. Now the number of words in the language has been very largely increased since the early part of the seventeenth century, and yet, first, the words in ordinary use are on the whole much the same as they were then; and, secondly, we have opened no fresh sources of any importance since that time from which to increase our stock of words.[1] As to the first point, the language of the Bible was, as we saw, old-fashioned in 1611. And yet the number of words in it which have disappeared, or have changed their meaning, since the translation (or revision) was made is extremely small compared with the whole number. *Ear* (plough), *scrip*, *mete* (measure), *leasing* (lying), are among those which are gone. *Wont, come to pass*, are almost entirely obsolete. *Fowl* no longer means 'any bird'; and *offend* does not give the notion of 'causing a difficulty' to some one. But the bulk of the words used both in the Authorised Version and in Shakespeare are still quite

[1] But Greek is much more largely drawn upon.

familiar to us. No doubt the cause of this partly is that Modern English is to a very large extent modelled on our translation of the Bible; but the fact remains the same.

The ways in which our stock of words has been increased in the last three centuries are chiefly these [1]—

(a) By the formation of words from Latin and Greek, mostly as terms for new discoveries or inventions, or for the purpose of accurate naming and classification in Science. Of the first kind are words like *electricity* (*electrum*, ἤλεκτρον, amber, which is 'electric' when rubbed), *telegraph* (τῆλε, far, γράφω, write), *phonograph* (φωνή, sound, γράφω, write), *omnibus* (= 'for all'). To the second class belong words like *cryptogamous, silicious, hydrogen, vaccinate, autonomy*. But though the number of these new words used in the different sciences is very large, the source from which they come is not a new one. We have before had plenty of words borrowed from Latin, and some from Greek, from a very early period of our language. Only we have certainly been bolder in recent times. If the words which we require are not to be found in Greek or Latin, we form them, sometimes contrary to the rules of the language. *Telegram*, for instance, is an impossible form, and should be *telegrapheme* (τηλεγράφημα in Modern Greek). However, it answers the purpose, and few people are vexed by its incorrectness. Sometimes we do actually invent new compound words out of English itself to describe new inventions; for instance, *rail-road, rail-way, steam-boat, iron-clad*. But these are quite the exception; English has for centuries been most shy of compounding from its own resources, and prefers either to borrow or to manufacture the required words from the dead languages.

(b) A good many new words have come in from French since 1625, and especially since the Restoration (1660), as others had been doing before them ever since the Norman Conquest. Sometimes these have assumed a more or less

---

[1] Skeat, *Etymological Dictionary*.

English form, or at any rate are pronounced as English words; as, for instance, *disservice, glacier, impromptu, irretrievable, vacillation*. As was said before, there were so many French words in the language already that the new ones did not look strange, and were readily received. But sometimes, or for a time, they retained their French pronunciation, as is still the case with *beau, dénouement, ennui, pique, unique, abattis, glacis, mêlée*. *Army-corps* for *corps d'armée* is a compromise. It is compounded as an English word, but *corps* is pronounced as French. It is impossible to say how long a word may be in the language before it conforms in pronunciation. We have seen already that *honour* and *hour* still leave out their H as a mark of their French origin, and have done so for 500 years. *Beau, glacis*, and *pique* retain their French pronunciation, though the youngest of them has been naturalised for nearly two centuries. Words incompletely established in English are often written in italics.

And this brings us to those French words which have tried, so to speak, to become recognised in our language and have not yet succeeded. Many of these are not in the least required, they do not 'supply a want.' *Surtout* for *great-coat*, or *over-coat*, seemed at one time to be established, it has even been written as English, *surtoot*. *Paletot*[1] appeared also to be naturalised. These words are now seldom used in speech or writing. Of somewhat the same kind are the more modern intruders, such as *dot, fiancée*, neither of which is in the least needed in our language, since they mean respectively nothing in the world but 'dowry,' and 'betrothed' or 'intended,' which last word seems to be getting obsolete like its English predecessor. *Menu* too appears to be establishing itself to the exclusion of *bill of fare*. Some writers show a great liking for such words as these, and for French idioms too which are unnecessary. Of this something more will be said under the head of style.

---

[1] Found in Middle English in another form which is now extinct.—Skeat, *Etymological Dictionary*.

(c) Besides these we have received some contributions from other European languages besides French; a number from Italian, especially words connected with music or with some other art; as, for instance, *piano(-forte)*, *quartet*, *trio*, *arcade*, *balustrade*, *façade*, *caricature*, *fresco*; a few from Spanish, such as *mosquito*, *quadroon*, *tornado*; and a sprinkling from some other languages, among which are *hussar*, *shako*, from Hungarian, and *howitzer*, from Bohemian.[1] Many of these have come to us through French. Our debt to German is surprisingly small. Except those German words which have come to us through French, which are not very numerous, there appear to be only twenty-eight in all, and of these only *camellia*, *Dutch*, *fuchsia*, *hock*, *landau*, *meerschaum*, *plunder*, *poodle*, *quartz*, *shale*, *swindler*, *waltz*, *wiseacre*, *zinc*,[2] are in common use. So much then for English being derived from German!

(d) Just as we saw the words *cocoa*, *potato*, *tobacco*, appearing in English in the sixteenth century (p. 311), so trade, travel, and colonisation have since then given us words from a great variety of languages; for instance, *tea* from Chinese; *coffee*[3] from Arabic; *chocolate* from Mexican through Spanish; *tapioca* from Brazilian; *bamboo*, *gong*, *orang-outang*, *sago*, from Malay; *skunk*, *squaw*, *wigwam*, from the languages of the North American Indians; *chimpanzee* from West Africa; *bazaar*, *sash* (for a dress), *shawl*, from Persian; *chintz*, *shampoo*, from India.[4] From this last source come many words only used in connection with India, and therefore hardly a

---

[1] Skeat, *Principles of English Etymology*, Second Series; and *Etymological Dictionary*.

[2] Skeat, *Etymological Dictionary*. The list includes *all* words in English borrowed from German (except those which have come through French), not only those borrowed since 1625.

[3] On the edge of the earlier period.

[4] Skeat, *Etymological Dictionary*, and *Principles of English Etymology*, Second Series. Of course these are only some specimens of the words derived from these languages. We borrowed some words from Sanskrit (through other languages) much earlier, e.g. *hemp*, *pepper*, *ginger*. The Indian languages include, of course, some connected with Sanskrit (and so Indo-European), and some not allied to English at all.

part of ordinary English, such as *nullah* (a ravine), *râj* (rule), and *shikaree* (a man who gets his living by shooting, and by acting as guide to sportsmen). Other Indian words, such as 'to *jink*,' a technical term for a 'pig' or boar turning, many of which are to be found in some articles in *The Field*, and in books written by Anglo-Indians, have, of course, at present no sort of settled place in the English language, though they are used by the English in India.

(4) Next we come to style, which, as we leave the fifteenth century further and further behind, becomes more and more almost the only mark by which we can distinguish the English of different periods. And first of all, what is 'style'? Perhaps the clearest way of representing it to ourselves is to say that in any work, if we take away the 'matter,' the information which an author has to give us and the ideas which he wishes to convey, what remains is his style, the form of language, the mode of expression, in which these facts and thoughts are dressed. And since these facts and thoughts are conveyed in words, plainly the selection of words is a most important part of style. But it is not the whole of it. The words must be arranged in some order. How they shall stand is partly determined beforehand by the rules or practice of the language, especially where this is only slightly inflected, as English now is. The order of the words is one of the chief substitutes for inflexions; as, for instance, the nominative is usually distinguished from the accusative by its standing before the verb.[1] So far the order of words is a substitute for grammar in the language and cannot be considered as part of an author's style. He is not responsible for it. Still there is plenty of room left for a writer to exercise his choice as to the order in which words shall be placed. Now the placing of the words in a

[1] *e.g.* we *must* say, 'The man killed the gnat,' and not 'The gnat killed the man,' though, one would think, the sense might have shown us what is meant. On the other hand, where the nominative and accusative are different, the necessity for putting the words in a particular order is not so great. 'The gnat killed he' is an unnatural order of words and suggests (doggerel) poetry, but it is more possible English.

particular order gives emphasis to some words before others, especially if one of them stands in an unusual position; as, for instance, in the sentence—

Great is the Lord, and *greatly* to be praised.[1]

But the arrangement of the words also gives a rhythm or 'swing' to the sentence. Prose has rhythm as well as poetry, but it is usually not the same in two following clauses. If this is the case, it takes the character of rough metre, more especially if the sentences are marked off by any kind of jingle at the end of each.[2] But 'prose' of this sort is as a rule most carefully avoided.[3] We keep poetry and prose each to its own department. The difference between the rhythm of prose and the rhythm of poetry is that we *expect* the latter to recur, but not the former. Now each word of course consists of a certain number of syllables, accented and unaccented, and these are the units which compose the rhythm; every word does not count the same as another. Therefore the character of the words which an author chooses determines to a large extent the rhythm of his sentences, as do also his idioms, and the length or shortness of his sentences. Besides, certain kinds of words are appropriate to a particular style, long words (which in English are mostly derived from Latin) to a pompous style, short words to a rapid and vivid description of a scene or event. And of course there are many characteristics of style beyond this, such as the way in which sentences are grouped together in

---

[1] Psalm xlviii. 1.

[2] A sort of metrical prose or very rough poetry verging on prose was not uncommon shortly before and after the Conquest; as, for instance, in Ælfric's *Homilies*, and in the *Peterborough Chronicle* in its character of William the Conqueror. (Earle, *Saxon Chronicles*, 1086. This is *not* a part of the Chronicle which represents Peterborough English.) But as a general rule prose and poetry were at least as distinct in Anglo-Saxon as they are now.

[3] There are parts of *Lorna Doone*, and perhaps of Kingsley's *Heroes*, which are almost verse. Otherwise this style is only used to give a comic effect, like the blank verse in *The Rose and the Ring*, and in 'Mr. Punch's Moral Music-Hall Dramas, *Conrad, or the Thumbsucker*,' 9th August 1890.

paragraphs, and one of the most striking is the use of 'antithesis,' constantly opposing two statements or contrasting them with one another. Of this Macaulay is the great representative; it sometimes degenerates into a trick or mannerism with him, obscuring the admirable way in which he weaves sentences of varied length and construction into paragraphs.

Now it would be a great mistake to imagine that English prose before the sixteenth century was destitute of style. Even at the end of the ninth and in the tenth century it shows a distinct and fairly finished style, as in Alfred's works (pp. 151, 152), and in parts of the Anglo-Saxon Chronicles. The prose style at the end of the fourteenth and in the fifteenth century, as in Purvey's New Testament, 'Sir John Mandeville' (pp. 275, 278), Sir Thomas Malory, and Caxton (p. 296, etc.), is, for the most part, well marked, smooth, and satisfactory, and on this prose the translations of the Bible which we now use (the Prayer-Book Version of the Psalms, and the Authorised Version) are largely modelled. But in the sixteenth century the style assumes greater prominence, since, now that the great changes in the written form of English are over, it becomes almost our only mark of the progress of the language. And there is certainly a marked difference in the style of English prose at different periods. The prose of the sixteenth and early seventeenth centuries is different from the prose of the eighteenth, and this again from that of the nineteenth century. This is in some measure due to the difference in some of the words used, and (in the sixteenth and part of the seventeenth centuries) to some differences in the grammar, especially to the retention of *-eth* in the 3rd person singular, which gives a more weighty sound to the verb. But it is much more largely due to the different arrangement of words and clauses, and to the length or shortness of the sentences. The prose of the sixteenth century, as in Hooker's *Ecclesiastical Polity* (1594-97) has a different swing or rhythm from later English prose, and the sentences are as a rule far longer; and this is due in large measure to imitation of the style of Latin, in which learned men were then steeped, an influence which lost us our double negative (p. 346). Bacon's prose (1622)[1] has to a large extent the same character, and so have Milton's prose writings (1644), partly no doubt from imitation of earlier models, partly from the same Latin influence. But the style of the Bible, which is much more national, was acting to some extent as a corrective to this. And Bunyan and Defoe late in the seventeenth century were also the pioneers of a simpler style. Since the time of Milton English prose was, on the whole, more and more going its own way. The prose of the early part of the eighteenth century, as in *The Spectator*, is not like that of the sixteenth or seventeenth centuries. It seems to be advanced at least half-way towards our simpler modern prose.

But the progress in this direction was not uninterrupted. We now come to that mode of writing English which is associated with Dr. Johnson's name (1759), and which represents a reaction against the increasing tendency towards simplicity, though it is by no means the same as the Latinised prose of the sixteenth and seventeenth centuries spoken of above. The style which we connect with his name is a pompous way of writing, fond of long words, which are mostly derived from Latin, and seems carefully to avoid a simple expression, if a more high-flown one can possibly be used. It also prefers long sentences, though these are not so characteristic of it as stilted and unusual words. As a short example of this style we may take Johnson's own translation of a remark of his into the high-flown style—

> It has not wit enough to keep it sweet,
> It has not vitality enough to preserve it from putrefaction.

This sort of English is usually known as the 'Johnsonian' style, or even as 'Johnsonese.' But in justice to the author

[1] For specimens, see end of chapter. The dates given in the text are of these extracts.

whose name it bears we ought to notice some points in which this name is misleading.

(1) Johnson did not invent the 'Johnsonian' style. There is a good example of it, for instance, in the 'Bishops' Bible,'—

> Prepare your prepromised beneficence, that it might be ready as a beneficence and not as an extortion.[1]

And the Douay Bible, in its original shape, is in some places more 'Johnsonian' than Johnson, for instance—

> I think that the passions of this time are not condigne to the glory to come.[2]

(2) It is only in some of his works that the 'Johnsonian' style appears in anything like perfection, while in others, such as the *Lives of the Poets*, though the style is not so simple as we like to have it now, it is still vigorous, stately, and satisfying.

(3) Even where he is stilted or 'Johnsonian,' he shows a certain power over the language which redeems his writing from absurdity.

(4) Finally, the better side of his style has certainly served as a model to much of the good English prose written since his time.[3]

On the other hand, there is no doubt that a mass of writers of inferior ability, in trying to copy Johnson, imitated little else but his mannerism, which they reproduced in an exaggerated form without any of his mastery over language, a result for which Johnson himself can scarcely be held responsible. The 'Johnsonian' style thus produced is, as has been said, a pompous style. It is not a reproduction of the Latinised style of the sixteenth and seventeenth centuries. The long sentence is not its most essential characteristic, but

---

[1] 2 Corinthians ix. 5. Eadie, *The English Bible*, vol. ii. p. 99 ; see p. 317.
[2] Romans viii. 18. Eadie, *The English Bible*, vol. ii. p. 131 ; see p. 317.
[3] See Earle, *English Prose*, on the whole subject of Johnson—a work to which I am greatly indebted in all this part of my subject.

rather a stilted and unnatural choice of words. It is much further removed from ordinary talk than prose usually is, though of course no one writes quite as he speaks. This pompous prose shows a self-conscious striving to be dignified, chiefly by the use of long and unusual words, which are generally borrowed from Latin. In this attempt it often fails, and becomes merely ridiculous. It is often said that a style is hard to parody in proportion to its excellence, and this is to some extent true. Mannerism or affectation is peculiarly easy to get hold of and caricature. The following is a very excellent parody of the pompous style in verse :—

> The torrid orb of Phœbus from the pole
> Demits his candid rades on siccid sole ;
> On arid camp a turb of juvents ludes,
> While sudant humour from their limbs exudes.
>
> Aspice the turb, relinquent now their games,
> With rapid vestiges 'neath virid rames,
> Concur to lave their pells in gelid und,
> And shouts lætific from their gules effund.
>
> . . . . .
>
> What though with planging sound some plane do fall
> Upon the liquor ? Them doth not appal
> The ventral dolour ; no ludibrious verb
> Their fixed proposit can at all conturb.
>
> Oh beate lusors ! Oh, how suave to merge
> Beneath the latice ! Thence refect to surge,
> And cumb quiescent on umbrageous sell,
> Leging a recent, luteous-terged libell ![1]

This is, of course, an exaggeration, as all parodies are. It may be construed with the help of a Latin dictionary. Prose specimens of Johnson's own style, and of the 'Johnsonese,' which is its caricature, will be found at the end of the chapter.

More recently there has been a reaction in English prose

[1] From the *Marlburian*, 29th June 1889, A. S. Warman and A. H. Cherrill.

in the direction of greater simplicity. This corresponded and was partly due to the increased simplicity of the poetical style of Wordsworth, Coleridge, and Scott, in the early part of this century. The example was also set by the more natural English prose of Scott's novels (1814). English prose is now much nearer to the spoken language, both in its preference for sentences of moderate length, more or less artistically combined in paragraphs, and in the general simplicity of the words which it uses, and the influence of the 'Johnsonian' style (as developed by Johnson's inferior imitators) has almost passed away. Some persons have even an exaggerated horror of words derived from Latin, which are sometimes useful and even indispensable. It is not Latin words, in their proper place, that make a style heavy or give it an over-learned air, but piling them up where more ordinary words would do equally well.

In a book by a master of English style, published in 1887, are to be found within a few pages the words *clarity, meticulous, symphonious*. But these do not affect the general style of the work. Put them into a single sentence, and see what the result would be! However, in spite of the marked tendency of the best recent English prose towards simplicity, even now there are some traces of the 'Johnsonian' style remaining in English. Sentences are still to be found especially in newspapers, like the following:—

 An apocryphal victory in a fratricidal strife.
 Once a place of mundane assemblage.

And the comments of the *Times* on Thackeray's *Kickleburys on the Rhine* (see end of chapter) show to what lengths the 'Johnsonian' style has sometimes gone in fairly recent times.

Now the love of a long or hard word for its own sake is as illogical and vulgar as the old woman's attachment to 'that blessed word Mesopotamia.' Since the first end of language is to express one's meaning clearly, it is a pity to use words derived from Latin where common English ones would do. 'The juvenile portion of the community,' or, 'the male progeny of human kind' have no more meaning than the one word *boys*. A 'sacred edifice' is merely a *church*, and 'lead to the hymeneal altar' is no more expressive than *marry*. It is worse still to degrade Latin words, to deprive them of half their meaning in order that one may be able to drag them in so as to give a sort of false dignity to a subject, as when a vulgar murder is called a 'tragedy,' or sudden death a 'fatality.' But it is saddest of all when a Latin word is used quite incorrectly, as when some writers imagine that to *predicate* means to *predict*. In such a case one is really sorry for the writer. He might have written *foretell*, and then no one would have known that he was ignorant of Latin.

We have now to a large extent given up using Latin words in profusion. But some writers have taken up with French words instead.[1] Here it is not the length that is of importance. The shortest French word will suit them as well as a longer one. Of course, if a French word has a different meaning or shade of meaning from any English word, it may be useful and worthy of introduction, like many of its predecessors. Otherwise there is absolutely nothing to be said for it. *Résumé* is nothing but 'abstract' or 'summing-up.' *Double entendre* (which is not even correct French!) is constantly used to mean nothing in the world but a pun. And the less a word is recognised in English the more offensive is its unnecessary use. Besides, such words are read as if in inverted commas, and spoil the continuity and rhythm of the sentence. In such sentences as—

(A town) embowered in *bosquets* of trees
—Whispered Eugenius with a *malin* air,—[2]

---

[1] Of course these remarks do not apply to the words thoroughly naturalised in the language, especially Norman or Anglo-French words. We cannot get on without these, and there is no reason why we should try.

[2] *St. James's Gazette*, 21st June 1890. Sometimes even Italian and Spanish (!) words are introduced in this way. The use of foreign words unnecessarily has been well caricatured by Mark Twain in *The Tramp Abroad*.

it is difficult to see why 'clumps' or 'groves' should not be used in the first, and 'sly' in the second sentence.

The same is the case with French idioms, for instance—

> The power of all the griefs and trials of a man is hidden beneath its words. It is the representative of his best moments, and *all that there has been* about him *of soft*, and gentle, and pure, and penitent, and good, speaks to him for ever out of his English Bible.[1]

This is of course *tout ce qu'il y a été de.* It is a French, and by no means an English idiom, and might quite equally well be expressed in ordinary English.

In the same way we sometimes meet with a door or window 'giving' on a street (French *donner*) which means nothing at all but 'opening' or 'looking' on it. Such a use of French words and idioms inevitably leads to the uncharitable conclusion that the author, like his remote ancestors, brings them in in order to display his knowledge of French, 'to be more y-told of.'

Since German has been more studied in England, we occasionally meet also with an intruder from 'the fatherland,' such as *Zeitgeist*, where 'spirit of the age' would do as well. Only German words have not yet become the fashion. It has been the practice of English to admit French words if they could show cause for being naturalised,—sometimes too without reason,—while, as we saw, few German words have been adopted into English, in spite of the original relationship between the two languages. If acquaintance with German were to lead us once more to make good native compounds as that language still does, it would be an unmixed advantage, just as in the happier attempts which Carlyle has made in this direction, and which poets make occasionally.

A few extracts are given at the end of the chapter from authors who have had more or less reputation for their prose style, both in order to show what English has been like at

[1] Faber, quoted in Eadie, *The English Bible.*

the different periods, and more especially to illustrate in some measure the remarks on English style just made. They will be no more than are absolutely necessary, and certainly omit many authors (such as Bunyan and Defoe, who anticipated the simpler style of English prose) whose works are as famous as any of those of which specimens are given. But these extracts are only intended to illustrate in outline the main current of English prose style.

On the style of English poetry from the sixteenth century it is certainly dangerous to make general remarks. Only this may be said, that to a certain extent but not altogether it runs parallel with our prose. Just as we saw tendencies in English prose at particular periods, so in poetry we might say that the immediate influence of Latin and Greek models, as it would be felt by scholars who really knew Latin and Greek literature, is very powerful in Ben Jonson (died 1637) and Milton (died 1674), though not in Shakespeare.'[1] The classical influence did not cease with Milton, but degenerated more and more into a mere conventional mannerism. Thus the poems of Dryden (died 1700) are more modern in appearance than Milton's, but are in reality more artificial (the classicism of the greater poet, as in *Lycidas*, having become a part of his nature); and as Dryden is, so is Pope (died 1744), and eighteenth-century poetry in general. This poetry is much hampered by fixed rules, some of them derived from the French, and by a classical dress. At the beginning of the nineteenth century Wordsworth, Coleridge, and Scott broke through many of these traditions, and set the example of a more natural kind of poetry which has been followed by later writers.

[1] This is the meaning of Milton's lines in *L'Allegro*—
  Then to the well-trod stage anon,
  If Jonson's *learned sock* be on,
  Or sweetest Shakespeare, Fancy's child,
  Warble *his native wood-notes wild.*

HOOKER

'ECCLESIASTICALL POLITIE' (V. 30)

1597

[1] Hauing thus disputed whether the surplice be a fit garment to be vsed in the seruice of God, the next question whereinto we are drawne is, whether it be a thing allowable or no that the Minister should say seruice in the Chancell, or turne his face at any time from the people, or before seruice ended remoue from the place where it was begun. By them which trouble vs with these doubts we would more willingly be resolued of a greater doubt, whether it be not a kinde of taking Gods name in vaine to debase religion with such friuolous disputes, a sinne to bestow time and labour about them. Things of so meane regard and qualitie, although necessarie to be ordered, are notwithstanding very vnsauorie when they come to be disputed of; because disputation presupposeth some difficultie in the matter which is argued, whereas in things of this nature they must be either very simple or very froward who neede to be taught by disputation what is meete. When we make profession of our faith we stand; when we acknowledge our sinnes or seeke vnto God for fauour, we fall downe, because the gesture of constancie becommeth us best in the one, in the other the behauiour of humilitie. Some parts of our Liturgie consist in the reading of the word of God, and the proclayming of his lawe, that the people may thereby learne what theyr duties are towardes him; some consist in wordes of prayse and thanksgiuing, whereby we acknowledge vnto God what his blessings are towards vs; some are such as albeit they serue to singular good purpose euen when there is no Communion administred, neuerthelesse being deuised at the first for that purpose are at

---

[1] The extracts down to Johnson inclusive use the long *s* (very much like an *f*), except at the end of words.

the Table of the Lord for that cause also commonly read; some are vttered as from the people, some as with them vnto God, some as from God vnto them, all as before his sight whom we feare, and whose presence to offend with any the least vnseemelines we would be surely as loath as they who most reprehend or deride that we do.

LORD BACON

'THE HISTORIE OF THE RAIGNE OF KING HENRY THE SEUENTH'

1622

BVT PERKINS *Proclamation* did little edifie with the people of *England*; neither was hee the better welcome for the companie hee came in. Wherefore the *King of Scotland* seeing none came in to PERKIN, nor none stirred any where in his fauour, turned his enterprise into a *Rode*;[1] and wasted and destroyed the Countrie of *Northumberland*, with fire and sword. But hearing that there were Forces comming against him, and not willing that they should find his Men heauie and laden with bootie, hee returned into *Scotland* with great Spoyles, deferring further prosecution, till another time. It is said, that PERKIN acting the part of a *Prince* handsomely, when hee saw the *Scottish* fell to waste the Countrie, came to the King in a passionate manner, making great lamentation, and desired, That that might not bee the manner of making the Warre; for that no *Crowne* was so deare to his mind, as that hee desired to purchase it with the bloud and ruine of his *Countrie*. Whereunto the King answered halfe in sport; that hee doubted much, hee was carefull for that that was none of his, and that hee should bee too good a *Steward* for his Enemie, to saue the *Countrie* to his vse.

---

[1] Southern form of *raid*. See 1 Samuel xxvii. 10.

MILTON

'AREOPAGITICA; A SPEECH OF MR. JOHN MILTON FOR THE LIBERTY OF VNLICENC'D PRINTING'

To the Parlament of England

1644

Yet that which is above all this, the favour and the love of heav'n we have great argument to think in a peculiar manner propitious and propending towards us. Why else was this Nation chos'n before any other, that out of her as out of *Sion* should be proclam'd and sounded forth the first tidings and trumpet of Reformation to all *Europ*. And had it not bin the obstinat perversnes of our Prelats against the divine and admirable spirit of Wicklef, to suppresse him as a schismatic and *innovator*, perhaps neither the *Bohemian Husse* and *Jerom*, no nor the name of Luther, or of Calvin had bin ever known: the glory of reforming all our neighbours had bin compleatly ours. But now, as our obdurat Clergy have with violence demean'd the matter, we are become hitherto the latest and the backwardest Schollers, of whom God offer'd to have made us the teachers. Now once again by all concurrence of signs, and by the generall instinct of holy and devout men, as they daily and solemnly expresse their thoughts, God is decreeing to begin some new and great period in his Church, ev'n to the reforming of Reformation it self: what does he then but reveal Himself to his servants, and as his manner is, first to his English-men; I say as his manner is, first to us, though we mark not the method of his counsels, and are unworthy. Behold now this vast City; a City of refuge, the mansion house of liberty, encompast and surrounded with his protection; the shop of warre hath not there more anvils and hammers waking, to fashion out the plates and instruments of armed Justice in defence of beleaguer'd Truth, then there be pens and heads there, sitting by their studious lamps, musing, searching, revolving new notions and idea's wherewith to present, as with their homage and their fealty the approaching Reformation: others as fast reading, trying all things, assenting to the force of reason and convincement. What could a man require more from a Nation so pliant and so prone to seek after knowledge. What wants there to such a towardly and pregnant soile, but wise and faithfull labourers to make a knowing people, a Nation of Prophets, of Sages, and of Worthies. We reck'n more than five months yet to harvest; there need not be five weeks, had we but eyes to lift up, the fields are white already. Where there is much desire to learn, there of necessity will be much arguing, much writing, many opinions; for opinion in good men is but knowledge in the making. Under these fantastic terrors of sect and schism, we wrong the earnest and zealous thirst after knowledge and understanding which God hath stirr'd up in this City.

ADDISON

PAPER IN THE 'SPECTATOR' ON 'PARADISE LOST'

12th Jan. 1712

THERE is another Circumstance in the principal Actors of the *Iliad* and *Æneid*, which gives a particular Beauty to those two Poems, and was therefore contrived with very great Judgment. I mean the Authors having chosen for their Heroes Persons who were so nearly related to the People for whom they wrote. *Achilles* was a *Greek*, and *Æneas* the remote Founder of *Rome*. By this means their Countrymen (whom they principally proposed to themselves for their Readers) were particularly attentive to all the Parts of their Story, and sympathized with their Heroes in all their Adventures. A *Roman* could not but rejoice in the Escapes, Successes and

Victories of *Æneas*, and be grieved at any Defeats, Misfortunes or Disappointments that befel him ; as a *Greek* must have had the same Regard for *Achilles*. And it is plain, that each of those Poems have lost this great Advantage, among those Readers to whom their Heroes are as Strangers, or indifferent Persons.

MILTON'S Poem is admirable in this respect, since it is impossible for any of its Readers, whatever Nation, Country or People he may belong to, not to be related to the Persons who are the principal Actors in it ; but what is still infinitely more to its Advantage, the principal Actors in this Poem are not only our Progenitors, but our Representatives. We have an actual Interest in every Thing they do, and no less than our utmost Happiness is concerned, and lies at Stake in all their Behaviour.

JOHNSON

THE PRINCE OF ABISSINIA ('RASSELAS')

1759

The Great Wall of China and the Pyramids

'We have now, said Imlac, gratified our minds with an exact view of the greatest work of man, except the wall of China.

'Of the wall it is very easy to assign the motives. It secured a wealthy and timorous nation from the incursions of Barbarians, whose unskilfulness in arts made it easier for them to supply their wants by rapine than by industry, and who from time to time poured in upon the habitations of peaceful commerce, as vultures descend upon domestick fowl. Their celerity and fierceness made the wall necessary, and their ignorance made it efficacious.

'But, for the pyramids no reason has ever been given adequate to the cost and labour of the work. The narrowness of the chambers proves that it could afford no retreat from enemies, and treasures might have been reposited at far less expence with equal security. It seems to have been erected only in compliance with that hunger of imagination which preys incessantly upon life, and must be always appeased by some employment. Those who have already all that they can enjoy, must enlarge their desires. He that has built for use, till use is supplied, must begin to build for vanity, and extend his plan to the utmost power of human performance, that he may not be soon reduced to form another wish.

'I consider this mighty structure as a monument of the insufficiency of human enjoyments. A king, whose power is unlimited, and whose treasures surmount all real and imaginary wants, is compelled to solace, by the erection of a pyramid, the satiety of dominion and tastelessness of pleasures, and to amuse the tediousness of declining life, by seeing thousands labouring without end, and one stone, for no purpose, laid upon another. Whoever thou art, that, not content with a moderate condition, imaginest happiness in royal magnificence, and dreamest that command or riches can feed the appetite of novelty with successive gratifications, survey the pyramids, and confess thy folly!'

SIR WALTER SCOTT

'WAVERLEY'

1814

Rose Bradwardine's Accomplishments

Miss Rose now appeared from the interior room of her apartment to welcome her father and his friends. The little labours in which she had been employed obviously shewed a natural taste, which required only cultivation. Her father had taught her French and Italian, and a few of the ordinary authors in those languages ornamented her shelves. He had endeavoured also to be her preceptor in music; but as he began with the more abstruse doctrines of the science, and was not perhaps master of them himself, she had made no proficiency further than to be able to accompany her voice with the harpsichord: but even this was not very common in Scotland at that period. To make amends, she sung with great taste and feeling, and with a respect to the sense of what she uttered that might be proposed in example to ladies of much superior musical talent. Her natural good sense taught her, that if, as we are assured by high authority, music be "married to immortal verse," they are very often divorced by the performer in a most shameful manner. It was perhaps owing to this sensibility to poetry, and power of combining its expression with those of the musical notes, that her singing gave more pleasure to all the unlearned in music, and even to many of the learned, than could have been extracted by a much finer voice and more brilliant execution, unguided by the same delicacy of feeling.

THACKERAY

'VANITY FAIR'

1848

Sick-bed homilies and pious reflections are, to be sure, out of place in mere story-books, and we are not going (after the fashion of some novelists of the present day) to cajole the public into a sermon, when it is only a comedy that the reader pays his money to witness. But, without preaching, the truth may surely be borne in mind, that the bustle, and triumph, and laughter, and gaiety which *Vanity Fair* exhibits in public, do not always pursue the performer into private life, and that the most dreary depression of spirits and dismal repentances sometimes overcome him. Recollection of the best ordained banquets will scarcely cheer sick epicures.

Reminiscences of the most becoming dresses and brilliant ball-triumphs will go very little way to console faded beauties. Perhaps statesmen, at a particular period of existence, are not much gratified at thinking over the most triumphant divisions; and the success or the pleasure of yesterday become of very small account when a certain (albeit uncertain) morrow is in view, about which all of us must some day or other be speculating. O brother wearers of motley! Are there not moments when one grows sick of grinning and tumbling, and the jingling of cap and bells? This, dear friends and companions, is my amiable object—to walk with you through the Fair, to examine the shops and the shows there; and that we should all come home after the flare, and the noise, and the gaiety, and be perfectly miserable in private.

THE MODERN 'JOHNSONIAN' STYLE

'The Kickleburys Abroad'

(Extract from the *Times* in Thackeray's Preface to the second edition of the *Kickleburys on the Rhine*, 1851)[1]

It has been customary, of late years, for the purveyors of amusing literature—the popular authors of the day—to put forth certain opuscules, denominated 'Christmas Books,' with the ostensible intention of swelling the tide of exhilaration, or other expansive emotions, incident upon the exodus of the old, and the inauguration of the new year. We have said that their ostensible intention was such, because there is another motive for these productions, locked up (as the popular author deems) in his own breast, but which betrays itself, in the quality of the work, as his principal incentive. Oh that any muse should be set upon a high stool to cast up accounts and balance a ledger! Yet so it is; and the popular author

---

[1] Thackeray's own retort on the critic will well repay reading; but the extract speaks for itself.

finds it convenient to fill up the declared deficit, and place himself in a position the more effectually to encounter those liabilities which sternly assert themselves contemporaneously and in contrast with the careless and free-handed tendencies of the season by the emission of Christmas books—a kind of literary *assignats*, representing to the emitter expunged debts, to the receiver an investment of enigmatical value. For the most part bearing the stamp of their origin in the vacuity of the writer's exchequer rather than in the fulness of his genius, they suggest by their feeble flavour the rinsings of a void brain after the more important concoctions of the expired year. Indeed, we should as little think of taking these compositions as examples of the merits of their authors as we should think of measuring the valuable services of Mr. Walker, the postman, or Mr. Bell, the dust-collector, by the copy of verses they leave at our doors as a provocative of the expected annual gratuity—effusions with which they may fairly be classed for their intrinsic worth no less than their ultimate purport.

MACAULAY

'History of England'

1849

Opinions of a Modern Royalist before the Great Rebellion

Neither party wanted strong arguments for the measures which it was disposed to adopt. The reasonings of the most enlightened Royalists may be summed up thus: 'It is true that great abuses have existed; but they have been redressed. It is true that precious rights have been invaded; but they have been vindicated and surrounded with new securities. The sittings of the estates of the realm have been, in defiance of all precedent and of the spirit of the constitution, intermitted during eleven years; but it has now been provided that henceforth three years shall never elapse without a

Parliament. The Star Chamber, the High Commission, the Council of York, oppressed and plundered us; but those hateful courts have now ceased to exist. The lord lieutenant aimed at establishing military despotism; but he has answered for his treason with his head. The primate tainted our worship with Popish rites, and punished our scruples with Popish cruelty; but he is awaiting in the Tower the judgment of his peers. The lord keeper sanctioned a plan, by which the property of every man in England was placed at the mercy of the crown; but he has been disgraced, ruined, and compelled to take refuge in a foreign land. The ministers of tyranny have expiated their crimes. The victims of tyranny have been compensated for their sufferings. Under such circumstances it would be most unwise to persevere in that course which was justifiable and necessary when we first met, after a long interval, and found the whole administration one mass of abuses. It is time to take heed that we do not so pursue our victory over despotism as to run into anarchy. It was not in our power to overturn the bad institutions which lately afflicted our country, without shocks which have loosened the foundations of government. Now that those institutions have fallen, we must hasten to prop the edifice which it was lately our duty to batter. Henceforth it will be our wisdom to look with jealousy on schemes of innovation, and to guard from encroachment all the prerogatives with which the law has, for the public good, armed the sovereign.'

CHAPTER XXIII

ENGLISH DIALECTS AT THE PRESENT DAY

The Southern (or South-Western) dialect—The West Midland dialect—The Northern dialect—East Midland, or 'standard' English.[1]

IN the last few chapters, on English since 1500, we have been speaking of 'standard' English only, and it might almost seem from them as if there were no other dialect of English now in existence, but that the other dialects, having contributed more or less to colour the literary East Midland dialect, and thus having made their mark upon it, had died out, leaving no traces behind them but these contributions to our 'standard' English, and some differences of pronunciation in various parts of the country.

As a matter of fact this is far from being the case at present. They are not so distinct as they once were. They have been influenced by literary English, especially through the schools, where it is literary English, the English of books, that the children learn. And they have been affected more and more by each other on and near the borders of each. But there are still an almost infinite number of varieties of dialect in England, and these may still be grouped under the

---

[1] 'On the Dialects of Monmouthshire, Herefordshire, etc.,' by Prince Louis Lucien Bonaparte, *Transactions of the Philological Society*, 1875-76. 'The Dialect of West Somerset,' by Frederic Thomas Elworthy, *Transactions of the Philological Society*, 1875-76. *A Glossary of the Dorset Dialect, with a Grammar*, by William Barnes. *Poems and Songs*, by Edwin Waugh. *Lancashire Lyrics*, edited by John Harland. *Horæ Momenta Cravenæ, or the Craven Dialect exemplified in two Dialogues*, by a Native of Craven.

main heads of Southern, West Midland, Northern, and East Midland.

(1) The Southern dialect.

We will place the Southern dialect first as the 'decayed gentleman' of the company. It has seen better days. Its dominion has now been greatly narrowed. No longer is it to be found in all its glory in Kent as in the days of Dan Michel and Caxton (pp. 263, 285). We must not look for it anywhere near the capital, but far within its old borders in Dorset and Somerset and Devon. It is now so 'fallen from its high estate' that for centuries it has been regarded as the typical 'rustic' speech. One of the old poems in *Percy's Reliques* is a conversation between Truth and Ignorance, Truth being an advocate of the Reformation, and Ignorance a benighted Popish rustic. Truth speaks the East Midland dialect or literary English, and Ignorance broad Somersetshire, thus—

Ignorance

Chill tell thee what, good vellowe,
    Before the vriers went hence,
A bushell of the best wheate
    Was zold vor vourteen pence;
And vorty egges a penny
    That were both good and newe;
And this che zay my zelf have zeene,
    And yet ich am no Jewe.

Truth

Within the sacred Bible
    We find it written plain,
The latter days should troublesome
    And dangerous be, certaine;
That we should be self-lovers,
    And charity wax colde;
Then 'tis not true religion
    That makes thee grief to holde.

Ignorance

Chill tell thee my opinion plaine,
    And choul'd that well ye knewe,
Ich care not for the bible booke ;
    'Tis too big to be true.
Our blessed ladyes psalter
    Zhall for my money goe ;
Zuch pretty prayers, as there bee
    The bible cannot zhowe.

Truth

Nowe hast thou spoken trulye,
    For in that book indeede
No mention of our lady
    Or Romish saint we read :
For by the blessed Spirit
    That book indited was,
And not by simple persons,
    As was the foolish masse.

Ignorance

Cham zure they were not voolishe
    That made the masse, che trowe ;
Why, man, 'tis all in Latine,
    And vools no Latine knowe.
Were not our fathers wise men,
    And they did like it well ;
Who very much rejoyced
    To heare the zacring bell ?

Truth

But many kinges and prophets,
    As I may say to thee,
Have wisht the light that you have,
    And could it never see :
For what art thou the better
    A Latin song to heare,
And understandest nothing,
    That they sing in the quiere ?

Truth is a little hard on the poor man, and inclined to be priggish. He seems rather to overstate his case when he says that there is no mention of 'our Lady' in the Bible. But we are not now concerned with the sentiments but with the language. Here, then, we have not only the V for F, Z for S, which were and are characteristic of the Southern dialect (p. 263), but also the old-world form *ich* for 'I,' both separate, and also in *chill* (*I will*), *chould* (*I would*), *cham* (*I am*). So too in *King Lear*, when Edgar pretends to be a rustic, he says—

    Chill not let go, zir, without vurther 'casion.

And

    Chill pick your teeth, zir : come ; no matter vor your foins.[1]

Thus, then, even in Shakespeare's time, the Southern dialect, the lineal descendant of Alfred's West Saxon, was considered as the typical speech of a rustic. And at the present day the rustic in *Punch* nearly always speaks a kind of conventional Somersetshire. This Southern (now South-Western) dialect is still in existence, and it is in many points a most antique form of English.

First, as to the sounds of the dialect. What was said in the last chapter on English pronunciation will show that many of the sounds of the (West) Somersetshire dialect are much more like Old English than those in our modern literary English are. Besides, it has 'split vowels' like the EA, OA of Anglo-Saxon—*tae-ŭr* (to *tear*), *dae-ŭlur* (*dealer*), *drae-ŭr* (*drear*), and *a-nō-ŭd* (*known*), *nō-ŭrt* (*naught*). Though these are not in the same words as those which have the EA and OA respectively in Anglo-Saxon, the way of speaking is evidently the same. And the V for F, Z for S, as in *vlog* (*flog*), *vork* (*fork*), *zix*, *zee*, have been already mentioned.

Next, as to the grammar. In the Old English verb we saw

[1] *King Lear*, IV. vi. 240, 250.

English Dialects at the Present Day 389

that some verbs ended in -*ian* (p. 106), e.g. *lufian, ich lufige, hi lufiað* (to *love, I love, they love*). The traces of this are still preserved in the Somersetshire verbs *mowy* (*mow*), *rocky* (*rock*), *scaaly* (*scald*). The termination of the 3rd person singular of the verb is not a mere -*s* but -*es*, or rather -*ŭs*—*walkŭs, burn-ŭs*[1] = *walks, burns*, much as it was in Robert of Brunne. But this is one of the contributions of the Midland dialects. It is an exotic in Somersetshire. In other parts of Somersetshire, however, as well as in North Devon, the proper Southern inflexion of the 3rd person singular is still preserved (*talketh, loveth*), which is now quite extinct in ordinary English. Past participles have the prefix *a*- (the corruption of *ge*-), as in *a-bin* (*been*), *a-taich* (*taught*). We have seen this prefix before in Barnes's Dorsetshire poems (p. 94). Then too the personal pronouns are in some points very old-fashioned. *Ich*, or something like it, must certainly have been common a century or two ago. At present the word is represented by *utchy*, which seems to survive only in the mouth of a few old men in one or two parts of Somersetshire; *utchill, utchood*[2] (I will, I would) are also in existence.

A (or *ŭ*) is commonly used for *he* in Devonshire and parts of Somerset, as in *a goo-uth, a talketh*. We last saw this in Shakespeare, as a relic of the Southern dialect (p. 344). So too *un* (= *hine*, see p. 113) is used for him—*I zeed un* = I saw him. *Thick* or *thicky* (*þilke*, p. 295) for 'that' is still in common use, and *that* is only used of neuters or things in the abstract, as in such a sentence as 'I daedn' zay *that* thae-ur' (p. 112). This last sentence also contains the old negative *ne*. Our own form is *didn't* = *did not*.

Then too the adverb supports our explanation of -*ly*, as in *plainly*, given early in the book (p. 12). '*Ard-like* is *hardly, quiet-like, quietly*, and so on.

[1] Both the forms in -*y* (*e.g.* mowy), and in -*us* (*e.g.* walkus), are, for some reason, only used in neuter verbs.
[2] *Uch* is another Southern form in Middle English besides *ich*.

Thus Somersetshire is not only an old-fashioned form of English, but distinctly represents the old Southern dialect among the dialects of England, the Dorsetshire and Devonshire dialects being closely allied to it.

(2) Next we come to the West Midland dialect, which has had a more equable career. It has never held a commanding position like the Southern dialect, nor, like it, become a byword. It is a very interesting variety of English. It now includes the speech of Southern Lancashire, Cheshire, and Shropshire, and we will take Lancashire as its representative, since this variety has something of a literature.

First, as to the sounds. It is curious to find 'split' vowel-sounds here too, such as *greawnd* (*ground*), *eawt* (*out*), *neaw* (*now*), though the Midland or Mercian dialect of English before the Conquest used them far less than did Southern or West Saxon. Besides this, the old sound of the I survives in very many words, such as *neet* (*night*), *dee* (*die*), *breet* (*bright*), and so on, and that of OU or OW in *groo* (*grow*).

In the grammar there are some most archaic forms, of which the most noticeable is the Midland plural of the verb in *-en*, not unfrequently used, though, as we saw, it died out of literary English in the fifteenth century; for example, 'yo *seen*' (you *see*), '*dun* yo' (*do* you), 'they *comen*,' 'they *knawn*' (*know*), 'they *han*' (they *have*), or, abbreviated, *we'n*, *yo'n*, *they'n* (*we, you, they have*), *they'rn* (for *they weren*); as, for instance, in the lines—

> Mi wage sin' then, yo *seen*, 's kept two,
> An' so, yo're sure *we'n* had no fat;
> *We'n* ne'er complain'd, *we'n* made it do;
> Bo' could we save owt eawt o' that?[1]

Besides this, the Lancashire dialect keeps some old 'strong' forms of verbs which we have made weak, such as *crope* (*crept*), *lope* (*leapt*).

[1] *Lancashire Lyrics*, edited by John Harland.

English Dialects at the Present Day

In the pronouns the most remarkable thing is the preservation of *hoo*, or *'oo* (*héo*, p. 113), for 'she,' as in the verse—

> Nan had fritter't away o' th' for-end of her life,
> For *hoo*'d flirted o' round, though *hoo*'d ne'er bin a wife.
> But one day, when *hoo* fund *hoo*'re turn't thirty year owd,
> *Hoo* began a-bein flayed *hoo*'d be left out i' th' cowd.[1]

This *hoo* is the most distinct mark of Lancashire being the representative of the West Midland dialect, *she* having supplanted it in East Midland before Chaucer's time. But the two Midland dialects had much in common. And it is chiefly the characteristics which they once shared which have been preserved, so that the Lancashire dialect in many respects reminds us of the English of Chaucer and Wycliffe, in such words, for instance, as *shoon*, *een* (*eyes*), *nobbut* (= only), *brids* (*birds*), *axe* (*ask*), and in '*tone* fro *tother*,' the T in each case being a relic of the neuter article.

(3) After what was said of Lowland Scotch in chapter xvi., it is not necessary to prove once more that the Northern dialect is still alive. One variety of Northumbrian was, as we then saw, for centuries the language of the Court and literature of an independent kingdom, and is even now something more than an ordinary dialect. And besides, in the northern counties of England, including part of Yorkshire, there are still varieties of speech more or less akin to Lowland Scotch, and derived, like it, from the old Northumbrian dialect. There is still to be found in the speech of the northern counties the old A in such words as *lang*, *strang*, *laith*, *sair*, just as we saw it in the Northern Psalter of the thirteenth century, 'I *is*,' 'thou *is*,' as those forms are used by Chaucer's Northern clerks, and 'thou *sees*,' 'thou *tells* me,' like the Northumbrian verb before and after the Conquest (pp. 85, 260). And Charlotte Brontë, in *Shirley*, makes her Yorkshire squire

---

[1] *Flayed* = frightened. Edwin Waugh, *Poems and Songs*.

say *sul, suld* (for *shall, should*), much like our thirteenth-century Northumbrian poet, or like a modern Scotchman.

(4) Lastly, the East Midland is represented by literary English, the language of books and of educated persons in speaking, and a dialect very much like this is spoken northwards from London as far as the middle of Lincolnshire—that is to say, in the old home of the East Midland dialect.

APPENDIX A

RACE AND LANGUAGE

WE cannot of course assume that the Indo-Europeans, before or after they split up, were pure-blooded.

As to the original Indo-European language, there may be foreign elements in it which we are not likely to detect. But, however this may be, the fact that a nation, or a mass of tribes, has a language with little or no foreign admixture does not necessarily imply that there is no mixture of foreigners in the race. The French are the most familiar instance of this. Though they are mainly Celtic in race, with only a very small Roman and German element in their blood, their language is practically corrupt Latin, with a certain proportion of German words, but with only the very smallest tinge of Celtic. And Spaniards, Portuguese, and, above all, Roumanians can have only a very small share of Roman blood in their veins, though their languages are 'Romance.' These are probably extreme instances. But at all events the Indo-Europeans, or the separate tribes after they became divided, *may* have absorbed any number of foreigners. There is, for instance, evidence to show that they absorbed a race of short, dark-haired men in the west of Europe (those who lived in our islands are often called Ivernians), though no certain trace of the language of this people is to be found among their conquerors.—See Schrader, *Sprachvergleichung und Urgeschichte*; Brachet, *Historical French Grammar*; Rhys, *Celtic Britain*.

APPENDIX B

THE ENGLISH OF THE CONTINENT

It may be interesting to have a specimen of the English which stayed at home, in the form which it afterwards assumed. A specimen of North Frisian would be a nearer relation of our language, but Lübeck is not very far from the part whence our ancestors came.

Low German (or Platt-Deutsch) is now after a long interval being written once more to some small extent, though of course it will never again be more than a local dialect.

The specimen given is the Parable of the Sower, from St. Matthew's Gospel (xiii. 3-9), made in Low German according to Luther's translation.

DAT NYE TESTAMENT JESU CHRISTI

D. Mart. Luth.

Lübeck. 1615

Vnde he rĕdede tho en mannigerley / dŏrch Gelykenisse / vnde ſprack: Sŭe dar ginck ein Saedtſeyer vth tho seyende. Vnd in dem alse he ſeyede vell etlick an den Wech. Do quemen de Vŏgele / vnde fretent vp. Etlyck vell in dat ſtenige Landt / dar ydt nicht veel Erde hadde / vnd ginck drade vp / darŭmme / dat ydt nene depe Erde hadde. Alse ŏuerst de Sŭnne vpginck / vorwelckede ydt / Vnde de wyle dat ydt nene Wŏrtelen hadde wardt ydt dŏrre. Etlick veel vp ein gudt Landt vnd droech Frucht / Etlick hundertvoldige / etlick ſŏſtichvoldige / Etlick dŏrtichvoldige / Wol ohren hefft thohŏrendĕ / de hŏre.

> We have taken a few words from this 'continental English,' through trade connections with North Germany. *Groat* (=4d.) is apparently a certain example of a word from Bremen. (It is found in Chaucer.) But these words are, as a rule, not easy to distinguish from native English, for the same reasons as those stated on pp. 306-308. They are still harder to distinguish from Dutch words, that language being most closely akin to the North German dialects.

APPENDIX C

THE KENTISH DIALECT

This is a difficult subject. It does not appear to 'come out' quite right, since what we know of the history of the tribe does not seem to square with the character of its language.

Bede, in his *Ecclesiastical History* (chapter xv.), has evidently no doubt that Kent was settled by Jutes, and that these came from the district to the north of the Angles. In this case one would expect the Kentish dialect to have more affinities with Northumbrian and Mercian (the Anglian dialects) than it actually shows, and even to be more nearly related to Danish than Anglian originally was. Now, a good many of the peculiarities in its vowels agree with the Mercian dialect, but it certainly afterwards was a form of Saxon or Southern English. We may therefore suppose one of the following alternatives :—

(1) That Bede was mistaken as to the place from which the Jutes came.

But as he must have had means of information, from tradition or otherwise, which we do not possess, this would be a very dangerous theory to take up without strong evidence for it, which is not forthcoming.

(2) That the dialect (possibly owing to some movements of population of which we know nothing) was not what one would expect from the position on the Continent of the tribe speaking it.

This is possible, but there is no proof of it.

(3) That there was a mixture of some other tribe among the invaders of Kent. The leaders may have been Jutes, but it does not follow that all who came with them were. That the different English settlements did not all consist each of a single tribe is practically proved by this fact. We are told that Frisians settled in England at the same time as

the Saxons, and North Frisian (as spoken in the islands off the west coast of Schleswig) is more closely allied to English than any other Continental Low German dialect, and yet none of the different settlements are described as Frisian. But there is no proof of any mixture of race in Kent.

(4) That the dialect of the Jutes in Kent became altered by imitation of the Saxon on its borders.

It is true that Kent was for a long time an independent or semi-independent kingdom, and, one might think, could maintain and fix its own dialect. The West Saxons of Gloucestershire, Worcestershire, and Herefordshire retained the Southern character of their dialect under somewhat similar disadvantages (see pp. 77, 281), though they became part of the kingdom of Mercia. But they were not surrounded by those who spoke another dialect. The neighbourhood of Middlesex and Sussex, and afterwards the supremacy of Wessex and of West Saxon might well influence Kentish. And as Kentish becomes more and more like West Saxon this is probably the main solution of the problem.

If (as Mr. Sweet believes) the differences between the dialects were originally slight, and increased after the tribes speaking them settled in England, the problem is an easier one (see pp. 16, 118 note 4).

There do not seem to be any traces discoverable of a special dialect of any kind in the Isle of Wight, and in the mainland near it. But as this was a small isolated settlement, and was very soon absorbed in Wessex, there is nothing strange in this.
—*Encyclopædia Britannica*, Ninth Edition, Articles 'England,' 'English Language'; Sweet, *History of English Sounds, New English Grammar*, etc.

APPENDIX D

NOTE TO PAGE 167

Professor Skeat (*Principles of English Etymology*, Second Series, pp. 21, 22) says—

'I believe that these lines are usually misunderstood. Chaucer is merely stating a linguistic fact, viz. that the Prioresse, being one "of the old school," naturally spoke such Anglo-French as was usually spoken and taught in her nunnery at Stratford, a French excellent in its kind, and in some respects more archaic and truer to the Latin original than the French of Paris, which had but lately risen into importance as a literary language. And this is all. It is difficult to have patience with the newspaper-writers to whom this is a perennial jest, and who are utterly incapable of distinguishing between the language of the English Court under a king who claimed to be *also king of France*, and the poor jargon taught by the second-rate governesses of the last century, who pretended to teach "a French never spoken in France," nor indeed anywhere else. It is charitable to suppose that those to whom this is a joke for ever have no idea what nonsense they are talking. Chaucer must have known—indeed no one knew better—that Anglo-French could boast a literature of its own. His own Man of Lawes Tale is taken from the Anglo-French Chronicle of Nicolas Trivet.'

I am quite conscious that it is audacious for me to disagree with such an authority on the history of the English language as Professor Skeat, and am therefore all the more pleased to find that Professor Earle (*English Prose*, p. 295) takes something like my own view of the lines. Speaking of such words as *déshabille*, he says—

'I expect that it will amuse and interest my readers to find that French of Stratford-atte-Bowe is not yet an extinct species among us. In the thirteenth and fourteenth centuries there were in England many old French words, some distorted and all antiquated, which had been French once, but were so no longer; and such words were used as decorations of their English speech by those who, like Chaucer's Prioresse, studied the old-fashioned airs of politeness.' And then follow the three lines of Chaucer in dispute.

Now whether the Prioresse's French was continuous or fragmentary, in sentences or single words, is perhaps not of much consequence. It was probably both as occasion required. But I cannot help thinking that this is one of the places where Chaucer is 'smiling' at some one or other of the characters in the Prologue, as when he says of the Merchant, who evidently thought himself a person of considerable importance—

But sooth to say I not (*ne wât*, do not know) what men him calle.

And the parallel of 'Marlborough French' (though the date of this nickname is much earlier) seems to me to lend much support to the view that Stratford-atte-Bowe French was thought of by Chaucer as something more or less absurd, as a peculiarly English form of Anglo-French; not that the name had become proverbial, but merely because such French was local or 'provincial.' In the country even Anglo-French would degenerate. Thus the lines need not be a laugh or smile at Anglo-French in general, though even this might be safe at a time when it was rapidly going out of fashion, and when the King (Richard II.) himself spoke Continental French instead of it. (Skeat, *Principles of English Etymology*, Second Series, p. 7.)

APPENDIX E

VERBAL SUBSTANTIVES AND PRESENT PARTICIPLES IN '-ING'

This is a very difficult and confused subject, the confusion beginning, in some points, in the twelfth century or earlier. Only the heads of the matter will be given here.

We will first state the elementary facts from which the forms and uses of the Verbal Substantives and Present Participles are to be explained.

There were in Anglo-Saxon and later—

(1) An infinitive in -*an*, e.g. *fyllan* (to fill), later *fyllen, fylle, fyll.*

(2) A dative of the infinitive in *-anne, enne*, e.g. *to fyllenne* (see pp. 95, 154).

(3) A present participle in *-ende*, e.g. *fyllende*, later *fyllinde, fyllinge, fylling*. The change to *-inge* is first found in Layamon (see p. 225).

(4) A verbal substantive in *-ung*, e.g. *fyllung* or *fylling* (a filling, or fulfilling).

Now the dative of the infinitive (2) became confused with the present participle (3) both in its earlier and later form (*-ende, -ing*). But this use died out in the fifteenth century, so that we need not attempt to derive English idioms (*e.g.* 'fell to *eating*,' verbal substantive) from it.

The main thing to remember is that the dative of the infinitive became merged in the simple infinitive by losing its special termination, *fyllenn(e)* being the same as *fyllen*, and then the termination of the infinitive was lost as well. Thus 'to *sow*,' in the Parable of the Sower, is the descendant of 'to *sáwenne*.'

We are now left with (1), (3), (4).

The infinitive, with or without *to*, (1) and the verbal substantive (4) are often used in exactly similar ways; as, for instance—

Returning were as tedious as *go* o'er.[1]

To give gold to you is *giving* fuel to him.[2]

Both are really verbal substantives, and there is nothing strange in their being used as alternatives. But the verbal substantive in *-ing* also lies at the root of those expressions where a present participle active seems to be used passively, for instance—

The bread is baking,
The bath is filling,
The breakfast is getting ready.

---

[1] Shakespeare.   [2] Sir Walter Scott.

In the earliest English the verbal substantive is used with a preposition, for instance—

<blockquote>Ic wæs on huntunge,
I was on hunting, or a-hunting</blockquote>

(like Latin *inter venandum*), *on* being abbreviated to *a-* just as it is in *on board, a-board, on sleep*,[1] *a-sleep*.

Now in some cases this preposition with a verbal substantive could be replaced by the present participle, of similar form, but of course without the preposition; as, for instance—

<blockquote>Ic wæs huntende,</blockquote>

or later,

<blockquote>I was hunting.</blockquote>

The only difference then, in the form of the words, after the present participle had taken a similar form to the verbal substantive, was that the first expression has an apparently meaningless *a-* before it. This was therefore dropped, and the expression

<blockquote>I go fishing</blockquote>

is really shortened from the form in the Bible—

<blockquote>I go a-fishing,[2]</blockquote>

and this abbreviation was extended to verbs where shortening the phrase makes nonsense, strictly speaking. Thus

<blockquote>While the ark was preparing</blockquote>

is an abbreviation of the expression in the Bible

<blockquote>While the ark was a-preparing (or *in preparation*),[3]</blockquote>

fishing and *preparing* being both verbal substantives in their origin. And in the same way the similar expressions referred to above may be explained.—See Morris, *Historical Outlines of English Accidence*; Koch, *Historische Grammatik der Englischen Sprache*; and Kington Oliphant, *Old and Middle English*.

[1] Acts xiii. 36.
[2] St. John xxi. 3.
[3] First Epistle of St. Peter iii. 20.

INDEX

A, changes to O in English, 89, 210-213, 235, 247, 248, 333
    changes in its pronunciation, 352-354
    in Sanskrit, 34
a- 254 note, App. E; and see *ge-*
a (pronoun = *he*), 344, 389
Ablative, in Indo-European language, 52
    lost in Old English, 102
-*able*, 6, 190
Accent in English, 11, 12, 201-208
    in French, 201-207
    in Indo-European, 24, 90
    influence of, 12, 24, 55, 57, 58, 201-208
Accusative in Gothic, 71
    in Greek, 71
    in Indo-European, 52
    in Latin, 71
    in Old English, 102
    in Old High German, 71 note
    use of, in Old English, 115, 116
Addison. See *Spectator*
Adjective, declension of, in Chaucer, 272
    declension of, in Old English, 108
    declension of, in Orm, 236
    declension of, in *Peterborough Chronicle*, 229
    declension of, in Purvey, 276
    declension of, in Robert of Brunne, 259
    declension of, in Robert of Gloucester, 262
    declension of, in sixteenth century, 338

Adjective, declension of, in Southern English, 262
    declension of plural in -*s*, 190 note, 338
    declension of, 'weak' or definite, 108, 109, 236, 272, 276
    See also -*e*
Adverbs in -*e*. See -*e*
    in French, see -*ment*
Æ in Old English, 121
    lost in England after Norman Conquest, 183
Ælfric, 157, 366 note
    specimen of, 178
African languages, words in English from, 364
Agriculture, terms of, chiefly English, 197, 198
-*ai*, in future of French verbs, 56
Alfred the Great, history of, 123, 124
    literary work of, 128-130, 170
    quoted, 122, 128, 129
    specimens of, 147, 151, 152
am. See verbs in $\mu\iota$
American languages, words from, in English, 311, 364
Analogy, 5, 55-57, 91, 92, 189, 190, 237-239, 332-335. See also 'Strong' Verbs
Analytic tendency, in language, 82, 83, 95, 116, 184, 185, 230
-*ance*, 190
Angles, 18, 76-78, 105, 118, 126, and App. C
Anglo-French, character of, 160-163, and App. D

Anglo-French, how widely used in England, 158-160, 163, 164, 166, 167, 281 note
   idioms in English, 184-186
   influences English spelling, 174, 181-184, 229, 236
   literature in, 171
   specimens of, 172, 173, 279, 280
   used in schools, 166, 167
   words from, 138, 143, 160-163, 168, 186-208
Anglo-Indians, words used by, 364, 365
Anglo-Saxon. See West Saxon
Anglo-Saxon Chronicles, 124, 129, 171, 175, 184, 186, 187, 226-231
   specimens of, 153, 175, 176, 228, 229
Arabic, 22, 23, 103 note
   words in English from, 310, 311, 364
Aramaic, words in English from, 310
Architecture, terms of, from Anglo-French, 194
are, 98 note, 133
Article, definite, 108-113, 230, 239, 263
   definite in Old English, 108, 111-113, 134
   in Dan Michel, 263
   in Lancashire dialect, 391
   in Layamon, 246
   in Orm, 239
   in *Peterborough Chronicle*, 230
   origin of, 111-113
   indefinite, 114
-*as*. See -*es*
-*ap*. See -*eth*
Avon, 79
axe (*ask*), 218 note
   used by Purvey, 277
   used by Tyndale, 345
   used in Lancashire, 391

BACON, style of, 368, 376
Barnes (William), 17, 94, 130, 389
Be, conjugation of verb in Old English, 98, 99 note
Bede, 121, 146, and App. C
Béowulf, 157
   specimen of, 150

Bible, 'Authorised Version,' a revision, 318, 319
   'Authorised Version,' adjectives in, 338
   'Authorised Version,' double negative in, 346
   'Authorised Version,' double superlative in, 345
   'Authorised Version,' influence of, 7-9, 362
   'Authorised Version,' its debt to Wycliffe and Purvey, 274, 318, 319
   'Authorised Version,' its use of relatives, 341-343
   'Authorised Version,' obsolete words and meanings in, 7, 61, 313 note, 348, 361, 362
   'Authorised Version,' projected, 317, 318
   'Authorised Version,' pronouns in, 114, 339-343
   'Authorised Version,' specimen of, 326
   'Authorised Version,' subjunctive in, 100
   'Authorised Version,' substantives in, 101, 102, 336, 337
   'Authorised Version,' verbs in, 330, 331, 333-335
   Bishops', 317, 369
   Douai, 317, 369
   Geneva, 316, 317
   'Great,' 316, 317
   in Old English, 121, 132, 133, 148, 149, 154, 155
   Revised Version, 319. See also Coverdale, Matthew, Tyndale, Vulgate, Wycliffe and Purvey
Bohemian, words in English from, 364
Books, behind spoken language, 2
   influence of, on language, 9, 177, 385
Borrowed words, 5-7, 19, 20, 41, 42, 78-80, 127, 128, 137-145, 160-163, 168, 175, 186-208, 216-218, 230, 231, 243, 302-313, 361, 365, and see Danish, French, Latin, etc.
both appears in English, 231, 242
Bourne, 255

Index 403

Brazilian, words in English from, 364
'Breathed' letters, 4, 92, 93, 358
Bunyan. See *Pilgrim's Progress*
Burns, 251, 253 note
-by, 123

C, changed to CH in English, 30, 120, 214-218, 235, 247
    hard in Old English, 120
    softened in French, 34 note, 39 note, 182
    turned into K in English, 182, and see K
Cædmon, 121, 128, 134
    specimen of, 146
Caesar, 45, 68, 69
Cambridge, 285
Cambridgeshire dialect, 226, 285
Canterbury, 120, 262 note
-caster. See *Ceaster*
Caxton, 285 note, 290 note, 291, 293-302, 367, 386
    changes Y to G, 294, 295
    his spelling, 299, 300, 332, 351
    specimen of, 296-298
    uses *their*, *them*, 293-295
Ceaster, 79, 80, 138, 140, 141
Celtic, blood in the English, 79, 80, and App. A
    languages, 22, 23, 33, 36-41, 48-51
    languages, words from, in English, 79, 80, 144, 309, 310
CH, in Anglo-French, 162, 181, 215, 216
    (see C), derived from C in English, 214-218, 235
    the spelling due to Anglo-French, 216
Changes of meaning in words, 7, 11, 12, 61-64, 188, 189, 304, 305, 313 note, 347
Charlotte Brontë, 391, 392
Chaucer, 267-273, 284-292, 303, 311, 313, 391, and App. D
    accent in, 202-204
    adjectives in, 272, 273, 287
    clips N, 291
    -e in, 271, 272, 287, 288
    French words in, 194, 200, 201-204, 270, 271

Chaucer helps to make East Midland 'standard' English, 267, 268, 273, 284-286
    his dialect, 269, 270, 284
    imitated by Spenser, 268, 285 note, 320
    keeps double negative, 346
    medical terms in, 194
    pronouns in, 241, 265, 269, 270
    quoted, 167, 188, 202-204, 284 note, 287, 290-292, and App. D
    specimen of, 270, 271
    substantives in, 272
    verb in, 271-273, 287-290, 331
    Y for G in, 273
Cheshire dialect, 224, 266, 390
Children, language of, 2-4, 60, 91
Chinese, 58, 59
Chronicle. See *Anglo-Saxon* and *Peterborough*
Cimbri and Teutones, 70
Coleridge, 6, 374
Compound words in English, 5, 136, 137, 145, 192 note, 362, 373
    disused in English, 192, 197, 362
Coverdale, his translation of the Bible, 316, 337, and see Bible, 'Great'
Cowper, 355, 356
Cuneiform Inscriptions, 36
CW written QU, 182, 229

D, changes from, or to, 4, 25-27, 40, 92, 93, 307
    inserted for ease of pronunciation, 109
Dan Michel of Northgate, 262-264, 270, 285, 386
Danes, 76 note
    settle in England, 122-125
Danish (or Norse), 33, 49, 51, 61, 66-68, 98 note, 105
    influence of, on English, 122, 123, 125-128, 130, 133-135, 144, 145, 214 note, 216-220, 230-232, 238, 242-244, 247, 254, 291, 307
    keeps C hard, 216
    keeps G hard, 219, 220
    keeps SC hard, 217, 218

Danish, words in English from, 127, 128, 144, 145, 214 note, 216-220, 230, 231, 243, 254 note, 307
Dative case, in English, 100-102, 105, 106, 113, 114, 229, 230, 240, 272, 276, 290 note
   in -φι or -m, 38
   in Indo-European language, 52
   takes the place of the accusative in pronouns, 114, 180, 240
   uses of, in Old English, 115, 116. See also -e, them
Defoe, style of, 368, 374
Demonstrative pronouns, 111-113, 239, 295
Derby, 231, 244
Devonshire dialect, 14, 17, 24, 386, 389, 390
Dialects become languages, 15-18, 32, 37, 39, 170
   connected with Latin, 33, 37, 170, 393
   formation of, 8, 15, 16, 39
   of English, 14, 17, 77, 85, 86, 94, 98 note, 112-114, 118, 119, 125-135, 144-156, 158, 174, 176, 177, 210, 213-218, 220, 223-270, 283-285, 293-295, 327-329, 341, 385, App. C, and see Devonshire, East Midland, etc.
   of French, 160, 161
   of German. See Teutonic
   of Greek, 25, 33, 37
did, 87, 92
Dorsetshire dialect, 17, 94, 130, 386, 389, 390, and see Southern dialect, West Saxon
Double comparative in sixteenth century, 345, 346
   consonants shorten a preceding vowel, 93, 234
   negative in English, 325, 345, 346, 368
   superlative in sixteenth century, 345
Dryden, 374
Dual, in personal pronouns, 113, 114, 240, 241
   in verb in Gothic, 68, 72
'Durham Book,' 133-135
Dutch, 306-308, and see Low German

D, Ð, 121

E, omitted inside words, 292, 293
   (long) changes in its pronunciation, 353, 354
-e, becomes a mark of quantity, 235, 300
   confusion in writing, 249, 250, 287-290, 299
   dropped in adverbs, 10, 55, 347
   dropped in Northumbrian, 249
   effects of its loss, 347
   in Caxton, 299
   in Chaucer, 271, 272, 287, 288
   in Dan Michel, 263
   in Kyngestone's letter, 279, 280
   in Layamon, 246
   in Orm, 236-238
   in Robert of Gloucester, 262
   in Sir John Mandeville, 278 note
   in Wycliffe and Purvey, 276
   loss of, 10, 55, 93, 208, 229, 230, 237, 288-292
   marks adverbs, 10, 55, 272
   marks plural of adjective, 229, 236, 259, 262, 272, 276, 287
   marks plural in the verb, 259, 260, 262, 271
   marks 'weak' adjective. See Adjective, 'weak'
   of dative, 229, 230, 237, 266 note, 272, 287, 290 note
   of infinitive, 259, 262, 266 note, 271, 276, 278 note
   of 'weak' perfects dropped, 93
EA, changes in its pronunciation, 300, 355, 356
   (split vowel) in Old English, 121
   (split vowel) in Somersetshire, 388
Ease of pronunciation, desire for, 4, 15, 25, 34, 199, 288-291
East Anglian dialect, 224, 295, 353
East Midland dialect, adjectives in, 229, 236, 259, 272, 273, 276
   Danish influence on, 128, 132, 133, 135, 144, 145, 216-220, 230, 231, 238, 241-243, 247
   dislikes compound words, 192, 197
   inserts H wrongly, 360
   keeps some C's hard, 214-216

Index 405

East Midland dialect, keeps some G's hard, 220
  keeps some SC's hard, 216-218
  midway between North and South, 214, 253, 265, 282, 284
  parent of 'standard' English, 127, 128, 132, 133, 135, 144, 145, 214, 215-220, 226, 228-244, 250, 255-260, 266-280, 283-301, 314, 348, 392
  pronouns in, 259, 269, 270, 276, 293-295
  SC softened in, 217
  specimens of, 228, 229, 232-234, 257, 258, 270, 271, 275, 278-280
  spoken in London, 269, 284, 285,
  substantives in, 229, 230, 236, 237, 259, 272, 275, 276
  verbs in, 229, 238, 239, 259, 260, 265, 271, 272, 276, 277, 287, 288, 290-293, 328-333, 335
  where spoken, 224, 226, 255, 256, 269, 283-285, 392
-*ed*. See Participle, past, Verbs, 'weak'
Edward I., his knowledge of English, 165
-*en*, in adjective (suffix), 91
  in adjective, 'weak' form. See Adjective, 'weak'
  in infinitive, 229, 259, 271, 276, 290, 320, App. E
  in past participle, 91, 291, 292, 334, 335
  in plural of substantives, 101, 102, 190 note, 237 note, 348, 391
  in plural of verb, 86, 229, 238, 259, 260, 271, 276, 290, 291, 320, 327-329, 390
-*es* (or -*s*), in genitive of adjectives and substantives. See Adjective, Genitive, Substantive
  in plural of adjectives, 190 note, 338
  in plural of present tense and imperative, 85, 248, 260, 327-329
  in plural of substantives, 100, 101, 103, 134, 190, 236, 259, 271, 272, 275, 292, 293, 337, 338

-*es* (or -*s*), in 2nd person singular, 85, 86, 185, 260
  in 3rd person singular, 85, 134, 259, 260, 265, 327, 348, 389
Esk, 79
-*ess*, 190
Essex, 77
-*eth* (-*aþ*), in plural of imperative, 85, 189, 190, 248, 272, 276, 280, 290
  (-*aþ*), in plural of present tense, 84, 85, 238, 260, 262, 265, 327-329
  (-*eþ*), in 3rd person singular, 84, 85, 238, 260, 265, 327, 360, 367, 389
Exe, 79

F, in Old English, changed to U or V, 181, 229
  See also V
'Five Boroughs,' 124
Franks, 78, 79, 125
French (the name), 105
  derived from Latin, 18 note, 33, 37, 55, 56, 198
  dialects of, 160, 167, App. D
  English words borrowed from, 19, 20, 31, 186-208, 231, 270, 271, 302-305, 309, 310, 313, 362, 363, 372
  German words in, 79, 198
  idioms from, 184-186, 373
  letters in, 279, 280
  plural of adjectives, 190 note, 338
  words in Lowland Scotch, 254. See also Anglo-French
Frisians, 18, 33, 67, 68, 76-78, 118, 119, App. C
-*ful*, 11, 12, 53, 54
Future, how supplied in English, 95, 96

G, dropped in pronunciation, 357, 358
  changed back from Y, 295, 344, 345
  history of, 218-221, 235
  in Anglo-French, 162, 181, 221
  softened, 34, 120 note, 218-220, 235, 273, 277, 344, 345, and see Y

ʒ, ȝ, 183, 219, 221, 222, 240 note, 295 note
   written as Z, 221, 222
Gaelic. See Celtic Languages
Ge- (y- or i- or a-), 94, 133 note, 189, 220, 231, 238, 245, 262, 263, 270, 276, 280, 320, 329, 389
Gender, in English, 103, 115, 180, 237, 238
Generalisation in meaning of words, 62, 63
Genitive, adverbs formed from, in English, 109
   in English, 100, 101, 103, 108, 109, 114-116, 134, 184, 185, 237, 272, 273, 275, 292, 293, 337-340
   in Indo-European language, 52
   use of, in Old English, 114-116
German dialects. See Teutonic
   literary or High, 14, 25, 26, 65-67, 83, 92, 94-96, 100, 102, 103, 106-109, 111, 208, 214, 215, 288, 289, 364, 373
   (literary or High), English words borrowed from, 364, 373
Gerund in English, 95, 154, 263, and App. E
GG softened, 220, 221
GH, 182, 183, 219, 221, 283, 358
Gloucester, 80, 208
Gloucestershire, 131, 224, 281
Gothic, 33, 66-68, 71-74, 87, 92, 95, 96, 98, 102, 105-107, 109
   does not show 'mutation plurals,' 105
   English not derived from, 109
   nominative in, 102
   passive in, 72, 96
   reduplication in, 87
   specimen of, 74
   subjunctive in, 98
   weak perfect in, 92
Goths, 71, and see Gothic
Government, terms of, from Anglo-French, 166, 168, 193
Gower, 286
'Gradation' in the verb, 88-90, and see Verbs, 'strong'
Grammar learnt unconsciously by imitation, 3, 4
Greek, 22-30, 33-35, 37-39, 41, 42, 48-51, 57

Greek, dialects of, 25, 33, 37, 38
   words in English from, 5, 6, 137, 141-143, 194 note, 305, 310, 311, 362
Grimm's law. See Sound-Shifting
GU, 161, 221

H, dropped, 24, 114, 199, 241, 358-360
   dropped in English words derived from French, 199
   guttural in Old English, 28, 29, 182, 183, 358 note
   spelt GH or ȝ, ʒ. See GH, ȝ
   wrongly inserted, 359, 360
Hampshire dialect, 118, 130, App. C, and see West Saxon
Hampton Court Conference, 317
have, tenses formed with, 96-98
-head, 12, 59
Hebrew, words in English borrowed from, 310
hem, 113, 240, 241, 259, 265, 269, 276, 293-295
Henry I., his knowledge of English, 164
   II., his knowledge of English, 165
   IV., letter to, 279
héo, 113, 241, 265, 294, 391
her (here, hir). See *hem*
Herefordshire dialect, 77 note, 131, 224
hers, 348
hi (hii, hig), 113, 219, 260, 262, 281 note, 294
hight. See Passive Voice
hine, 113, 114, 245, 389
his, genitive of *it*, 113, 240, 241, 339, 340
hit, 113, 241, 259, 281 note, 338, 339, 360
Hoccleve, 286, 289
hoo. See *héo*
-hood. See *-head*
Hooker, 367, 368, 375, 376
Hungarian, 20, 22, 23
   words in English from, 364

I, change in its pronunciation, 353, 354
   modifies a preceding vowel, 103-107

I written for J, 282 note, 327
I (pronoun, *ic*, *ich*), 113, 114, 230, 240, 388, 389
i-. See *ge*-
-ian, verbs in, 106, 107, 389
ic. See *I*
ich. See *I*
Icelandic. See Danish, Norse
Idioms in English, from Danish, 243
  from French, 184-186, 373
  from Latin, 346, 368
  obsolete since sixteenth century, 345-348
Imitation of others' speech, 2-4, 9, 15-17
Imperative in *-eth*. See *-eth (-aþ)*
  in Northumbrian. See *-es*
Indefinite article. See Article
Indian languages, 33, 36, and see Sanskrit
  languages, words in English from, 311, 364, 365
Indo-European language, 22-64, 86, and App. A
  language, character of, 32-34, 52, 53
  language, divisions of, 32-40
  language, origin of, 53-64
  language, proof of its existence, 22-31, 48-51
  people, its home, 46, 47
  people, its life, 41-46
Infinitive, form of, in English, 95, 271, 320, and App. E. See also *-e*, *-en*
Inflexions, an essential part of Old English, 115, 116
  applied to French words, 189, 190
  confused in *Peterborough Chronicle*, 227, 228
  decay and loss of, 82, 83, 126, 127, 133-135, 177-180, 208, 229, 230, 236-244, 248-253, 258, 259, 270, 273, 276, 277, 287-291
  displaced by phrases, 184, 185, 230
  influence accent, 205, 206
  irregular in children, 3, 4, 91
  not borrowed, 6, 20
  origin of, 53-60

Inflexions, sapped by accent, 208
-ing, 206, 225, and App. E
Instrumental case, in English, 67 note, 102, 108-110, 239, 240
  case, in Indo-European, 38, 52
Iranian, 33, 36, 46, 48-51
Irish. See Celtic Languages
Isle of Wight, 77, 118, and App. E
it. See *hit*
  (genitive), 339, 340
Italian, words in English from, 309, 364
its, 114, 338-340
itself, 339, 340
Ivernians. See App. A

J, in Anglo-French, 162, 181
  takes the place of I (consonant), 282 note, 327
  written for I, 230, 282 note
John of Trevisa. See Trevisa
Johnson, Dr., 368, 369, 379, 380
'Johnsonian' style, 368-372, 382, 383
Jonson, Ben, 291, 320, 334, 374
Jutes, 76, 77, 118, and App. C

K, dropped in English pronunciation, 4, 357, 358
  (or hard C), softened in French, 39 note
  (or hard C), softened in Sanskrit, etc., 28, 29, 34, 38, 39
  once sounded in *knave*, etc., 4, 283, 358
  written for C in English, 152, 182, 236
  See also C
Kent, 76, 77, 118, 119, 285, 286
Kentish dialect, 76, 77, 119, 132, 156, 224, 263, 285, 286, 297, 298, 386, and App. C
Kyngestone, letter of, 279, 280

LANCASHIRE dialect, 14, 17, 77, 79, 80, 112, 124 note, 201, 224, 241, 266, 390, 391
Latimer, 319, 320, 324, 325, 327
Latin, 22-41, 48-51
  books written in England, 121, 122, 168-171

Latin, English words borrowed from, 5, 6, 19, 30, 31, 79, 80, 137, 144, 187, 205, 274, 304, 305, 362, 368-372
   idioms in English, 346, 368
   influence of, on English style, 368, 369, 374
   position of, in England after Norman Conquest, 168-171
Law terms from Anglo-French, 166, 168, 193
Layamon, 225, 244-247, 343
Leicester, 124, 141
Leicestershire, 123
-*less*, 12, 53, 54, 59
Lilleshall. See Myrc
Lincoln, 80, 124, 231, 244
Lincolnshire, 123, 226, 231, 244, 255, 348, 392
Literature, in Middle English, 171, 285 note, 367
   in Old English, 119-122, 128, 129, 131, 132, 157, 251, 252, 367
   See also Ælfric, Alfred the Great, Chaucer, etc.
Lithuanian, 22, 33, 35, 38-40, 48-51, 57
Locative, in Indo-European language, 52
   wanting in Old English, 102
London dialect, 269, 270, 283, 285, 289
Low German, 18, 33, 40, 66-68, 76, 211 note, 268, 306-308, App. B, and see Frisians, Jutes, etc.
Lowland Scotch. See Northumbrian
-*ly*, 12, 54, 55 note, 57, 82, 389
Lydgate, 286, 289

MACAULAY, 94, 367, 383, 384
Malay, words borrowed from, in English, 364
Mandeville, Sir John, 278, 287, 288, 367
Marlborough, 167, 398
'Matthew, Thomas,' translates Bible, 316. See Rogers
Medicine, terms of, from Anglo-French, 194
-*ment*, in French adverbs, 55, 57, 82 note
   suffix to substantives, 190

Mercia, 118 note, 123, 124, 225
Mercian dialect, 17, 86, 118, 132, 133, 135
   how far influenced by Danish, 128, 133, 135
   nearer to Modern English than West Saxon, 132, 133
   specimens of, 148, 155
   where spoken, 118, 132
   See also East Midland, West Midland
Middlesex, 77
Middle voice. See Reflexive voice
Midland dialect, 17, 265, 391, and see Mercian, East Midland, West Midland
Milton, archaisms in, 94, 102
   number of words used by, 191
   old accent in, 204
   poetical style of, 374
   prose style of, 368, 377, 378
   uses *its*, 340 note
   uses *writ*, 332
mine, 113, 114, 240, 343, 361
my. See *mine*
Myrc, 264-266

N, dropped in inflexions, 290-292, 299, 332, 334
   restored, 291
ne (negative), 346, 389
New words, formation of, 5-7, 10-13, 53-64, 136, 137, 145, 192, 362
Nominative case, -*s* of, in Gothic, 71, 72
   in Indo-European language, 52-54
Norfolk, 123, 224, 295
Norman Conquest, its effects on English, 156-209, 215, 216, 218, 221, 223, 224, 363
Norman-French. See Anglo-French
Norse, 33, 49, 51, 61, 66-68, 73, 92, 98 note, 105, 125, and see Danish
North American, words in English from, 311, 364
Northamptonshire, 123, 226, 348
Northern dialect. See Northumbrian
Northumberland, 135, 251, and see R
Northumbria, 77, 78, 119-123, 251-253

Index

Northumbrian dialect, 17, 78, 85, 98 note, 125-128, 133-135, 146, 177, 213-215, 217, 218, 220, 225, 226, 247-254, 260, 282, 284, 348, 391, 392
    Danish words in, 127, 128, 254
    decay of inflexions in, 127, 133-135, 248-253, 289
    drops -e, 248, 249, 289
    early writings in, 119-122, 128, 133, 146, 157, 251, 252
    French words in, 254
    how influenced by Danish, 125-128, 133-135, 243, 252, 254
    imperative in, 248
    keeps A for O, 213, 250, 251, 253, 391
    keeps C (or K) hard, 214, 215, 235
    keeps G hard, 219, 220
    keeps Old English guttural H, 182
    keeps SC hard, 217, 218
    Old English words retained in, 254
    plural of nouns in -es or -s, 134, 190
    plural of verb in -es or -s, 85, 248, 260, 327-329
    present participle in, 248
    pronunciation of, 134, 135, 213-215, 217-220, 225, 253, 291, 352-354
    pronunciation of, affects 'standard' English, 134, 135, 213-215, 217-220, 225, 253, 284, 354
    retains Old English pronunciation, 253
    S for SH in, 250, 251 note, 391, 392
    specimens of, 146, 247, 248
    the parent of Lowland Scotch, 17, 134, 251-254
    3rd person singular of verb in -es or -s, 85, 134, 259, 260, 265, 327
    uses *I* (pronoun), 230
    where spoken, 133, 225, 252, 256, 391
    See also *hers, I, ours, þai, those*
Nottingham, 124
Nottinghamshire, 123
Nut-brown Maid, 202

O changes in its pronunciation, 212 note, 213, 353
    derived from A, 210-213, 235, 247, 248, 250, 271 note, 281, 295
Occleve. See Hoccleve
of replaces genitive, 184, 185
OI changes in its pronunciation, 356, 357
Onomatopœic formation of words, 60
Origin of language, 53-64
Orm, 185, 231-244, 255, 259, 270, 293, 295, 296, 342, 343
Ormulum. See Orm
ours, 348
-*ous*, 190
Ouse, 79, 123, 353
Oxford, 283-285

PARTICIPLES, English, past, 91, 92, 96-98, 206, 291, 292, 329-335, and see *ge-*
    English, present, 94, 95, 206, 225, 248, App. E
    Latin without inflexion, 330
Passive voice, how supplied in English, 96
    in Gothic, 72, 96
    in Indo-European language, 52, 53
    traces of, in English (*hight*), 96
Paston Letters, 295 note
Percy's Reliques, 386, 387
Perfect. See Verb, 'strong' and 'weak'
Persian, 33, 35, 36, 38, and see Iranian
    words borrowed from, in English, 311 note, 364
Personal pronouns, 111-114, 230, 240-242, 259, 260, 262, 265, 266, 269, 270, 276, 293-295, 299, 338-344, 361, 388, 389, 391. See *I, thou, he, hi*, etc.
Peterborough Chronicle, 226-231, 244, 255, 359, 366 note
Phrases used for inflexions. See Analytic Tendency, Inflexions
Pickwick, 261, 262
'Pidgin-English,' 58, 59

Piers Plowman, 266 note, 285 note, 294 note
Pilgrim's Progress, 5, 9, 63, 368, 374
Platt-Deutsch. See Low German
Plural, of substantives formed by mutation, 103-107
    not marked in some neuters in English, 107, 336, 337
    See also *-e, -en, -es, -eth*, Adjective, etc.
Poetry, archaisms of, 94, 96, 101, 102, 109, 112, 174-176, 204, 246 note, 320, 329, 336-338, 340, 360, 361
    in Old English, 157, 174-176, 366 note
    in Old English, specimens of, 146, 147, 150, 175, 176
    in Old English, uses old-fashioned words, 174-176
    modelled on Latin verse, 231
    old-fashioned accent in, 204, 205
    See also Béowulf, Cædmon, etc.
Pope, 200 note, 356, 374
Portuguese, words borrowed from, in English, 309
Possessive case, 3, 114, 185, 240, 337-340
    pronouns in English, 114 note, 240 note, 241 note, 338-340, 343, 361
Prayer-Book of 1549, 315, 316, 319-324
    of 1549, borrows from 'Great Bible,' 315, 316, 323
    of 1549, how formed, 319
    of 1549, its use of relatives, 342
    of 1549, specimens of, 321-324
    of 1549, uses *you* as nominative, 341
    of 1662, 7, 315, 316, 319, 342 note
Printers' rhymes, 351
Printing affects English spelling, 300, 351
Pronouns. See Demonstrative Pronouns, Personal Pronouns, etc.
Pronunciation, English, 8, 84, 120, 121, 134, 135, 162, 182, 183, 200, 201, 209-221, 225, 253, 295, 300, 350-361, 388, 390

Pronunciation, English, desire for ease of, 4, 288-291
    English, how discovered, 120, 200, 201, 351, 352, 354 note
    of Middle English, 181-183, 200, 201, 209-221, 352-354
    of Modern English, 350-360
    of Old English, 84, 120, 121, 182, 352-354, 358 note, 388, 390
    traces of former, 120, 182, 210-213, 253, 300, 352, 353, 388, 390
    See also A, etc.
Prose, English, owes a debt to Alfred the Great, 128, 129
    how distinct from poetry, 366
    style of, 366-374
Provençal, 33, 56
Psalms, 'New Version' of, 356, 357
    Prayer-Book Version of, 315, 316, 323
Purvey. See Wycliffe and Purvey
Pytheas, 70

Q, in Anglo-French, 162, 182
    in Indo-European, 29, 30
    appears in English, 182, 229

R, dropped in English, 3, 358
    influences vowels, 210, 213, 356
    pronunciation of, in Northumberland, 17, 24
Reduplication, 86
    in Gothic, 87, 92
    in the English perfect, 86-90, 92
Reflexive voice, in Gothic, 72
    in Indo-European, 52, 53
    See also Passive voice
Relationships, names of, 19, 20, 192
Relative pronouns, 111-113, 239, 245, 341-343
Religion, terms of, from French and Latin, 196, 197, 274
    terms of, in Old English, 141, 145
Robert Manning. See Robert of Brunne
Robert of Brunne, 255-260, 265, 267, 273, 294, 354 note
Robert of Gloucester, 260-262, 270, 291 note, 293, 328, 338, 359, 360

Index

Rogers, John, 316
Romance languages, 18 note, 33, 37, 170, App. A, and see French, Italian, etc.
Roots, 57-61
   invented in modern times, 64 note
Runes, 69, 119, 120, and see p, þ
Rushworth Gospels, 132
Ruthwell Cross, 134

S, dropped in Greek, 3
   for SH. See Northumbrian
-s. See -es
Sanskrit, 22, 23, 25-30, 33-36, 38, 39, 42, 46, 48-51, 90, 114
   antiquity of, 34, 35
   English not derived from, 34, 35
   words in English borrowed from, 311 note, 364 note
Saxon Shore, Count of the, 77
Saxons, 18, 51, 67, 76, 77, 118, 269, App. C, and see West Saxon
SC, change of, 216-218, 235
Schleswig-Holstein, 18, 76, 77, 79; see also Low German
scho, 265, 266
Scott, Sir Walter, 6, 205, 250, 251, 310, 334, 361, 374, 380, 381
Semitic languages, 103 note
   words in English borrowed from, 141, 310, 311, 364
Sempringham, 255
SH, derived from SC. See SC
Shakespeare, 8, 9, 13, 114, 145, 305, 315, 320, 325-331, 334-336, 338-340, 342-348, 374
   adjective, plural with -s in, 338
   archaisms in, 94, 96 note, 101, 102, 109, 204, 329, 336-338
   date of his plays, 320
   Midland plural in, 328, 329
   Northern plural in, 85, 328
   number of words used by, 191
   old accent in, 204, 305
   poetical style of, 374
   pronouns in, 185, 338-344
   Southern dialect in, 328, 388
   specimen of 'First Folio,' 325, 326
   subjunctive in, 336
   substantives in, 336-338
   uses *a* (pronoun), 344

Shakespeare uses double comparative, 345, 346
   uses double negative, 346
   uses double superlative, 345
   verbs in, 85, 327-331, 332 note, 334-336
shall, 95, 96
she, 112, 241
   used as substantive, 347
Sheridan, 185
-ship, 12, 53
Shropshire dialect, 224, 264, 390, and see West Midland
Slang, 8, 9, 64 note, 308 note, 347 note, 348, 357
Slavonic languages, 22, 23, 33, 36, 38, 39, 42, 48-51, 128 note
Somersetshire dialect, 130, 263, 352, 353, 386-390, and see Southern Dialect
Sound-shifting in Indo-European languages, 24-31, 114, 137, 138
   in Teutonic languages, 25, 26, 30, 40, 66, 307
Southern dialect, 114, 177, 180, 213-215, 217, 218, 220, 224, 225, 230, 238, 241, 243 note, 244-247, 249, 259-266, 268-270, 273, 280-284, 291 note, 293, 294, 299, 314, 327-329, 341, 344, 348, 386-390
   clips N, 291, 299, 332
   its influence on 'standard' English, 270, 291, 332, 348
   once spoken in London, 269
   pronouns in, 262, 269, 270, 293, 294
   specimens of, 179, 244, 245, 261, 263, 281, 282
   uses U for Y, 225
   uses V for F, 263, 270, 388
   verb in, 260, and see *-eth* (*-aþ*)
   where spoken, 224, 256, 269, 283
   See also West Saxon
Spanish, words borrowed from, in English, 308, 309, 364
Specialisation in meaning of words, 61-63, 145, 305
Spectator, 368, 378, 379
Spelling, 'etymological,' 199, 200, 303

Spelling in Middle English, 181-184, 200, 210, 234, 236, 249, 289, 290, 351-354
  in Modern English fixed by printing, 300, 327, 330, 350, 351, 354-360
  in Old English, 84, 120, 131, 132
  in Orm, 234, 236
  phonetic (experimental), 183
  See also -e
Spenser, 285 note, 320
  archaisms in, 94, 96 note, 320, 329
  does not write the English of his time, 285 note, 320
  imitates Chaucer, 268, 285 note, 320
  old accent in, 204
Sport, terms of, from Anglo-French, 194-196
Stamford, 124
'Standard' English, 9, 14-17, 267-269, 283-384, 392
  at first more Southern in character, 269, 270, 314, 348
  before the Conquest. See West Saxon
  in the sixteenth century, 314-348
  origin of, 226-244, 250, 255-260, 266-280, 283-286
  specimens of, 296-298, 321-326, 375-384
  See also East Midland
Stevenson, 251
'Strong' verbs. See Verbs
Style, in Modern English poetry, history of, 374
  in Modern English prose, history of, 367-374
  what it is, 365, 366
Subjunctive, in Middle English, 262, 272
  in Modern English, 100, 335, 336, 360
  in Old English, 93, 98, 99
Substantives, declension of, in Chaucer, 272
  declension of, in Old English, 100-107
  declension of, in Orm, 236-238
  declension of, in *Peterborough Chronicle*, 229, 230

Substantives, declension of, in sixteenth century, 336-338
  declension of, in Wycliffe and Purvey, 275, 276
  French, declension of, in English, 190
  See also -e, -en, -es, Dative, etc.
Surrey, 77, 118, 132, 269
Sussex, 77

TACITUS, 42, 68, 69
Teutonic languages, 33, 65-75, 81-83. See Gothic, Sound-shifting
  pronoun in, 67
  substantive in, 66, 67
  verb in, 66-68, 81-83, 92, 95, 96
  people, 68-70, 73
Tennyson, 157, 268
Þ, þ (TH), confused with Y in writing, 183, 222, 297 note, 324, 325
  loss of, 183, 222
  origin of, 120, 121
  written TH in Middle English, 183, 259
  written TH in the Oldest English, 121
þæt. See *that*
þai, 247, 248, 257 note, 260
þam. See þai
þe (definite article). See Article, definite
  (relative). See Relative Pronouns
þilke (*thilke*), 295, 389
þú. See *thou*
þý, 99, 108-110, 239, 240
TH, changed to D. See Sound-shifting in Teutonic Languages
  changed to T, 235
  from DH, D, T. See Sound-shifting in Indo-European Languages
Thackeray, 127 note, 381, 382
Thames, 77, 79, 118, 131, 132, 224, 269
that, 26 note, 27, 40, 57, 66, 108, 111, 112, 236, 239, 245, 277, 341, 389, 391
the, see Article, definite ; for þý, see þý
their. See *they*

Index

them. See *they*
these, 295
they, 240-242, 260, 262, 265, 270, 276, 293-295
thine, 113, 114 note, 240, 343, 361
tho, 108, 271 note, 295, 343
those, 295
thou, ~~113, 114, 181,~~ 185, 340, ~~361~~
thy. See *thine*
to-, prefix in verbs, 94, 192 note
Tone. See Accent
'tother, 111, 277, 391
Trevisa, John of, 164, 268, 281
    specimen of, 281, 282
Tyndale, character of his English, 318
    specimen of, 321
    strong verbs in, 318, 331, 332
    translates New Testament, 315, 316, 319
    uses *ax,* 345
    uses *hit,* 339
    uses Southern plural, 328
    uses *thine* before a consonant, 343
    uses *tho,* 343
    uses Y for G, 344, 345

U (vowel), becomes OU, 181, 240 note, 353
    changes in its pronunciation, 353
    in Devonshire, 17, 24, 107, 121
    written for Y, 225
    (consonant), in Norman-French, 161
    written for V, 181, 182, 259, 300 note, 301, 327
Ulphilas, 71, 74
'un. See *hine*
Usk, 79
Utchy. See *I (ic, ich)*

V, for F, 263, 270, 348, 388
    written for U, 181, 182, 259, 300 note, 301, 327
Verbs, in East Midland Dialect. See East Midland
    in Gothic, 67, 68, 72, 87, 96
    in Indo-European, 23, 52, 53, 56, 57, 59, 86, 87, 89, 90
    in μι, 23, 35, 56, 57, 72, 85, 86

Verbs, in Modern English, 327-336, 360, 361
    in Southern dialect. See Southern dialect and *-eth (-aþ)*
    lose terminations in fifteenth century, 287-292
    'strong' become 'weak,' 5, 91, 239, 330, 331, 335
    'strong,' changes of, 89, 277, 332-335, 361
    'strong,' origin of, 86-91
    'weak,' 5, 91-93, 239, 292, 293, 329, 330
    'weak' become 'strong,' 91 note, 335
    'weak,' origin of, 92, 93
Vocabulary, English, 10-13, 19, 30, 31, 60-64, 79, 80, 127, 128, 135-145, 160, 161, 163, 164, 168, 186-208, 212, 214, 216, 217-220, 230, 231, 243, 254, 270, 271, 274, 302-313, 318, 361-365, and see Danish, French, Latin, etc., and Compound words, New words
Vocative case, in Indo-European, 52
    lost in English, 102
'Voiced' letters, 4, 92, 93, 217 note, 358
Vowels, modified by anticipation, 103-107, and see A, etc.
Vulgate, 132, 133, 139 note, 148, 169, 170, 187 note, 247, 273, 274, 304, 317

W, dropped in pronunciation, 4, 357, 358
    used as vowel, 182, 220
    written for þ, 182
þ written UU (VV), 120, 182, 229
Wace, 172, 244, 255
War, terms of, from Anglo-French, 193, 194
Wars of the Roses, 354
Watts, Dr., 356
'Weak' verbs. See Verbs
Welsh. See Celtic Languages
Wessex, 77, 123, 124, 129, and see West Saxon
West Midland dialect, 224, 225 note, 230, 264-266, 390, 391
    pronouns in, 265, 266, 391

West Midland dialect, specimen of, 264
   verb in, 260, 265, 390
West Saxon dialect, grammar of, 84-117
   loses its position as the 'standard' dialect, 174-179
   represented by South-western dialects, 94, 114, 130, 132, 386-390
   specimens of, 75, 147, 149, 150-154, 175, 176, 178
   the 'standard' dialect before the Conquest, 128-132, 156, 157, 174-177, 253
   vocabulary of, 79, 80, 128, 136-145
   where spoken, 77, 131
   See also Southern dialect
WH becomes W, 358, 359
what, 110, 341, 342
which, 113 note, 245 note, 341-343
Whitby, 121, 123 note
who, 110, 245 note, 341-343
whom. See *who*
whose. See *who*
why, 110, 240
-*wick*, 80, 140 note, 141, 145
will (auxiliary), 95, 96
William the Conqueror, 157-159, 168, 169, 176, 252, 261, and see Norman Conquest
Wiltshire dialect, 130, 190 note, 268, 294 note
Winchester, 79, 86, 175, 176, 285

Worcestershire, 77 note, 131, 224, 225, 244
Wordsworth, 374
Wycliffe and Purvey, 17, 24, 111 note, 273-277, 283-287, 290, 318, 319, 332, 333, 391
   debt of 'Authorised Version' to, 274, 318, 319
   help to make East Midland 'standard' English, 273, 283-286
   introduce religious terms into English, 274, 318, 319
   pronouns in, 276
   specimen of their translation, 275
   'strong' verbs in, 277, 331-333

Y, replaces G, 120 note, 218-222, 273, 277, 295, 344, 345
   vowel, history of, 107, 121, 215, 216, 219, 220, 225
   written for Þ, 183, 222, 297 note, 324, 325, and see *ge*-
y-. See *ge*-
ye, 113, 114, 185, 240, 340, 341
Yorkshire, 123, 251, 282, 284, 391, 392
yours, 348

Z, in Anglo-French, 162
   in Old English, 121
   written for Ȝ, ȝ, 221, 222
   written for S in Southern dialect, 263, 388

THE END

Printed by R. & R. CLARK, *Edinburgh.*

www.ingramcontent.com/pod-product-compliance
Lightning Source LLC
Chambersburg PA
CBHW020543300426
44111CB00008B/769